THE REPORT OF THE PRESIDENT'S COMMISSION

★ AMERICANS ★ OUTDOORS

THE LEGACY, THE CHALLENGE

With Case Studies

Island Press
Washington, D.C.
Covelo, California

GV
191.4
P74
1987

Library of Congress Catalog Number 87-80384
ISBN 0-933280-36-X
Printed in the United States of America

Published by:
  Island Press
  1718 Connecticut Avenue, N.W.
  Suite 300
  Washington, D.C. 20009

Cover and book design by Tim Kenney Design, Inc.

Acknowledgement: Island Press gratefully acknowledges the permission granted by Market Opinion Research to include survey material produced by them for the President's Commission on Americans Outdoors. The survey was made possible by a generous contribution from National Geographic Society.

iv

Contents

CONTENTS

Case Studies

Foreword to the
Island Press Edition

WILLIAM K. REILLY
President, World Wildlife Fund and The Conservation Foundation

Over the past two decades, millions of us have had the opportunity to enjoy long stretches of public beach, expansive wilderness areas, mile upon mile of scenic river, carefully-restored historic sites, hiking trails, and a great many state and local parks, all of which might not have existed had it not been for the vision of a government commission most Americans have never heard of.

In 1962, the Outdoor Recreation Resources Review Commission (ORRRC), chaired by Laurance S. Rockefeller, released a report that helped launch the modern environmental movement. After three years of study, ORRRC concluded that the nation's recreational patterns were being transformed dramatically by expanding population, increased leisure time, greater mobility, and growing affluence. America, ORRRC warned, was fast outgrowing its existing outdoor resources.

Rockefeller and his fellow commissioners proposed bold and imaginative steps to meet the explosive growth they had anticipated in the demand for many types of recreation. Over the years many of their ideas became realities. The federal Land and Water Conservation Fund has added nearly $6 billion worth of parks and other public recreation lands and facilities to local, state, and federal holdings. National systems of wilderness areas, hiking trails, and wild and scenic rivers have been established. The public has gained access it otherwise would not have had to hundreds of miles of oceanfront. Federal assistance has enabled states and localities to protect places of exceptional scenic, historic, recreational, or natural interest—places that otherwise might have been irretrievably lost, and that tens of thousands of visitors have subsequently enjoyed.

The book you are about to read is another important legacy of ORRRC, whose members foresaw the need for periodic reexamination of the adequacy of America's outdoor resources. In 1983, Laurance Rockefeller again took the lead by convening a small group of conservation and recreation leaders, under the chairmanship of Henry Diamond, former commissioner of the New York State Department of Environmental Conservation, to revisit the issues ORRRC had explored twenty years earlier.

The group found that outdoor pursuits had become, if anything, more important in our society, and that America's recreational habits and needs had indeed changed a great deal in the interim, as ORRRC had predicted. The private sector's role as a purveyor of recreation had grown substantially, and states and localities were funding outdoor facilities in innovative ways. Most significant, the review group found that after two decades of clear improvement in the quantity of recreational resources, retrenchments in government funding at all levels in the 1980s threatened the integrity of the country's recreational infrastructure. Deep federal cutbacks in the Land and Water Conservation Fund and its pending expiration were of great concern to the conservation community. Many of the National Park units authorized in the 1960s and 1970s remained unfinished. State and local park systems had expanded greatly during that period, but their care and maintenance had suffered considerably from federal and state funding cuts.

These findings led the Rockefeller review group to recommend a comprehensive government appraisal of the nation's recreation policy and resources. When attempts to authorize the effort stalled in Congress, President Reagan was prevailed upon to establish a special Commission by Executive Order. *Americans Outdoors: The Legacy, The Challenge* is its final report.

Under the able leadership of Chairman Lamar Alexander, Governor of Tennessee, and Vice Chairman Gilbert Grosvenor, President of the National Geographic Society, the Commission discovered some significant and surprising changes had occurred in the nation's outdoor recreation habits since the early 1960s. Public demand for many types of outdoor recreation had grown dramatically; participation in some activities in the late 1970s exceeded levels projected by ORRRC for the year 2000. Community parks, natural areas, and other recreational resources in urban areas—where 80 percent of all Americans will live by century's end—had become the only outdoors most of us know. Even the traditional American vacation had been redefined. "Getting away from it all" now often means a long weekend trip to a state park or other nearby facility, not a two-week stay at some distant attraction.

The Commission has a great deal to say about the enormous contribution the outdoors makes to the quality of our lives, our sense of community, our economy. It is the setting in which we pursue health and adventure, solitude and camaraderie, and our connections to the natural world. So central is it to the American way of life that "we take the outdoors for granted," the Commission observes, and therein lies a problem. "We assume it will always be there, not recognizing that its maintenance depends on each of us."

Americans Outdoors warns that "the quality of the outdoor estate remains precarious." Open space, wildlife, and wetlands are being lost, often because their value does not register in the economic calculus of development. Pollution threatens the quality of air, land, and water. Heavy visitor loads and inadequate funding strain recreation facilities and services. Opportunities for outdoor recreation, as for so much else, are unduly limited for the poor of the central cities, the elderly, and the handicapped.

The President's Commission on Americans Outdoors offers more than 60 recommendations responding to the problems and opportunities it documents. Vindicating the Land and Water Conservation Fund, the report proposes a federal trust fund that would provide $1 billion annually to maintain and expand resource protection and recreational activities—the minimum the Commissioners felt was required—and earmarks a significant portion to stimulate grass-roots innovation and experimentation. The Commission envisions a new system of "greenways" along scenic highways, riverways, and trails, linking communities and cities, and the expansion of the federal estate. Parity should be given to recreational use of national forests and Bureau of Land Management lands the Commissions argues. *Americans Outdoors* calls for new efforts to mitigate the many threats to valued resources in the national parks arising from activities outside park boundaries. Implicit in many of the Commission's proposals is the view that the severe falloff in recreational funding in recent years needs reversing.

In searching for the means to implement its recommendations, the Commission looked first to the concerns and resourcefulness of local communities. One of the report's central themes is that America's outdoor estate can be best utilized and protected through partnerships forged among citizens and governments at all levels, the private sector, and the conservation community. Given current budgetary realities, and the variety and quality Americans expect in recreational resources, the federal government cannot be expected to bear all of the burden. The Commission has nonetheless affirmed a crucial federal role in funding, leadership, and resource husbandry.

The President's Commission on Americans Outdoors began and ended in controversy. Underrepresented on the Commission itself, conservationists and environmentalists worried that the final report would over-emphasize private commercial development of outdoor resources, endorse a very limited federal role, and downplay resource protection. As the report neared completion, however, reservations about its contents were voiced most strongly by inholders and commercial interests.

Americans Outdoors is a consensus document. It reflects the diverse make-up of the Commission and its staff, the views of hundreds of Americans who testified at hearings around the country, and the insights of dozens of experts who prepared background studies. Many of my colleagues in the conservation community and I do not espouse all of the report's recommendations; we wish some of its proposals had been more ambitious. The Commission has not adequately treated some issues that I feel need urgently to be addressed—for example, the need to take a broader, ecosystem approach in managing protected areas.

Americans Outdoors deserves a wide readership, and Island Press is to be commended for making the full report available in a timely manner. The President's Commission has made an important contribution to our understanding of the nation's outdoor recreation needs and resources. It is a much needed initiative at a time when many in the conservation community expected less. I suggest that we take this report seriously and work to see its vision translated into a new era of outdoor stewardship as accomplished and beneficial as the last.

Washington, D.C.
February 1987

Editor's Note

President Ronald Reagan, on January 28, 1985, issued Executive Order 12503, creating an advisory commission to review outdoor recreation. Fifteen members of the President's Commission on Americans Outdoors were appointed, including officials of local and state government, members of Congress, and citizens representing diverse interests in outdoor recreation. The President appointed Governor Lamar Alexander of Tennessee as Chairman. National Geographic Society President Gilbert Grosvenor served as Vice Chairman. Commission members named twenty prominent citizens as senior advisors to the Commission to assist them in their work.

The Commission was charged by the President with reviewing public and private outdoor recreation opportunities, policies and programs, and making recommendations to ensure the future availability of outdoor recreation for the American people. The report of the President's Commission on Americans Outdoors was completed in January 1987 and is addressed to the President, to members of Congress, to governors, mayors, and county officials, and most important, to the people of the United States of America.

The body of this volume is the final report of the President's Commission on Americans Outdoors, which was transmitted to the President on January 28, 1987. However, as the reader will quickly discover, this is an unusual government report, in content and in format.

As it began its work, the Commission made two decisions which influenced the nature of its final report. First, the Commission decided to go to the American people to elicit their views about how current and future needs for outdoor recreation might better be met. The Commission heard from hundreds of individuals who appeared at hearings around the country, and many others who submitted letters and informal papers. Extracts from some of these contributions, reflecting the broad spectrum of views and concerns expressed by people from all walks of life, are included with the text of the report in this edition. They provide invaluable context for the Commission's findings and recommendations.

Second, the Commission decided that its report would not be aimed primarily at Washington policy makers. Rather, the Commission wanted, in the words of Chairman Lamar Alexander, to "start a prairie fire of concern and investment, community by community" across the country. To inspire local action, the report includes dozens of brief case studies and examples of initiatives being taken by communities around the nation to solve problems and seize opportunities. Thus the report is also the "working manual" for the prairie fire.

This ISLAND PRESS edition includes the complete text of the final report, and most of the additional material which accompanied it, although some redundancies have been edited out. The text of the report itself has been copyedited for clarity; but neither meaning nor substance has been changed. However, the material is complex, so to assist the reader, different typefaces have been used.

The report itself is in four parts with several chapters within each part. This material appears in roman type, and the Commission's recommendations and "action" items are designated by solid black bullets (●).

Interspersed with the text of the report, delineated by the following rules: ═══════════ , and also at the end of each chapter, is other material relating to the Commission's work. *In italics, are extracts from testimony by the more than 1000 people who presented their views at hearings throughout the country, as well as statements pertinent to the report made by various individuals.*

Also included in a compressed roman typeface is material from a variety of sources including research undertaken by the Commission staff and extracts from case studies prepared for the Commission. This too is either integrated into the text of the report, but clearly delineated from it, or placed at the end of chapters.

The summary of key issues and recommendations prepared for the Commission by parallel State Commissions, as well as a summary of the proceedings of a national conference on Recreation and the American City, cosponsored by the Commission, are included as appendixes.

At the end of the volume is the full text of twelve selected case studies solicited by the Commission.

Americans Outdoors
The Legacy, The Challenge

Report of the
President's Commission

PRESIDENT'S COMMISSION ON AMERICANS OUTDOORS

P.O. Box 18547
1111 20th St. N.W.
Washington, D.C. 20036-8547

January 28, 1987

The President
The White House
Washington, D.C. 20500

Dear Mr. President:

It is with pleasure and pride that we submit this report of the President's Commission on Americans Outdoors. It contains our recommendations for policies and programs to assure adequate outdoor recreation opportunities for Americans into the next century.

The recommendations represent a consensus of the Commission on findings, basic principles regarding public and private sector responsibilities, and policies and programs. Although we represent diverse views and backgrounds, we were able to objectively consider the problems, and adjust our individual views to achieve general agreement. Because this is a consensus report the absence of a member's separate views does not necessarily indicate that there is unanimity on the details.

In preparing this report we had the benefit of the views of literally thousands of Americans who testified at our hearings or wrote to us, as well as contributions from hundreds of experts in the field of outdoor recreation and resources management.

Increasingly, outdoor recreation occurs close to home, in or near towns and cities where 80 percent of us soon will live. So, more and more, the solutions must be found close to home. We have concluded that the best way to assure that Americans will have adequate outdoor recreation opportunities is through a prairie fire of concern and investment community by community. State and local governments will play a major role, but implementation of our recommendations ultimately will depend on the efforts of thousands of individual citizens, non-profit organizations, and businesses.

There still is a need for a strong outdoor commitment from the nation's capital: to safeguard the environment, to expand recreational opportunities on federal lands, to protect and improve the federal estate, and to provide money to support state, local and private sector efforts.

Achievement of the goals set forth in this report will require a partnership among governments at all levels and private sector organizations and businesses and industry. We are confident that the American people will rise to this challenge.

Respectfully,

Lamar Alexander

Chairman

Gilbert Grosvenor	*Charles Jordan*	*Stuart Northrop*
Frank Bogert	*Wilbur LaPage*	*Sally Ranney*
Sheldon Coleman	*Rex G. Maughan*	*Morris Udall*
Derrick Crandall	*Patrick Noonan*	*Barbara Vucanovich*
J. Bennett Johnston		*Malcolm Wallop*

The President's Commission on Americans Outdoors

MEMBERS

Chairman
THE HONORABLE LAMAR ALEXANDER
Governor of Tennessee

Vice Chairman
GILBERT GROSVENOR
President, National Geographic Society
Washington, D.C.

THE HONORABLE FRANK BOGERT
Mayor of Palm Springs, California

SHELDON COLEMAN
Chairman of the Board, The Coleman Company
Wichita, Kansas

DERRICK CRANDALL
President, American Recreation Coalition
Washington, D.C.

THE HONORABLE J. BENNETT JOHNSTON
U.S. Senator, Louisiana

CHARLES JORDAN
Director, Department of Parks and Recreation
Austin, Texas

DR. WILBUR LAPAGE
Director, New Hampshire Division of Parks and Recreation
Concord, New Hampshire

4

The President's Commission on Americans Outdoors

STAFF

Executive Director
VICTOR H. ASHE

Deputy Executive Director
LORAN FRASER

Associate Director for Management
KENT MAYS

Associate Director for Federal Lands and Waters
CLAY E. PETERS

Associate Director for Research and Studies
WILLIAM SHANDS

Associate Director for Trends and Forecasts
GEORGE SIEHL

Associate Director for State and Local Systems and Resources
BARRY S. TINDALL

Director of Public Affairs
EDWIN S. DARRELL

Editor
DAY LOHMANN

	JAMES GASSER	
SHELIA BRIGGS	DIANNE HAM	MICHAEL ROGERS
WILLIAM BURLEIGH	WILLIAM A. HILLMAN, JR.	HAL SALWASSER
TED DINKEL	AUDREY HOFFER	RODGER SCHMITT
MICHAEL ENSCH	JOHN LUGAR	LAURA SZWAK
RONALD FOWLER	WARD LUTHI	PATRICIA THOMAS
THOMAS GARLAND	WILLIAM MASON	GWEN WILLIAMS

BARBARA GROHMANN served from October 1985 to December 1985; C. LYNN EDWARDS from October 1985 to January 1986; JOYCE KELLY from October 1985 to April 1986; JAMES GILTMIER from December 1985 to May 1986; ELENA BURBANK from January to August 1986; KAYE MORGAN from August to October 1986; and DIANE WALKER from October 1986 to December 1986.

The President's Commission on Americans Outdoors

SENIOR ADVISORS

LOIS ANDERSON
President, Gadabout Tours, Inc.
Palm Springs, California

ROBERT O. ANDERSON
Retired Chairman of the Board, Atlantic Richfield
Roswell, New Mexico

WILLARD W. BROWN
Director, AmeriTrust, Co.
Cleveland, Ohio

ANGELA B. BUCHANAN
Former Treasurer of the United States
Irvine, California

HOWARD (BO) CALLAWAY
Former Secretary of the Army
Denver, Colorado

JAMES CALLOWAY
Director of Recreation and Leisure Studies, Gallaudet College
Washington, D.C.

MARION CLAWSON
Senior Fellow Emeritus, Resources for the Future
Washington, D.C.

HENRY DIAMOND
Partner, Beveridge and Diamond
Washington, D.C.

6

BENJAMIN EMORY
President, Land Trust Exchange
Bar Harbor, Maine

DREW LEWIS
Chairman and Chief Executive Officer, Union Pacific Railroad
Former Secretary of Transportation
Omaha, Nebraska

RICHARD NUNIS
President, Outdoor Recreation Division, Walt Disney Corp.
Laguna Beach, California

PAUL PRITCHARD
President, National Parks and Conservation Association
Washington, D.C.

DANIEL A. POOLE
President, Wildlife Management Institute
Washington, D.C.

NATHANIEL REED
Former Assistant Secretary of Interior for Fish and
Wildlife and Parks
Hobe Sound, Florida

WILLIAM REILLY
President, World Wildlife Fund and The Conservation Foundation
Washington, D.C.

WILLIAM RUCKELSHAUS
Partner, Perkins Coie
Former Administrator of U.S. Environmental Protection Agency
Seattle, Washington

RICHARD TRUDEAU
Former General Manager of East Bay Regional Park Authority
Lafayette, California

STEWART UDALL
Former Secretary of the Interior
Phoenix, Arizona

DOUGLAS WHEELER
Executive Director, Sierra Club
San Francisco, California

JOHN WHITTAKER
Assistant to the President, Union Camp Corporation
Former Undersecretary of the Interior
Washington, D.C.

The American Outdoors

The majesty of the Great Outdoors helped make America, and Americans, what we are today. No mere coincidence matched a national character of independence, of resourcefulness, and of generosity, with a land of splendor, vastness, and inspiration.

We find that the outdoors is a wellspring of the American spirit, vital to our belief in ourselves as individuals and as a nation. It has influenced our music, literature, science, and language; molded our history, heritage, and national outlook. It has served as the training ground of athletes and philosophers, of poets and defenders of American ideals. It is the reward of blending freedom and responsibility.

Each generation must therefore ensure to the next, the inspiration of the outdoors' dignity, power, and elemental freedom; the opportunity to participate in its challenges of discovery and personal involvement; and the fulfillment to be found in its endless opportunities for physical release and spiritual renewal.

We believe that the outdoors is a statement of the American condition. The recommendations of the President's Commission on Americans Outdoors reflect our shared commitment to keep that statement strong and vital, with a vigilance no less than that which guards our American freedoms.

. . . .

Chapter 1

Americans Outdoors

Our charge

In 1985 President Reagan asked us to look ahead for a generation and see what needs to be done for Americans to have appropriate places to do what they want to do outdoors.

This is our report to the President.

It is also a call to action to mayors, state legislators, governors, the Congress, and the private sector—corporations, landowners, small businesses and not-for-profit organizations. Most of all, however, we seek to turn the spotlight on the efforts and ideas of millions of Americans working together in their neighborhoods, communities, towns, and cities to build quality environments and spaces for play, regeneration, health, and enrichment in the outdoors.

America's strength is in her people and her land

This report is about Americans—our needs, our potential, our creativity, energy and desires: Americans in communities across the nation, working together to find imaginative new ways to make their own communities the kinds of places in which they want to live, work and play; helping each other as volunteers; teaching their children. They are America's strength, and it is to Americans in communities across the land that we look for leadership to meet our needs of tomorrow.

It is about the Outdoors. We call it "the Great Outdoors," and in many other ways do we Americans declare our affection for the world beyond the hearth. The love of open-air activity is rooted in our frontier history, reflected in our heroes, celebrated in our arts. "If you would understand me," exclaimed Walt Whitman, "go to the heights or watershores." He spoke for an entire nation.

It is our obligation to pass on to future generations an unimpaired legacy of the American Outdoors.

Our goals as a Commission were to find what outdoor recreation means to the American people, and to recommend ways to make sure our governments, our communities, and our actions as individuals reflect the values we attach to it. We seek the establishment of enduring processes—private and public—to meet our outdoor recreation needs, today and in the future.

We were directed to assess future needs for land, personnel, information, and money; to explore opportunities for innovative partnerships between the private sector and government in providing outdoor recreation opportunities and protecting outdoor recreation resources; and to evaluate how outdoor recreation contributes to our health, our economy, and our environment.

Here is how we went about it.

We went to the people

We listened to Americans, more than one thousand of them who testified at eighteen public hearings in every region of the United States, people who wrote to us, who called and met with us. We visited public and private recreation sites in communities across the country, and listened to those who operate and those who use these areas. These Americans shared with us their ideas, their concerns, and their hopes for the future.

Twenty distinguished leaders served as Senior Advisors to the Commission, and reviewed and commented on draft papers and report outlines.

Through a generous contribution from the National Geographic Society, Market Opinion Research conducted a nationwide telephone survey of 2,000 Americans, to ask their recreation activities and preferences, and their views on recreation policy. With help from the National Park Service, we drew on the expertise of public and private leaders in eight strategic planning sessions in cities around the country.

More than three hundred technical experts were organized into five study teams and they submitted over 150 technical papers. Another 100 researchers expert in virtually every aspect of recreation and resources management searched relevant literature and prepared 71 summary papers. We solicited 24 case studies of ways in which problems are being solved and opportunities realized.

We received seven hundred concept papers from citizens sharing their ideas for the improvement of our recreation estate. Recreation commissions, councils, and agencies in all 50 states provided us with reports and information. The National Association of State Outdoor Recreation Liaison Officers assembled data on public recreation areas from state recreation plans.

Special events were sponsored for the Commission. A workshop on recreation on private lands was convened by Senator Malcolm Wallop. A national conference, "Recreation and the American City," was sponsored by the City of Baltimore and the U.S. Conference of Mayors. The Conservation Foundation held two workshops on land issues.

From the Executive Order

What the President Directed Us to Do

In conducting its review, the Commission shall examine:

○ Existing outdoor recreation lands and resources and the land and resource base necessary for future outdoor recreation;

○ The roles of the federal, state, county and municipal governments in providing outdoor recreation opportunities, protecting outdoor recreation resources, and meeting anticipated outdoor recreation conditions;

○ The role of the private sector in meeting present and future outdoor recreation needs, and assess the potential for cooperation between the private sector and government in providing outdoor recreation opportunities and protecting outdoor recreation resources;

○ The relationship between outdoor recreation and personal and public health, the economy, and the environment;

○ The future needs of outdoor recreation management systems, including qualified personnel, technical information, and anticipated financial needs;

○ The relationship of outdoor recreation to the broader range of recreation pursuits and its implications for the supply of and demand for outdoor recreation resources and opportunities;

○ Underlying social, economic, and technological factors that are likely to affect the demand for and supply of outdoor recreation resources, including trends in disposable income and demographic characteristics of the United States.

We found needs, and we found opportunities. We found commitment, and we found answers

More than anything else, we found in Americans a love of the land, and a shared conviction that it is our legacy for the future. We found that recreation is important to people in their daily lives, and that most of them cannot imagine a world in which they did not have access to the outdoors. We found that Americans are willing to work, and to pay, to see that quality outdoor opportunities continue to be available to them, and to their children's children.

The Great Outdoors is still great. But we found that we are facing a deterioration of the natural resource base, and of the recreation infrastructure. Accelerating development of our remaining open spaces, wetlands, shorelines, historic sites, and countrysides, and deferred maintenance and care of our existing resources, are robbing future generations of the heritage which is their birthright. We are selling the backyard to buy the groceries, and we must increase our investment today to protect what we have.

We believe that the place to start, in meeting our outdoor recreation needs for the future, is in our communities. Americans living together and joining in associations across the country—this is where the tremendous strength and vision of our people will be tapped. We recommend a prairie fire of local action to sweep the nation, encouraging investment in outdoor recreation opportunities and rededication to the protection of our great natural heritage. We urge Americans to form coalitions, to build together a shared vision for the future, and act to make it happen.

We believe that we must enter a new age of partnerships, among private businesses, non-profit organizations, local associations, and all levels of government. The private sector holds immeasurable potential for the delivery of outdoor recreation. And Americans are willing to work as volunteers to help build and maintain our outdoor recreation estate.

We have a vision for delivering outdoor recreation opportunities close to home for all Americans: a network of greenways, created by local action, linking private and public recreation areas in linear corridors of land and water. Greenways can bring access to the natural world to every American, and can eventually, if we act now with speed and with foresight, link our communities and our recreation areas together across the nation.

We believe that there is a clear need for local, state, and national governments to put a higher priority on outdoor recreation and preservation of American open space—the American people feel they should. We also believe the creative private sector can do more. But most of all, we need that prairie fire of action and concern from communities across the land. They will show the way, and make it happen.

This is our obligation, and our opportunity

Theodore Roosevelt once said that nothing short of defending this country in wartime "compares in importance with the great central task of leaving this land even a better land for our descendants than it is for us. . . ." The Great American Outdoors, like the freedom we cherish, requires eternal vigilance.

We can write a new chapter in the shaping of America, linking our pioneer past with our post-industrial future, by proper use and care of the Great American Outdoors.

We can and must create opportunities for future generations, by preserving and nurturing the natural world which is their legacy, before we lose it forever.

The Outdoor Recreation Resources Review Commission (ORRRC) and Its Lands and Waters Legacy

This report and its recommendations builds on the foundation laid by the Outdoor Recreation Resources Review Commission (ORRRC), which left a legacy of achievement on behalf of all Americans seldom matched in government.

Twenty-five years ago ORRRC's landmark report *Outdoor Recreation for America* galvanized public support for new outdoor recreation initiatives: the establishment of new national systems of wildernesses, trails, and rivers; creation of a fund that has helped purchase millions of acres of local, state, and federal recreation lands and waters; and establishment of an outdoor recreation agency which, until it was folded into the National Park Service in 1981, provided national leadership in numerous outdoor recreation initiatives. With impetus from ORRRC's work, the nation made tremendous progress in increasing outdoors opportunities.

ORRRC believed that its proposals would satisfy our outdoors needs into the next century. But by the late 1970s, participation in some activities had surpassed the rates ORRRC projected for the year 2000. It became apparent that dramatic changes in our population, life-styles, and the national economy, required a new examination of Americans' outdoor recreation needs.

Rockefeller's Policy Review Group Paved the Way

Americans Outdoors grew out of a broad-based citizen concern over the future direction of outdoor recreation. At the urging of a number of individuals and organizations, Laurance S. Rockefeller, the chairman of ORRRC, in 1983 convened seven leaders in recreation policy as the Outdoor Recreation Policy Review Group, with Rockefeller himself serving ex officio. Two of its members served on this Commission. A third now is director of the National Park Service.

The Policy Review Group concluded first, that outdoor recreation is more important than ever in American life—as a fundamental expression of our national character, for its benefits to individuals and society, and its significant contribution to the nation's economy. Second, even in the face of increased demand for outdoor recreation, governments at all levels have been retrenching and providing less recreation opportunity. Third, the private sector is doing more, and could do even more with government cooperation.

What was needed, the Policy Review Group concluded, was a review and revitalization of government policy and an assessment of the increased outdoor recreation role of the private sector. It recommended the creation of a new outdoor recreation resources review commission to conduct a comprehensive assessment of outdoor recreation in America.

Governors Established State Commissions

Commission Chairman Lamar Alexander called on his fellow Governors to establish state-level outdoor commissions to examine outdoor recreation needs, opportunities and problems. Twenty-five states responded by establishing commissions or holding governor's forums. Another seven had such groups already in existence or had held conferences in 1984-85 in anticipation of a national study.

The purpose of the call was to stimulate action at the local and state levels on behalf of the outdoors. More than 2,000 people testified at hearings or participated in meetings and conferences sponsored by the states in 1986. A broad base was laid for action in the future.

The states' processes also provided invaluable insights for the President's Commission. A total of 32 states submitted reports to aid us in our studies. The New Jersey Department of Environmental Protection, on behalf of the National Association of State Outdoor Recreation Liaison Officers, compiled summaries of priority needs and problems from all 50 states, and presented it to the Commission.

. . . .

Chapter 2

The Outdoors Is Great, But There Are Problems: Commission Findings

Outdoor recreation in a dynamic society

If there is a single word that describes Americans outdoors, it is *diversity*. We go outdoors for many reasons: to keep physically fit, for excitement, to have fun with family and friends, to get away from other people, to experience nature and to learn. Nearly 50 percent of Americans describe themselves as "outdoors people", and another 16 percent consider themselves a combination of indoors and out. It is a rare American who does not engage in some form of recreation outdoors.

Outdoor recreation is not limited to physical activity. Our mental faculties are challenged when we study nature or delve into history at a Civil War battlefield or other historic site. We calm and refresh and renew ourselves as we reforge our ties with the natural world—links that can offset the stresses of modern society.

We recreate in many ways and in many places and we can do some things both indoors and out. Outdoor recreation is distinctive, however, because it involves experiencing, in some way, the natural environment: land, water, air, trees, plants, wildlife, and combinations of resources and landscapes.

Americans have a rich outdoors heritage

We celebrate the outdoors in our literature, art, and music. Our cultural heritage includes Henry David Thoreau's accounts of his rambles around New England, Mark Twain's tale of Huck Finn's escapades on the Mississippi River, the adventure stories of Jack London. We are enriched by Aldo Leopold's contemplative essays about the central Wisconsin landscape, the lyrics of Walt Whitman, the Arctic rhymes of Robert Service, and the poems of Robert Frost.

Visually, the outdoors has stimulated the talents of artists and photographers ranging from Currier and Ives and their picturesque outdoors scenes, to Thomas Moran and his paintings of the Yellowstone country, to Frederick Remington, to the incomparable Ansel Adams. Musicians too have found inspiration in the outdoors, among them Aaron Copeland ("Appalachian Spring"), Ferde Grofé ("Grand Canyon Suite"), Virgil Thompson (who composed the score for the Depression-era film classic "The River"). Folksingers exemplified by Woodie Guthrie and Pete Seeger have sung its glories.

Today we benefit from an outdoors legacy left by scores of men and women—Theodore Roosevelt, Gifford Pinchot, John Muir, Stephen Mather, Bob Marshall, John D. Rockefeller, Jr., Aldo Leopold, J. N. "Ding" Darling, and Lady Bird Johnson—whose vision matched the greatness of the resource. All worked to conserve and protect forests, parks, wildlife, and the nation's beauty.

Others, like Frederick Law Olmsted, Sr., Jane Addams, and Jane Jacobs, argued for creation of urban parks and open space for the relief and refreshment of people in crowded cities. Many men and women, past and present, have helped establish public parks and wildlands which are envied worldwide and which have served as models for similar systems in dozens of countries.

We benefit as well from the energies and visions of those, like L.L. Bean, who have pioneered the development of recreational equipment, facilities, and services which make the outdoors enjoyable.

But as we examined the state of the outdoor recreation estate in America today, we found problems as well as opportunities. We face a deterioration of the natural resource base and of the recreation infrastructure, due, in part, to too much use with too little attention.

Here's what we found

These are some of the things we learned from the American people.

Americans place a high value on the outdoors; it is central to the quality of our lives and the quality of our communities.

Outdoor recreation provides significant social, economic, and environmental benefits. Because these benefits are difficult to assess in dollars, recreation and resources protection suffer in competition with other programs for public and private dollars.

High quality resources—land, water, and air—are essential to fishing and boating, camping and hiking, skiing and bicycling, hunting and horseback riding, and every other outdoors activity.

Quality of the outdoor estate remains precarious. People continue to misuse and abuse resources and facilities. We are becoming aware of more pervasive long-term threats such as toxic chemicals, water pollution from non-point sources, groundwater contamination, and acid precipitation.

○ We're losing available open space on the fringe of fast-growing urban areas and near water. Wetlands and wildlife are disappearing.

○ Wild and free-flowing rivers are being dammed, while residential and commercial development is cutting off public access to rivers in urban areas.

○ With more people doing many different things outdoors, competition for available lands and waters is increasing; to accommodate these pressures we will have to better manage what we have.

○ The quality of recreation services delivery is inadequate. Though some services are improving, much remains to be done.

○ Inadequate funding for staff, development of facilities, and maintenance limits recreation use of some public lands.

○ People in central cities have a harder time experiencing the outdoors.

○ Barriers to investment prevent the private sector from reaching its potential as a recreation provider.

○ Resources management and recreation programs offered by public and private providers are not coordinated as well as they should be.

○ The liability crisis is limiting our opportunities to enjoy the outdoors.

○ We don't have a good overall picture of what we have; we lack systematic monitoring of resource conditions and public needs.

Perhaps the biggest problem is that we take the outdoors for granted; we assume it will always be there, not recognizing that its maintenance depends on each of us.

Aggravating these problems is a population increase of about 2.2 million persons a year—the equivalent of a Houston and a New Orleans. By 2010, the nation's population is expected to reach 283.2 million [Bureau of Census medium growth projections], an increase of about 44 million over 1985, or the equivalent of adding a California and a New York. We found that Americans care deeply about these problems, and are willing and anxious to dedicate more of our individual and national resources to addressing them. There is a love of our outdoor heritage which rings loud and clear across the country.

Our hope with this report is to spark the prairie fire of concern and investment in the great outdoors. Our objective is to inspire a celebration of the outdoor resources and values which are the legacy of all Americans, and a rededication by each of us to making sure that they will be available for future generations.

Chapter 3

We Benefit From Outdoor Recreation In Many Ways

What the outdoors means to us

There was nothing but lands, not a country at all, but the material out of which a country is made.

WILLIAM HARTER

Symbols of the outdoors characterize our country—national and state symbols, streets and towns, heroes. We seek the outdoors to get away from it all, to escape, to renew and refresh. Perhaps this is our modern way of expressing the freedom our forefathers sought in searching for a new life.

The total value of the outdoors for recreation is difficult to describe, let alone price. Price denotes short-term value. A sunset, a rainbow, an ocean wave, a 500-year old tree are priceless recreational commodities. The real value of the outdoors lies in its vitality—the way in which it enhances our lives.

When a sports program keeps a teenager away from drugs, when a neighborhood park offers a friendly gathering place for older people, when families learn to appreciate each other on a camping trip, when a jogger adds years to her or his life, how do we place a price on it? The value is life itself. As John Muir said a century ago,

Each year thousands of nerve-shaken, overcivilized people find that going to the mountains, forests, and deserts is sort of like going home. These areas are useful not only as fountains of timber and water but fountains of life.

Why are we concerned about the values of outdoor recreation?

The outdoors and Americans' use of the outdoors for recreation are essential elements for a healthy, productive, enduring society. However, Americans take their resources for granted.

We can provide some figures of the economic values to society, but in most cases, the greatest values of the outdoors are intensely personal, and cannot be expressed in dollars.

We are losing beachfronts, wooded areas, river banks, and green spaces at an accelerating rate. The value of a solitary walk along the beach or a family picnic in the woods cannot compete in quantifiable measures with the economic value of these resources for housing and commercial uses.

We can measure bits and pieces of the recreation benefits picture: the amount various activity enthusiasts spend, the amount a recreation resource or facility brings into a community's economy, or how important people say recreation activities are to them. It is difficult to put the pieces together, however, for developers, community leaders and other decision-makers to appreciate the entire impact of a recreation investment on an area's economy.

When a mayor says he would prefer his community have access to an interstate highway which attracts industry rather than a waterway which attracts recreation dollars, he has lost sight of the total value of the recreation resource. It is only when social benefits and quality of life factors are quantified and added into the benefits equation that recreation can compete economically with other development.

What must we do?

First, we need to improve the measures of values of recreation resources, using terms similar to those which measure the values of competing investments. Then, we have to complete the economic analysis, comparing these values with those of alternative proposals.

We must also increase the public's awareness about these values. In a 1986 survey, most adults did not recognize that recreation and park areas brought in money or reduced crime in their communities. Social actions involving economic development, housing, crime prevention, health, safety and overall environmental quality and improvement must reflect the values we hold for the outdoors.

Outdoor recreation is important to achieve our individual, community and national goals

Outdoor recreation helps us accomplish personal goals—fitness and longer life, family togetherness, friendship, personal reflection, and appreciation of nature and beauty. As the outdoors leads to the attainment of personal goals, it becomes a stimulant or catalyst for the achievement of the nation's social goals: health, education, employment, family cohesion, economic vitality, environmental quality.

Outdoor activity: a foundation for health

Health is the primary reason American adults say they engage in outdoor recreation. Healthy people constitute a productive work force, effective armed forces, and a motivated citizenry.

Americans spent $355 billion, or about $1,500 per capita, on health care in 1983. If increased recreation participation could reduce that figure by just five percent, the national savings would amount to more than $15 billion.

One-third of all disability payments administered by the Social Security Administration are for cardiovascular disease. Of the nearly 700,000 Americans who die of a heart attack every year, 200,000 are men in their most productive years—between 45 and 65. The American Heart Association estimates a cost of $100 million a year to replace these workers.

To reduce these costs, businesses have instituted health promotion programs for employees. These programs pay off: New York Telephone Company estimated a net savings of $2.7 million annually from its health promotion and fitness programs. In a 1986 nationwide survey of all businesses with at least 100 employees, one-half sponsored some health promotion, ranging from elaborate facilities to comprehensive wellness programs. To further reduce health investments, companies are beginning to make these facilities available to employees' families and to retirees, as do military fitness and recreation programs.

Stress relief is as important to good health as physical fitness. Stress is a forerunner of many human illnesses, including cancer and cardiovascular disease. Outdoor settings stimulate personal reflection and help people deal with traumatic life events, difficult personal decisions, and general stress. One study showed that patients viewing natural scenes recovered from surgery more quickly than those viewing developed landscapes.

Health, "Wellness" and Recreation

There is growing agreement among physicians and medical researchers about the substantial contributions of active exercise programs to people's physical and mental health.

The Public Health Service's 1986 report, *Annual Review of Public Health*, cites 43 studies finding positive links between regular physical activity and the prevention of heart disease. Clinical studies have also demonstrated that vigorous physical fitness activities are effective in controlling depression, anxiety and other psychological ailments.

Despite an increasing number of such findings and people's common sense awareness that exercise is good for them, health officials estimate that less than 20 percent of American adults engage in regular exercise of sufficient intensity to improve cardiovascular performance.

Many in the health professions also feel that today's *average* youth gets significantly less healthful exercise than earlier generations.

The medical profession is focusing more and more on disease prevention, going beyond the traditional notion of simply curing illnesses once they occur. This leads to the general approach of promoting *wellness*, through positive changes in personal lifestyles including improved diet and exercise. Wellness involves the avoidance of disease by individuals who accept responsibility for maintaining their own bodies and minds. Americans are discovering that, by adopting more healthful lifestyles, they can often do more to protect themselves *before* an illness occurs than doctors can *after the fact*.

Shape up, America! Get going and get fit

Wellness and recreation are closely linked. Just fifty years ago, physical exercise was much more an obligatory part of daily life for a people engaged mostly in labor-intensive farm and factory jobs and lacking many of the "labor-saving" devices that we now take for granted. In the 1980s, exercise is discretionary for most Americans. We work mainly in service jobs that involve little physical exertion. We can take the car instead of walking, the elevator instead of the stairs. When we do get exercise, it is almost always on our own time, usually during periods set aside for recreation.

The crucial role of parks and recreation programs in disease prevention and health promotion is recognized by the Surgeon General's latest report, *Promoting Health/Preventing Disease: Objectives for the Nation*. It recommends development of more fitness related recreation facilities by both governments and private entities, including programs for fitness in the workplace.

Recreation creates jobs and economic vitality in our communities

Recreation is big business. In 1984 American consumers spent $262 billion on recreation and leisure, $100 billion on outdoor recreation. Outdoor recreation resources, facilities, and activities generate economic activity. Some examples:

Seventy firms relocated or expanded their business in Arizona, creating 27,800 jobs and $970 million in indirect salaries and wages. Chief executive officers of these firms said that they chose Arizona for its "outdoor lifestyle and recreation opportunities."

The East Bay Regional Park District (EBRPD) in California employs 300 permanent and 200 seasonal employees. The park system generates about $38.2 million of economic benefits to the community every year, with $16.3 million from user fees and property taxes. (Richard Trudeau, former Director, EBRPD) o The total economic impact of over 11,000 organized recreation camps in the United States is over $2.5 billion. (Armand Ball, Boston hearing).

o Ski areas produce total revenues of $2.75 billion. (Jim Branch, Boston hearing).

o Marina del Rey, a man-made recreational harbor near Los Angeles, California, accounts for 8,000 jobs, $24 million to the county, and $10 million to the state. (Robert Leslie, Seattle hearing).

o A three-field softball complex in Lewiston, Maine, with an initial cost of $150,000 added $160,000 to the local economy in one year. (John Picher, Boston hearing)

o The nation is losing half a million acres of wetland habitat a year. Senator Bennett Johnston testified that wetlands added $20 to $40 billion a year to the national economy. For Louisiana, the decline of wetlands has resulted in a loss of $145 million a year in sport and commercial fish and wildlife resources.

o Snowmobiling accounts for $1.3 billion in expenditures annually. (Robert Ellsworth, Denver hearing). Boaters spent $13.75 billion in 1985 for equipment and other needs. (Robert Leslie, Seattle hearing). Fishermen spent $17.3 billion and hunters spent $8.5 billion in 1980 to pursue their sports. (James Ruch, Reno hearing). White-water rafting produces $60 million each year in Colorado alone. (Doug Freeman, Denver hearing). The annual sales of new recreational vehicles accounts for $6 billion. (David Humphreys, Indianapolis hearing).

Recreation can compete economically with other land uses

We were told:

o Over the next 50 years, the Chattahoochee National Forest in northern Georgia will produce $108 million from timber and $637 million from recreation. (Bryan Ripley-Hager, Atlanta hearing).

o The benefits to local citizens of four urban parks in Worcester, Massachusetts, exceeded the annual operating costs of the parks by 4.5 to 1. (Thomas More).

o The recreation benefits from lands managed by the U.S. Forest Service equalled the total management budget of the agency ($1.8 billion). (1985 Annual Report to the Chief of the Forest Service).

In 1982 governments at all levels invested $8 billion in recreation and park programs, or $103 for every American household. Users of these government programs received total benefits of $26 billion—a benefit/cost ratio of three to one. (Richard Walsh, literature review paper).

Methods for assigning economic value for recreation resources are improving. The Public Area Recreation Visitors Survey (PARVS) project attempts to define the economic impacts and values of state, national, and local parks.

The outdoors stimulates tourism

Why do people visit Colorado? Our research tells us that the number one reason is the scenery.

DAN LOVE
Executive Director
Colorado Tourism Board

Tourism is a powerful economy, the third largest industry in the country. Outdoor places are destinations for many traveling Americans.

According to a 1986 Market Opinion Research survey, three-fourths of American adults traveled outside their communities to parks on all-day trips. More than one-fourth (28%) of these adults visited parks and recreation areas ten or more times a year.

In 1984, Americans took more than one billion trips at least 100 miles long within the United States. These trips generated business receipts of $225.1 billion, 4.7 million jobs, and $13.6 billion, $8.9 billion, and $2.7 billion in federal, state, and local revenues, respectively.

In 1984 people from other countries spent $100 billion in the United States, not including air fares. In a Gallup survey of potential foreign travelers, visiting scenic places was ranked at or near the top of vacationers' objectives.

More than 600,000 Americans took a bicycle vacation in 1985, and spent $17 per day if they camped and $50 per day if they stayed in motels.

Outdoor recreation enhances environmental quality

Recreation has helped stimulate our efforts to maintain and enhance the quality of our environment. The Outdoor Recreation Resources Review Commission demanded that rivers be cleaned up. Standards based on recreation uses, such as fishable and swimmable, were subsequently written into clean water laws. As rivers become cleaner, waterfronts prove to be recreational and economic assets to communities.

Wilderness areas represent "insurance premiums" that insure availability of wildland recreation in the future. They also contribute to clean air, clean water, and preserve gene pools of species and ecosystems. These areas are barometers which are used to monitor environmental changes.

As early as the late 1800s, Frederick Law Olmsted planned major park systems in Boston, Chicago, and several other cities as large green areas that were "lungs of the city." Trees and open spaces reduce air pollution.

The outdoors is habitat for plants, animals and people

When I hear of the destruction of a species, I feel just as if the works of some great writer had perished.

THEODORE ROOSEVELT

Like winds and sunsets, wild things were taken for granted until progress began to do away with them.

ALDO LEOPOLD

Wildlands preserve a variety of plants and animals that may be essential for future human survival. Species as yet unknown or unresearched may hold the key to future food, medicine, and fibre sources. As David Brower says, "Wilderness holds the answers to questions we have yet to ask."

Wildlife has economic value as a recreation asset. Nearly half (93 million) of the U. S. population watched, photographed, or fed birds and other wildlife, according to the 1980 National Survey of Fishing and Hunting. In addition, there are 64 million people who fish and 22 million that hunt. In 1980, these sports enthusiasts spent $41 billion to fish, hunt and observe wildlife.

The American public also values wildlife for its own sake. The Aransas National Wildlife Refuge in Texas is the wintering grounds for over half of the world's population of whooping cranes. Participants in a national survey were willing to pay $1.24 each every year to support the refuge as a home for this endangered bird, even though they never intended to visit the area. Wild animals are symbols of our nation. What effect would the extinction of the bald eagle—the symbol of our nation—have on Americans' optimism for our country's future? States adopt trees, birds, and flowers that reflect their state's special identity. Natural symbols define American tradition.

Recreation is vital to the prosperity of our families and children

There is little statistical evidence that families who play together, stay together; however, the public believes it. In a 1982-83 national recreation survey, adults said their children determined how much time they spent in outdoor recreation. In another study, healthy, functioning families said that they strengthened family ties by doing things together outdoors.

Lifestyle changes occurring in the past 25 years have drastically influenced the lives of children. There are ominous signs that the lives of children are troubled. About 20 percent of all children under age 18 live below the official poverty line, compared with 12 percent of the adult population. According to the National Children and Youth Fitness Study (NCYFS) (1984), children's health and fitness levels are declining.

Children depend on safe, available places to play. Children also need open spaces to roam and explore wild lands. The NCYFS found that physically fit children depended on services and facilities of community organizations, such as religious organizations, local park and recreation departments, and private organizations.

Parents, participants, and organizers recognize the value of camps and youth-serving organizations as character builders for youth. A 1986 study by the University of California at Los Angeles found that teens did not use drugs if drug use conflicted with their self-images. Public and private recreation services provide opportunities for youth to feel good about themselves—to learn new skills, to gain confidence, to become winners.

Recreation helps prevent crime

We moved 21 years ago into a neighborhood which was considered very run down. As you had the beginning of gentrification, stones would be thrown resentfully. We built a small park—basketball court, some benches, a place where you could at least throw some balls around. The stone throwing stopped. That's why I'm convinced, firsthand, that there's a direct relationship. You don't throw stones when you've got balls to throw around.

ARTHUR J. HOLLAND
Mayor
Trenton, New Jersey

In 1979 the U. S. Office of Juvenile Justice and Delinquency Prevention generally rejected the use of recreation programs because of "their repeated failure to demonstrate effectiveness in reducing delinquency." Since then, many agencies have made an effort to document the positive outcomes of recreation programs.

Participants in STEP, an outdoor program in Florida for juvenile offenders, showed a lower rate of repeat offenses (52 percent) than did five other non-outdoor programs. Participants in Passport to Adventure, a camping program for preadolescents with behavior problems, showed improved behavior and less supervision needed two years after completing the program. Outdoor programs tend to be more successful with troubled youth than non-outdoor programs, because every participant faces a natural challenge equally. The rock being climbed is just as hard and the rain just as wet to every climber.

Outdoor programs lead to civic pride and social unity

Community leaders use recreation programs and outdoor settings as means to accomplish other community goals. For example, McKeesport, an economically depressed town in southwestern Pennsylvania, revitalized a waterfront park and included programs—outdoors movies, festivals—to draw people downtown. Shops began to reopen, and downtown became a center of economic and community life.

Boston began First Nights, a program on New Year's Eve that featured a street festival of games and food. The program was intended to provide an alternative to alcohol-related activities. Nine other cities around the country have adopted the program.

For many recent immigrants, the first contact with other community residents is in recreation programs or parks. New immigrants use community parks frequently. Outdoor settings provide a novel environment that nurtures social exchange and interaction.

Outdoor places foster a spirit of belonging— to communities, among generations

Outdoor settings offer heritage—a connection among individuals and among communities across time. A connection between generations—"the search for points of continuity"—is a strong underlying theme in societies undergoing rapid change.

A private garden owned by a wealthy resident of Barrington, Rhode Island had served as a public park for weddings, graduations, and other community events for 50 years. The owner sold the property to a developer, and a citizens group appealed successfully to the new owner to retain the garden for civic functions.

Some trails follow the routes of early travelers; in some places, wagon tracks from the Santa Fe and Oregon Trails are still visible. These "souvenir places" allow visitors to transcend time and wonder if those early travelers experienced similar feelings inspired by the landscape.

Yet it is more than simply landscape that maintains bonds between generations and over time—it is activity as well. Ninety percent of hunters learned their skills from their fathers.

The outdoors is an investment in our education

The great outdoors is worth preserving as the textbook from which [the natural tale] can be deciphered and taught.
HOLMES ROLSTON

The outdoors is a learning environment for many professions. Wilderness areas in particular are living museums of natural history. The study of science is enhanced by an appreciation of the natural forces of the earth—the geology that formed the Grand Canyon and botanical features shaping the Everglades.

Even a modest neighborhood woods provides a laboratory for individual exploration. Bil Gilbert, a writer for *Sports Illustrated* magazine, told us that "just messing around" in outdoor spaces is important, especially for children, to learn about nature and develop respect for it.

The outdoors enriches our culture

There is nothing more practical in the end than the preservation of anything that appeals to the higher emotions of mankind.

THEODORE ROOSEVELT

The outdoors stimulates creative expression: poetry, philosophy and religion, among other forms. From Winnie the Pooh's "100-Aker Woods" to Huckleberry Finn's life on the great Mississippi River, children share the experience of beauty and wonder of the outdoors through stories.

Impressionism in the world of art grew from the artists' desires to portray what they felt, not just what they saw. Many of the Impressionists painted outdoor scenes.

The outdoors has provided the setting for many treasured artworks—paintings, photographs, novels, poems, essays, symphonies—that describe the nation and stimulate pride in our great land. The legacy and heritage of the United States of America are built on the beauty and bounties of this country's natural resources—spacious skies, amber fields of grain, purple mountains' majesty, and shining seas.

Shape up America! Get going and get fit. I don't care how old you are. You're never too old or too young to start. I want you to get out and work out. All of you! Run. Walk. Swim. Jog. Bicycle. Play tennis. I'm tired of excuses! I want action!

GEORGE ALLEN
Chairman
President's Council on
Physical Fitness & Sports

The advantage of using parks and recreation programs [for health promotion] is that they provide readily available, low-cost resources which are generally accessible, may be sustained over time, and have a preexisting administrative structure and financial base.

*Priority Strategies for the
Promotion of Physical Activity*
1986, U.S. Center for Disease Control
Atlanta, Georgia

City-Fit is a Comprehensive Fitness Program

The City-Fit program in New Rochelle, New York is a national model for public health and recreation. City-Fit is a highly successful, community-wide approach to fitness that includes fitness programs in the city's parks and recreation centers, a travelling fitness van, extensive education and publication programs on exercise and nutrition, a Farmers' Market with emphasis on healthful diet, citywide Walking Tours and fitness seminars and wellness events.

Recreation Policies Should Promote Wellness

We believe that private and public recreation policies, resources and programs should be better directed toward helping all Americans achieve the state of wellness. No single public agency or private organization can effectively address the broad spectrum of public health needs. Diverse recreation programs that require people to use their legs, arms, lungs and minds should be available to support the full array of personal health and wellness goals.

Future strategies to restore and maintain a healthy nation must recognize the crucial role of recreation resources:

● Public and private recreation providers must actively promote the health and wellness benefits of recreation.

● All health authorities and medical practitioners should incorporate regular recreation activities into their health promotion programs.

● Businesses and industry should fully recognize the contribution of recreation programs to the health and productivity of their employees.

● Congress and the Executive Branch should review public health policies, laws and regulations to ensure that recreation's contribution to public health is acknowledged and supported.

Public Area Recreation Visitors Survey (PARVS)

PARVS is a cooperative project, initiated in 1982, to gather data about visitors to recreation areas. Twelve state agencies, five federal agencies, three universities and several national organizations have cooperated in developing and managing PARVS. The survey results in data that assess the economic impacts and values of recreation areas. The survey also provides travel, recreation and demographic profiles of visitors. More than 20,000 visitors have been interviewed. For example, preliminary data from PARVS show that visitors to Assateague Island National Seashore in Virginia and Maryland spend a total of $68 million per year on their trips.

A frequently expressed motivation for participation in outdoor recreation is escape. This is described in a variety of ways, from "seeking a change of pace," to "getting away from it all," to "giving the mind a rest," to "blowing off steam." We are all in need of a change from the daily routine from time to time. Outdoor recreation is significant in its ability to fulfill these needs by providing a setting which is often in sharp contrast to everyday life. Those settings are often open, quiet, less demanding and probably have a lot more natural features and fewer man-made features than our normal environment. Further, in participation we are generally in control of the circumstances of our routine, such that we are not continually confronted with demands or needs to respond to others' wishes. We can do more for ourself, and thus find a restoration of the sense of control over our life. It is particularly significant that this motivation is one that appears to be on the increase.

RICHARD SCHREYER
Utah State University

One way to measure the health of a society is to measure the health of its citizens. Preventing the diseases of our society would, I believe, be a hopeless task without places to be alone, or places to play with our children, or places to walk with a friend.

DR. RUSSELL HOVERMAN
University of Texas
Austin hearing

Recreation is an important economic asset and stimulant to the sagging traditional economies of a large part of rural America.

BRUCE BABBITT
former Governor of Arizona

Compared to future generations, the present generation may be the least advantaged with respect to economic growth and technology, but the most advantaged with respect to resources and the environment. As a minimum, each generation should leave the environment no more polluted than when it arrived.

IAN BARBOUR
*Technology, Environment, and
Human Values*

My family and I often spend sunny, summer Sundays picnicking or fishing. This time is very family oriented. It gives us time to get away from telephones and televisions, and experience wildlife. Many memories have been made on those Sundays.

JENNIFER MILLER
Minneapolis hearing

It costs over $30,000 a year to keep a kid in jail and many times they come out worse than when they went in. We are spending $3.33 per child a year for recreation and they are better for it.

EDWIN COLVIN
Shaftsbury, Vermont
Boston hearing

My favorite outdoor activity is horseback riding because, as I ride, I learn about the landscape and about my ancestors from my father, who rides with me. My feelings toward this sport are very intense because I seem to be brought back in time—the time of my grandfather's life in the early twentieth century. To me these times are magical.

SARA WILANDER
age 12

We must all have some sense that our private lives connect to the larger meanings of our social circles and our community's public life. A central function of leisure settings and services is to provide that necessary connection.

WILLIAM BURCH
Yale University

Angling has a sizable impact to local economies in the United States. During 1980, anglers spent an estimated $17.3 billion dollars on their sport, $412 per fisherman and an estimated $20 per day. Of that total it is estimated that $7.8 billion was spent solely on freshwater angling and $2.4 billion on saltwater angling. Among the total expenditures made by all anglers, food and lodging accounted for $3.9 billion, transportation for $3 billion, and fishing equipment for $2.5 billion. Licenses, dues, subscriptions, rentals, and special equipment made up the remaining expenditures. Economic studies have shown a multiplier effect associated with angling expenditures that range from 1.7 to 2.6.

MICHAEL MANFREDO
Oregon State University

It's not just fun and games

When the hospital board bemoans the high costs of health care, we must be there to remind them that the hikers and the bikers are not crowding our trails just for the scenery. We do more for the physical, mental and spiritual wellness of the population than any hospital could ever hope to accomplish.

Recreation is not only big business, it is good for business. When the Convention and Visitors Bureau talks of tourism, we must be there to remind them that what tourists like to do is what we do best. One of our chief products is enjoyment, and nothing brings tourists and their dollars to a town like the promise of a good time.

Every kid cannot dunk a basketball; every kid cannot hit a home run. We create silly little games so that everybody wins. We are there to make sure that at least one time in his life, he will run home to say, "Mom, today I was number one." And so when they ask why do we engage in those silly little games, we must be there to remind them that we are in the business of building self esteem.

When the police chief asks for more officers, we must remind the decisionmakers that recreation is more than funt and games. On a daily basis we engage thousands of young people in constructive and positive activities. Were it not for the opportunities we provide, those idle hands and energetic bodies may well turn to less constructive and less positive activities. It is cheaper to recreate than to incarcerate.

When the Human Relations Commission makes its report of the State of Race Relations, we must remind them that we break racial barriers everyday. We provide opportunities for people of different races and ethnic backgrounds to taste victory, only after they have set aside those artificial barriers of color and status and work together as a unit, each contributing some unique and necessary talent. If they can do it on the courts and on the playing fields, just maybe they can do it in society.

COMMISSIONER CHARLES JORDAN
from an address to the 1986
Congress of the National Park
and Recreation Association

Recreation is very, very important for disabled individuals, not just for all the reasons that it is important for non-disabled individuals . . . but recreation is a rehabilitation tool. We have found in our programs that individuals who become disabled often go through a real identity crisis, and they go through a period where there's a lot of self-doubt, and lack of confidence. We have found that recreation gets them back on the road to recovery by increasing their self-confidence, and increasing their strength so that they can compete in the marketplace. We believe recreation is even more important for the disabled person than it is for the non-disabled person.

KIRK BAUER
Washington, D.C. hearing

To create a motivated society

Today I will take the whole concept of parks and recreation out of the fun and games business and link it with probably the most significant issue that this country has to face today. I quote from John Gardner, "The task of the moment is to recreate a highly motivated society. If we fail in that, forget the rest."

Now the reason that recreation is so important is that the work ethic and the whole concept of work has so changed. With specialization and interdependence, the average worker does not find a sense of identity, a sense of challenge and a sense of purpose that are the guts of any motivational experience.

Business has discovered that the most productive and the most highly motivated workers are those who possess significant, and challenging, and fulfilling lives apart from their jobs. What we do with our lives off the job can be of far greater significance in kindling the spirit of self confidence and optimism, that are keys to a highly productive, highly creative employee.

In recreation, you do find these opportunities of choice. You find the opportunities of significance and identity, of challenge and purpose, and the ultimate purpose, whether I'm quoting from Karl Marx or from Thomas Jefferson, is a sense of fulfillment within society.

The parks and recreation movement is providing people with opportunities for fulfillment, for challenge, and for identity that they're no longer finding in their work. In doing that, we're making a very real contribution to resolving the most significant issue this country does face, the recreation of a highly motivated society.

WILLARD BROWN
Indianapolis hearing

A Blind Woman 'Sees' Her Mountain

I am amazed that in 1986 I still hear providers tell me that they don't know why they should make their parks or programs or services accessible to the blind because "no blind people ever come here." The attitude screams, "Keep Out!" How little they know about people who are blind and our ability to see the beauty around us.

Professionals ask me why someone without sight would be interested in seeing a mountain or watching the sun as it rises over the ocean. It is sad that they clearly believe that beauty can only be experienced through the eyes. How I would have loved to have had some of these people with me when I went to the top of Mt. Wildcat in New Hampshire where I first experienced a mountain.

Since I was a small child and read Heidi *on my talking book machine I longed to understand the depth and breadth of a mountain, and one day 25 years later that became a reality for me. I boarded a gondola and went to the summit. On the way I leaned as far as I could out my window which was against all the rules, and listened intently to the trees as they passed me by. This ride actually ascends the face of the mountain, and that enabled me to sense the rock formations in front of me, smell the pines, hear the wind rustling through the trees and listen to a wonderful mountain stream as it descended the mountain twisting and spiralling beneath me. How can I describe to these skeptical professionals the joy I felt at standing on top of this mountain listening to its silence and seeing it not with my eyes, but with every part of me.*

As I moved about on top of my mountain I saw areas thick with vegetation. The flowers felt beautiful and soft as I looked at them, but probably the most wonderful sight my mountain held for me occurred on my second visit.

When I revisited the mountain last summer (I had to get another mountain fix), I found a tree lying full on the ground. I looked at its trunk.

Descending the mountain provided
me with the opportunity to drop
heavy stones from the gondola's
window, and listen to them rolling
down, down, down.

I had obviously seen tree trunks before, but what was wonderful was that for the first time in my life I saw the top of a tall pine tree. I've never had sight so tops of trees were mysteries to me.

Descending the mountain provided me with the opportunity to drop heavy stones from the gondola's window, and listen to them rolling down, down, down.

The trees rose up to greet me, the air became warmer, and soon I was at the base.

I still have one stone from my mountain. It now sits in the dried arrangement I've made for my living room. This stone and the cassette tape I made of the mountain serve as my photographs. I wish I could share them with all of you.

Blind and visually impaired persons will be best served when service providers and professionals stop viewing our blindness through their eyes. We lead normal, healthy and active lives. We work hard and we want to play hard as well.

While you who see stand at a distance and view the mountain, I go to the top and become one with it.

Those with sight admire the sun as it rises above the horizon. I listen to the sounds created by daybreak and feel the increase of light and warmth and become part of the total experience.

It's true, I don't see the beautiful colors, but what's color—when you have a world with sounds and smells and feelings around you to absorb. Blindness allows me to use the gift of imagination. I created my own beauty in the space around me.

You see your world as it is. I see the same world as I want it to be in my own mind's eye.

Who can tell then whose appreciation is greater?

DONNA VENO
Washington, D. C. hearing

Chapter 4

What Do We Want To Do For Outdoor Recreation?

We expect that three major trends will be evident in what we do for outdoor recreation by the year 2000:

○ the rate of growth in outdoor recreation activities will slow;

○ pursuit of physically active recreation will increase;

○ there will be growing diversification of recreation activities.

Nearly everybody goes outdoors for recreation

In 1959, the Outdoor Recreation Resources Review Commission (ORRRC) asked Americans if they went outdoors for recreation. Ninety percent of the people said yes. A quarter century later, nearly the same percentage (89%) said yes, a total of 188 million people. Since children under twelve are not included in the total, this figure is low. Those people who said they do not go outdoors for recreation were typically elderly, poor, less educated, ill or lived alone.

Although overall participation in outdoor recreation activities continues to grow, the rate of growth has decreased significantly in recent years, according to Dr. Marion Clawson, senior fellow emeritus with Resources for the Future and a Senior Advisor to the Commission. While participation had been increasing at the rate of 10 percent per year following World War II into the 1970's, the rate is now between three and four percent annually. This may be partially due to the aging of our population, and a decrease in the rate of population growth as a whole.

While this might be taken as a sign that demand and recreation supply are approaching balance, that emphatically is not the case. Increasing interest in outdoor recreation opportunities close to home, where available resources and facilities are perceived as crowded already, especially on weekends, complicates the problem. (See Figure 1).

Why people go outdoors for recreation

The reasons people go outdoors for recreation are as diverse as we are (See Table 1). Fitness and health related reasons are the most commonly cited, according to the Market Opinion Research survey. Other reasons people engage in recreation include: to be with other people, to experience excitement, to enjoy nature and the outdoors, and to escape. Children tend to motivate adults to spend more time outdoors.

We are living longer, with the average life expectancy for women expected to reach 92 years by 1990. According to the Surgeon General, half of the deaths which occur are the result of lifestyle behavior—choices in nutrition, exercise, smoking and accidents.

In a 1985 Louis Harris survey of disabled citizens, life satisfaction is directly related to the frequency and quantity of recreation activity engagement. Fitness is increasingly important to the disabled. Several national organizations promote athletic competition for disabled groups. This promotion has helped increase awareness among disabled persons about fitness and their abilities. As technological innovators focus on increasing the mobility of these people, the demand from this group may rise considerably.

What Americans do for recreation

The outdoor activities we choose are as diverse as our population: walking in the neighborhood, reading under a tree, backpacking in the wilderness, playing soccer in a field (See Table 2). Most Americans enjoy swimming, walking, fishing, team sports and bicycling. The fastest growing activities are canoeing, swimming, boating, walking, bicycling, and snow skiing. The move toward physically demanding activities is one of the more dramatic changes in participation patterns to have occurred since 1960 (See Figures 2 and 3). Many of these popular and fast growing activities take place in linear corridors—roads, rivers, sidewalks, and snow paths.

Time, location, family demands and other circumstances do not always allow us to do the things we most enjoy, so we substitute other activities. Outdoor recreation activities we do most often are those activities ORRRC described as "simple pleasures"—walking, driving for pleasure, sightseeing, swimming and picnicking.

Where people go outdoors

People seek different recreation places and activities to match different reasons for participating. Some of these places may be outdoors, some indoors (See Figure 4).

Why We Choose a Recreation Area

Attributes adults consider, in rank order, when choosing parks, beaches and other outdoor recreation areas.

Rank	Attribute
1	Natural beauty
2	Amount of crowding
3	Restroom facilities
4	Parking availability
5	Available information
6	Picnic areas
7	Cultural events
8	Fees charged
9	Concessions
10	Organized sports
11	Guided activities

Source: 1986 Market Opinion Research Survey, "Participation in Outdoor Recreation Among American Adults and the Motivations Which Drive Participation."

People seek pleasant surroundings. Natural beauty is the most important criteria in choosing park and recreation areas, followed by amount of crowding. Built amenities such as developed picnic areas, restrooms, and parking are also important criteria people use to choose favorite recreation places.

Close to home may be coming to characterize a great deal of the outdoor recreation interest of the American public. We are taking more trips, up 8 percent between 1969 and 1983, but the average duration of trips for social and recreation purposes is down 19 percent over the same period. (See Figures 5 and 6).

People use local or community parks and recreation areas most often. Visitation to state park areas has grown steadily over the last 25 years. Day use of these areas has grown more than overnight use. People are taking more trips to public areas that last less than six hours. In 1960, most trips lasted five days or longer.

Visitation at other public areas has also increased (See Figure 7). The National Park Service reports generally level or declining visitation to remote park areas, but greater visitation to areas near population centers.

Population trends drive what people do for recreation

We are a constantly changing mosaic in America. Since ORRRC, we have increased in number, become far more mixed ethnically, and moved in large numbers to the South and West. As we change our lifestyles as a whole, the way we spend our leisure time also changes.

The average U.S. household has changed drastically in its composition and size during the last few decades and will continue to change. In 1910 the average household consisted of 4.5 persons; that number has now shrunk to 2.7 and is likely to decline still further. Recreation as a means to get together with others will become more important.

As family size declines, basic changes in the composition of our households are occurring. Single parent households (13% of all households) are far more common than they were 20 years ago. Almost half (46%) of all children born in the late 1970s will spend part of their youth in a one-parent family. In addition, some population experts are predicting a baby boomlet with as many as 4 million children born per year through 1995.

As children are often a motivating force for adult recreation, the amount or nature of recreation demand may be changed. Absence of a spouse and time pressures on a single parent may prevent children from being provided outdoor recreation opportunities or learning recreation skills. Yet, some single parents say they spend more of the time they have in recreation because of their children. Some traditional outdoor recreation activities predominantly taught by fathers, such as hunting, may experience declines.

Teenagers Are Most Active

Teenagers (aged 12-17) are by far the most active in recreation—in number of activities and days of participation—than any other age group. Teenage boys played baseball, basketball, soccer, tennis and driving off-road vehicles frequently; girls played softball, tennis and volleyball frequently. Both boys and girls also backpacked and snow skied often.

Teenagers also began more outdoor recreation activities than any other age group. Girls especially showed the greatest initiation in outdoor recreation activities, particularly wilderness camping and backpacking, during their teenage years.

Youth is a period when individuals build leisure capital that can extend or limit their life-long opportunities.

KENNETH ROBERTS
British researcher

Lifecycle determines how much time people spend on outdoor recreation. Young singles, young couples, and married couples with young children typically increase the time they spend in outdoor recreation. Those who have not changed or reduced the amount of time they spend include married couples with grown children, older singles and widows. Job pressures and health tend to reverse these trends. Children spend twice as much of their free time on recreation as adults.

Elderly people constitute an increasing percentage of our population. The over 65 population will increase from 12 percent of the population to between 18 and 24 percent by the year 2030. The median age in 1970 was 28; by 2000 it will be 36. Over the next 25 years newly retired persons will be better educated, more widely traveled, more politicized, and actively involved in the community. All of these factors are associated with high outdoor recreation activity.

People tend to continue the recreation behaviors they have begun before age 40. Consequently, the best estimate of elderly leisure patterns depends on the activities done before retirement rather than after retirement. On this basis, the next two generations will be highly visible users of outdoor recreation areas.

The fertility rate is down, but legal immigration is adding about 450,000 to our numbers each year. Many people from foreign countries use recreation resources differently, thus creating new challenges for providers.

Although the rate of population growth is slowing, there are implications for outdoor recreation as that population redistributes itself around the country. By the year 2000, 60 percent of the population will live in the South or West. The West, with massive acreages in federal ownership, will have an easier time in meeting recreation space requirements in a gross sense, although land availability in urbanizing areas will remain a problem. In the South, there is not such an extensive federal land buffer.

People are moving from metropolitan to non-metropolitan areas. If they expect the same park and recreation opportunities and services they left behind in the cities, there will be a clear increase in demand in these growth areas. However, as these areas become subdivided or developed, land becomes unavailable for use as a recreation resource for existing metropolitan areas.

Technology expands our options for playing outdoors

The development of new technologies is one of our country's great economic strengths. Many technological innovations have been targeted to or adapted for the outdoor recreation market. Inflatable rafts and lightweight camping gear were among the earliest innovations, followed by hang gliders, sailboards, and an expanded array of off-road vehicles. We look for lands and waters to use this new equipment.

Aerospace technology has produced fiberglass laminates used for skis, lightweight reflective clothing and blankets appropriate for camping, and titanium frames used for racing bicycles. The rubber industry improved the inflatable rubber raft, a vestige of World War II, and made major recreation corridors of some of our rivers. These products increase demand by making recreation activities more accessible to people, easier to learn, and safer.

Recreation activity has provided its own energy to spur technology. The explosion of joggers and runners in the past decade has led to a technological boom in shoe design and manufacture, to the point where we now have shoes with on-board computers.

There have also been developments in leisure technology for the home which may diminish the demand for outdoor recreation. Large screen televisions, improved stereophonic equipment and personal computers make homes entertainment centers. In a symposium on future trends sponsored by Johnson Wax, the participants concluded, "The American home will take on increased importance as the year 2000 approaches—it will serve as workplace, entertainment center, fitness center, school, and even hospital."

The personal computer and rapid development of information networks are technological innovations likely to have profound impact on how people learn about recreation opportunities. About 34 million modems, devices which allow computers to communicate through telephone lines, are expected to be installed by the end of 1990, and many will serve home computers. People will use computers to make reservations or other arrangements to use recreation facilities, and to learn outdoor recreation skills.

Three major factors influence recreation demand

Since the 1960s, three factors, beyond population level, have significantly affected the demand for outdoor recreation. These factors are leisure time, income and mobility. Other factors closely correlated with levels of recreation activity are age and education.

Leisure Time—The President's Commission heard early in its life that we have experienced a thirty percent loss in leisure time, about eight hours per week, since the 1970s. There are age, sex and ethnic differences in these findings, but generally the trend in leisure time is downward. However, the Commission also heard the amount of leisure time we spend on recreation activities has remained constant.

Work Week Increases, Leisure Time Declines

Louis Harris and Associates (1985) found that the median workweek length increased from 43.1 hours in 1975 to 47.3 hours in 1984. Median time for leisure was down from 24.3 hours in 1975 to 18.1 hours in 1984. Part of the reason for this may be corporate cautiousness about the economy, leading to a tendency to work present employees longer hours rather than hire additional ones. Leisure time may also have declined due to a higher percentage of women in the labor force. Time devoted to working, commuting, going to school and studying is also growing as more adults go back to school and women combine family and housework with jobs. Additionally, the number of hourly workers is declining with a shift to a service sector economy and there are more salaried workers today who generally work longer hours. Women, according to the Harris Survey, have 15.6 hours of leisure per week while men have 20.3.

GEOFFREY GODBEY
The Pennsylvania State University

On the other hand, retirement is coming earlier for most Americans. Less than one out of four Americans waits until age 65 to retire. Added to longer life expectancy, leisure is increasing for older citizens.

Income—We have to pay for many forms of outdoor recreation—for equipment, use of an area or facility, or transportation to an activity site. Thus, the ability to pay becomes an important factor influencing recreation demand, particularly in the case of privately provided resources. People with higher incomes serve as trend setters fopr ap broader base of recreation users over time—tennis, golf and sailing being examples. As women continue to advance toward economic equity, they will likely become leaders in recreation activity trends.

There was a gradual decline in median family income, measured in constant dollars, during the 1970's and early 1980's, but this trend reversed starting in 1982. There is also a trend showing a shrinking middle class, those persons earning between $15,000 and $35,000 per year, resulting in a more polarized income distribution pattern. This bi-modal pattern may lead to a greater demand for private recreation resources among people with higher incomes, with a corresponding need for publicly provided resources for lower income people. Not only has there been an increase in income between 1962 and the present, there has been an increase in the share of disposable personal income (DPI) spent on recreation, broadly defined. In 1985, the share of DPI going to recreation was 6.4 percent.There is a significant public acceptance of user fees and charges at public recreation areas. This finding supports the public's willingness to spend money for recreation in general.

Mobility—Our freedom of movement expresses itself in our recreation choices as much as in any other aspect of our lives. While the cross-country auto trip was a common element in middle class America in years past, it has become less so in the past decade. This decline is reflected in fewer visits to remote areas of the National Park System, and is shown directly by statistics on shorter recreation trip lengths (See Figures 6).

The semi-disappearance of passenger trains, deregulation of airlines, completion of an extensive interstate highway system, evolution of comfortable tour buses, and resurgence of interest in cruise ships are some of the major events in public recreation travel since 1962. The absence or expense of public transportation, however, has been cited as a significant barrier to outdoor recreation participation in some areas and for certain people. Fifty-six percent of people with a physical disability said that their disability limited their mobility and prevented them from attending cultural or sporting events or from socializing with friends outside their homes. Despite higher fuel prices, smaller autos and a deterioration of highway conditions in recent years, the automobile remains the principal means of transportation to recreation destinations.

The Disabled Want to Participate Fully

More than 14 percent of noninstitutionalized Americans have physical disabilities. Another 12 percent have either visual or hearing impairments. In a Louis Harris survey of American adults who have a physical disability, over half have annual incomes of $15,000 or less, in comparison with a quarter of the nondisabled public.

Today, disabled people are generally more able than they were 20 years ago. Technology and public accommodations have all improved. However, with these improvements, expectations have also been raised. Disabled people can now recognize that we have the responsibility to be contributing, productive members of society. Yet, disabled people in exchange for assuming this responsibility are also demanding the opportunity to be involved in the mainstream of life, to participate fully in community activities, and to enjoy the benefits of our great democracy."

LEX FRIEDEN
National Council on the
Handicapped

As Our Values Change, So Do Our Recreation Choices

America's prevailing social values have changed dramatically over the years, affecting recreational needs and choices.

In the 50s, leisure people measured success in economic and status terms and time was considered a reward that was earned from work. Affluence and a continuing stable economy were taken for granted. A new social consciousness evolved during the 60s and 70s which dampened the search for economic achievement in favor of more socially productive activities. Minority and women's rights were part of this agenda, as was a concern for preservation of the environment. Leisure was seen as the dominant route to self-fulfillment, and each American had the "right" to leisure.

Tough economic times in the late 70s brought most baby boomers out of the clouds and into serious working lives. Neotraditional values have formed as the new economic agenda blends with the social agenda of the previous decade. Today, people are more programmatic and less optimistic, and a new emphasis on moral and ethics is emerging.

Americans have less time for leisure but nevertheless a strong commitment to personal excellence through fitness activities. They have less desire to participate in many types of sports, instead wanting to perfect a few activities. "Winning" at work and at play, is important, so leisure time is often used to enhance skills that will bring personal rewards.

Today's fast-paced, highly-technological society has produced new stresses and pressures. The home is seen as a sanctuary from stress, and travel for leisure is frequently closer to this home base. The focus on family and children has returned, causing parents to investigate and scrutinize the amenities their communities offer. Recreation programs need to be flexible, allowing participation before work, during lunch hours, or after work. Amenities such as child care are increasingly important.

Consumer demand for outdoor recreation opportunities will be on the rise in the next decade, and many retirees will be heavy users of recreation facilities. Quality is the watchword for the 90s and beyond, because leisure time is scarce—but very important—in American society.

ANN CLURMAN
Yankelovich, Skelly and White/
Clancy, Shulman, Inc.

Our Strategic Planning Process and What It Found

Strategic planning involves assembling people with special knowledge of a subject to elicit their views of future trends, issues and optional solutions to determine a future course of action. The President's Commission on Americans Outdoors, with the assistance of personnel from the National Park Service, used this process to:

○ Involve individuals with a special knowledge and interest in outdoor recreation issues;

○ Identify broad social trends believed likely to occur during the next 20 years;

○ Discuss recreation issues related to these trends;

○ Generate possible options to resolve these issues for consideration by the Commission.

The process included two sessions in Washington, D.C. in December 1985 to identify trends; eight sessions at different field locations; and a final, capstone session in Annapolis, Maryland in July 1986. Field locations were selected to include different regions of the country with varying outdoor recreation resources. The sessions were held in Palm Springs, California; Tampa, Florida; Dayton, Ohio; Asheville, North Carolina; Houston, Texas; Colorado Springs, Colorado; Renton, Washington; and Bloomington, Indiana.

A total of 213 individuals participated in the strategic planning sessions. Participants in the field sessions represented businesses, organizations, and private citizens within a given state or region. The capstone group was drawn from a national base, thus providing a new perspective. The capstone group reviewed the top ranked issues from the field sessions, added any elements they thought were lacking, and ranked the new list in order of importance.

Trends

Two groups met in Washington, D.C. on December 2-3, 1985 to identify the broad social trends expected to affect American life to the year 2000 and beyond. The first group consisted of futurists, policy analysts from several fields, environmentalists, conservationists, industry representatives and other experts. These experts served as the primary identifiers of trends.

The second group was made up of public and private recreation providers. They provided expert views on the supply of recreation and identified additional trends.

The sessions resulted in identifying nearly 60 trends. Participants chose ten trends they felt were the most significant.

1. *Changing social and demographic composition:* American society is aging, increasing its ethnic mix and its education level, changing its work patterns and creating new centers of population.

2. *Fluctuating energy availability and cost:* Travel and tourism, and recreation activities dependent on energy, will continually be faced by uncertainties based upon day-by-day changes in world market and political conditions.

3. *Technological innovations:* New products and new ways of doing work greatly increase the choices for using leisure time, but can also change demands on recreation providers.

4. *Shifts in political power closer to the people:* State and local governments have shown initiatives in problem solving and assuming responsibilities while the federal government has been reducing its regulatory and financial assistance roles.

5. *Increased accountability of institutions, leaders:* People are increasingly participating in public processes to plan programs and formulate policies. Private institutions are being required to make available more information on products and plans.

6. *Concern for the environment:* Public interest and involvement in environmental protection issues remains high, with more emphasis now being placed on threats to personal environmental health and safety than on threats to nature.

7. *Creation of innovative partnerships:* Cooperative efforts between and among public and private sectors are developing to more efficiently meet public demand for recreation and other services.

8. *Shifts in economic strengths and weaknesses:* A domestic shift in employment from manufacturing to services and information is changing the time and money available for recreation.

9. *Changes in recreation and leisure:* Development of new equipment, changes in lifestyles and the variability of the leisure fashion of the moment place strong pressures on the ability of providers to respond to these changing demands.

10. *Changes in transportation systems:* Near completion of the interstate highway system, deregulation of airline and bus travel, and smaller automobiles are changing how, when, and where we travel for pleasure.

Issues

Participants in the field sessions verified the above trends and listed issues relating to recreation and outdoor opportunities arising from these trends. Groups identified between 25 to 50 issues in each session. Participants then voted on the ten issues which they felt were most important. The eight field sessions resulted in the following ranking of recreation issues.

Issue	Total Votes
1. Protection of natural resources and open space	131
2. Conflicting uses of recreation lands and waters	130
3. Roles of providers	110
4. Liability	88
5. Physical access to open space	85
6. Funding operations, maintenance, capital improvements	84
7. Alternative funding sources	69
8. Benefits of recreation	67
9. Acquisition of open space	67
10. Land use planning	54
11. Social access to open space	52
12. Partnerships	50
13. Data base needs	48

No single issue finished in the top ten issues for all eight of the field sessions. Liability came closest, finishing in the list of top ranking issues in seven of the eight sessions.

The rank order of issues varied widely among the eight sessions, reflecting the differences between large urban areas and smaller cities, the lack or presence of extensive federally managed lands, and many other factors.

Both field and capstone participants agreed that the importance of resource protection and problems with conflicting uses were the most important issues. However, the capstone panel in comparison with the field panels placed an increased importance upon the need for funding and expressed less concern with liability problems.

Capstone participants also discussed access as a single issue, which differed considerably from the way in which field panels clearly separated physical barriers to access from sociological and economic constraints. If the votes for access, including physical and social, were combined from field and capstone sessions, access would be the top ranking issue nationwide.

Table 1. Main reasons for participating in outdoor recreation

What are the main reasons you participate in outdoor recreation? *(Top Mentions Only)*	*Total Sample*
Enjoy/Enjoyment/Fun	36%
Exercise/Keep in shape	25
To be outdoors/Outside/Just to get out	22
Health/Healthier/For the health/Feel good	15
Fresh air	12
Be with people/Friends/Camaraderie/Socialize	8
Be with family/Son/Children/Spouse	6
Relax/Relaxation	5
Sunshine/Need the sun	5
Nature/Like nature	3
Claustrophobia/Hate to be confined in the house	3
Like sports	2
Pass time/Helps pass the time/Keep busy	2
Weather	2
Clear mind/Take mind off work	2
Scenery	2
Individualism/Be by myself	1
Always did/Grew up	1
Get away from work/Diversion from work	1
For work/Working/Work purposes	1
Enjoy wildlife/Animals	1
Competition	1
Nothing/I don't participate	3
Don't know/Refused	4
(BASE)	(2,000)

Table 2. Rank order of adult participation 1 or more times past year

1986 % Participation	Sometimes Often Very Often	Often/ Very Often
Walking for pleasure	84%	(50)
Driving for pleasure	77	(43)
Sightseeing	77	(34)
Picnicking	76	(28)
Swimming outdoors	76	(43)
Ocean, lake, river	(63)	(30)
Outdoor pool	(58)	(28)
Visit zoos, fairs, amusement parks	72	(17)
Attend outdoor sports events	60	(22)
Visit historic sites	59	(14)
Fishing	51	(25)
Bicycling	46	(17)
Camping	45	(21)
Tent Camping	(29)	(9)
Recreational vehicle	(22)	(8)
Other camping	(17)	(5)
Softball/baseball	43	(16)
Running or jogging	42	(17)
Attend outdoor plays/concerts	42	(11)
Bird watching, nature study	35	(15)
Tennis outdoors	30	(10)
Basketball	27	(10)
Motor boating, water skiing	27	(15)
Day hiking	27	(12)
Driving off road vehicles/snowmobiles	24	(11)
Canoeing/kayaking/rafting	22	(5)
Golfing	22	(10)
Football	21	(6)
Hunting	21	(11)
Backpacking	17	(5)
Sledding	17	(4)
Horseback riding	15	(3)
Sailing or windsurfing	15	(4)
Downhill skiing	14	(5)
Ice skating	12	(3)
Soccer	10	(3)
Cross country skiing	8	(3)
(BASE)	(2,000)	

Figure 1. National population trends in summer participation in selected outdoor recreation activities (12 years and older), 1960–1982

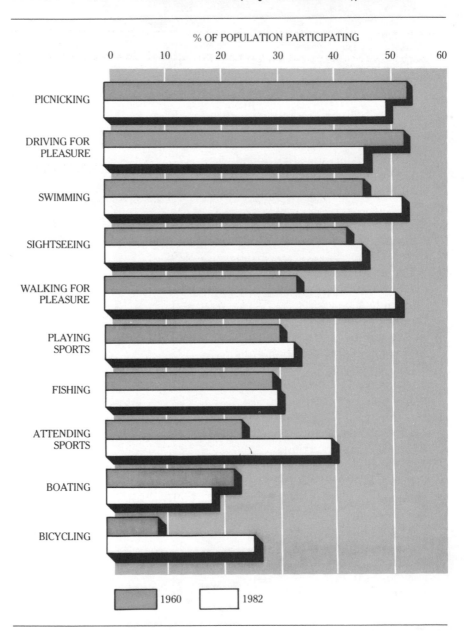

Source: 1960, 1982 National Recreation Surveys.

Figure 2. Percentage change, summer participants in 9 rapidly growing activities, 1960–1982

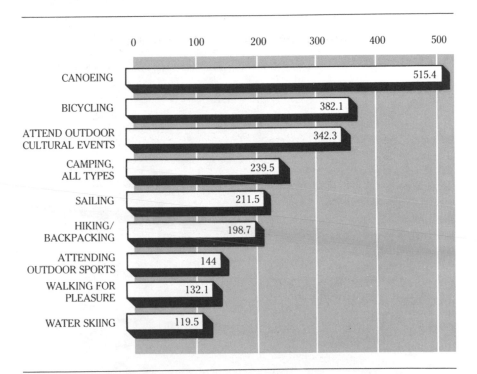

Source: 1960, 1982–83 National Recreation Surveys. Growth percentages based on rounded percentages of population participation.

Figure 3. Estimated number of participants in selected outdoor recreation activities, 1973–1982

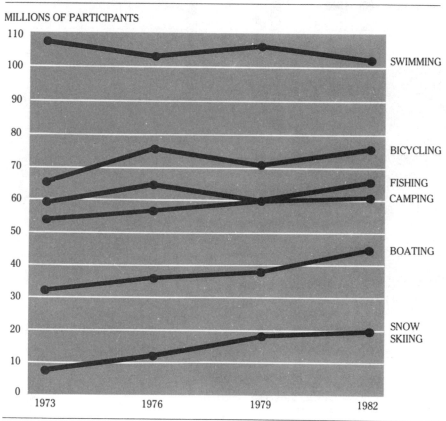

Source: A.C. Nielson, 1982. Ranking of Popularity of Participation in Sports Measured, 1973–1982, News release.

Figure 4. Where people recreate "often"—public areas.

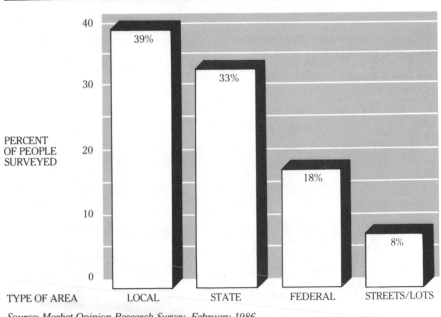

Source: Market Opinion Research Survey, February 1986.

Where people recreate often—private areas.

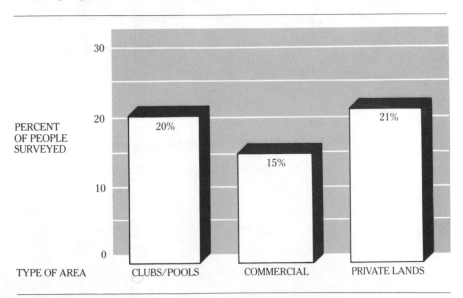

Figure 5. Comparison of distribution of visitors to public areas by time away from home for two surveys, 1960 and 1985.

PERCENT

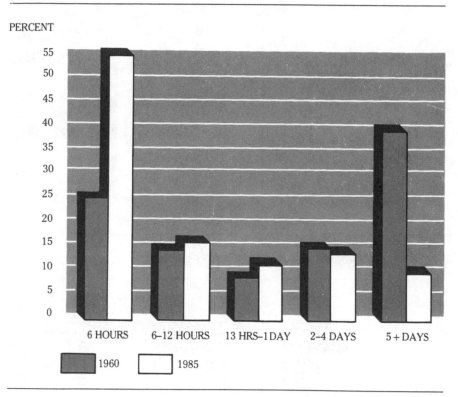

Source: ORRRC Study Report #5, Table 14: Public Area Recreation Visitor Survey, preliminary results, Summer 1985.

Figure 6. Comparison of recreational trips, 1972 and 1982, by outing type and oneway travel miles

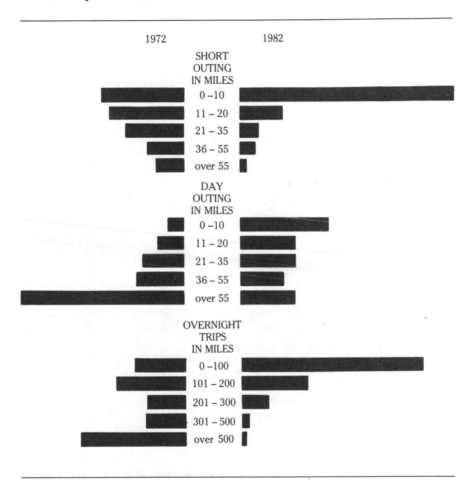

1972   1982

SHORT
OUTING
IN MILES
0 – 10
11 – 20
21 – 35
36 – 55
over 55

DAY
OUTING
IN MILES
0 – 10
11 – 20
21 – 35
36 – 55
over 55

OVERNIGHT
TRIPS
IN MILES
0 – 100
101 – 200
201 – 300
301 – 500
over 500

Source: Cordell and English, 1985; 1972, 1982 National Recreation Surveys.

Figure 7. Visitation to federal land, 1965–1984 by agency.

MILLIONS OF VISITOR HOURS

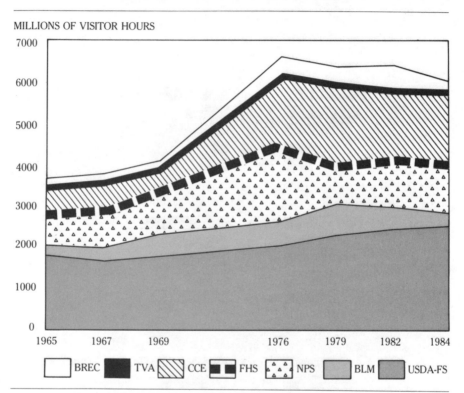

Sources: Selected Outdoor Rec. Statistics, BOR: Federal Recreation Fee Reports; Agency
Visitation Files.

Chapter 5

Do We Have Places To Go for Outdoor Recreation?

Private and public lands constitute our recreation estate

Two-thirds of our nation's lands are privately owned, and we use a lot of it for recreation—our own, that of community associations, and land owned by farmers and ranchers who offer various opportunities. We have more publicly-owned recreation land than any other nation—a measure of our country's size, affluence, and especially the foresight of earlier Americans.

We know the extent of the public estate and what it offers. But, we know relatively little about the number of acres open to the public or opportunities offered by private property owners.

The public recreation estate: vast—and West

The distribution of public recreation lands varies tremendously among regions and states. More than 778 million acres of public parks, forests, wildlife refuges and gamelands, and other lands are available for recreation. Of that total, 460 million acres are in the contiguous states and Hawaii; the remainder is in Alaska. One third (34%) of the contiguous United States is public recreation land.

Western states have a disproportionate share of public lands because of the concentration of federal lands in that region. Almost 38 million acres of Idaho, 71 percent of its land area, is in public—largely federal—ownership; nine other western states and Alaska have between 33 and 85 percent of their total land acreage as federal lands.

There is less public land in the East, and a few states have almost none. Illinois, the most populous state in the Midwest, has less than 3.5 percent of its 35 million acres in public ownership.

Figures 1 through 4 show total acres and regional distribution of public land managed by federal, state, county, and municipal governments. The federal government is by far the largest landowner, with 708 million acres, or 90.9 percent of all public recreation land. While municipal parks comprise but a fraction of the acreage, they account for more than 60 percent of all recreation areas.

National parks are dedicated to resources preservation and recreation for present and future generations

When we think of the great outdoors, many of us picture the Grand Canyon, Old Faithful, or Yosemite's Half Dome. Of all the federal lands, only the National Park System (76 million acres) is dedicated exclusively to the preservation of natural and historical areas for public recreation and education.

The National Park System is the most varied of the federal land systems. The 337 units include the great national parks, national seashores and lakeshores, dozens of small historic and cultural sites, and several metropolitan recreation areas, such as the Gateway National Recreation Area in New York City and the Golden Gate National Recreation Area in San Francisco. However, more than two-thirds (53 million acres) of the system's acreage is in Alaska, and in the lower 48 states, the majority is located west of the Mississippi River.

Most federal lands have multiple uses, including recreation

Federal lands administered by the U.S. Forest Service and the Bureau of Land Management provide outdoor recreation along with timber production, range forage, watershed protection, wildlife habitat, and mineral extraction.

While the bulk of the 191-million-acre National Forest system is located in the West, every resident of a major metropolitan area in the East is within a day's drive of a national forest. In the West, the national forests often are the backyards of major urban centers; residents of Denver, Salt Lake City, Albuquerque, Phoenix, Los Angeles, Portland, and Seattle can be in a national forest in an hour or less.

The Bureau of Land Management (BLM) is the largest national landowner, with over 337 million acres nationwide. The bulk of these lands are in 10 western states (175 million) and Alaska (161 million). All lands are open to the public for recreation, but some are geographically isolated or have access blocked by surrounding private lands.

Eighty-five percent of the 90 million acres managed by the Fish and Wildlife Service are in Alaska. However, there are 425 National Wildlife Refuges in 49 states. The Fish and Wildlife Service dedicates its lands first to habitat protection, fish hatching, and wildlife breeding, but the public may use many areas for fishing, hunting, birdwatching, walking, nature study and other wildlife-related recreation activities.

Three other federal agencies manage lands and waters primarily for flood protection, navigation, power production and irrigation, but also provide extensive water-related recreation opportunities.

The Corps of Engineers manages almost 4,000 recreation sites on 10 million land and water acres. It is one of the major suppliers of boating opportunities in the United States. The Corps leases many of its reservoir areas to state and local park agencies, who share the costs of facility development.

The Bureau of Reclamation administers six million acres of land and water, including 355 recreation areas in 17 western states. The Bureau directly manages 49 recreation areas and has cooperative agreements with state and local governments for administration of another 242 reservoir sites.

The Tennessee Valley Authority manages 600,000 recreation acres at reservoirs and adjacent sites in six southeastern states and the 170,000-acre Land Between the Lakes Integrated Resources Management Area in Tennessee and Kentucky.

States also manage parks and multiple-use lands

States administer 61.8 million acres of state parks and recreation areas, forests, and wildlife areas. These include 5,300 state parks, 721 state forests, and 7,400 wildlife areas, as well as a variety of natural, historic, and cultural areas, and reservoir and river recreation sites.

There are nearly 10 million acres in the park systems. State parks generally are fairly large areas in rural locations, with developed campgrounds and other facilities.

Thirty-nine states have their own forest systems totalling 20 million acres, but only twelve systems exceed 200,000 acres. Michigan, Idaho, Minnesota, Pennsylvania, Arizona, Alaska and Wisconsin have the largest state forest systems. State forests, just as national forests, are managed for multiple uses, including recreation.

All but four states have designated fish and game or wildlife areas and these total 19.9 million acres. Some of these areas are much larger than average state park systems. They are major resources for hunters and anglers, but their availability for general recreation activities, such as hiking and canoeing, varies according to their degree of accessibility and development.

Local recreation areas are smaller, but more numerous, and close to home

Municipal, county and regional parks and forests account for the largest number of recreation sites but a much smaller number of acres. Many sites in urban areas are quite small neighborhood parks. There are 67,685 municipal parks totaling almost 3 million acres. Counties administer more than 17,000 recreation areas of various types with a total area of 5.1 million acres. Municipal and county parks account for much of America's daily recreation close to home.

County parks are distributed throughout the nation, but county forests are located mainly in Wisconsin, Illinois, Alaska and Minnesota.

The 500,000 acres of regional parks and forests included in the local total are unusual in several ways. Most of the 2,780 regional park, forest and recreation areas are administered by regional authorities that provide recreation for two or more counties in a metropolitan region. The Huron-Clinton Metropark Authority in the Detroit area manages about 27,500 acres in five counties. The East Bay Regional Park Authority in California, provides 57,000 acres in and around the sprawling metropolitan complex of San Francisco-Oakland.

Often, these multi-county regional authorities manage large areas on the urban fringe. They focus on protection of key regional resources, such as river valleys or forested areas, and have an important influence on maintaining open space in the face of urban growth.

River, trail, and wilderness systems have grown

In addition to, and often within, public lands are specialized resource systems, established over the past 20 years as a result of the recommendations of the Outdoor Recreation Resources Review Commission. These include national systems of wilderness, wild and scenic rivers, and trails.

Rivers and trails have unique values for "linear" outdoor activities such as canoeing, hiking, rafting and trail riding. They also serve as vital links within and between areas available for other recreation uses. In the last 15 years, state and federal governments have increasingly recognized the values of wild, scenic and recreational rivers and of scenic and historic trails.

The national government has designated 73 river segments totalling 7,365 miles for protection under the National Wild and Scenic Rivers program enacted in 1968; states administer 753 of these miles. States report almost 6,000 additional miles under some protection to preclude uses that conflict with public access and enjoyment.

Local, regional and state agencies administer almost 35,000 trail miles, including 776 National Recreation Trails (8,100 miles) recognized by the Secretary of the Interior. There are 13 designated National Scenic or Historic Trails stretching more than 23,500 miles.

Trails Are Important

According to 13 national surveys conducted between 1959 and 1978, trail-related activities consistently rank among the ten most popular out-

door recreation activities. Historically, trails in the United States are not the result of conscious recreation planning decisions. Consequently, many trail routes pass over private property or along public rights-of-way and are subject to disruption and environmental degradation as development threats grow. This susceptibility is of particular concern as public interest in trails continues to grow at a rapid rate.

In part, the National Trails System Act of 1968 was a response to these pressures as between the years of 1978 and 1980 it provided the impetus for the designation of almost 19,000 miles of national trails. This represented 75 percent of the trail-miles up to that point. This expanded the system to include more than 500 trails totaling 25,000 miles, although it must be noted that only about 40 percent of these miles are "on the ground —rather than on a planner's map.

LAWRENCE R. KLAR, JR.
AND JEAN S. KAVANAGH
University of Massachusetts

The National Wilderness Preservation System, established in 1964, includes almost 90 million acres within National Forests, Parks, Wildlife Refuges and other federal natural resource areas in 44 states. About two-thirds of wilderness acres are in Alaska, with the remaining third spread in 43 other states. The largest areas outside Alaska are in the Mountain and Pacific states.

Nine states have established wilderness systems to maintain portions of state park and forest lands in an undeveloped, "forever wild" state. Wilderness areas supply not only primitive camping, backpacking and nature study opportunities, but important scientific benchmarks against which the condition of America's land can be measured.

Public land acreage is not the best measure of recreation opportunities

Public acreage totals are a better measure of *potential* than of *actual* outdoor recreation opportunity. Four factors affect whether people can use a recreation area: whether people can get to it (accessibility); necessary facilities; necessary services, including information about available opportunities; and whether other areas are available that offer similiar opportunities.

Distance from where people live is only one measure of accessibility. Almost half of all federal lands are located in Alaska, but the accessibility of a particular outdoor recreation area is also affected by the availability of roads, other transit routes or access points; places to park; and buses, trains, planes or other public transportation.

Much of the federal estate is relatively remote from population centers and difficult to reach. Some parcels are blocked by private land. In urban

Campgrounds—A Major Recreation Resource

Campgrounds can range in accommodations from very rustic, small units in forest environments to highly luxurious campgrounds with a broad range of resort-type recreation activities and facilities. The Woodall Company estimates there are approximately 17,000 campgrounds in the United States in 1986. Of this total, 12,000 are private campgrounds, and 5,000 are public. They also estimate there are currently over 1.3 million campsites in the United States. If this figure is multiplied by the average amount of money needed to develop one campsite ($3,500), it can be seen that the total capitalization value of campgrounds in the United States today is approximately 4.5 billion dollars. This figure underscores the importance of campgrounds as a component of outdoor recreation resources in Amerrica today.

HERBERT E. ECHELBERGER
U.S. Forest Service
AND DOUGLAS N. MCEWEN
Southern Illinois University

areas, public recreation sites may not be accessible because of the lack of public transportation.

While some activities (backcountry hiking and camping) may not require facilities, for many (swimming, boating, baseball, camping, golf, or tennis) developed facilities are essential. These range from the simple—primitive campgrounds, woodchip trails and pit toilets—to the elaborate—resort lodging, cable car ski lifts and visitor centers. Some facilities, such as comfortable areas to eat and sleep, enhance our enjoyment of recreation experiences, but may not be essential. Many developed recreation facilities have deteriorated due to age and heavy use, or have become obsolete because of changing demands.

Program services, ranging from information on opportunities to coaching a particular sport, equal recreation land and facilities in importance for many people. We throng to places we know about or which have been publicized. Some national parks and wilderness areas are intensely used, even overused, while other outstanding areas are only lightly visited because they have attracted little attention.

Education and interpretation are important services. Many of the values of magnificent natural areas or historic sites may be lost to visitors unless they are "opened up" by a guidebook or interpreter. The finest beach will be of little use for swimming if families are afraid to use it because there are no lifeguards. Special programs to encourage participation are as important as wheelchair ramps or elevators to bring people with disabilities into the mainstream of recreation opportunities.

The private sector supplies many of our recreation needs

The private sector manages recreation lands, offers services that transport people to recreation areas, conducts courses that teach recreation skills, provides comfort services on public lands and produces equipment that allow people to enjoy all kinds of recreation activity. Availability of private lands, recreation facilities and services is a major factor in determining actual recreation opportunity. The private sector has the ability to respond to the diverse recreation demands of the public quickly. Private providers perform many services that make public lands accessible and more enjoyable to the public.

Nonprofit groups, such as youth clubs, church groups, community associations and other independent, voluntary organizations, fill important recreation needs, particularly in urban areas. In a number of suburban areas, homeowner-sponsored community associations provide key sports facilities. In the Northern Virginia suburbs of Washington, D.C., for example, community associations own and operate over 200 swimming pools.

Nonprofit organizations, such as The Nature Conservancy and the Land Trust Exchange, have the ability to act quickly to protect important recreation and habitat lands. Five hundred local land trusts have been established in the past ten years.

We know that private lands and facilities are an important and integral part of the overall supply of outdoor resources. We do not know the extent of private recreation opportunities. The rapidly changing state of private recreation supply makes a comprehensive inventory of private areas and services difficult.

The private sector is a major recreation supplier for certain kinds of activities. There are more than 10,000 private campgrounds, for instance. Six hundred privately operated ski areas, some located on leased public lands, provide almost all the downhill skiing opportunities in the nation. The National Golf Foundation reports 4,789 private golf courses, making the private sector a major provider of this activity, as it is for boating through marina facilities.

Many activities, including hunting, long-distance hiking and camping, depend heavily on the use of private farm and forest lands. Private lands and facilities are also more critical in eastern and midwestern states where public land acreage is small in relation to nearby populations.

There are still problems

Americans have made generous investments in private and public recreation opportunities over the last 20 years, but a number of problems remain.

o Despite progress in protecting some natural resources, key open space areas such as wetlands, shorelines, and farmland are being lost or closed to the public at the rate of one to two million acres each year.

o Urban development pressures and rising property values are reducing the number of private recreation opportunities available to the public. Facilities, such as marinas and campgrounds, located on particularly important recreation resources (water, ridge tops), cannot compete with pressures to convert to higher-profit residential and commercial uses. Independent, non-profit agencies have closed key recreation facilities in urban neighborhoods. Farmland once open for hunting is being closed to the public.

o Developed public recreation facilities have deteriorated because of age and heavy use, or become obsolete due to changing demands.

o Development of close-to-home recreation facilities, such as swimming pools, playfields, courts and trails, has not kept pace with population growth; many such facilities are overloaded during periods of peak use. Older facilities, and even some new ones, are not made accessible to people with physical handicaps.

o Budget freezes and cuts have made it difficult for public recreation agencies to staff programs and services essential to full use and protection of parks and facilities. Services that inform people about recreation opportunities, encourage activity participation, interpret natural resources, and teach or coach new participants have particularly suffered.

o Complementary relationships between public and private recreation lands and facilities are not as effective as they should be because information is lacking about what the private sector provides, and because uncoordinated public and private programs make partnerships difficult to establish and sustain.

Despite these problems, our existing recreation lands and facilities are an incomparable base on which we can build to meet future recreation needs. How American people and American resources can translate these needs and problems into opportunities is the subject of the following pages.

Figure 1. Acres of public recreation land

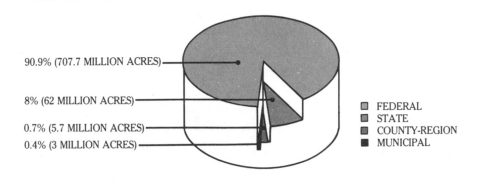

90.9% (707.7 MILLION ACRES)

8% (62 MILLION ACRES)

0.7% (5.7 MILLION ACRES)

0.4% (3 MILLION ACRES)

FEDERAL
STATE
COUNTY-REGION
MUNICIPAL

Figure 2. Numbers of recreation areas

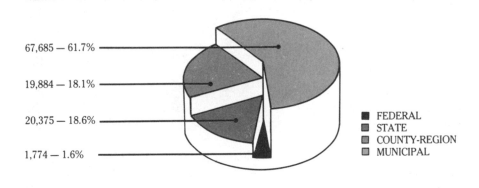

67,685 — 61.7%

19,884 — 18.1%

20,375 — 18.6%

1,774 — 1.6%

FEDERAL
STATE
COUNTY-REGION
MUNICIPAL

Sources: Fed. Agencies, NASORLO — 1986.

Figure 3. Public recreation land by region.

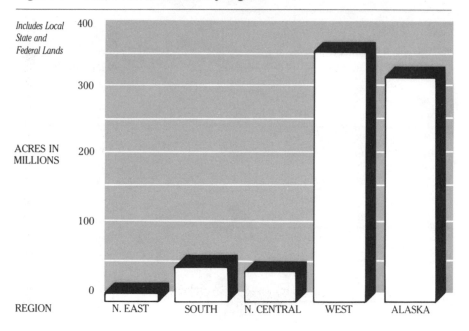

Includes Local State and Federal Lands

ACRES IN
MILLIONS

REGION

N. EAST   SOUTH   N. CENTRAL   WEST   ALASKA

Figure 4. Public recreation acres per 1000 people.

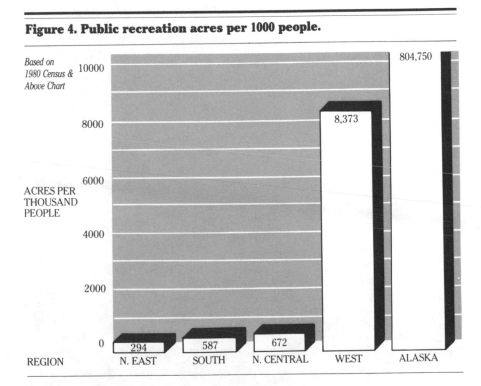

. . . .

Americans: The People

"Life, liberty and the pursuit of happiness" were the three inalienable rights Thomas Jefferson claimed for the American people in the Declaration of Independence. For more and more Americans, the pursuit of happiness leads to the Great Outdoors. We find blind people on mountaintops, "seeing" wind and trees and rushing streams in a whole new way. We heard about a 70-year old man running his 50th consecutive Boston Marathon. Our choices of the things we do in the outdoors are as diverse as we are.

We found an excitement abroad in the land: Americans coming together to plan for their future and to shape their environments. Volunteering, a tradition as old as barnraising and quilting bees, has risen to new levels. The political decisions which affect our lives are increasingly made close to home. We are finding the leadership for accomplishing our dreams in our communities, in our friends, neighbors and associates. We are finding it in ourselves.

We listened to thousands of people, and we heard one thing above all. Americans prize the outdoors, and are eager to do more to see that they have opportunities to enjoy it, and that their grandchildren will as well. Americans care about helping each other, and about the world we leave to future generations.

We want to capture that spirit of the American people, in a prairie fire of action to protect the outdoors and provide recreation for the future. Local coalitions can look ahead to see what community members will want to do outdoors, plan what needs to be done, and then get on with it. Local concern and investment will do more than anything else to preserve outdoor opportunities for Americans tomorrow. We call upon the President to light the prairie fire, and lead the crusade. But it will become reality in our communities.

An outdoor ethic is essential to ensure that our efforts to preserve and enjoy the outdoors are carried forward by future generations. We must understand that all our actions affect the outdoors and the other people we share it with, and learn to accept our responsibilities as stewards.

Our schoolchildren must learn about the importance of the natural world, and their places in it. Nature is a book waiting to be opened, which those with experience can share with those wanting to learn. All our citizens should be aware of the importance of meaningful leisure in their lives, and of the values of the outdoors for health, economic security, social cohesion, and inspiration. We can go a long way toward meeting our conservation and recreation needs by tapping the willingness of millions of Americans, young and old, to work together for a common good. Outdoor corps to build trails and greenways, maintain parks, and protect the environment can be a cornerstone in reshaping the outdoors.

We are concerned with the quality of the experience Americans have in the outdoors, and that is at least partly dependent on the quality of services they receive. Services—transportation, safety, information, activity leadership, food and lodging—play a critical "gateway" role in getting people into the outdoors. Public satisfaction with services is declining, and this needs to be addressed.

"To speak of the outdoors is also to speak of the true greatness of America, a greatness that is found in the spirit of its individual citizens, a spirit that can be fired by the opportunities of challenge to be found in the outdoors. It has been a spirit that has been characterized by those unique human qualities of self-confidence and self-reliance, of tenacity, of enterprising curiosity and, above all, a sense of compassion that when shared in common have been the source of the nation's strength and vitality."

WILLARD BROWN
Mentor, Ohio

Chapter 1

We Must Ignite a Prairie Fire of Local Action

We recommend

● Community by community, across America, we form coalitions for action. We must organize to invest in recreation opportunities for the future and to protect our outdoors heritage.

● Mayors and other local officials lead your communities by building a plan of action. Define a vision for the future, list your recreation assets, and identify your tools. Then decide what needs to be done, and go to work.

● Governors create Governor's Councils to promote outdoor recreation. Find out what people in your state will want to do in the outdoors twenty years in the future, or fifty. Explore what needs to be done, to make sure they will have appropriate places to do those things. Draw a blueprint for action to meet tomorrow's needs.

● The President launch a nationwide celebration of Americans Outdoors, a program that looks forward for Americans Outdoors of the future.

We need the great outdoors close to home

The phrase "the Great American Outdoors" usually conjures up images of the front range of the Rockies, or Lake Tahoe, or the Great Dismal Swamp. But the fact is that the Great American Outdoors is just down the block as well. It's the community park, the town commons, the local streamside. The Great American Outdoors is in your backyard, too.

The outdoors is important to us in many ways, but most of all in the places where we live, work, and play. And people care most about helping to make things happen on the street where they live.

All across the country, people are putting muscle and ideas to work

★   In *Ohio*, biking, hiking, and equestrian groups helped build the Buckeye Trail, a 1,200-mile riding and hiking trail across the state. In *California*, voters set up the Midpeninsula Regional Open Space District, which has protected nearly 21,000 acres of open space and over 110 miles of trails in heavily populated San Mateo and Santa Clara Counties. In Phoenix, *Arizona*, farmers granted easements along their irrigation canals for a 125-mile metropolitan bikeway. When accounting personnel in *Oregon's* Ochoco National Forest cut the time needed for their bookkeeping work, they used their free time to take over maintenance duties for a forest campground that was scheduled to be closed for lack of staff. In Multnomah, *Oregon*, local citizens helped renovate an abandoned school as a community recreation center. In Denver, *Colorado*, the developer of an office park surrounded his development with acres of open space for wildlife habitat.

★   The Sheboygan, *Wisconsin*, members of the local Izaak Walton League Chapter went door-to-door with a video tape campaign promoting a conservation ethic and encouraging private landowners to open their lands for recreation. In *New York City*, more than 1,000 volunteers from grade school children to senior adults planted more than 60,000 flower bulbs in Central Park. More than 80 *Utah* communities have inventoried their communities' trees and organized tree-care programs. In *Indiana*, the AMAX coal company donated land to the state for a 12,500 acre fish and wildlife area. In central *Texas*, citizen volunteers raised money to buy Wild Basin of Bee Creek, a unique example of Texas hill country located only six miles from the state capitol building in Austin. In *Washington* state, the Washington State Snowmobile Association and the Washington Nordic Ski Federation jointly prepared a Winter Recreation Code of Ethics. In Warren, *Vermont*, Sugarbush Inn and the Ottauquechee Land Trust arranged to transfer development rights to protect 150 acres as a conservation area. In Pleasanton, *California*, the Kaiser Sand and Gravel Company donated a quarry to the local park district; the quarry now is an award-winning park.

★ In *Minnesota*, city, state, and federal agencies and local industries cooperated to establish a national wildlife refuge along the Minnesota River only minutes from downtown Minneapolis. In *Arizona*, more than 4,000 volunteers have spent more than 58,000 hours maintaining trails on the Tonto National Forest. In *Colorado*, guides and river runners on the Yampa River report sighting of the endangered peregrine falcon as part of the state's Peregrine Falcon Reintroduction Program. In Portland, *Oregon*, local officials and neighborhood groups turned a downtown parking lot into recreation open space. Each Saturday in spring, the Murray (*Utah*) High School football team plants trees along city streets. In Pocahontas County, *Iowa*, local citizens, the Iowa Natural Heritage Foundation, and public agencies teamed up to protect one of the state's largest remaining virgin prairie sites. A special Horse Patrol of the Backcountry Horsemen of *Washington* promote minimum impact use by backcountry and wilderness area trail riders.

★ In Houston, *Texas*, more than 80 local volunteers developed long range goals and an action plan to increase the number of local parks. In Carthage, *Mississippi*, volunteers planted more than 12,000 dogwood trees along a local highway to create a scenic "dogwood trail." In Oxnard, *California*, after neighbors helped renovate Colonia Park, use increased 400 percent. In *Vermont*, the Catamount Trail Association is developing a 280-mile cross-country ski trail across the state as a part of a trans-state ski trail from Massachusetts to Quebec. The *Maine* Coast Heritage Trust has acquired more than 100 scenic islands that surround Acadia National Park to protect island ecosystems and vistas from the park. In Dubuque County, *Iowa*, a local nonprofit community group maintains a county-owned conservation/recreation trail on 25 miles of abandoned railroad right-of-way. A Senior Citizens Park Maintenance Corps maintains parks in Revere, *Massachusetts*; the parks are cleaner and the volunteers are happier. In Shaftsbury, *Vermont*, 25 volunteers raised money to buy a 65 acre tract for a community park. In *Denver*, the non-profit Platte Greenway Foundation has raised more than $14 million to restore the South Platte River in the city.

The special places that are important to us, the programs and facilities we rely on for recreation, will not be available to our children if we don't act now to see that they are. It is up to us to make sure that future generations will be able to track a deer in the dawn stillness, or see the ice crystals fly as children skate up a country stream.

We will light a prairie fire

The Commission believes that Americans across the country can light a prairie fire of action, to protect what is important to us, to build for the future. This is the single most important recommendation we can make. Americans working together in their own communities will spark a renaissance of caring about our great outdoors.

When the prairie fire catches and burns, we will create a lasting corps of people who care about environmental quality and scenic beauty. We can build a movement of Americans investing in recreation opportunities for the future.

Why local action?

All across America, people are taking more control over the decisions and actions which affect the quality of their lives. Political authority is increasingly centered at the state and local levels. Volunteer activity continues to escalate. People know their own needs best, and are best qualified to make decisions to meet them.

We need recreation opportunities close to home. We are taking shorter vacations these days. Piling the kids and dog into the station wagon for a three-week visit to a national park is no longer the standard. We are travelling shorter distances, for shorter periods of time.

We know that open spaces, scenic beauty, and safe, clean places to play, are critical pieces of the fabric of our lives. They must be provided, and safeguarded, by the members of our communities.

"Communities" can mean communities of interest as well as geographic communities. We form associations with other people of similar interests, such as sport clubs, neighborhood associations, and nonprofit organizations. These groups can function as communities in designing a vision for the future of outdoor recreation, and an action plan to get there.

How does the prairie fire begin?

We need to spark excitement and creativity about caring for the outdoors. There are as many different ways for this to happen as there are communities in America. What works for Hardin, Montana might not be the best answer in Houma, Louisiana.

The best answer is to involve all the members of your community, and set your own priorities. We can give you some ideas of things Americans have already done in some places. We can recommend a focal point to provide coordination and assistance to communities. Then it's up to you.

Organize for action

To spark a renewal of values and an awareness of roots, 800 communities in Tennessee celebrated "Homecoming '86." Homecoming was "part reunion, part history lesson, and part good old-fashioned hoe-down." Each community identified what makes it special or unique. Then they looked ahead ten years and thought about what they would like the community to be. Next they planned—and carried out—a community project to preserve or enhance that special quality. And they invited everyone home to celebrate.

Homecoming '86 helped boost tourism and economic development in Tennessee. But it did something more important than that. It increased Tennesseans' pride in their heritage. It sharpened their determination not to lose those things that are precious to them. And it brought them together in communities, to act.

We think that will work for Americans Outdoors. Each community should organize to draw up a plan for the future of outdoor recreation in their community. Select a chairperson to coordinate and promote the action.

Then, begin to build coalitions. Involve everyone who is interested in the outdoors and recreation, and the many more who might like to be. The people who join you will become the core of a new, activated constituency for the outdoors. Develop an agenda which will interest people with many different points of view.

Involve civic groups, garden clubs, neighborhood associations; local officials and planners, boy scouts and girl scouts; sporting clubs, conservation organizations, and recreation associations. Most importantly, go to all the citizens or members of your community who care about the places where they live and work and play. They will have ideas no one has asked them for.

Develop a dream

Your agenda? First, develop a dream. Define a vision. Look forward for twenty years, or fifty, and decide what you want the future of the outdoors to be like in your community. What kind of recreation opportunities do you want coming generations to have?

Think about what it would mean if that stream valley cove where the old folks take the grandchildren for picnics is lost as development advances. Would it make people feel differently about living here if a park with a fountain or a place for kids to go for organized sports took the place of that vacant corner lot? Do your children learn anything about the natural world in school? Can people with special needs feel a part of the community by participating with others in planning and enjoying recreation programs?

Make it happen

Decide your priorities, and set your goals. Then, plan to make it happen. You might go about it like this:

o Develop a list of all your community's outdoor recreation assets. Include buildings, people, institutions, lands, and waters and special places. List everything that already contributes to the outdoors experience in your community.

o Analyze the tools available to you to get from where you are to where you want to be. You may need new ones. Evaluate your authorities for shaping growth and development and your environmental quality regulations. Nonprofit land trusts can help set aside needed open space. Teachers, park and recreation personnel, neighborhood associations all have special skills to offer.

o Now, build a plan of action. Determine the changes and actions that will be necessary in order to make your dream of the future a reality. Many ideas are contained in this report. Make a list of all the projects to undertake. Then, go to work.

Here are some ideas

Many, many ideas for possible community action are presented throughout this report. The Greenways are an obvious, exciting place to start.

Every town, city, or neighborhood can benefit by the addition of green sanctuaries for walks, running, horse and bicycle rides, and enjoying nature. With a Greenways system, you can multiply the value of these areas many fold by linking them up with other parks in other communities.

Development of an outdoor ethic is an essential task which should be undertaken by every geographic community and every community of interest. The Commission has challenged every community to develop a code of ethics suitable to its needs and to work actively toward reflecting that ethic in actions. Each community should take responsibility for shaping growth so that recreation needs are considered and met. Planning for outdoor recreation should take place before development happens, not afterwards. Most tools for shaping growth are most effectively and appropriately employed at the local level.

The ideas which you can use are almost limitless. Others presented in this report include rivers protection. This can be closely tied with your local greenway, and will help to protect your town's water supply as well. Scenic beauty projects to control unsightly billboards and junkyards or planting trees and flowers will make both visitors and residents feel better about your community. The establishment of outdoor corps of youth, senior citizens, or other volunteers will help to spread a conservation ethic while completing important outdoors projects.

Put it to work

Boundless horizons mark the work which you can undertake in your communities. We probably haven't even thought of the best ideas yet. Your own creativity will best spark the prairie fire. Your commitment will make it last.

Mayors and local officials, and organization directors, should play a key catalyst role in making the steps outlined here happen. We make the following specific recommendations to the nation's Governors, and the President, as well.

Governors should establish Governor's Councils to find out what people in your state will want to do in the outdoors into the twenty-first century and what actions need to be taken to provide appropriate places to do those things. Many states have already launched, or completed, this critically important step. If you have, take the next step. Put those recommendations into action.

Our recommendation to the President is that he lead the prairie fire.

• Launch a nationwide celebration of Americans Outdoors.

• Challenge each of America's 40,000 communities to invest in the outdoors in their community.

• Recognize 100 model Great American Outdoors Communities, and share their successes with the rest of the nation.

• Invite the nation's governors to a Presidential Conference on the Outdoors, like Teddy Roosevelt did in 1908. Ask them to create Governor's Councils on the Outdoors, and to help launch the prairie fire.

General George S. Patton once said, "Don't tell people how to do something—tell them what needs to be done and they will surprise you with their ingenuity." We believe that Americans working together, in the places where they live and in the groups to which they belong, will find ways to protect our magnificent outdoor recreation heritage; to be sure that all Americans have access to the recreation opportunities they need to be productive, active citizens; and to make the outdoors a central part of the world we leave for all future generations.

Although we might like to spend a lifetime in a favorite park, we spend most of our time at our daily work and with routine family matters. What people need are more of the park resources they crave in parks that are closer to home and work . . . The National Park Service cannot provide all of our urban park needs and desires. The community must. We need community "reference points": playgrounds and parks, pools and fountains, even tree-lined boulevards that make driving to work so pleasant. We need great community parks like those created for our enjoyment by Olmsted and his generation. I grew up in Kansas City, a community that provided green oases. Someone with foresight made sure these reference points existed in my neighborhood.

For two weeks each summer, my family vacationed at lakes or visited the national parks and national forests. We loved these special places. But we were there for only a two-week vacation. We spent the other 50 weeks living in a community that, fortunately, had enough green reference points.

PAUL PRITCHARD
National Parks and Conservation
Association

Somewhere in the last 30 years the nation has lost, or failed to nurture and develop, the underlying strength of a local approach to conservation.

JOYCE KELLY
Defenders of Wildlife

Chapter 2

We Need An Outdoor Ethic

Our country has become so greatly urbanized that there are now millions of adults and children who have never seen a wild turkey or black bear, have never been inside a 19th-century log cabin, or never camped or walked a woodland trail.

ELIZABETH THACH
Tennessee Valley Authority

We recommend

● Each geographic community and community of interest develop an outdoor ethic and work toward reflecting that ethic in personal and organizational actions.

● Educators make the environment an integral part of each child's basic education.

What is an outdoor ethic?

An outdoor ethic means personal involvement in the outdoors as an essential part of life. It means a sense of appreciation for, and obligation toward the air, land, water and living things of the earth. It includes statesmanship, courtesy for others using the outdoors, and stewardship; our obligation to ensure future generations' enjoyment of our natural heritage.

Our contact with the outdoors may be extensive, as in our recreation; or brief, as we dash between classrooms and office buildings. It can be vicarious, as we watch a blue jay in a tree through a hospital room window, or read a novel about outdoor adventure. Our interactions with the outdoors help to shape our commitment to its care.

The most powerful ethics are unwritten, and individual. They direct our actions in the outdoors and affect decisions about community priorities made in voting booths across the country. An outdoor ethic reflects pride in our country.

We must instill in every American a sense of ownership of the outdoors, and a commitment to maintaining outdoors opportunities for the future. Our objective is an aware, educated, sensitive, and activated outdoor constituency.

Different approaches

Suppose a subdivision is planned for a piece of land which has a pond. Four people petition the developer for the same action—to save the pond—for slightly different reasons.

One person stresses the need for conservation of the pond. She addresses our responsibility—as individuals and as a society—to protect the quantity and quality of natural areas passed on to future generations.

Another emphasizes the environmental relationship between the pond, the living creatures it supports, and present and future residents of the area. He warns of the consequences of disturbing parts of the web.

The recreation advocate points out that the pond can be used for many things, such as ice skating, fishing, nature study, and picnicking. The area can be designed and managed to promote safe and courteous behavior.

The fourth petitioner stresses our need for meaningful use of our leisure time. Quality places for quiet reflection or physical activity are necessary for this.

We recommend that as individuals and communities across America develop their outdoor ethic, they include each of these approaches.

Our society benefits from an outdoor ethic

The National Governors' Association in August 1986 adopted a policy statement saying, "The Governors believe that preservation, conservation, and wise management of the earth's natural resources is critical to the human capacity for sustained economic development and quality of life."

Broad adoption of an outdoor ethic will increase the benefits to our society of a healthy, productive resource base, and a vigorous recreation economy. Communities will be more attractive places to live, work, and play. Americans will have more and better recreation opportunities. A variety of outdoor habitats will be preserved for future generations.

Recreationists need to be educated and then constantly reminded of their responsibility to the outdoors.

JACK LORENZ
Izaak Walton League of America

Why do Americans, who love the outdoors so much, do so much to jeopardize its future? Are we oblivious to the insults we scatter in the form of trash along our country roads—or worse yet along trails to our scenic natural sites? How did we ever come to expect others to clean up after us at our campsites? Because we exhibit so little respect for the outdoors, we run the risk of converting our federal, state, and local recreation programs into law enforcement efforts. Enough! We can do better. We need to educate all Americans to their rights to enjoy the outdoors—and their responsibilities to use the outdoors well.

COMMISSIONER DERRICK CRANDALL

The use of the world is finally a personal matter, and the world can be preserved in health only by the forbearance and care of a multitude of persons.

WENDELL BERRY
"The Unsettling of America"

For the past 100 years—especially during the past 25—we have emphasized the role of government in conservation and have given little attention to the individual. We have not developed a land ethic in the minds and hearts of citizens in a manner and scale that complements public programs.

LARRY TOMBAUGH
Michigan State University

The people of this country should love their land and treat it with care.

COMMISSIONER SHELDON COLEMAN

With the widespread growth of an outdoor ethic, private landowners will be more willing to make their land available for recreation. Resource degradation through ignorance or overuse will decrease. Conflicts among different kinds of users will be lessened as people learn to be considerate of others and better care for the land base. We will be able to accomodate more people in the outdoors, with fewer impacts on the resource.

We need to do more to build an American outdoor ethic

Many Americans already subscribe to an outdoor ethic. Thousands of volunteers work on public lands. Membership of outdoors and conservation groups is growing. We have statutes which punish those who litter, pollute our air and water, kill endangered species, or destroy valuable ecosystems.

But there are signs that many people do not share this respect, or are unaware of the effects of their actions on the outdoors. Vandalism in parks costs municipalities over $500 million a year. Park rangers, who traditionally help people learn about the natural world, are asked to perform law enforcement duties instead. Conflicts among different recreation groups seriously degrade recreation opportunities for all.

And the outdoors itself suffers from our misuse. We fill wetlands for housing and build shopping centers over historic battlefields. We find trash in the middle of the ocean and on the tops of our highest mountains. We create air pollution which obscures the grand views in some national parks and wilderness areas. We cannot drink from our streams.

How do we promote an outdoor ethic? With information and experience

People shape and change their values based on information and experience. Information is a powerful tool. We need basic knowledge about the importance of the outdoors, and the interdependence of living things. And we need direct experience of the outdoors to forge an emotional commitment.

A few states have laws on the books requiring environmental or natural resources education. A requirement for outdoor education in schools represents an investment in the future protection of resources. As the State of Indiana reported to us, "Conservation education and outdoor ethics are the thread that holds together the future of outdoor recreation."

Secretary of Interior Donald Hodel's Take Pride in America campaign is a partnership of state and federal agencies, designed to foster local activities which increase public awareness of the need for wise use of our land. Other means for imparting information to the public include mass media, community groups and organizations, and outdoor places themselves.

Each park, like everyman's university, must serve as a center of knowledge and enlightenment . . . must be a hotbed of scholarship, learning, teaching, seeking, searching, inquiring, delving, discovering and understanding.

TED SUDIA
Senior Scientist
National Park Service

Public land managers have a responsibility to make park and recreation areas outdoor learning centers. Programs, signs, guidebooks, brochures, and personal example can all help promote an ethic about the proper use of the outdoors.

General knowledge about the outdoors is important, but direct experience is required to truly build an emotional response and greater commitment. There is no substitute for getting people into the outdoors. Let them feel exhilaration on a glistening snowy slope, a sense of heritage sharing a favorite fishing hole with a child. A blind person sees the outdoors through touch, sounds, and smells that inspire just as much commitment and exhilaration. We must make outdoor places available close to people's homes—so that their experiences in the outdoors will help lead them to adoption of an outdoor ethic.

Experience in fields, streams, and meadows should supplement outdoor education in the classroom. Outdoor corps, adopt-a-park and other volunteer programs give people the chance to participate in planning and stewardship of outdoor opportunities.

Who can help promote an outdoor ethic?

We want to build individual awareness and promote responsible action through communities and coalitions of interest. A variety of partnerships will be necessary to reach a broad audience in achieving this goal.

Non-profit organizations and associations have long lead the way in making information available to the public to promote an outdoor ethic. Organizations such as the Izaak Walton League, the National Wildlife Federation, and the Audubon Society have skills, materials, and experience to contribute.

Private landowners play an important role in the education of the American public, particularly hunters and fishermen. They can promote, and require, responsible behavior on their land.

Private recreation providers reach a large number of people: one of every two Americans over eleven years old visits a fair, amusement park, or zoo sometime during a year. Messages about conservation, environmental protection, and the impact of human activities upon wildlife can be informative and entertaining in these areas. The San Diego Zoo, for instance, teaches wildlife conservation principles in a recreation setting.

Recreation equipment manufacturers and sellers can provide a message about the safe and proper use of equipment—safe for the user, for others enjoying the outdoors, and for the environment. The motorcycle industry publishes literature on outdoor ethics and landowner relations that is distributed free to purchasers by dealers.

Recreation activity and enthusiast groups can develop codes of conduct for their sport or activity. The Good Sam Club, a group of vehicular campers, urges members to leave campsites cleaner than they found them. The United States Hang Gliding Association has worked for over ten years to instill respect for property owners. The Boy Scouts and Girl Scouts have a long tradition of teaching outdoor skills and providing young people their first experiences in hiking and camping.

The recreation and tourism service industry, including travel agents, outfitters, park concessioners and others, serves as a highly effective information source to many recreation users.

Parks, recreation and natural resource professionals are looked to as stewards, as teachers, and as leaders. They need to work to establish an outdoor ethic within their agency, institution, or business.

Community leaders can insist that government decisions consider conservation and recreation values equally with others such as economic development in achieving community objectives.

Corporations can sponsor environmental exhibits or messages or other informational material as a public service.

Recreation skills teachers can teach courtesy and resource impacts as part of their instruction.

• We recommend that the President recognize the importance of an outdoor ethic to the health of the country in the annual State of the Union message.

And if we succeed . . .

Commissioner LaPage stated it this way: "a true outdoor society . . . would surely reflect a different set of conditions than those which we address in 1986." Decreased costs for clean-up, healthier functioning natural systems, more diversity of recreation opportunities, are only a part of what we can expect.

We also will be able to do in our own day as Mike Harvey, counsel for the Senate Energy and Natural Resources Committee challenged us,

> *what Theodore Roosevelt did 80 years ago and Franklin Roosevelt did 50 years ago; we must expand the concept of conservation to meet the problems of a new age . . . to make sure that the national estate we pass on to our descendants is green and flourishing.*

With a broad-based outdoor ethic, we all become stewards of our estate. And future generations, as well as our own, will be richer for it.

Conservation Commandments

1. Study the land so that each acre may be used wisely according to its capabilities and treated according to its needs.

2. Guard well the living soil, that it may continue to nurture man:

   Clothe it lovingly with vegetation, hold on to it tenaciously, restore its fertility and organic content, improve it as a legacy for posterity.

3. Revere water, the lifeblood of civilization:

Retard it on the surface, trap it in the soil, guard its purity zealously.

4. Cherish forests that they may:

Conserve water, shelter wildlife, provide for our needs, restore our tranquility.

5. Respect all living things as having a role, however humble, in the balance of nature.

6. Provide living museums, samples of primeval America, to be managed by nature alone, so that they may:
   Serve as reservoirs of wild species that may be needed tomorrow, provide control areas against which man's efforts at management may be measured.

7. Learn to live in harmony with nature in an ecological symphony, a mutually beneficial dependency.

M. GRAHAM NETTING
Director
Carnegie Museum, Pittsburgh
Powdermill Nature Reserve and
Bioscience Center
Ligonier Valley

Winter Recreation Code of Ethics

1. I will respect the rights of all winter recreationists to enjoy the beauty of the winter wonderland. I will respect public and private property.

2. I will park considerately, taking no more space than needed, without blocking other vehicles and without impeding access to trails.

3. I will keep to the right when meeting another winter recreationist. I will yield the right-of-way to traffic moving downhill.

4. I will slow down and use caution when approaching or overtaking another.

5. I will respect designated areas, trails, use signs and established ski tracks.

6. When stopping, I will not block the trail.

7. I will not disturb wildlife. I will avoid areas posted for the protection or feeding of wildlife.

8. I will pack everything I packed in and will not litter.

9. I realize that my destination, objective and travel speed should be determined by my equipment, ability, the terrain, weather, and the traffic on the trail. In case of emergency, I will volunteer assistance.

10. I will not interfere with or harass others. I recognize that people judge all skiers or snowmobilers by my actions.

WASHINGTON STATE
SNOWMOBILE ASSOCIATION
Shelton, WA

The National Wildlife Federation Creed

I pledge myself, as a responsible human, to assume my share of man's stewardship of our natural resources.

I will use my share with gratitude, without greed or waste.

I will respect the rights of others and abide by the law.

I will support the sound management of the resources we use, the restoration of the resources we have despoiled, and the safe-keeping of significant resources for posterity.

I will never forget that life and beauty, wealth and progress, depend on how wisely man uses these gifts . . . the soil, the water, the air, the minerals, the plant life, and the wildlife. This is my pledge!

Operation RESPECT Works

In 1979 the Westvaco Corporation decided to close its 300,000 acres of timber land in Virginia to the public, due to the irresponsible behavior and actions of visitors. The Izaak Walton League organized a council of landowners, recreation activity groups and others to ensure appropriate user attitudes. Operation RESPECT—Responsible Educated Sportsmen Promoting Ethical Behavior—took the message of responsible behavior on private property to the public through magazines, newspapers, and newsletters across the state. Westvaco's lands remain open today as a result.

Storyteller Extols Virtues of a Clean Chesapeake

Folksinger and master storyteller Tom Wisner celebrates the heritage of Chesapeake Bay, and extolls the virtues of a clean and healthy environment, in workshops and programs for people of all ages. His words and music, shared in schools, museums, and special gatherings, are designed to lift the spirits and kindle a sense of respect and stewardship for the American Outdoors.

Creating awareness and helping Idahoans and out-of-state visitors to understand the many values and recreational uses that underlie the state's recreation/tourism attractions are important. The potential effects of information and education programs should not be underestimated, whether they focus on reducing conflict between recreation users, instilling a land ethic, teaching our youth to appreciate the values of wildlands, historical artifacts, and wildlife, or advertising local events, lodging and outfitting and guiding services.

Report of the Commission on
Idahoans Outdoors

Hostels Foster Appreciation and
Conservation of Natural Resources

Along the coast of California and on Cape Cod and the offshore islands of Nantucket and Martha's Vineyard are chains and clusters of hostels. Within these chains and clusters are hostels on public lands and hostels owned or leased by American Youth Hostels, Inc. Hikers and cyclists are the predominant users of these hostel networks. While the hostels provide access to trails, shores, dunes and other fragile ecosystems, they also provide "how-to" and "how-not-to" information about enjoying these resources.

Staff of the hostels provide policing and maintenance support in concert with public and private agencies. The result is: 1) low environmental impact from the recreationists in the system; 2) the stimulation of dispersed utilization of these resources grows, this combination of benefits may be employed in other situations where a delicate balance between use and enjoyment on the one hand and protection on the other must be maintained.

For example, the Coastal Zone Management benefits which are derived from this public/not-for-profit cooperation which has been pioneered in California and Massachusetts could be obtained in more than 20 other states in the future. The coastal access mitigation program which sets aside funds derived from developers of high impact programs on the coastline can direct monies to protection of natural and recreational resources by low-impact programming.

ROBERT B. JOHNSON
American Youth Hostels
Boston hearing

· · · · · · · · · · ·

Chapter 3

Schoolchildren Should Learn About the Outdoors

We recommend

• As part of the prairie fire, local coalitions encourage school boards to provide education programs about our natural environment in schools. Curricula should reflect the "4 R's"—Reading, 'Riting, 'Rithmetic, and Resources.

• Local, state and federal recreation and natural resources agencies engage in educational activities, through teaching in school classrooms, providing incentives to bring schoolchildren to the resource, and offering educational activities for visitors to their areas.

• Physical education programs include outdoor activity skills and proper use of the natural resource to ensure its protection.

Why should we be concerned about our children learning about the outdoors?

If a student can read, balance a checkbook, and write a paragraph, the school system has given him or her basic skills to succeed. But if a student litters, dumps fertilizer in the neighborhood creek, or cuts down too many trees, he or she may not be aware that these actions hurt wildlife, pollute drinking water, and cause soil erosion.

As Elizabeth Titus pointed out at our Boston hearing, "education is cheaper than maintenance, or trying to correct a problem." Outdoor education will help create an activated citizenry which is more effective at preserving environmental quality and protecting natural resources. Conflicts and accidents in the outdoors should also decrease as we learn how to employ outdoor skills safely.

Teaching young people about the outdoors is a long-term investment in the future quality of our natural environment. It is our insurance that our actions will continue to protect our outdoor estate.

What is outdoor education?

Education about the outdoors covers many topics.

Nature study, begun in schools in the latter part of the 19th century, focused, in the words of one writer, "on the artsy things and mere rambles in the countryside [to] put the child into intimate and sympathetic contact" with nature.

Conservation and *resources education* had its roots in 1935, when the National Education Association issued the following statement:

Realization of the basic importance of these resources (forests, soils, grasslands, water, minerals, oils, fish, game and scenic beauty), determination to utilize them for the common good through long-range planning, and general knowledge of appropriate remedial and preventive conservation procedures are among the marks of an educated citizenry.

The same statement emphasized the role of schools in taking "responsibility for checking the ravages upon the heritage of the nation." Conservation theory recognizes the need to conserve the habitat for a diversity of plants and animals, and promotes wise use and management of resources.

Environmental education focuses on the interaction between human beings and the natural environment. In the late 1960s, public awareness increased about the problems of air, water, noise, and landscape pollution. Other problems noted include overpopulation and excessive energy demands. Environmental education instructs students in the impacts of their actions on others and on the environmental web.

What is environmental education for kindergarten students?

It's a game called "Everybody Needs A Home." Children learn that animals, just like people, need homes, too. Homes for many animals are not just houses, but the outdoors itself—arranged in a way suitable for the animals' needs for water, shelter and space.

. . . for elementary school children?

In "Animal Poetry," students go outside and imagine themselves as animals. They then write poems to express how they felt. The wildlife experience serves as the inspiration for the poem.

. . . for high school students?

"What You Wear Is What They Were" is an activity where students analyze their clothes according to the natural resources from which they are derived. Students recognize environmental consequences of clothing preferences while learning about renewable and nonrenewable resources. (Project Wild)

The goal of environmental education is: To produce citizens who are: knowledgeable about the natural environment and people's interaction with it; aware of the problems threatening the environment and possible solutions to these problems; and motivated to work and resolve problems.

Leisure education teaches the "worthy use of leisure time," an 1897 principle of public school education. Academicians and recreation professionals have observed that some Americans do not learn how to use their leisure in satisfying, constructive ways. Courses include recreation skills, such as canoeing, soccer or nature photography, and knowledge about recreation places to enjoy these skills. Such courses are particularly important for young people, the elderly, and the disabled. It also includes the responsible use and enjoyment of recreation resources.

What makes an effective outdoor education program?

Education is most effective when it affects people's daily lives and decisions. Current trends in outdoor education are to fuse environmental education into all courses of study at all levels of schooling, from kindergarten through college. Thus math principles can be taught by tree sampling, or political science by locating a hypothetical waste disposal facility.

An important component of environmental education is field work. Pike's High School in Indiana created an outdoor classroom by developing a park adjacent to the school. Said one teacher: "What we have done is taken a piece of the township and literally preserved it and given students an opportunity to see the changes over a long period of time—to be a part of it, not just visit." In this "classroom," students study nature as well as people and their recreation behavior.

Students also benefit from the experience of those who work and study in natural and recreation areas. Natural resource and recreation professionals should be encouraged to share their knowledge with students, both in the classroom and on-site in outdoor areas. Schools should take advantage of the classroom potential of our nation's natural areas.

The states have a responsibility to promote education about the outdoors

Environmental education has chiefly persisted as a community effort. A few states require environmental education in public school classrooms. Many more states list environmental or conservation education as an objective of the public school system, but have no requirements or guidelines which implement its inclusion.

Wisconsin requires each school board to develop a curriculum plan for environmental education, and to integrate environmental education activities into all subjects, particularly art, health, science and social studies.

The state will withhold up to 25 percent of state aid from a school district that does not comply. Wisconsin also lists environmental education as a necessary part of a teacher's certification.

Minnesota requires a separate curriculum on the environment in elementary schools and mandates integration of environmental education principles into other subjects.

California provides grants to agencies and local school districts to support outdoor education, and incorporates education about the environment in curricula at all grade levels and in all major subjects.

Tennessee has used a small amount of state funds and staff to create Project C.E.N.T.S.—Conservation Education Now for Tennessee Students. The program makes conservation education curricular materials, such as those of Project Wild and Project Learning Tree, and teacher training, available to teachers and supervisors throughout the state system. Enthusiastic response has demonstrated that a real demand for environmental knowledge exists among students, teachers, and school administrators.

Private organizations and partnerships have done exciting work

Some of the most creative and innovative education programs have been developed by private organizations and public/private partnerships.

Project Learning Tree, begun in the late 1970s, is one of the oldest public education cooperative projects. Sponsored by the American Forest Foundation and the Western Regional Environmental Education Council, it provides curricular materials to teach students awareness of their responsibility to the environment. The program is available in 43 states and has reached more than 90,000 educators.

Project Wild was inspired by Project Learning Tree. It is an interdisciplinary program emphasizing wildlife, established as a joint project of the Western Association of Fish and Wildlife Agencies and the Western Regional Environmental Education Council. Activities prepare young people from kindergarten through high school for decisions affecting people and wildlife and their shared home, planet Earth.

The Alliance for Environmental Education is a diverse group of nongovernmental organizations in such fields as education, wildlife, youth, utilities, and other services. The organization plans to create a network of information clearinghouses at universities throughout the country.

The Yosemite Institute is a private, non-profit residential program with campuses located in Yosemite National Park and the Golden Gate National Recreation Area. Students learn about science and nature and our connection with the environment. The outdoors is the classroom. The institute combines art, poetry, philosophy, history and literature to relate the outdoors to human endeavors.

The Human Environment Center in Washington, D.C. sponsors programs and activities encouraging minority students to enter careers in recreation, natural resource management, and other environmental fields.

The National Outdoor Leadership School teaches outdoor skills, such as backcountry camping and canoeing. The school pioneered the teaching and development of practical conservation techniques designed to reduce the impact of recreation activities on natural resources.

Leisure Match, a computer system in libraries that informs children about things to do during their leisure time, was developed by the University of Massachusetts and the Parks and Recreation Department of Hartford, Connecticut.

The federal government should support the states and private efforts

From 1970 to 1980 the Department of Education conducted a program authorized by the Environmental Education Act of 1970. During this time, the department awarded about 780 grants totaling $26 million. Purposes included research, pilot projects in curriculum development, information dissemination, personnel training, establishment of ecological study centers, and provision of study materials for the mass media.

Funding dwindled in the late 1970s, and although the Act was reauthorized in 1978, it was not funded. In 1981 the Act was combined with 27 other programs into Chapter II of the Educational Consolidation and Improvement Act, which provides block grants to states. Environmental education remains an approved area of funding for state block grants in education.

The Education for Economic Security Act is designed to provide staff development opportunities for educators in school systems and higher education. Science and math education are now eligible. Title II of this Act should be amended to include "environmental, outdoor, and conservation education" as well.

The Secretary of Education should acknowledge environmental, outdoor, and conservation education as important basic education. The Federal Interagency Committee on Education, and Subcommittee on Environmental Education, should be directed to catalyze cooperative efforts in support of environmental education.

Many can help

Environmental education specialists can use the media creatively to reach young people. The National Geographic Society has developed a computerized game in which school-aged children design a zoo, taking into account staff concerns, visitor satisfaction and animal needs. "Wildways," developed by Control Data Corporation, is a 20-30 hour computer course about wildlife conservation.

Private businesses can promote outdoor education programs in their communities and develop educational materials that reach a broad audience.

Recreation activity and conservation groups can create and support partnerships, such as Project Wild, to promote education in their members, schools, and the general public.

Textbook publishers can encourage writers to infuse environmental principles into all appropriate subject areas.

Universities can require that graduates take one credit of environmental education; take an active role in incorporating environmental education in continuing education courses; and promote recreational skill development and leisure education.

Youth organizations and senior citizen groups can teach outdoors appreciation, and leisure and recreation skills. Outdoor activity should be encouraged.

Public and private land managers can promote the use of their outdoor areas as classrooms.

Equipment and materials manufacturers and sellers of outdoor products can join in educating the public about the outdoors. The Dupont Company, a supplier of fiber fill to manufacturers of sleeping bags, has developed a booklet about camping with children.

We commend

o States, such as Wisconsin, Minnesota and California, which require environmental education in elementary and secondary school curricula.

o Partnerships, such as Project Wild and Project Learning Tree, for creative and aggressive efforts to reach all schoolchildren with fun, imaginative and informative programs.

o Private companies, such as Dupont and the Coleman Company, for taking an active role in educating the public about the outdoors.

We all need outdoor education

Schoolchildren are by no means the only ones who should learn about the outdoors. For the next twenty years, senior citizens will be shaping our social decisions. We must encourage partnerships to reach all people. Our goal is to establish the foundation for an environmentally informed public. A more informed public will protect its investment in the outdoors.

*When you put a child in the outdoors with the proper catalyst, the out-
doors becomes a book, a book that will change that child's life forever.*
WILBUR LAPAGE
Commissioner

*I would like to propose mandatory education to the public on topics
like reducing stress from our lives by escaping into nature, to learn more
about the variety of plants and animals God created and that so few of
us are even aware of, and finally how to use our parks for family time,
relaxation, exercise and countless recreation activities.*
VANESSA LESTER
Teenager from Minneapolis

*To build a society and economy that will preserve the environment,
we need first to build the environmental knowledge and sensitivity of our
people. We cannot expect to maintain a wholesome etnvironment unless
our people are envirornmentally informed.*
S. DAVID FREEMAN
Former Chairman
Tennessee Valley Authority

*In the recreation business the hope is that people, by their own ac-
tions, will preserve the aesthetic landscape and eliminate unnecessary resource damage. The land-management agencies and private property
owners will not be forced to rely completely on closures, restrictions, regulations and law enforcement to maintain the recreation land base.*
ROBERT OSET
Concept paper

*No environmental education program should come up with a series
of correct answers, for the answers to environmental problems shift as the
economy and technology allow. The contribution that environmental
education can make is of a rational approach to the problems and an
understanding of consequences of a variety of alternative solutions.*
W. V. MAYER

*Environmental education provides alternative ways of thinking—a
synthesis—which colors and affects the humanities, language, social sci-
ences, history, economics, and religion . . . gives ecological perspective
for every aspect of learning.*
U. S. OFFICE OF EDUCATION

. . . .
Outdoor Corps Can Help Communities With Local Action

We recommend

● Mayors, county officials, governors, and state legislatures establish outdoor corps programs to encourage youth and citizens of all ages to dedicate a period of their lives to the stewardship of natural resources.

● Conservation and volunteer organizations provide technical and financial assistance to support local, state, and non-profit outdoor corps.

There is work to be done and people to do it

Americans are willing to work to put their ideals into action. We work to help others, to improve our surroundings, and for personal satisfaction. Our world is a better place because of it.

Our communities have identified tremendous backlogs of conservation projects. At the same time, there are many, many Americans, young and old, who are willing to work in parks, forests, and other public lands principally for personal satisfaction. Organizing these people into outdoor corps will help to meet conservation needs, achieve social goals, offer opportunities for personal fulfillment, and help build an awareness of our responsibilities for resource stewardship.

Outdoor corps will help spread a conservation ethic

A frequently-remarked benefit of the Peace Corps program, in addition to its remarkable accomplishments in other countries, is the creation of an informed citizenry at home. Peace Corps volunteers learn about other peoples, their values and world perspectives. They learn the importance of recognizing that our way is not the only way of seeing things. And they bring that understanding back home.

Volunteers organized into outdoor corps, to undertake conservation projects, will do more than get more miles of trails built and city parks cleaned up—although that is important. They will constitute an informed citizenry. They will form a core of Americans to whom the importance of taking care of our outdoor resources has become a personal matter. They can spread the outdoor ethic.

Outdoor corps workers learn the whys and wherefores of resource stewardship. In activities like wildlife habitat improvement, trail design, and erosion control projects, they gain hands-on experience of the need to care for our outdoor assets. Like Peace Corps volunteers returning from overseas, they will pass that understanding on to others.

Outdoor corps perform needed services

The need is acute for the types of activities which outdoor corps can offer. Recreation and conservation agencies at every level report severe staff shortages, hindering their delivery of essential development, management, and rehabilitation services. Researchers warn us that under-staffing of parks creates the perception of abandonment, which leads to a downward spiral of vandalism and fears for public safety.

Outdoor corps can, and do, help meet these critical public needs, usually at great cost savings. Illustrative comments on the work of some existing conservation corps:

> I estimated that it would take the crew a week to do the cross-country ski trail project, based on my experience with city crews over the last 20 years. But this crew [Wisconsin Conservation Corps] is incredible, and they finished the project in two days.
> Wisconsin County Engineer

> What I did not realize at the time I agreed to the project was that when the East Bay Conservation Corps says they will work, they mean hard work. The total amount accomplished by your corps members in just over a day of work would take our small staff weeks to match, or literally thousands of dollars if done by outside contractors.
> Director, Yosemite Institute

What is an outdoor corps?

An outdoor corps is a team of volunteers of any age group. It may be teenagers building campgrounds or bridges, or senior citizens serving as interpreters at the neighborhood park.

Most importantly, outdoor corps provide a way to accomplish important work which needs to be done. And they build a corps of citizens who have learned about caring for outdoor resources.

An important advantage to agency managers who utilize outdoor corps for project assistance is that under a corps structure, managers can count on continued availability of the corps workers. Members are encouraged to make a commitment, for a summer, six months, or a year, to an organization that is on-call for many services. They can be assigned long-term responsibilities as well as short-term tasks.

There are 40 existing local, state, and non-profit conservation corps. Many of these programs pay an hourly wage and/or expenses of the volunteers. Several are based on the federal model of the depression-era Civilian Conservation Corps, although they are essentially grassroots efforts.

The current 16 state and 21 local corps are targeted to resource improvement. Their primary focus is accomplishing work badly needed in their own communities, while achieving social goals. Essential public projects are completed, while participants receive work and educational experiences that might not be otherwise available to them.

Because of relatively hard manual labor and low pay, there is commonly an orientation to youth in these corps programs. Recent graduates and dropouts are attracted by the opportunity to acquire job experience and skills.

There is also substantial interest by older Americans and retired workers in service programs within their communities. This is evidenced by programs such as the Revere, Massachusetts, Senior Citizen Corps, and the federal Retired Senior Volunteer Program (RSVP). Many more seniors might be recruited if there were opportunities for outdoor work available to them.

Right now, there's a real, growing emergence of these programs nationwide . . . in response, basically, to two major problems in today's United States. One—there is a huge level of unemployed youth between the ages of 16 and 24. Two—there is a very large backlog of conservation and maintenance work on public lands and facilities throughout the U.S. which, because of budget cuts, cannot be done. Conservation corps can pretty much meet both of those needs in one organization.

JOANNA LENNON
Executive Director
East Bay Conservation Corps

Here are some examples

The Iowa Youth Corps operates year-round volunteer conservation programs, an in-school service Corps, and a community volunteerism grant program. The Corps works with county conservation boards, school boards and other local agencies. It currently sponsors about 2,500 teenage volunteers each year. In 1985, workers completed 60 major park and conservation projects and provided more than 260,000 hours of volunteer labor in 89 of Iowa's 99 counties. Projects include construction and repair of canoe accesses, trails and trail bridges; soil erosion control projects; landscaping park and school grounds; building wildlife shelters and playgrounds; and conducting plant and animal surveys.

The Wisconsin Conservation Corps employs young people between the ages of 18 and 25 for one year at the minimum wage. Work crews with seven to ten members assemble each morning at sites near their homes all across the state and work under trained crew leaders. Upon completion of their one-year service, graduates can receive either a $1,000 scholarship or a $500 cash bonus. With a current budget of $2.5 million, the Corps employs 600-700 full-time crew members each year. Since its beginning in 1983, some 125 manual construction projects have been completed. These include building campgrounds, boating facilities, cabins and visitor centers in state and local parks and forests; planting and thinning trees, restoring prairie habitats, monitoring water pollution, reducing soil erosion, tagging waterfowl and deer, and restoring historic buildings and other properties.

The Student Conservation Association, a non-profit organization founded in 1957, recruits and places approximately 1,000 high school and college students every year. Assignments are made to federal, local and state natural resource management agencies and private organizations, in 250 areas nationwide including Alaska, Hawaii and the Virgin Islands. Volunteers are assigned on an individual basis for a specific job for which they meet the qualifications. Transportation to and from the project site is provided where needed by the Association; housing is provided by the agency. SCA receives approximately 25 percent of its funding from philanthropic sources, 75 percent from fees for services. SCA receives roughly 50 percent more requests for volunteers than it is able to fill.

The Senior Citizen Park Maintenance Corps of Revere, Massachusetts, employs 25 to 30 retired residents at minimum wage to work part-time in city parks each summer. The Corps does landscape and maintenance work in neighborhood parks. Vandalism and litter has decreased with the presence of Senior Corps members in the parks. Many Corps members now work voluntarily in the parks in their spare time. Their experience has sparked a new sense of ownership and stewardship. Corps members now watch over "their" parks on a daily basis, and provide an example of caring for the entire community.

The California Conservation Corps, begun in 1977, is the oldest existing state program. With an annual budget of about $36 million and an average enrollment of 1,700, it completes 1,800 to 2,200 projects a year. New corps members attend a 3-week training academy before assignment. The state runs 17 residential and 24 non-residential work centers, including a crew permanently assigned to Yosemite National Park for trail maintenance and improvement projects. A study of the California Corps estimated that the Corps returned $1.65 in benefits for each dollar spent.

Helping outdoor corps to grow

Despite reputations for "hard work at low wages," many state and local corps have waiting lists of applicants two to three times larger than annual openings. The California Conservation Corps often receives ten or more applications for specific job slots, even in good economic years like 1985. Project sponsors in California also indicate that there are enough annual conservation projects to justify a corps two to three times larger than the current 1,700 members.

We've received many, many more requests from states, organizations and other levels of government to create volunteer organizations than we've been able to respond to. When we have started organizations, we've gotten tremendous community response. What it amounts to is that people seem to be sitting back and hoping that someone's going to coordinate projects, and when there's a nucleus of an organization that does plan and coordinate a project, it's very well attended, and it's really created a lot of publicity and a lot of interest in the communities.

ROGER L. MOORE
Director
National Volunteer Project
Appalachian Mountain Club
Boston hearing

Community outdoor corps programs have produced thousands of critical improvements and restorations in parks, forests and wildlife habitats in recent years. Many identified conservation needs could be met by creation of more outdoor corps in states and localities across the country. We recommend:

● Mayors, county officials, governors, and state legislatures establish outdoor corps programs to encourage youth and citizens of all ages to dedicate a period of their lives to the stewardship of natural resources.

● Conservation and volunteer organizations provide financial and technical assistance to support local, state, and non-profit outdoor corps.

● The federal government's primary volunteer agency, ACTION, explore possibilities for "subcontracting" some of its national efforts to local and state outdoor corps.

● The two major national service programs, Volunteers in Service to America (VISTA) and the Retired Senior Volunteer Program, consider matching grants to support local or state outdoor corps.

● Financial and technical assistance to encourage innovation in such areas as recruiting skilled adults and senior citizens to provide experienced guidance to young corps members, and establishing linkages between corps programs and volunteer organizations.

The creation of a public sector/private sector National Volunteer Corps would create an opportunity for the American public to contribute their time, talents, and skills in the conserving and managing of America's natural resources, and would involve all sectors of society: government, business and industry, conservation organizations; but the program would essentially be run by volunteers for volunteers. All sectors can provide leadership. Additionally, each has skills and expertise it can share with the others; the land managers can provide the opportunities and tools; the business community can provide organizational structure funding; and the volunteers the energy and enthusiasm.

GERALD COUTANT
U. S. Forest Service
Concept Paper for the
Commission

Chapter 5

Volunteers Play Vital Roles

We recommend

● Local officials, mayors, governors and private sector managers support volunteering, develop incentives and remove barriers to encourage Americans to volunteer in outdoor recreation. The goal is to double volunteer efforts in conservation and recreation by the year 2000.

● Current laws and regulations be reviewed to enhance mechanisms for using volunteers in national parks, national forests, and all federal agencies.

Volunteering is part of our American heritage

From barn raising and crop harvesting to parents helping children and neighbors helping neighbors, Americans have always volunteered. An early incentive for helping others was the knowledge that at some point there would be the need for others to come to our aid. By helping others, we helped ourselves.

Budget and staffing cuts over the last decade have challenged the ability of professionals to meet recreation needs in a responsive way. Volunteering has increased, and managers now find themselves working with new partners in providing outdoor recreation.

Volunteers support communities and contribute to our economy

President Reagan stated in his 1986 State of the Union address that volunteers contributed an estimated $74 billion to the American economy. A 1985 study found that retired senior volunteers were better off socially, mentally, and physically than they would have been without the volunteer experience. Once again, by helping others we help ourselves.

Opportunities for community volunteer action vary widely, from Keep America Beautiful to the National Youth Sports Coaching Association, to the National Volunteer Project of the Appalachian Mountain Club to the Student Conservation Association. There are countless associations dedicated to a neighborhood or a particular park, and adopt-a-park and adopt-a-trail programs.

Volunteer organizations, with the assistance of providers, develop a community spirit and pride of accomplishment at the grass roots. The local level is where efforts to encourage volunteering should be strongest.

So much work remains to be done in this unfinished and imperfect world that none of us can justify standing on the sidelines. Especially in a society like ours, volunteering is an expression of democracy in its purest form. For the volunteer is a participant, not a looker-on, and participation is the democratic process.

EUNICE KENNEDY SHRIVER

. . . volunteerism is not a fad but a viable, long term solution to providing many recreation services. The success and importance of volunteer activities today are far exceeded by their potential for the future. Volunteer programs require a great deal of effort to initiate and sustain, and they are not free. However, when approached properly, these programs can have broad long term benefits that far outweigh costs.

ROGER MOORE
Appalachian Mountain Club

Volunteers are out there but we don't cultivate their talents

Organizations exist throughout all levels of government and the private sector to promote and support volunteers. However, we think we can do more. We need to double our efforts over the next decade to meet the challenges of tomorrow.

In 1985, of the 67 million hours donated by 348,000 National Retired Senior Volunteer Program volunteers, only 3.6 percent were in recreation related activities. A 1985 poll conducted by the Volunteers for Outdoor Colorado indicated that 40 percent of those surveyed would volunteer in the outdoors if asked. Eighty-two percent felt that local organizations are best suited to provide for community needs.

The 1982-83 National Recreation Survey found that 16 percent of people over age 60 said they had an outdoor recreation skill they could teach. However, only a quarter of these people taught the skill, mostly to family and friends. The most common reason older people said they did not teach the skill was because they had not been asked.

Managers can better support volunteers

Though managers have begun to turn to volunteers in order to fill the void left by budget cuts to outdoor recreation programs, they are sometimes reluctant to delegate real responsibility to volunteers. Furthermore, employees have expressed concern that volunteers are replacing important employee functions, reducing opportunities for entry level positions and advancement. Volunteers must not be seen simply as a cure-all for staff cut-backs.

There is a thin line between effective utilization of volunteers and the negative effect volunteers can have on employee morale. Jeannette Fitzwilliams of the Virginia Trails Association observes:

> At this time when people are fighting to keep their jobs, volunteers can be seen as a threat. Furthermore, it is not human nature for a manager to share responsibility; he has to make a conscious effort to do so. Yet [parks] do not exist in a vacuum; they are part of a community. Cooperation and partnership will do more for a manager's image than if he tried to do everything all by himself.

Volunteers can do more than menial tasks

The Appalachian Mountain Club believes that cooperation between volunteer organizations and public agencies offers many advantages. Agencies must spend a good deal of time on tasks that must be repeated year after year—recruiting, training, supervising. Volunteer organizations can perform these tasks along with many administrative ones and provide a continuity not easily achieved by the agencies.

Volunteer organizations are not always afforded equal opportunity to bid on public contracts. While some contracts have been awarded to non-profit groups to manage park facilities, there are relatively few such cases. We recommend that public agencies and the private sector remove obstacles to competition for the chance to provide services to the American public. There should not be a penalty for being a nonprofit.

We need volunteer program leadership

Community, state, federal and private sector leaders must actively develop and encourage volunteering. We recommend that organizations, particularly those providing services or products for outdoor recreation, create staff positions responsible for the development of volunteer programs.

We recommend that policy statements and legislation be developed to nurture volunteering through:

• support for an expanded role by volunteer organizations in providing outdoor recreation opportunities;

• tax laws which allow deductions for contributions to volunteer organizations;

• deferment or partial forgiveness of student loans repayment, and/or work requirements, for students who volunteer in parks and outdoor corps;

• encouragement to government agencies and private groups to include volunteer programs in their organizational structures;

• training programs within agencies and organizations to develop understanding of volunteer program potential and to teach volunteer management skills;

• annual recognition, sponsored by governors, city and local officials and the federal government, of volunteers in outdoor recreation who have worked for the betterment of their communities;

• encouragement to the private sector to offer incentives to employees to volunteer their time to assist in providing outdoor recreation opportunities in their communities;

• protection for volunteers from legal liability and tort claims and coverage for injuries sustained while volunteering;

• provisions for minimal expense reimbursements to those volunteers less able to pay for their transportation or other incidentals (senior citizens and the less fortunate);

• encouragement to and authority for land managers to delegate real responsibility to volunteers.

Private organizations and businesses should encourage employees to serve their communities as volunteers. The IBM Corporation loans employees to community organizations as part of their community awareness and support ethic.

We need to review current laws to promote volunteering

The National Park Service's Volunteers in the Parks and the U.S. Forest Service's Volunteers in Forests programs are good examples of positive emphasis on volunteering by federal agencies. However, these laws do not apply to all federal agencies. They do not encourage agency partnership development and cooperation with local profit and nonprofit groups and organizations, and they do not provide minimum budget levels for federal agencies to initiate and strengthen volunteer efforts. Neither the Bureau of Reclamation nor the Tennessee Valley Authority have volunteer authorities. Current statutes should be reviewed to address these opportunities.

The Bureau of Land Management received specific authority for volunteer programs through a 1984 amendment to the Federal Land Policy and Management Act. In 1981, 64,000 hours were donated to the agency. By 1985 the figure was 371,000 hours, valued at $3.2 million—a return of 10 to 1 over the costs to manage the program. This growth occurred without any full-time field staff devoted to development of volunteer programs. In two Bureau of Land Management districts the volunteer work-years were as much as 27 percent of the full-time staff work years.

Potential volunteers can't find the right information

Volunteers seeking opportunities to assist with outdoor recreation programs are not always able to get enough information. An agency or organization may not know about opportunities outside its own programs. There is no central volunteer information service for outdoor recreation.

Independent agency programs should develop direct working relationships with other agencies. When one agency cannot provide an opportunity for a volunteer, a referral should be made to another agency which can. This would require information sharing and cooperation—partnerships for the benefit of all. We recommend the establishment, with local communities, states and the federal government being equal partners, of a clearinghouse for volunteer information and opportunities.

Volunteering promotes respect for and knowledge about the outdoors and how people behave in the outdoors. Local volunteer groups are proving that people really believe Woody Guthrie's words, "This land is your land, this land is my land." Volunteers must be given leadership, real responsibilities and acknowledgment in order to foster a true feeling of accomplishment and to maintain viable ongoing programs.

National Leadership Helps Develop Local Action

The National Volunteer Project (NVP) of the Appalachian Mountain Club was formed in 1982 with private foundation grants to foster the development of local volunteer organizations. The NVP program founded six independent groups around the country—Volunteers for Outdoor Colorado, Outdoor Washington, Florida Trails Association, Trail Information and Volunteer Center, Volunteers for the Outdoors in New Mexico, and Tahoe Rim Trail Fund. The purpose of these organizations is to foster a partnership with federal, state, and local providers. The NVP does all recruiting, training, and supervising of the volunteers. The providers supply financial assistance through grants, concessions, or contracts. This kind of relationship between the local community and a national entity generates local impetus and interest in volunteer projects.

Volunteers Manage the Appalachian Trail

The Secretary of the Interior in 1984 gave the Appalachian Trail Conference overall responsibility for management and protection of the Appalachian Trail. The Conference and its 31 member clubs have long led volunteer efforts to provide public services that might otherwise be considered the responsibility of government. With 18,000 members nationwide, ATC's responsibilities include assigning sections of the Appalachian Trail to its member clubs and ensuring that they do a good job of management and maintenance. ATC's assuming management for the 60,000 acres along the Appalachian Trail was a unique effort in transferring broad management responsibilities for public lands to a private, nonprofit organization.

Traditionally, minority groups of all sorts have found it difficult to become involved in volunteering, sometimes because they were not made to feel welcome, sometimes because they did not have the carfare it took to reach or work in an agency across town or money for lunch. Neighborhood volunteer centers and reimbursement of expenses are two methods that have enabled these groups to volunteer.

ISOLDE CHAPIN WEINBERG
National Center For Voluntary Action

For volunteers to perform well, they need to have a sense of responsibility. Too often government agencies have seen volunteers as inexpensive, unskilled laborers, not as a tremendous resource waiting to be tapped. Under-utilized volunteers rarely develop a solid sense of stewardship or participation. On the Appalachian Trail, where the clubs are clearly in the hot seat of responsibility, there is a remarkable level of commitment and resolve to do well. Public land managers must be willing to have faith in volunteer organizations with good track records. In some cases specific legislation will be necessary to give volunteer groups significant responsibility.

LAWRENCE R. VAN METER
Potomac Appalachian Trail Club

Several urban recreation agencies could not function effectively without the public's efforts. With the initiation of the Gramm-Rudman Act and the general trend of reduced federal support for local services, the reliance on volunteerism will only increase in the coming years. The support and recognition of the public's effort must be continued at all levels of government.

LAWRENCE ALLEN
Temple University

. . . .

Chapter 6

We Can Improve the Quality of Services

We recommend

● Public recreation providers develop visitor services plans which integrate all visitor services, including information, activity programs, and health and safety, and which incorporate feedback from visitors to ensure quality.

● Public recreation services be improved through development of partnerships.

● Creation of state recreation information clearinghouses to provide the public with information on recreation opportunities.

● Planning and design of recreation areas and programs be sensitive to the needs of special populations, and action be taken to provide information, access and other services.

Services are an integral part of an outdoor experience

Services provide a critical "gateway" role for recreation lands and facilities. Just as roads and airplane routes give physical access to recreation resources, so services are needed to overcome intellectual, emotional and sometimes social barriers to full participation in recreation activities.

Outdoor resources are generally recognized for the major attractions they offer—beautiful landscapes, unusual natural features, sports and recreational opportunities. However, public services play an important role in visitor's enjoyment of outdoor experiences.

Recreation services may be very basic (such as keeping restrooms clean and stocked with towels), or they may involve intensive use of skilled staff time (such as sports coaches, wilderness guides). The quality of service usually depends on the availability and quality of service staffing.

Services that are well planned and well delivered are unobtrusive; poorly planned, inadequate services can spoil everything. Well planned services can increase visitors' appreciation and enjoyment of recreation resources, and can make visitors partners with providers in the conservation and preservation of those resources.

The quality of recreation services can be improved

Forty-six percent of the public feels only "somewhat satisfied" with the recreation programs and facilities available to them. A total of 14 percent is dissatisfied. Blacks and Hispanics report higher incidences of dissatisfaction. According to the 1977 National Urban Recreation Study, "at the neighborhood level . . . the presence or absence of accessible, competently-staffed, diverse and year-round programs are critical determinants of citizen satisfaction."

Public recreational areas face staff and budget cutbacks, and private areas are limited by what the market will bear. For people who are able and willing to pay, options have increased with demand; private sector investment has grown, and the public sector is increasingly charging for services. Services for people who are unable to pay are decreasing significantly, as are some informational and educational services.

People cannot take advantage of a recreational experience when they do not even know that it exists; they cannot enjoy activities when they lack the knowledge, skills, or encouragement that may be necessary to participate. Fear of crime and the perception of abandonment will keep people away from recreation areas, parks, and forests.

The private sector has led the way

Commercial providers were early in recognizing the marketing value of such recreational conveniences as electrical hookups and sewage pumpout stations for recreational vehicle campers, fuel stations for boaters at marinas, and equipment rental programs for snowmobilers, skiers, and campers which allow people to try out a sport before buying equipment. Such conveniences have proved attractive to the many people who are willing to pay for them.

Concessions have played a vital role in providing services for the public in national parks. For many concession owners it represents a commitment of time and labor over many years, over lifetimes or generations. In some park units the concerns of the concessioner predate the concerns of the National Park Service and conservation groups in preserving the resource.

Sno-Park Program Improves Access

In the late 1980's, many areas that had been developed for Washington State's 10,000 snowmobilers, cross-country skiers, and snowshoers were often inaccessible because of snowed-in parking lots and a lack of regular trail grooming. Because no government funds were available for snow removal in these areas, the state adopted licensing legislation in 1971 to provide a reliable source of fee revenues for facility operation, enforcement, and safety programs.

When funding and distribution under the 1971 Snowmobile Act proved inadequate, user groups supported enactment of a winter recreation parking program (the Sno-Park Program) in 1975 and revisions of the Act to ensure adequate revenue and fair distribution of funds.

With more than a decade of cooperation between user groups and state and local governments, Washington State provides a model that ensures support services essential for access to winter trails.

It is a fact that the privately owned enterprise meets the bulk of the public's demand! I feel that it is very important that we survive, because we are the mom and pop operation, providing canoe recreation on our natural resources. We try to keep a low profile, nestled in the woods, blending in with nature, providing services, quality equipment so the public can experience our natural water-ways. I feel we contribute to those natural resources. We are not only there to service the public, but we provide river patrol, river clean-ups, river safety, canoe instructions, etc. If we don't provide a good quality experience we are out of business and the public will lose their recreational opportunities on our water-ways. We also [disperse visitors] . . . When we feel a certain section has too many canoes to give that customer a quality experience, we divert our customers to other sections of the river. Without a quality experience, we are out of business.

DONNA E. STOUT
Concept paper

Health and safety come first

The most basic function, recognized by public and private managers at every level, is protecting the health and safety of visitors. If visitors to recreation areas feel unsafe, they are unlikely to stay long or to return.

Protection of public health and safety includes preventing personal injury and crime (such as traffic control, lifeguards at swimming pools). It also involves education (such as safety signs and warning literature about hazards), testing and treating swimming and drinking water, and information programs to prevent littering and vandalism. Protective services also include "comfort" functions—restroom and food facilities.

A visible presence allays fears

The 1986 Market Opinion Research Survey found that "feeling safe from crime" is a major concern among urban residents. One-fourth of urban respondents said that they were not satisfied with the perceived level of safety in the community recreation areas available to them.

Staffing cutbacks in all recreation areas contribute to public perceptions of abandonment and increased fear of crime. The presence of uniformed rangers, concessions personnel, and professional activity leaders reassures visitors that they and their children will have some supervision and protection.

With staff and visitors absent, opportunities increase for antisocial behavior, creating a cycle of abandonment. Increased involvement by volunteers from user groups and nearby residential areas can help to break the cycle, but they have not and cannot entirely fill gaps caused by inadequate staffing.

On-site contact with personnel may also be the most effective way of meeting another critical service need: information. Recent surveys in wilderness areas reveal that even backcountry users enjoy having contact with rangers at trailheads to provide advice on specific opportunities, education on appropriate wilderness practices, and a demonstration that the provider "cares."

On-site interpretation is important information

The National Park Service interpreters' motto is "Through interpretation, understanding; through understanding, appreciation; through appreciation, protection." Educational and interpretive programs are an essential element of visitor services. These services represent a direct opportunity to promote an outdoor ethic in visitors, and encourage stewardship of resources.

Backcountry Users Want Information

A summary of wilderness and backcountry user preferences reported that a majority seems to want information. About 60 percent of the users of four wilderness and backcountry areas favored maps and information pamphlets, and that about two-thirds supported the presence of rangers in the backcountry. Since then, a growing body of research has indicated widespread desire for information services among users of dispersed recreation settings.

JOSEPH W. ROGGENBUCK
Virginia Polytechnic and State University
AND SAM H. HAM
University of Idaho

Cooperating associations—nonprofit entities that provide educational services in the national parks—often fill the gap created by the prohibition of direct sales of educational materials in the parks by the National Park Service. There are currently more than sixty cooperating associations in the national parks, and similar nonprofit associations assist at some Forest Service, Fish and Wildlife Service, and Corps of Engineers areas.

Coordinated information services are necessary

For an individual or family to take full advantage of recreation options, three things are required:

○ information on resources and activities available

○ skills education

○ an easy way to communicate with providers for reservations

Information services can also provide education about the values and appropriate uses of natural resources and leisure time. Effective use of information and education tools can increase the quality of recreation experiences, reduce social conflicts and resource impacts, and reduce management costs.

With improved information, the public can make better use of recreational opportunities, increasing individual and social benefits from outdoor recreation. Better information can also serve to distribute visitors among recreation areas, relieving the pressure on stressed resources, enhancing visitor enjoyment, and reducing user conflicts.

At present information is fragmented and diffuse

There are many current sources of information on activities and areas. Public recreation agencies, state tourism offices, private organizations like the American Automobile Association and publishers of travel guides all provide information services. Yet it is difficult for the potential consumer to get information on the full range of opportunities available. A family planning a vacation trip from New Hampshire to Texas must contact many different agencies and seek out innumerable private sector providers.

Lack of necessary skills or an understanding of what equipment is required and how to use it also limits opportunities. A number of organizations, from recreation agencies to schools to membership groups like the Audubon Society and Sierra Club, to commercial enterprises, offer skills training. However, it is difficult for the potential consumer with no knowledge of the activity to find these providers.

Finally, when one has learned of activities and sites, and has gained the necessary skills, the process of reserving a motel, campsite, or of making arrangements with a back-country outfitter or river rafting guide can be tedious and expensive.

The technology is available for a recreation information system

Technology available today makes a comprehensive information system integrating public and private recreational opportunities feasible. The challenge is to organize and capitalize on it.

There are proposals to address some of these needs. The National Park Foundation has completed an exploratory study of a centralized visitor information and reservation system. Twenty-three states have established some kind of visitor information/reservation system, but these do not address all visitor information needs. American Express has proposed establishing a computerized file of providers who could be contacted through an 800 telephone number.

We recommend that states take the lead in developing recreation opportunity data bases, or contracting their development. Some components of the system may develop independently as the private sector identifies markets and opportunities, along the model of the existing information and reservation network of airlines, hotels, and car rental agencies.

Activity leaders encourage people to participate

Activity leadership consists of programs and the people to run them. The provision of public recreation services began with an emphasis on programs and activities, providing constructive leisure alternatives for people, especially in the cities. Such programs are especially important for certain groups that need special encouragement or learning to participate.

Training of recreation professionals in recent years has tended to stress management and administration skills, sometimes at the expense of activity leadership training. Salary level increases for activity leadership personnel have not kept pace with those of recreation executives, facility managers, and marketing professionals. Rewards for activity leaders should reflect their central importance in bringing recreation to people.

Access for everyone should be a goal

The National Park Service's 1982-83 Nationwide Recreation Survey revealed that "inadequate transport or too far to go" was among the top five barriers to participation in recreation activities. Moreover, the 1975 U.S. Department of Transportation Recreation Access Study found that recreation areas, both urban and rural, were poorly served by public transportation. A 1977 sample of 45 metropolitan jurisdictions found that only half offered regular transportation services to major, community-wide recreation areas, and that service was usually reduced on evenings and weekends, when recreation needs are greatest.

Access to public recreational facilities for people with physical disabilities has increased in the last ten years with the openings of new areas and retrofitting of older facilities, eliminating stairs, curbs, and other immediate barriers. However, progress has been slow. Getting to recreation sites is still a major problem not only for the handicapped but also for children, the elderly, and people who do not own cars.

We need to improve our ability to measure services quality

There are serious gaps in our ability to measure service quality and its importance to participants. Despite some pioneering research and demonstrations in measuring services effectiveness, few management agencies analyze user perceptions of service quality.

The National Park Service has a strong legal mandate to provide visitor services in its areas, as well as a long tradition of concern about the quality of services. Concessioners have played a vital role. But as Field and Machlis note in a management study team paper, even in the National Park system:

> There is no human resources management plan. There are few national policies that define the responsibilities of the park superintendent to the client, and those that do exist refer mainly to physical health and safety. There is no [plan] that integrates natural and cultural management with human resources management. Until there is a human resources management plan, management functions cannot be evaluated in any meaningful way.

Information about services quality is collected by various organizations in a piecemeal way. The U.S. Forest Service has called for a "national recreation quality index." The following lists suggestions of indicators or data elements useful for a systematic assessment of quality of services at any level (municipal to national) for any provider (public and private).

○ General public's perceptions of the quality of recreation opportunities

○ Perception of quality of recreation opportunities by people who use the services, including crowding, facility appearance and maintenance, and assessment of staff

○ Hours of operation

○ Users' perceptions about safety, crime, and accident reports

○ Participation and non-participation by various groups

○ Variety of opportunities and programs

○ Location of opportunities in relation to where people live

○ Work force descriptions, including educational experience, in-service training, membership in professional associations, and length of service.

○ Amount of research and planning on service quality

Feedback from visitors should be incorporated in a timely manner into comprehensive visitor services plans. An index to measure services quality should be established and published annually.

● We recommend establishment and annual publication of a Recreation Quality Index to provide continuing information on the quality of recreation and natural resources for the American public.

Park Alert Reduces Vandalism

In the late 1970's, several parks in Evansville, Indiana, were scenes of increasing vandalism and abandonment. In 1981 the city and park user groups initiated the Park Alert program, which included high-visibility park police patrols and volunteer monitoring of antisocial behavior. In the schools, an educational junior park ranger program was instituted. Within two years, Evansville reported substantial reductions in vandalism and in fear of crime in the parks.

Park Outreach Includes Transportation

The value of transportation is illustrated by the experience of the East Bay Park Regional District in the San Francisco-Oakland, California, metropolitan area. In cooperation with mass transit authorities and local businesses, the district initiated a program several years ago to provide outreach to young, elderly, and handicapped residents, including transportation to the parks.

According to former park district director Richard Trudeau, many of the participants "did not know they had a desire to . . . [visit the parks] until it was offered." But in 1985 the program served 20,000 participants, many of them shut-ins, who would not have been able to visit the parks without the program.

Encouraging Use of Recreation Areas

The Market Opinion Research survey found that for adults, availability of information was an important determinant in recreation site selection. Word of mouth was the most frequent source of information listed.

How do providers reach potential users of their facilities? Public providers rely on public service announcements, radio, direct mail, and newsletters. Private providers utilize direct mail,

117

radio, and the yellow pages to market their services. ("Managed Recreation Research Report," *Recreation Sports and Leisure*, August 1985.)

The city of Hartford, Connecticut is utilizing Rec-Trek, an interactive computer program for children and teens. Children use the computer to find out about sports, arts, activities games, and other forms of recreation. Some people have likened the personalized system to "recreation counseling by computer." The system also records information about users, and turns that information into management reports.

Tram, Volunteers Reduce Traffic

As a nationally renowned area for wildlife and bird watching, the Santa Ana National Wildlife Refuge in Texas was experiencing such heavy visitation that the quality of the experience was reduced for everyone.

To reduce crowding on a scenic road through the refuge, the Fish and Wildlife Service bought an open-air tram to carry visitors through the area. The Frontera Audubon Society contracted to supply trained seasonal staff to drive the tram and volunteers to present interpretive programs. The nonprofit group's costs are covered by a nominal user fee.

Constraints on the Mentally Retarded

Individuals with mental retardation hold leisure interests that are in keeping with those of the general population (i.e. they are interested more in community activities than home activities); however, more of their free time is spent around the home than appears to be true with the general population. Based on an extensive analysis of the lives of 108 children, some of whom were mentally retarded and some of whom were not, all of the children were similar in their patterns of recreation activities. The reason many people with mental retardation are not utilizing outdoor recreation facilities seems to stem from the constraints placed on them by the public's attitude.

Persons with mental retardation do not participate in recreation as often as individuals without mental retardation. One reason for the lack of participation is the overall lack of recreational opportunities for this population. Of 128 agencies providing services to individuals with mental retardation, 68 percent indicated that they offered less than adequate or no leisure skill training for their clients. The majority of the agencies surveyed indicated that they could improve programs if appropriate instructional materials and professional expertise were made available to them.

JOHN DATTILO

Disabled Join the Olympics

I'm a paraplegic in a wheelchair. During the day I work as a counselor in the D.C. Public Schools and Special Education. My students are physically handicapped and chronically ill. They are as young as three years old. In the evenings, weekends and summers I'm Executive Director of New Life, Incorporated. It's an organization that my wife, Brenda, and I founded 15 years ago to offer handicapped youth the opportunity to participate in competitive sports. We have programs for youth in D.C., Maryland and Virginia. Our children use wheelchairs for participation in programs and activities. Among our ranks are many world-class athletes and five record holders who are as young as five years old.

In 1984, something pretty remarkable took place. The International Sports Committee for the Disabled, which is made up of disabled sports federations from countries from all over the world, urged the International Olympic Committee to include in the 1984 Olympics some exhibition sports competition for disabled competitors. These events would be historic in that never before had disabled athletes taken part in the Olympic Games.

As a result, amputee skiers performed at the Winter Olympics at Sarajevo, and wheelchair racers competed in the Summer Olympics in Los Angeles. I had firsthand involvement in Los Angeles, as I was fortunate to be named USA Olympic Wheelchair Track Coach. We had three men and women on the USA team.

There was one girl who I had coached since she was seven years old. Her name is Sacajuwea Hunter. Saca, as we are fond of calling her, was 14 years old at the time, and she is a double amputee. She was the youngest athlete on the entire USA contingent, disabled or able-bodied. More importantly, she was a favorite of the able-bodied Olympic team members.

It is important to understand that on a Saturday morning at that Los Angeles Memorial Coliseum amidst a crowd of 90,000 spectators, and millions watching via satellite, the world's able-bodied became aware that disabled people can also be athletes. That, of course, went a long way in educating the able-bodied that disabled people have the same aspirations and dreams as normal people. I was proud to be a part of the 1984 Olympics, and now all of our kids have as a goal to be part of the 1988 Olympics in Seoul, Korea.

BILL GREEN
D.C. Department of Recreation
Washington, D.C. hearing

What we see is an alarming lack of participation among the disabled population in mainstream recreation programs. A recent survey indicates that approximately 80% of disabled people in this country do not partici- pate in recreation programs, and I think that's very disturbing. If you take the U.S. Census figures that there are 24 million disabled people in this country, that means 19 million are not being served, and even from a com- mercial point of view we think that people should just sit up and start taking recognition of the fact that there is a large population group here that can both benefit from recreation and also can provide economic input as far as being paying customers in the recreation environment.

KIRK BAUER
Washington, D.C. hearing

. . . .

Outdoors: The Resources

"Land," Will Rogers said, "They ain't making it anymore."

Our nation is blessed with, and visitors come from around the world to marvel at the majesty of our mountains, deserts, canyons, rivers, forests, shores, and plains. We Americans have access to an outdoor estate which is unparalleled in richness and diversity.

But a castle is only as royal as the care lavished upon it, and future recreation opportunities will depend on our success in preserving the quality of our natural resources. The American outdoors, like freedom, requires vigilance and care.

We have examined the state of our outdoor estate and found it, while improved in many areas, still imperiled. We need a strong conservation ethic and strict enforcement of strong environmental laws to protect our investment in the future.

Soon 80 percent of us will live in cities, and those who do will especially require access to natural sanctuaries within easy reach of home, for exercise, for rest, for reflection and renewal. In the concrete jungles of our cities we lose touch with the real world of trees, birdsong, small mammals and babbling brooks—links that strengthen us to cope productively with the stresses of modern urban life.

We have a vision for allowing every American easy access to the natural world: Greenways. Greenways are fingers of green that reach out from and around and through communities all across America, created by local action. They will connect parks and forests and scenic countrysides, public and private, in recreation corridors for hiking, jogging, wildlife movement, horse and bicycle riding. If the creativity and enthusiasm and love of land of Americans are truly unleashed, greenways will link our communities coast-to-coast, from sea to shining sea.

Water is a backdrop for most of our favorite recreation activities— swimming, skiing, fishing, boating, hunting, surfing, sailing. Wetlands and floodplains are nurseries which cradle the incredible variety of plant, animal and fish life which enriches our lives and our recreation pursuits. Some of our rivers are being polluted and unnecessarily dammed, our wetlands filled, our floodplains paved over. Our shorelines are increasingly closed off to public access by unplanned development. Society pays the long-term costs, and we all lose.

Driving for pleasure remains our number two outdoor pasttime. A drive in the country with the kids and a picnic is still an American tradition. Through the establishment of a network of scenic byways, states and communities can protect stretches of the American countryside, and bring economic benefits to communities nearby. Country roads are an inheritance from the people who came before us, and they lead us to historical and scenic spots which help soothe the soul. We need to collect and keep them.

Some of our federal lands and waters are threatened by pollution, by spreading development, by crowding and overuse. We are the beneficiaries of these national treasures, and obligated to pass them on to future generations.

The recreation potential of our federal lands, which encompass nearly a third of our nation's land base, is not fully realized. We must search for ways to resolve competing demands on our public lands, to more effectively utilize and manage them for the full spectrum of uses which they are capable of supporting. Recreation does not have to conflict with the traditional uses of multiple use lands. The American people tell us that management of the public estate should reflect the high premium which Americans give to outdoor recreation.

. . . .

Chapter 1

Outdoor Recreation Depends on Healthy Resources

We recommend

• Strong local, state, and federal environmental quality laws, regulations, and policies be strictly enforced. Recreation should be explicitly recognized as a beneficiary of clear air, clean water, pleasing landscapes, and abundant and diverse wildlife.

Environmental quality is key to outdoor recreation

A quality outdoors is essential to fishing, boating, and camping; to hiking, skiing, and bicycling; to hunting and fishing and horseback riding, and every other outdoor activity. There is no outdoor recreational pursuit which does not depend, directly or indirectly, on the quality of the environment. If the waters are dirty, the game sparse, or the views impaired, our outdoor experience is not everything we expect it to be.

Recognizing the importance of environmental quality to outdoor recreation, we reviewed a number of reports prepared by federal agencies and environmental organizations. We found the glass both half full and half empty. We have made some progress, but serious problems remain.

We have made progress, but problems remain

Is America a cleaner place today than it was 50 years ago? Yes and no. Americans can once more swim safely in many of their lakes and streams. And city dwellers can breathe more healthful air in some parts of the country. But to date, most clean-up efforts have solved comparatively simple problems. Problems still facing us, such as toxic wastes or habitat loss, may be more complex, and will require integrated efforts to solve.

During the past three decades, the nation has made significant commitments to the quality of the environment. In many instances, there has been marked improvement. But major environmental problems still affect outdoor recreation, and their resolution will not be easy or inexpensive.

A quality environment requires constant vigilance and continuing investments in education, management, research, and monitoring. Local, state, and federal environmental quality laws, regulations, and policies must be strong, and they must be strictly enforced. Recreation should be recognized in policies, laws, and regulations as an explicit beneficiary of clean air, clean water, pleasing landscapes, and abundant and diverse wildlife.

Water

Success in cleaning up surface waters has been mixed. Many streams have improved, some dramatically: the "dying" Great Lakes are reviving; Atlantic salmon are returning to New England's Connecticut and Penobscot Rivers. The 1982-83 National Fisheries Survey found that 73 percent of the nation's rivers and streams have at least a minimum ability to support sport fish or other fish species of special concern. However, the survey found that the condition of 91 percent of waters had not appreciably changed since the last survey five years earlier. The trend is neither up nor down.

New contamination problems seem to be discovered almost daily. Recreation is inhibited by declines in fisheries, sewage spills, and contaminated groundwater. Groundwater quantity and quality has emerged as a serious long-term problem. The battle against water pollution is a standoff, varying from region to region and among localities within regions.

There has been progress in cleanup of point sources, such as urban sewage treatment plants and industry. However, non-point sources of pollution, such as agricultural and urban stormwater runoff, are increasingly serious problems.

Reservoir construction has shifted to smaller projects, but the conversion of free-flowing streams to flat-water continues. Some recreationists benefit, while others are trying to halt the loss of wild rivers and streams.

Air

Nationwide, air quality probably is better than it was 20 years ago. Some industrial sources of air pollution are being cleaned up. However, pollution remains a health hazard and inhibits recreation in major cities. Smog conditions have improved in some metropolitan areas. Yet smog incidents still occur in large cities under certain weather conditions, and urban pollution contributes to declining air quality over distant rural areas.

According to the Coalition for Clean Air, air pollution was a major concern in planning the 1984 summer Olympics in Los Angeles. That city experiences more days on which air quality is below health-based standards than does any other city in the United States. In fact, those standards are exceeded in Los Angeles during the summer months almost on a daily basis.

Wildlands hundreds of miles from cities and industries suffer from loss of visibility and acid deposition. Visibility is a major factor in recreation experiences. On some days one cannot see the north rim of the Grand Canyon from El Tovar on the south rim. All forms of outdoor recreation are influenced by the clarity of the air.

Acid precipitation is increasingly recognized as a problem in the United States. It is blamed for sterilizing lakes in the northeastern United States. Although the acidity of rainfall in the Northeast appears to have stabilized, it is still more than six times as acidic as rain falling in isolated locations around the world. Meanwhile, forests die, fisheries decline, and recreation suffers.

Increases in carbon dioxide and other gases in the upper atmosphere could alter regional climates and possibly lead to a significant increase in the average global temperature by the middle of the 21st century.

Biological diversity

Biological diversity is the variety of living things: variety in gene pools, species, and ecological communities. Diverse flora and fauna are important to the structure and function of ecosystems. A diverse ecosystem is a healthy ecosystem.

After a century of decline in the 1800's and early 1900's, due to forest clearing, land development and, in the case of some species, overhunting, wildlife and fisheries continue improvements that began after the 1930's. But the greatest continuing threat to all fish and wildlife species is loss and/or degradation of habitat.

Game and sport fish with high commercial and recreational values generally are on upward trends, although there are exceptions. For nongame species, the trend is not so optimistic. Habitat loss from development continues to be a major problem affecting a wide variety of wildlife species, especially those that migrate across international boundaries.

Approximately 80 percent of wildlife species are not hunted. More than 55 percent of the adult population participated in nonconsumptive enjoyment of wildlife in 1980. Many state and federal agencies have initiated programs to manage plants and animals that are not hunted, fished, or trapped. However, there is a serious imbalance in the funding of nongame programs when compared with the funding levels for game species.

There have been some well-known extinctions, such as the passenger pigeon, heath hen and Carolina parakeet. Other less glamorous species may ultimately represent the greater loss in terms of potential food, fibre and medicine sources for the future. Effective nongame programs could reduce the need for expenditures for recovery of endangered species by addressing problems before they become critical.

More common and perhaps of greater significance to recreation has been the extirpation of many species from large areas of the country. It is not likely, for example, that wild herds of bison, elk, moose, or bighorn sheep can be restored to all the areas they once inhabited.

The concern over biological diversity is international in scope. Trends toward genetic selection of crops and trees is reducing genetic diversity. The loss of tropical rainforest in Central and South America has seriously impacted the populations of a large number of migratory songbirds. A new species of perennial wild corn with significant potential for improving domestic production, recently discovered on a Mexican mountaintop, is a good example of an important species we might unknowingly lose forever.

Toxics and solid waste

It was once thought that hazardous waste disposal on land was relatively safe. This was based on the assumption that the substances would degrade into harmless products or stay where they were put. Both assumptions were wrong. Toxic substances continue to plague the environment. Production and consumption of pesticides and chemicals are up, and their residues contaminate many places.

Wastes from industry and municipalities continue to grow. Roughly 2.5 billion tons of solid wastes are generated annually in the form of mine tailings, forest residues, and crop wastes; refining and fabricating processes create an estimated 250 million tons of solid wastes per year. In 1978, 150 million tons of garbage and trash were generated by municipalities. Alarmingly, only eight percent of solid wastes are recycled. The rest ends up in landfills, dumps, and as litter.

Noise

Noise has increased as more mechanized equipment fills our cities, farms, trails, canyons, lakes, rivers, and snow-covered hills. One cannot escape man-caused noise even in wildernesses.

Energy

Since the 1960's we have seen two disruptions in the availability of gasoline that resulted in major changes in travel patterns and associated recreation and tourism. Stable and reliable sources of energy are vital to citizens' ability to enjoy recreation opportunities.

Energy consumption also has a strong impact on the environment. Choices about the fuels people consume, the technologies in which fuels are converted to useful work, and the methods selected to deal with waste products have profound and lasting effects on the environment, including human life and health.

We depend on many sources for our energy. Natural resources situated on public lands and, increasingly, on the Outer Continental Shelf provide a large share of our domestic oil and gas production. In electricity generation, nuclear energy has become relatively more important, especially in certain regions. However, its future is clouded because of economic problems and uncertainties about the safety of nuclear power plants.

Wildlife Recreation Is Popular

Wildlife-associated recreation is one of this country's most popular forms of outdoor recreation. In 1980, 42.1 million persons 16 years old and older fished, 17.4 million hunted, and 83.2 million took an active role in nonconsumptive forms of wildlife associated recreation (wildlife observation, photography, or feeding). In all 99.8 million persons, 59 percent of the population, enjoyed one or more of these recreational activities.

Observing, photographing, and feeding wildlife provide enjoyment to millions of persons in the United States, many of whom also fish and hunt. In 1980, 28.8 million nonconsumptive users aged 16 and older took trips of at least one mile from their home primarily for the purpose of observing, photographing, or feeding wildlife, spending $4 billion in the process. Some 69.4 million persons enjoyed wildlife in some way while on a trip taken for another purpose. Millions more enjoy wildlife-related activities around their homes. In 1980, 79.7 million individuals observed, photographed, or fed wildlife at home.

1980 NATIONAL SURVEY OF FISHING,
HUNTING AND WILDLIFE ASSOCIATED
RECREATION

Last year over 200,000 Minnesota citizens donated over $700,000 on their state income tax and property tax forms to help nongame wildlife. This year, in the sixth year of our checkoff program the donations are going up again. In spite of economically difficult time, people care so much about nongame wildlife that they have increased their donations for the past six years. This is a strong statement of local concerns for wildlife.

It is my feeling that federal policy and concerns have not shown any appreciable concern or commitment to the preservation and conservation of nongame wildlife. The best and cheapest programs for the protection of endangered species are good state programs to prevent nongame species from becoming endangered in the first place.

CAROL HENDERSON
Concept paper

WILDLIFE AND FISHERIES ENHANCEMENT

When explorers and settlers from Europe first came to America, they were astonished at the rich array of wild creatures in our lands and waters. Today we recognize that wildlife enriches our lives in many ways with aesthetic, scientific, cultural, educational, recreational and economic values, and as sensitive indicators of the health of our environment. Indeed they are components of the web of life which sustains us.

Corporate America Has an Important Role to Play

It is estimated that corporations control as much as one-third of America's 1.2 billion acres. Much of this land is not in immediate use and is well suited for wildlife habitat programs.

A number of companies, including Du Pont, Weyerhaeuser, Tenneco, and USX, have initiated their own habitat programs which can serve as demonstration projects. Environmental organizations such as the National Wildlife Federation and National Audubon Society also have active habitat enhancement programs.

Corporations support wildlife programs in other ways, too. Du Pont Corporation helps underwrite the bald eagle propagation project at the Patuxent Wildlife Research Center. The Miller Brewing Company supports the "Save the Eagle Program." The Shell Oil Foundation and Mobil Oil have made contributions toward the recovery of the Ridley's sea turtle in the Gulf of Mexico.

These corporate wildlife enhancement programs should be applauded and encouraged.

Wildlife Enhancement is Needed on Private Lands

Many private landowners provide innumerable benefits to wildlife. Landowners provide key habitat ranging from trees in city backyards to large farms. Ranchers in the West, for example, often feed wildlife from haystacks during severe winters. Private landowners can and should be encouraged to do even more.

Agricultural programs associated with crop production under the Food Security Act of 1985 should be strengthened to specifically enhance wildlife production and when possible provide for hiking and other kinds of low-intensity recreation. In implementing the Act, the Department of Agriculture should encourage incentives for hunting, fishing and other outdoor recreation activities on private lands on a lease or fee-for-access basis.

Local and state cooperation in federal programs such as the Resource Conservation and Development and county extension services should be strengthened by the establishment of boards at the county level specifically dedicated to wildlife and dispersed recreation programs. States should be encouraged to work with private landowners to develop land management plans in cooperation with state species management programs.

Incentives to private landowners for wildlife habitat protection or recreation could take the form of reduced property taxes, low interest loans, cost sharing, in-kind donation of expertise from state and federal agencies, or training on market opportunities for wildlife recreation.

Existing programs such as the Wildlife Restoration Act, Sikes Act, and Fish and Wildlife Conservation Act should be retained and strengthened. They have created working partnerships with the states, and have been successful in carrying out wildlife habitat programs.

Nongame Programs Need More Attention

The Fish and Wildlife Conservation Act of 1980 authorizes programs to enhance nongame species, but funds have never been appropriated for this purpose. In FY 1986, the Fish and Wildlife Service budgeted $1.4 million for nongame research. State fish and wildlife agencies devote approximately seven percent of their budgets to nongame programs. There is a critical need for funding to develop programs to address nongame issues.

A number of states have responded by establishing new programs for nongame wildlife. Thirty-one states currently have wildlife and wildlife-related income tax check-off programs. Since 1978, Colorado has raised more than $4 million for nongame wildlife with a tax check-off program.

The states have developed a variety of funding sources to support nongame programs, including sales taxes, sales of personalized auto tags, a special tax on car registrations and the establishment of endowment funds. In 1984 Missouri collected $48 million for wildlife with a one-eighth of one percent sales tax. The Market Opinion Research survey conducted for the Commission found that 64 percent of the American public support the funding of wildlife protection through taxes.

Federal Fisheries Programs Are Fragmented

In 1986, 60 million American anglers spent $25 billion dollars to enjoy their favorite sport, and participation continues to grow. The future of recreational angling is dependent upon the ability of natural resource agencies at all levels of government to protect the resource base, to find scientific solutions for problems limiting growth, and to provide innovative and resourceful fisheries management to meet future needs. Management of the nation's fisheries habitat and fisheries resources is shared by state, tribal and federal governments.

There are major shortcomings in the present federal fisheries structure. The collection, analysis and dissemination of fisheries information is deficient in quality and timeliness to effectively serve management of the nation's fisheries resources. Basic research in fisheries biology and ecology does not receive the sustained support essential to expand our knowledge base as an investment in future resource productivity.

The relative roles and responsibilities of federal, state, tribal and local governments lack definition and coordination. Development of coherent national programs has not been possible due to fragmented federal fisheries authority. In federal agencies such as the Bureau of Land Management, Corps of Engineers, Environmental Protection Agency, National Park Service, and U.S. Forest Service, fisheries-related functions are only one of the agency's responsibilities and may not receive adequate support.

131

We recommend the establishment of a single federal fisheries agency through merging of the National Marine Fisheries Service and the fisheries components of the Fish and Wildlife Service, to consolidate the presently divided marine, estuarine and freshwater protected species responsibility and fish-related estuarine habitat protection functions.

Fisheries Incentives Are Needed for Landowners

The implementation of tax relief options for persons owning water frontage in urban areas in return for easements for sport fishing access would expand recreational fishing opportunities for the public. In addition, there is a need to develop programs, perhaps within the U.S. Department of Agriculture, to supplement farm income through the creation of sport fishing opportunities on farmland.

Angling Opportunities for Senior Citizens Are Restricted

We received several hundred letters from retirees requesting support for a national fishing license. In our society today there are large number of senior citizens who are geographically mobile on a seasonal basis. The current rates set by the states for non-resident fishing licenses severely restrict opportunities for these people to enjoy sportfishing. We encourage the states to establish less prohibitive fishing license fees for senior citizens.

Protecting Historic and Cultural Resources

Many people find diversion and enjoyment in the cultural and historical resources of our state. The site may be of special historical significance, such as a Civil War battlefield, or it may have unknown or unexplored cultural values, such as an Indian burial mound. Visitors to many of the state's oldest parks, constructed by the Civilian Conservation Corps, are drawn to the timeless beauty and historical quality of the old stone walkways and pavilions. All of these areas provide an important and popular form of recreation.

. . . Arkansas' cultural heritage plays an important role in our overall recreation picture. Programs, such as the Historic Preservation Program, which include tax incentives are valuable tools and should be retained. Multiple-use concepts and cooperative efforts such as the proposed National Heritage Corridor for the Mississippi River Valley should also be pursued.

ARKANSASANS OUTDOORS: ISSUES
CRITICAL TO RECREATION IN THE
"NATURAL STATE"
February 1986

Chapter 2

Our Greatest Recreation Needs Are in Urban Areas, Close to Home

We recommend

● Citizens, businesses, and urban officials recognize the value of recreation to meeting community goals for livability, economic development, and healthy citizens. All Americans should have access to the outdoors close to home.

● Local governments place particular emphasis on meeting the needs of less mobile people who are often concentrated in urban areas, including those with physical and mental disabilities, the elderly, minorities, new immigrants, and others who cannot easily leave their neighborhoods.

● Communities devote more time, money and expertise to developing strong partnerships with neighborhood, corporate, and nonprofit groups to improve recreation resources in cities and to plan for future recreation needs. We must encourage Americans to discover and support their parks.

The urban environment is the great outdoors for most Americans

By the year 2000, eighty percent of Americans will live in metropolitan areas. Those of us who do will especially need access to the great outdoors; in concrete deserts we lose touch with the real world of trees, birds, small mammals, and plant life. We each need outdoor recreation opportunities close to home, where they can be a part of our daily lives.

The places where people are—cities and their urbanizing areas—are the focus of the most rapid changes in the physical environment, in society and in the economy. How we respond to these dynamic changes in urban areas will determine much of the future of Americans outdoors.

Recreation and the American City: A Special Conference

In May 1986, the Commission cosponsored a Conference on Recreation and the American City. Participants in eight topical round tables addressed a variety of issues from financing and managing urban recreation systems to the problems of protecting urban open space and serving special populations.

Findings

Dr. John G. Keane, Director of the U.S. Census Bureau, highlighted the rapid growth in the elderly, the immigrants, school age residents and single-parent households expected to occur mostly in urban areas over the next 15 years, and the needs implied by these changes for increasing urban recreation services. He also noted a resurgence of growth in a number of older urban areas, which had lost population between 1960 and 1980. Mayor William Collins of Norwalk, Connecticut, discussed his city's notable successes with corporate sponsorship of specific park maintenance and recreation programs, noting that the city-business partnership was based on mutual self-interest rather than charity. Collins said that cities must clearly define their own goals for open space and recreation, then match city needs with corporate interests by negotiating mutually beneficial arrangements to improve park and recreation amenities.

Peter Stein of The Trust for Public Land emphasized the amazing variety of natural features still present in cities as well as the potential of abandoned land in cities to be reclaimed as recreation spaces:

"From abandoned lots that have been reclaimed as food-producing community gardens to the majestic urban gems like Golden Gate Park in San Francisco and Central Park in New York, these urban open spaces often provide the only significant opportunities for city residents to come in contact with nature. These experiences are the foundation for an environmental awareness that carries over into all other phases of life. Contemplative time spent in an urban forest or in a near-urban wildlife refuge leads directly to a better understanding of the relationship between people and wildlife and an appreciation of natural diversity."

Conclusions

○ Stable sources of funding for development, renovation and acquisition of remaining open space are critical to most communities. Participants indicated strongly that state and federal governments should have a continuing role as stimulators of local investments.

○ Better planning and citizen involvement is essential to integrate recreation into the overall urban fabric of economic development, housing, historic preservation, health, transportation, and related concerns.

○ Stronger interagency and public-private partnerships are also critical for the survival of urban recreation systems. Coordination of programs between school and recreation agencies was the most frequently cited example, but better linkages to state and federal conservation and development programs are also a major concern.

○ Joint efforts with neighborhood residents, nonprofit service agencies and environmental groups are needed to involve citizens in direct stewardship of their parks and recreation programs.

○ To increase partnerships with corporate America, public officials must also increase their understanding about how private investment can help them reach their open space and recreation goals.

○ Recreation managers must continually adapt to the needs of changing populations to ensure provision of services to the many special people concentrated in cities.

City recreation areas and open spaces are essential links in our national network of outdoor resources, key components in a continuum that extends from small parks in crowded residential areas to pristine wilderness. Greenways can be the ties that link these separate areas together. Community-based programs that encourage use and appreciation of recreation resources will help to increase awareness of the need to safeguard all outdoor values.

Recreation is a critical part of good places to live and work

Urban parks are more than just play and conservation areas. Attractive parks, plazas and recreation facilities draw tourists and long-term private investment to communities. Parks and recreation areas are "escape valves" that improve mental health for harried city dwellers. Close-to-home recreation facilities and programs encourage active exercise that improves the physical health of urban America.

Communities must recognize that their goals for economic development, culture, and quality of life are closely tied to recreation. This recognition is key to building successful multi-purpose partnerships among many public and private agencies.

Urban natural areas introduce people to the outdoors

Cities are, by definition, places where nature has been altered. Natural areas in cities are essential contacts with the real world of earth, water, fresh air and sky for a people increasingly isolated from nature. They are "learning grounds" which point us toward greater appreciation of our nation's most spectacular outdoor resources.

The Audubon Society, the National Wildlife Federation, and others have pointed out the amazing diversity of natural features that exist within the boundaries of most major cities. Plants and animals continue to share cities with human residents—in parks, gardens, backyards, and on the many hillsides, streams and rivers that must coexist with concrete, steel and asphalt.

City residents may be introduced to natural systems through bird-watching, tree and wildflower observation or other wildlife identification activities on local park or school sites. According to the 1980 Survey of Fishing, Hunting and Wildlife-Associated Recreation, almost 80 million Americans showed an active interest in observing, feeding and enjoying wildlife within one mile of their homes.

Urban wildlife is a key educational as well as physical tie to the natural environment for urban people. Understanding the habits and haunts of birds or squirrels in the city is the first step toward understanding the natural and man-made forces that govern the natural environment of the nation and planet Earth.

Many urban residents have special recreation needs

Historically, organized urban recreation programs began with concerns about immigrants, children, and the poor. The needs of these groups for safe and wholesome recreation activities are still a major justification for public recreation services.

Close-to-home recreation is important for everyone, but it is particularly critical for less-mobile people who are often concentrated in cities. Recreation helps special groups overcome social isolation. Citizens with physical and mental disabilities are often isolated from the mainstream of society by social attitudes, as well as physical and economic barriers. Recreation programs can be a first step to break down these barriers.

Many elderly are also bound to their neighborhoods by needs for medical and other services or desires to be close to families and friends. Even though many senior citizens have more free time, higher incomes, and enjoy better health than ever before in our history, for a large number of older people this is not the case. Many have given up their cars or are reluctant to drive them, especially in busy urban areas. They are threatened by isolation from the rapidly changing world around them.

Racial minorities and new immigrants are heavily concentrated in cities—almost 60 percent of blacks, for example, and 53 percent of all Hispanic residents. Recreation serves to integrate people with diverse backgrounds and promotes harmonious living in crowded urban areas.

Younger children and their parents are equally dependent on close-to-home recreation programs. The needs of such special groups place particular burdens on cities and suburbs to provide outreach, transportation, and organized play, sport and social recreation programs.

Public budget cuts and greater emphasis on operating self-sufficiency threaten service to those who cannot afford to pay. Communities must continue their traditional roles as providers of services to the many special population groups concentrated in urban areas, by combining tax-supported programs with nonprofit and citizen volunteer efforts. Park and recreation providers must be facilitators, brokering services in partnerships with schools, senior citizen centers, youth and service clubs, and participants themselves, to ensure access to affordable leisure opportunities.

There are opportunities for reclamation

Because of the rapid changes typical of cities, many recreation areas are poorly located in relation to where people live, or inadequately designed for current needs. Barriers to movement such as intervening highways, industrial or commercial corridors, or lack of convenient public transportation, and poor condition or obsolete design of facilities may keep people away.

But the very pace of change also presents opportunities for recreation in cities. Land is often available as part of the regular turnover of land uses. We must look for ways to capitalize on opportunities to integrate recreation into our city life, as we redesign and revitalize degraded parts of our cities.

What local citizens and communities must do

The first step toward assuring adequate citizen support and resources for urban park systems is to recognize that outdoor recreation places and programs are key to making cities good places to live.

In urban areas, the "City as a Park" concept is a good tool for help in building the prairie fire of local concern and investment. This concept integrates recreation into all community services, including housing, school, health, transportation, crime prevention, historic protection and the arts and other efforts to enhance the natural and built environments.

New office complexes can incorporate plazas, walkways, gardens or rooftop recreation facilities, providing places for people to relax in the heart of business districts. Urban residents must work closely with local leaders to ensure that cities, suburbs and urban counties do a better job of integrating open space and recreation values into all community services' plans and budgets.

Remaining urban natural areas are prime candidates for *greenways*. Remnant stream valleys, lakeshores, floodplains, ridges and other areas where development has not yet occurred are invaluable pieces of the greenway network. Urban greenways may connect recreation resources, providing a natural walkway to private and public areas. They also give urban residents natural access routes to the surrounding countryside.

All who love the outdoors can help by protecting the natural riches in and near cities, and ensuring that urban residents have chances to appreciate them. This will be a key to building the outdoor ethic for 190 million urban Americans.

For the people of Boston, outdoor recreation can mean either a door-stop, a street corner, an alley or a neighborhood park with lawns, flowers and benches, a recreation area with ballfields, game courts or an urban garden. For us, the choice between these is clear, the benefits certain. Our parks and greenspaces are our outdoor living rooms. They are the places where we go to be alone, to think, to relax, to refresh the spirit in quiet contemplation of nature; the place we go to expend our extra energy, to run as far as we can, to play as hard as we can, to test our mettle in competition; the place we go to be with our neighbors, to catch up on local news, to celebrate special events, to sit and watch the world go by. Our parks are for all of us: the young and old, the rich and poor, the strong and the weak, for those well established and for those who have recently come to our city.

ROBERT McCOY
Boston Commissioner of Parks
Boston hearing

Center Provides Recreation for the Handicapped

San Francisco's Recreation Center for the Handicapped was established in 1952 to provide year-round recreation activities for disabled children and adults. This citizen-based effort was the idea of one individual, Janet Pomeroy, who established the center and has directed it for 24 years. The Center began with swimming and physical fitness programs in unused space provided by the San Francisco Parks and Recreation Department. It has increased its programs to serve adults as well as children and to provide comprehensive recreation and leisure education services to severely disabled people both at the center and in their homes.

With almost $9 million in donated funds, a new complex was completed on city land in 1977, including a large, therapeutic swimming pool, a day camp site, a skills development center, and a gymnasium. The Recreation Center for the Handicapped has pioneered applied research methods of organizing and administering recreation programs for the severely disabled, and is a model of public-private partnership. Over the years, local government has provided land and some operating revenues, while community donations have paid most development costs and volunteers have helped maintain program services.

Baltimore Sponsors Outward Bound

In 1986, Baltimore became the first city in the nation to host an Outward Bound program. Parks and People, a nonprofit foundation that supports Baltimore's park and recreation department, is sponsoring Baltimore-Chesapeake Bay Outward Bound. Like Outward Bound programs in rural and wilderness locations, Baltimore's effort offers challenging recreation experiences to young people and adults. It also reaches out more directly to city residents by operating close to the places they live. Sailing on Chesapeake Bay, climbing in the nearby mountains and learning about land and sea ecology increase understanding about the outdoors and improve leadership skills, teamwork and pride in each participant.

School-Park Partnerships Increase
Recreation Opportunity

For more than 60 years, joint "school-park" programs have proven one of the most productive and efficient partnerships for allowing multiple use of community resources and tax dollars. Independent boards of education operate and control billions of dollars worth of recreational facilities: sportsfields, swimming pools, gyms and playgrounds.

Milwaukee's 70-year-old Lighted Schoolhouse Program, operated by a municipal recreation division jointly funded by the school board and the city government, keeps school facilities open for community recreation after school hours, on weekends and in the summer. Portland, Oregon; Dade County, Florida; Grand Rapids, Michigan; and Birmingham, Alabama, among others, also operate successful park-school programs. Although fiscal restraints in recent years have made it difficult for communities to adopt these programs, the costs of such cooperation are small in comparison to the substantial benefits of using school facilities for public recreation.

Riverspark—The Hudson-Mohawk
Urban Cultural Park

Riverspark covers six communities along the Hudson and Mohawk Rivers north of Albany, New York. It is not a single or continuous site but rather a concept to unify a variety of resources along the two rivers and within six cities and towns. The communities share a heritage of natural and cultural features associated with the 19th century history of the region as an industrial center.

The Riverspark idea was adopted in 1977 by the legislative bodies of Troy and Cohoes, and four smaller communities. Goals and objectives for the park were established and a Commission of mayors was established to oversee planning and implementation. Shortly thereafter, the State Legislature designated the Hudson-Mohawk area as the State's first Urban Cultural Park. The four goals of New York's Urban Cultural Parks System include preservation, recreation, education and economic development.

Parks, historic sites and natural or open areas along the rivers were inventoried. Then a 28-mile Heritage Trail and bikeway (now designated a National Recreation Trail) was created on existing streets to link the key areas identified. The Commission's plan now includes seven historic "theme areas" and two visitor centers.

A tourism program for the area emphasizes guided bus, bicycle, and auto tours of key features—unique buildings, streets, natural areas, parks, squares and other public spaces along the Hudson-Mohawk corridors. Physical redevelopments, including adaptive reuse of old mills and warehouses for housing and commercial centers, creation of a new park, restoration of historic properties, have occurred. Special events and programs, such as bike and foot races, Community Heritage Days and educational programs for schools and adults, also focus on the river heritage.

*What once seemed dull, ugly or commonplace in our urban land-
scape appears as a rich tapestry embroidered from the lives and dreams
of earlier generations.*

PAUL M. BRAY
Riverspark founder

Clinton Community Garden— A Neighborhood Park

The Clinton Community Garden is one of 400 garden-parks operated by neighborhood groups in New York City on formerly abandoned or vacant lands. It began in 1978 with a few community residents who began to clear away debris from a rubble-strewn, half-block lot in Manhattan. By 1980, the site had been transformed into an award-winning garden where neighborhood residents could grow their own vegetables and flowers. A grass play area, green-house and shady area for sitting and socializing make the Clinton Community Garden into a complete neighborhood park.

When rising development pressures raised the possibility that the city-owned lot might be sold for a building development, a Committee to Save Clinton was established to create local support for protecting the site. More that $100,000 was raised by "selling" square inches of the garden to city residents and people across the country. Finally, in 1985, the City trans-ferred the property from its sale list to the Department of Parks and Recreation, which ensures its continued protection while allowing use by community residents at no cost to the taxpayer.

Some Parks Are Historic Resources

In the last decade, citizens and private groups have begun to focus on restoration of city park legacies, from historic recreation areas designed by Frederick Law Olmsted in the 19th century to the many downtown and neighborhood parks established between 1910 and 1940. Boston, Seattle, New York, and Detroit are some of the communities that have led this effort. Older park restoration is an indication that city residents are beginning to recognize the links between recreation, culture and economic revitalization in many older American cities.

The "City as a Park" approach is another manifestation of the connection between recrea-tion and every aspect of city life. This idea is now proving itself as a way to renew people's pride in their communities, and has led to the establishment of partnerships to restore parks and historic features and operate recreation programs.

Massachusetts, New York and Pennsylvania have state urban cultural park programs that link historic, recreation and economic revitalization. Streets, public gathering places, historic buildings, special natural features and even abandoned industrial areas are given new life as recreation resources.

It may be an oversimplification to say that the best cities have the best parks. Yet the most progressive cities in terms of social improvements and economic growth are able to show notable physical improvements in their outdoor domain. Minneapolis, Dallas, Seattle, Atlanta, San Francisco can be named as a few of those that, while dealing with social problems, have created new open spaces. Conversely, when parks are neglected, lack of civic leadership and a diminished quality of life can be assumed.

AUGUST HECKSCHER
*Open Spaces: The Life of
American Cities*

Chapter 3

A Vision for the Future: A Living Network of Greenways

We recommend

● Communities establish Greenways, corridors of private and public recreation lands and waters, to provide people with access to open spaces close to where they live, and to link together the rural and urban spaces in the American landscape.

A vision for the future

Imagine walking out your front door, getting on a bicycle, a horse, or a trail bike, or simply donning your backpack, and, within minutes of your home, setting off along a continuous network of recreation corridors which could lead across the country.

Greenways are your vehicle for this imaginary trip of the future, reaching out from communities all across America to link cities, towns, farms, ranches, parks, refuges, deserts, alpine areas, wetlands, and forests into a vast and varied network of open spaces.

Greenways are a way to provide open recreation spaces for every American, close to home. Greenways are our vision for the future.

What are greenways?

Greenways are local natural areas where recreation and conservation are among the primary values. They are fingers of green that come in many shapes and sizes. They may be in public or in private ownership, and may serve many purposes.

Greenways link people and resources. They can put recreation open space within a short walk from your home.

They come in many different forms: biking and hiking trails along abandoned rail lines; boating and fishing sites on ribbons of bright water restored from neglect; vacant lots for "just messing around" after school or work; belts of grasslands, shrubs, and forests surrounding and threading their way through cities and countrysides like a giant circulatory system;

and working farms and ranches. Greenways connect new and existing recreation and conservation areas, like parks and forests and refuges, and corridors to link them together.

Greenways do *not* mean new federal lands, or federal land use control. Our concept is not to propose a federal initiative. Greenways will be put in place by communities.

Why do we need them?

Our nation has already committed vast tracts of lands and waters, and invested enormous sums of money in our federal and state parks, forests, and reserves. They are world class resources, and they remain bulwarks in our recreation estate.

But they tend to be far from where people live, and limited in their ability to meet the growing diversity of America's recreation and conservation needs. Most Americans live in urban areas. They need open spaces close to home, and they need the pride that comes from realizing individual initiative. Greenways can meet those needs.

Greenways are a bold idea with the magic to stir people to action. Greenways themselves are not new. We want to encourage their spread across the American landscape, by focusing on their values to communities. A nationwide network could ultimately grow from local action in thousands of communities across America.

Some Greenways Are Already in Place

Among the hundreds of greenways already in place around the country are:

New York Staten Island Greenbelt

East Bay Regional Park, Oakland, California

Maryland Program Open Space

Illinois and Michigan Canal National Heritage Corridor

Yakima Greenway, Washington

Bicycle trail along Interstate 70 in Colorado

Here's what greenways can do for us, and for future generations

Greenways can achieve six major goals:

o Provide Americans with access to open spaces and wildlands for the widest possible variety of outdoor activities, close to home;

o Conserve elements of the great American landscape, in all its diversity, and the full potential for human interactions with that heritage;

o Build partnerships among private enterprise, landowners, and local governments and groups in recreation and conservation;

o Encourage local pride and celebration in the quality and availability of outdoor assets;

o Diversify and strengthen local economies and lifestyles through enhanced recreation opportunities; and

o Link urban and rural areas for the recreation and conservation of natural resources.

How is a greenway established?

Any site, public or private, that is managed in a predominantly natural state for conservation of resources and recreation opportunities can become part of a greenway. Privately-owned lands would be included in a greenway network only with the express cooperation and agreement of the landowner.

Communities should work together to decide where greenways would go in their community. What special tracts exist that hold quality recreation potential, or encompass a part of the cultural heritage of your town or area? Where would you like to preserve opportunities for future generations to enjoy the great outdoors? Places to look:

o River and stream courses;

o Abandoned rail lines (approx. 120,000 miles potential nationwide);

o Utility corridors;

o Wildlife migration routes and flyway corridors;

o Scenic roads and highways; and

o Trails, paths, parks, golf courses, floodplains, forests, refuges, and scenic countrysides.

A network of greenways can grow from existing recreation and conservation areas, enhancing their value by connecting them. For example, city and county parks, state parks and state wildlife areas, units of the national parks, forests, and public lands systems, and private lands managed at least partly for recreation, such as California's Ranches for Wildlife—all can enhance, and be enhanced by, a greenways network.

Local governments and coalitions should take the lead in

o Goal setting, inventories, and priorities;

o Implementation: landowner contact, and management coordination;

o Major funding and sweat equity;

o Operations and maintenance.

The national government can help

National leadership can help spark, and assist, local action.

o Champion and market the concept;

o Funding through LWCF or its successor: challenge grants, innovation grants;

o Technical assistance and information brokering to local groups;

o Enforcement of existing statutes on environmental quality and property rights.

These people are ready to help

The focus of greenways creation should be local groups and individuals, local governments, and local chapters of regional and national organizations. Many existing organizations stand ready to help, including:

o non-profit conservation organizations and local land trusts;

o civic associations;

o recreation, sport, and wildlife groups;

o commerce and tourism agencies;

o state and local highway agencies;

○ state fish and game, forestry, and recreation agencies;

○ local park districts and planning boards; and many more.

Here are some tools

Greenways for Americans will be based on getting the most from existing resources and programs, and tapping the power of market forces and individual initiative. A variety of mechanisms will be used to build the system:

○ recognition and registration of sites that already meet greenway purposes;

○ incentives to private interests to make lands and waters available for active and passive recreation, including law enforcement, protection of property rights, limitation of liability, and to encourage them to provide services that are better delivered by the private sector;

○ conservation reserves and conservation easements under provisions of the Food Securities Act of 1985 (Farm Bill);

○ challenge and innovation grants from LWCF or its successor, and from private corporations, foundations, and individuals to stimulate local matching funds, for acquisition and stewardship by local, state or nonprofit groups;

○ broader application of existing authorities and new partnerships to use abandoned rail lines and utility corridors, with landowner consent, for multiple-use recreation corridors;

○ local, county, or state recreation fees to fund operations and maintenance on public areas.

There will be many benefits from greenways

Greenways will have significant environmental, conservation, and economic benefits. Innovative design and management could achieve the following:

○ reduced flood damage;

○ wildlife habitat protection, and plant and animal conservation;

○ water table recharge in wetlands and healthy riparians;

o improved landscape aesthetics;

o enhanced community pride and identity;

o more effective use of limited land area for conservation;

o concurrent uses by compatible industries;

o enhanced awareness and appreciation for wildlands;

o more diverse local economies from tourism.

Greenways can link Americans

Greenways can draw people together in their communities to provide open spaces for all close to their own homes. They have the potential to be this country's most important land-based effort for conservation and recreation in the next several decades.

They can draw private and local entities into lead roles in provision of recreation opportunities. They can capitalize on the entrepreneurial spirit of Americans and give pride of accomplishment and responsibility to millions of people in every community. They can protect vital water, fish, wildlife, and recreation resources as integral parts of the growth of cities and communities. And, if greenways truly capture the imagination and boldness of the American spirit, they could eventually form the corridors that connect open spaces, parks, forests, and deserts—and Americans—from sea to shining sea.

They should form a framework of parks and forests connected by a series of paths and trails for general outdoor living.

BENTON MACKAYE
(1929)

People's visual expectations of publicly and privately managed landscapes are beginning to affect land-use decisions in many places and at different levels of government. The demands on these lands are many and diverse and are sometimes complementary but often cause conflict. They can range from providing "hard" natural resource values such as wood, forage and clean water to less tangible or "softer" resource-based values such as the sense of wilderness, the exhilaration of a mountain meadow, or the beauty of natural appearing and well managed scenery—an important component of the individuals' outdoor recreation experience.

Often, scenic expectations are not met in large landscapes when proper planning and design have not been accomplished or even consi-

dered. This has resulted in disappointing, dramatic and unexpected changes to the existing scene with little resemblance to a natural appearing or well ordered and healthy landscape. Thus, a less than fulfilling recreation experience, with a thorough understanding of the basic principles and concepts of large scale landscape planning and design applied similarly and in concert at all levels of government, these precious scenic resources can continue to provide a wide variety of resource opportunities and at the same time be assured of continued, albeit ever changing and well planned natural appearing landscapes.

BOB ROSS
Concept Paper

A Hiker's Greenway Odyssey

A good example of a regional greenways network that has evolved over the years and is still developing is the chain of local, regional, and national trails that begins in the District of Columbia and northern Virginia. Let's follow the theoretical odyssey of a hiker on the greenway network.

From Rockville, Maryland, he or she hikes through Rock Creek Park (which runs through the length of the District of Columbia), connects with the Mount Vernon bike trail (which runs 24 miles to George Washington's estate) on the Potomac River's western shore, turns west onto a trail network which runs a dozen miles through city stream valley parks in northern Virginia suburbs, then onto the 44-mile Washington and Old Dominion Railroad Regional Park into the Virginia foothills. From there it is only six miles to the Appalachian Trail.

On the Trail our hiker can head south, and eventually wind up at its southern terminus at Springer Mountain, Georgia, or turn north to Mount Katahdin, Maine. At Harper's Ferry, West Virginia, he or she could swing onto the Chesapeake and Ohio Canal and return to Washington, or go west to Cumberland, Maryland.

On this odyssey, our hiker or biker has traveled on local, regional, and national trails. Some of the trails are paved for bikes, and there are bridle paths, too. Along the route are numerous local, state, and national parks. In rural areas private farmlands provide a scenic backdrop. There are private and public campgrounds, or hotels and restaurants if one tires of a sleeping bag and trail fare.

Obviously, few people could or would take full advantage of the thousands of miles of connecting trails on one trip, or even in a lifetime. But on good weather weekends, thousands of people stroll, hike, bike, ride horseback, birdwatch, and picnic along stretches of the network near their homes.

Chapter 4

We Need Initiatives to Protect Rivers All Across America

We recommend

● A 2000 by 2000 Program: through local initiative, with state and federal support where appropriate, protect 2000 river and stream segments by the Year 2000. Cities and towns should clean up and revitalize their stream corridors. States should set up or enhance rivers protection programs to complement local action.

● The federal government consider ending subsidies for new development within floodplains, following the model of the Coastal Barriers Resources Act.

Water is more precious than gold

Water, as Forest Service researcher David W. Lime points out, "is a magnet for recreation and 'liquid' gold for a seemingly ever-expanding commercial, tourism, and service market." For many types of recreation water is the focal point—fishing, hunting, kayaking, boating, swimming, for instance. For others who like hiking, camping, bird watching, and sunbathing, water is an important backdrop.

Water recreation on flatwater lakes has traditionally been important in America—and still is. However, recreation use of our rivers and streams is increasing rapidly, and new attention to protecting these opportunities is needed.

The nation is blessed with abundant rivers: 3.2 million miles in the contiguous 48 states, and another 365,000 in Alaska. Rivers are the "lifeblood" of our continent—great biological systems which support diverse forms of life. Throughout our history, they have been the highways for exploration, migration, and commerce. And we use them as disposal systems for the byproducts of our industrialized society.

Thousands of stretches of rivers, streams, local creeks and runs provide refreshment and enjoyment to all Americans. Most communities have at least one stream of some kind which does, or could, serve as a visual recreation centerpiece. As a number of cities and towns have demonstrated, they can also be instruments of economic revitalization.

Our waters are cleaner but problems remain

The Clean Water Act has caused the restoration of many of the nation's once-polluted waterways. Salmon again are abundant in Oregon's Willamette. The Potomac, once declared unsafe for human contact, now is graced by windsurfers, sailboats, water skiers, and rowing shells. The Clean Water Act has served as one of the nation's most successful urban renewal programs, as communities redefine their downtowns or neighborhoods around newly-attractive riverfront parks.

While there has been some progress, many problems remain to be addressed.

o Nationwide, too many small streams and creeks have degraded through lack of attention and care.

o The recreation potential of the nation's urban rivers is frequently not realized. Industrial and commercial use of the urban waterfront typically walls off the river. Expressways, railroads and utility lines have been built along the shoreline, further cutting off access. Marinas and put-in points may be lacking.

o Many of the remaining wild and free-flowing rivers—a finite resource of high value—are being dammed for power and to supply water to urban areas and agriculture.

o Recreation users of the river also cause problems. Insensitive users litter shorelines, pollute the water, trespass on landowners' property, and trample sensitive vegetation.

We can establish local partnerships to clean up and protect our rivers

Rivers offer a particular opportunity—even necessity—for public-private partnerships. Rivers flow past lands in many ownerships, public and private. They flow through cities large and small, which can foul waters with sewage and industrial effluent, impairing downstream uses. The cooperation of all is required to protect and enhance river quality and access.

Private landowners along riverbanks have a particular interest in their use and care. Any efforts to protect rivers or open them to public use must be coordinated with local landowners. We need an ethic of respect for private landowners' rights and effective ways to control trespass, littering, and vandalism.

Private for-profit outfitters depend on rivers for their livelihoods, and uncounted numbers of businesses, local and national, manufacture and sell equipment for river use.

Volunteer groups who use a river often monitor its quality and use, and even clean it up. Not-for-profit organizations and for-profit businesses can forge links to identify what needs to be done and to provide the talents, muscle and money to do it.

Action might begin with the adoption of rivers by local coalitions—civic groups, conservation and user organizations, land trusts, local businesses. River clean-ups, development of parks and trails, and working for stronger river protection laws and zoning are possible projects. If just one river or stream in each of the 3000 counties in the country were adopted by local interests, the 2000 by 2000 goal would be surpassed in short order.

We can give special help to metropolitan rivers

Protection or enhancement of metropolitan rivers usually requires joint action by many localities and interests. Georgia's Metropolitan Rivers Protection Act, which has been used to preserve scenic and recreation values along the Chattahoochee River in metropolitan Atlanta, is a possible model. It works like this:

o The Atlanta Regional Commission, the metropolitan planning agency for the seven-county Atlanta region, prepares a comprehensive land and water use plan, coordinated with localities, for the Chattahoochee River Corridor.

o Land use changes approved by local government within the corridor must be consistent with the corridor plan.

o Proposed changes in land use and development are reviewed by the Commission before a local government acts. The final decision, however, rests with local governments.

The result is that citizens have a voice in the use and enjoyment of a community resource, and are assured of its availability for future generations as well.

● Special efforts should be made by cities and towns to clean up and revitalize the stream corridors which flow through them.

States can play a stronger role

States have played an important role in river protection. Today, 19 states have wild and scenic rivers programs, with over 200 rivers totalling more than 6000 miles. States also manage, alone or in partnership with federal agencies, a number of rivers in the National Wild and Scenic River System.

State programs vary in level of protection and approach. Some provide stronger pollution controls, zoning, or moratoria on damming or diversion of rivers in the system. Most systems provide for special signing, access sites, and information about recreation opportunities on the river.

These efforts can be used as guidelines for states drafting their own scenic rivers programs. However, current state river protection statutes are generally less stringent than the federal program. Existing state programs may need revitalization through stronger laws or increased staffing and budgets.

● States should inventory river resources and identify priority candidates for protection.

● Each state should institute or perfect a comprehensive statewide rivers protection program or system.

We can preserve floodplains

Floodplains are an integral part of river systems. Floodplains in their natural state provide for cleansing of pollutants in the rivers and floodwater storage, as well as recreation. Alteration or development of the floodplain eliminates or degrades these values.

Counties, municipalities, and states should examine their processes for controlling development in floodplains. The front line of protection for rivers and floodplains should be local action.

The federal government should review its role in subsidizing construction or other development in floodplains. The Coastal Barrier Resources Act, which barred federal subsidies and assistance to development on coastal barrier islands, is a model. The intent of the Act is to protect these fragile island systems and save the federal government money. The same principle should be applied to river floodplains.

We should protect free-flowing rivers for recreation

Increasing numbers of Americans are enjoying river recreation. Across the nation, free-flowing and scenic stretches of rivers—the Mokelumne in California, the Arkansas in Colorado, the Youghiogheny in Pennsylvania—are mobbed in season by white-water rafters. Rivers and streams on the national forests hosted 10.3 million recreation visitor days in 1985. River use continues to increase at a rapid rate.

Hydropower dams are a major threat to remaining stretches of adventure-class white water. Some 12 stretches of the best whitewater rivers in the Northeast and central Atlantic regions have pending proposals for hydroelectric development. These include the Black River in New York, the Kennebec and Penobscot in Maine, the Youghiogheny in Pennsylvania and

Maryland, the Cheat, Gauley and New in West Virginia, and the James in Virginia. But it is a nationwide problem.

Clearly, something needs to be done to check the continuing loss of whitewater recreation opportunities. Where states have taken action to protect a river, federal agency projects and programs should be consistent with the state action. This could deter the dams, hydro projects, diversions and channelization which transform free-flowing rivers and diminish whitewater opportunities. Water-release schedules of existing dams should take recreation concerns into account.

It is not just the nation's major whitewater rivers that are being dammed and otherwise altered, however. In 1986, Congress authorized 262 Corps of Engineers projects (with a price tag of $16.3 billion). Since 1978 there have been 6,000 applications for small hydro projects, many of them on small rivers and streams.

There has been some progress. In 1986, Congress amended the Federal Power Act to require that the Federal Energy Regulatory Commission (FERC) consider the environmental and recreation consequences of proposed hydropower development projects equally with power and economic benefits. Congress also barred federal subsidies under the Public Utilities Regulatory Policy Act for projects on state-protected rivers.

• FERC should be required to grant requests by government agencies and private parties for an adjudicatory hearing when recreation resources are threatened by a new hydropower proposal. FERC also should be prohibited from issuing licenses for new hydropower projects on river segments identified as special recreation zones in the Nationwide Rivers Inventory.

The federal wild and scenic rivers program should be reinvigorated

In 1968, Congress enacted the National Wild and Scenic Rivers Act. That Act declared it national policy ". . . that certain selected rivers of the Nation which, with their immediate environments, possess outstandingly remarkable scenic, recreational, geologic, fish and wildlife, historic, cultural, or other similar values shall be protected for the benefit and enjoyment of present and future generations."

Over the years, some 72 river segments, totalling 7,365 miles, have been brought into the Wild and Scenic Rivers System. In recent years, Wild and Scenic River designations have slowed, though the process is still working: the last Congress added segments of six rivers totalling 122 miles to the system, and designated five more for study. Significantly, the additions included the system's first southern blackwater streams.

However, the system is unbalanced geographically and incomplete. An estimated 80 percent of the current system's river miles are in Alaska, California and Idaho. The system includes few rivers in the nation's midsection, though river advocates say there are a number which qualify.

A Department of Interior nationwide rivers inventory, completed in 1982, identifed 1,524 river segments totalling 61,700 miles which possessed qualities which could qualify them for inclusion in the national system. This amounts to less than two percent of the river and stream miles in the coterminous states.

• River segments on federal lands which agencies have found to be eligible for Wild and Scenic River designation should have their suitability for inclusion in the system protected by existing authorities, management plans or other appropriate actions until Congress has had opportunity to determine final status of the river segment.

The National Wild and Scenic River System is designed to protect selected rivers of national significance only. Thus it is imperative that states have strong river protection tools of their own, so that river segments of less-than-national significance may be protected by state action and federal involvement is held to a minimum.

Most of the river segments in the system are there because of the work of vigorous local advocates. And that is where reinvigoration of the national rivers program must begin.

We can establish a network to provide information and help

Protecting rivers is a complicated task. People have to work with a number of political jurisdictions. There are many available tools, but often they require special knowledge of the law, or how to communicate with private landowners, or how to evaluate use pressures and problems.

Rivers advocates can establish a communications network to help each other. The American Rivers Conservation Council serves as a focal point for local and state rivers organizations. The American Wilderness Alliance Rivers Defense Fund helps coordinate citizen action for western rivers. The National Park Service provides invaluable technical assistance working with local groups and local governments around the country to help them achieve their river protection objectives.

• A central office should be established at the federal level to provide technical assistance to local and state agencies and private sector organizations and to provide a focus for river protection efforts.

We can learn to respect river resources and treat them with care

A river in flood is a formidable force. But a river is also vulnerable to abuse and misuse when used as a place to discard urban effluent or campers' wastes. If we are to truly enjoy the superlative recreation opportunities rivers provide, we must treat them with care. Rivers deserve a special niche in our individual outdoors conservation ethic. Environmental and outdoors education courses and public awareness programs should have a distinct element on rivers and their ecosystems. Only with a broad base of public knowledge of their processes and awareness of the threats they face will our rivers and streams continue to serve our recreation needs.

. . . Free-flowing river resources essential to white water sports are being destroyed by hydroelectric power development projects licensed by, or sponsored by, the Federal government. These losses are continuing although participation in canoeing, rafting, and kayaking has been growing rapidly. The combined effect of these two trends is to force more and more people onto fewer and fewer white water rivers. The result is crowding, safety problems, competition between private and commercial white water users, and other stresses on the resource base. As the resource base shrinks and demand grows, the stress and competition becomes increasingly intense.

REPRESENTATIVE OF THE AMERICAN
CANOE ASSOCIATION
Denver hearing

White Water Diminishes While Rafting Booms

Colorado rafters told us that the state's white water boating resource is shrinking at the same time demand for river recreation is booming. Recreation use of Colorado's rivers more than doubled in the last ten years, from 142,000 use days in 1976 to more than 350,000 in 1985. According to Pat Tierney, a Fort Collins, Colorado river outfitter, two of the state's most prized boating rivers, the Gunnison and the Dolores, have had white water recreation opportunities eliminated or greatly diminished by federally funded water projects . . . These projects have directly inundated canyons or reduced river flows to the point where floating is no longer possible.

The State should press vigorously for congressional designation of all additional qualifying Arizona rivers into the National Wild and Scenic River System.

The Governor should propose legislation to create a state wild and scenic river system. State Parks should conduct a rivers study of free flowing stretches in the state, including both those nominated by the Heritage Conservation and Recreation Service and any others that have not been identified to date for inclusion in a state wild and scenic river system.

Arizonans' Recreation Needs on
Federal Lands
GOVERNOR'S TASK FORCE ON
RECREATION ON FEDERAL LANDS

Rivers for Recreation Are a Scarce Resource

It is difficult to estimate the number of miles of rivers used for recreation, but the proportion of streams with enough volume for on-water activities is fairly small. The proportion of streams suitable for whitewater recreation is even more limited, as this requires not only sufficient volume but also the right combination of flow, gradient, and constriction to provide rapids which are exciting but still safely runnable. Because these same characteristics are often those which are most attractive for water impoundments, many whitewater resources have already been lost and others are threatened, and this trend seems likely to continue.

BO SHELBY
Oregon State University AND
DAVID W. LIME
U.S. Forest Service

Chapter 5

We Are Losing Wetlands and Shorelines

We recommend

● Increased cooperative efforts among private, local, state, and federal interests to protect and enhance wetlands.

● Public awareness efforts by local coalitions, private organizations, and states, as part of the prairie fire, to educate Americans about the many values of wetlands.

● States conduct or update inventories of relatively undeveloped shoreline areas and developed sites where public access is allowed.

Why are wetlands important?

Wetlands are a productive and invaluable public resource. Because of their important values, and because of the current rate of wetlands loss, the need to protect wetlands is critical.

Wetlands have values to mankind and to wildlife of which most Americans are unaware.

○ *Wetlands provide wildlife habitat.* Innumerable plant, fish and wildlife species, including many endangered species, depend on wetlands for spawning, breeding, nesting, or feeding. Alteration of wetland habitats is the single most important factor affecting the abundance of migratory waterfowl.

○ *Wetlands reduce flood damages.* Raging floodwaters which overflow streambanks into adjacent wetlands are slowed, trapped and absorbed by the wetlands like a sponge. The waters are then gradually released back into the stream, and into groundwater supplies.

○ *Wetlands cleanse polluted waters.* Wetlands filter and trap pollutants such as phosphorus, nitrogen, and suspended solids from waters which move through them. Many American cities actually use natural or artificial wetlands for secondary or tertiary wastewater treatment.

○ *Wetlands control erosion.* Roots of trees and shrubs stabilize stream banks and prevent bank erosion. Silt-laden streams which flow into wetlands deposit less of their sediment load downstream.

○ *Wetlands offer unique recreation opportunities.* Wetlands have irreplaceable aesthetic value to those who enjoy their solitude and natural beauty, and the wildlife they support. There is nothing quite like the wildness in a swamp, as you quietly dip a canoe paddle, fish, or watch and listen to the multitude of birds and other wildlife.

○ *Wetlands have tremendous economic value.* Wetlands contribute between $20 billion and $40 billion a year to the national economy. Several billion dollars a year are generated from wetlands-dependent sport and commercial fisheries harvest.

Two-thirds of the commercially important fish and shellfish species harvested along the Atlantic and Gulf coasts, and half of the Pacific coast species are dependent upon coastal wetland habitats for food, spawning and/or nursery areas. A commercial marine fisheries harvest valued at over $10 billion annually provides one economic measure of the significance of coastal wetland resources.

Wetlands need protection

Despite the undeniable importance of wetlands, losses continue at a tragic rate. Of the original 215 million acres that once existed, less than 95 million acres remain, and the annual loss exceeds 450,000 acres. Approximately 80 percent of the 25 million acres of bottomland hardwood forest in the Lower Mississippi Valley has been lost.

The Fish and Wildlife Service's national wetlands trends analysis estimates that over 80 percent of the wetlands lost between 1954 and 1974 in the United States were converted to agricultural uses.

Wetland landowners gain financially by converting wetlands to other uses. But the general public loses incremental flood and storm damage control, erosion control, water quality maintenance, outdoor recreation and fish and wildlife benefits. Destruction or alteration of wetlands deprives us of their values. The public at large often subsidizes wetland drainage, and thus bears the financial costs of drainage as well as losing environmental, economic, and recreation benefits.

Man's ever-increasing needs for food, fiber and energy continue to en-croach on Louisiana's natural environment at an alarming rate. Plans for the protection of this environment can be accomplished only with the proper understanding of the nature and imminence of the threat.

The plight of the loss of natural habitat in Louisiana is well docu-mented. According to U.S. Forest Service surveys, the north delta area of Louisiana in bottomland hardwoods decreased by 54 percent from 1954 to 1974. The south delta region lost 31 of its prime fish and wildlife habitat from 1935 to 1974.

The seven million acres of Louisiana's coastal wetlands are suffer-ing a similar fate but in a different manner. Today, erosion is destroying more marshland than is being renewed by sedimentation. Obviously efforts are needed that would preserve our unique habitat to meet not only our future recreation needs, but also our industries (commercial fishing, trap-ping, and tourism) that depend on this habitat.

DR. GERALD F. GUIDROZ
Chairman, Governor's
Commission on Louisiana's
Outdoors
New Orleans hearing

Some progress is being made

Public concern for wetland losses and support for wetlands protection is increasing. A 1982 Harris Poll found that 83 percent of the respondents felt that it is "very important" to keep the remaining wetlands free from further destruction. A 1985 Harris Poll analysis reaffirmed broad support for continued maintenance of wetlands, with an 85 percent majority of Americans favoring strict enforcement of the Clean Water Act and its asso-ciated wetlands protection authorities.

The Food Security Act of 1985 provides incentives to the agricultural community to protect wetland habitats. The "swampbuster" provision denies federal agricultural payments or other benefits to farmers who pro-duce an agricultural commodity in any crop year on converted wetlands. Since agriculture has been responsible for a majority of wetland losses during the past 30 years, this provision has great potential for reducing the rate of loss.

The Emergency Wetlands Resources Act of 1986 strengthens wetland conservation. A provision of this law requires State Comprehensive Out-door Recreation Plans under the Land and Water Conservation Fund Act to address federal and state acquisition of wetlands as an important out-door recreation resource. Other provisions include establishment of a National Wetlands Priority Conservation Plan for wetland acquisition, completion of nationwide wetlands mapping, and updating the wetland status and trends report.

There are opportunities to do more

We urge aggressive implementation of both the Food Security Act of 1985 and the Emergency Wetlands Resources Act of 1986. State and federal governments should place high priority on identifying, describing, purchasing and protecting the most important remaining wetlands. Local and state growth-channeling measures should be used wherever possible to halt further wetland destruction. Any existing tax or other incentives contributing to wetlands conversion should be removed.

We also recommend that states, localities and private organizations undertake to ensure that citizens and local leaders are aware of the importance of wetlands to outdoor recreation, as well as to clean water, flood control, and wildlife. Wetlands appreciation and protection should occupy a special niche in the outdoor ethics developed by Americans in our communities.

Other wetland protection efforts could include the following:

● Remove incentives, such as direct subsidies and tax code provisions, that promote alteration or destruction of wetlands. The Coastal Barrier Resources Act and the Food Security Act of 1985 represent positive approaches to removal of incentives to wetlands destruction.

● Develop a national program of wetland conservation to assist the Department of the Interior in achieving the goals of the North American Waterfowl Management Plan.

● Require federal land and water development and permitting and licensing agencies (e.g., Bureau of Reclamation, Corps of Engineers and Soil Conservation Service) to develop specific wetland conservation measures in all subsequent project planning, permitting, licensing and authorization reports.

● Require existing water resource development projects to have wetland conservation measures incorporated into their operation and maintenance programs.

● Develop programs to exchange publicly-owned uplands for private wetlands of equal value.

● Establish a consistent wetland mitigation policy. Projects involving unavoidable wetland modifications should have appropriate mitigation measures developed and implemented to ensure that no net loss of wetlands occurs.

A new shoreline initiative is needed

Open space along the ocean, Great Lakes and other shorelines of the nation continues to diminish under the rising tide of development. This is a long-term historical trend, and has been well recognized for decades. Not only is open space disappearing, but the development responsible for its loss severely reduces public access to the shoreline itself.

So we feel, at least as far as South Florida is concerned—and I think it's true throughout Florida and many other coastal states—that more importance, significance, has to be given to the acquisition of beach front so that it's provided for our public, and it remains in public ownership for generations to come.

DENNIS ESHELMAN
Director of Palm Beach County
Parks and Recreation Department
Orlando hearing

As a result, opportunities for many of America's favorite recreation activities—water-related—are being lost in the very places—the coasts—where our population is growing the fastest.

Many studies have been conducted to inventory shorelines resources and evaluate the potential for adding them to the public recreation estate. A significant number of federal seashore areas were acquired as additions to the National Park System in the 1960s as a result of such studies, and local and state jurisdictions have taken similar actions in recent decades.

Yet the demand for shoreline recreational open space continues to outpace supply. Within the next decade, most of the very last undeveloped shorelines with significant recreational qualities, particularly in populated regions, will disappear by preemption for development. As the supply continues to diminish, the price of what remains will escalate.

We need to mount a new nationwide effort to reassess the potential for protection of shoreline open space. Since all our need will not be met solely through acquisition, opportunities and problems of access short of public ownership must be explored. The states hold most of the legal authority in this area, and approaches vary widely from state to state.

A comprehensive shoreline study was undertaken by the U.S. Corps of Engineers in 1971. Since then, portions of the coastline have been reinventoried through 29 state coastal zone management programs funded in part by the U.S. Department of Commerce.

Updated inventories are urgently needed to identify all remaining relatively undeveloped shoreline areas, and developed sites where public access is allowed, for purposes of satisfying future water-related outdoor recreation needs. Inventories should be conducted by the states under criteria developed jointly by them, the Secretary of Commerce, and the Secretary of the Interior. A nationwide inventory should be published, including recommendations for actions designed to preserve remaining open space and provide shoreline access, developed cooperatively by all participants.

The federal government must push for total protection of undeveloped islands and areas, such as it has done with Cumberland Island here in Georgia.

BOB WOODALL
Atlanta hearing

If there is any problem with the wetland acquisition program, it is that it has not been successful enough. The U.S. Fish and Wildlife Service has produced several estimates of how much land must be acquired and managed in order to preserve our migratory waterfowl resource. In the recently released draft Waterfowl Management Plan, they call for the protection of 1.9 million acres of waterfowl habitat in the United States and an additional 3.6 million acres in Canada.

We must match wetlands acquisition programs with broad-based management programs to ensure that the wetlands we acquire will continue productively into the 21st century. The experience of the Jean Lafitte National Park in New Orleans has demonstrated that simple acquisition is not enough. We must balance acquisition with management and with mitigation for the preservation not only of those areas we acquire but of all our vast wetland resources in Louisiana. To achieve all these goals, we must have the cooperation of all branches of federal, state and local government, and of private land owners, if we will have the benefits of our wetlands for our children and grandchildren.

CONGRESSMAN JOHN BREAUX
New Orleans hearing

. . . .

Chapter 6

We Can Enjoy Scenic Byways and Thoroughfares

We recommend

● Local and state governments create a network of scenic byways, composed of scenic roadways and thoroughfares throughout the nation, and take action to protect these resources.

● The Congress establish an incentive program of matching grants to local and state governments to encourage scenic byways designations.

● Information concerning scenic byways be made available through partnerships between the private sector and all levels of government.

Americans like to drive on scenic roads

Americans are at home on the road. Pleasure driving to view the historic, natural, and pastoral qualities offered by many of our nation's secondary roads is an important part of recreation for a majority of our population, comprising some 15 percent of all vehicle miles driven.

Nearly half (43%) of American adults drive for pleasure, according to the 1986 Market Opinion Research (MOR) Survey underwritten by the National Geographic Society for the Commission. Driving for pleasure is second only to walking as a popular form of recreation activity by American adults. Americans seek a variety of sights as they drive: glimpses of mountains, lakes and rushing streams; small towns and farms; wildlife; covered bridges; and first-hand insights into the lifestyles of rural Americans.

As development spreads from urban cores, the rural countryside vanishes. We need to ensure that the character of our nation's land and water remains more than a memory. California, Oregon, and Tennessee provide excellent examples of how scenic roadway networks protect the countryside, through designation, conservation easements, and junkyard and billboard control.

Country roads, innocent of stop signs, advertising billboards, 18-wheel trucks, and the attention of road graders. We should be collecting them like diamonds, because they're not making any more of them. They're a last inheritance from the people who came before us and they lead to places that soothe the souls of city folks. They are our compensation for rush hour traffic.

ELIZABETH C. MOONEY
Country Adventures

Scenic byways: Links to natural and cultural treasures

Ed McMahon of the Coalition for Scenic Beauty told us, "Even a generation ago, a drive in the country was still an American institution. Families packed a picnic and a road map and set out to discover the wonders of rural America."

A scenic byways network begins with a local community's desire to protect the surroundings of some existing roadways and thoroughfares. These landscapes may be important to the historical development of a community, and may represent the best of the state's—and nation's—regional and local roadside scenes.

The network provides an opportunity for the pleasure driver to travel from community to community around the state along scenic byways. In some cases, the byway becomes a recreation destination in itself.

Walking trails, river walks, bike trails, and other recreational facilities complement the rural landscape and add to people's enjoyment of the outdoors. These amenities encourage people to experience the outdoors.

Bicycle Touring on the Increase

The Bicycle Federation estimates that 600,000 Americans took a bicycle vacation or extended tour in 1985 and this figure is expected to increase by 10 percent in 1986. More than one million cyclists participated in large scale organized one day rides in 1985. Participation in this type of event is expected to grow 15 percent in 1986. Bicycle tourists need good bicycle maps, overnight facilities (campgrounds, hostels and hotels) and information about bike access to scenic and recreational areas.

When cyclists travel beyond their own neighborhood, they are likely to seek out touring routes in scenic areas, such as coastal areas, rural forest and farmland areas, or following rivers or lakeshores. Also, many riders take shorter, day and weekend tours close to home, relying on bike routes or county road maps for route ideas and information.

CATHERINE G. MORAN
WILLIAM C. WILKINSON III
AND JAMES FREMONT
Bicycling Federation of America

Local communities create scenic byway networks

The purpose of a [scenic] byway program is a coordinated attempt to recognize a representative cross section of a state's most scenic and historic road corridors and place them together in a system in order to show visitors the diversity of its landscape.

RICHARD G. GIBBONS
Virginia Department of Conservation

Scenic byways keep travelers in state longer, increasing economic benefits to communities and states. They also help provide the impetus for preservation of special stretches of countryside with historic and scenic values. These potential benefits should encourage citizens to request that local and state governments create a scenic byways network that provides pleasant, recreational driving experiences.

Local communities, in cooperation with the state and federal governments, should develop their own criteria and standards for designating a scenic byway. These criteria and standards could include:

o examples of the area's historic, pastoral, and natural heritage;

o scenic views from either side of the designated byway;

o the presence of accessible recreation facilities and opportunities—trails, parks, picnic sites, boat ramps;

o signs of minimum size to inform travelers about the area's recreational and natural attractions, services, and history;

o minimal visual blight, such as billboards and junkyards.

After the criteria are established, communities, with the cooperation of the appropriate government agencies, could complete an inventory of the area's existing roadways to determine potential candidates for their scenic byways system. These local inventories could update the 1974 study, "Assessment of the Feasibility of a National Scenic Highways System." This report stated that the cost of protecting existing scenic byways was minimal compared with the cost of building new scenic highways.

The federal government can provide support to communities

To encourage scenic byways designations, Congress should establish an incentive program of one-to-one matching grants to state and local governments. This program could be funded initially from existing revenues of the Highway Trust Fund in fiscal years 1988 and 1989. Matching funds would be used to:

o protect the surroundings of the scenic byway, through growth-shaping tools and, where appropriate and necessary, purchase of scenic or other conservation easements (tax incentives for donations of easements should be developed as well);

o improve safety features of the byway;

o remove inappropriate signing and billboards;

o provide screening for areas along the byway that do not meet scenic criteria (e.g., junkyards);

o add information and designation signs;

o construct scenic vista and interpretive turnouts;

o add accessible picnic and sanitary facilities to turnouts if they are compatible with the scenic byways designation criteria.

From the local communities' nominations, state and federal governments will designate roadways and thoroughfares eligible for federal matching grant assistance. Local communities must participate actively in the continuing protection of their community's scenic byways.

A scenic byways network makes the best use of existing resources

A scenic byway network complements the interstate system. It offers a traveler the chance to take a scenic route for a portion of his or her trip, yet return to a major expressway to complete the trip. Intersecting scenic and major travel roadways lessen the need to develop extensive facilities and traveler amenities along the scenic routes. The features for which scenic routes have been designated must be retained.

The thrust of the program is to protect and preserve *existing* examples of our scenic roadway heritage. Thus, funds under this program would only rarely be used to develop new roadways or modify roads to meet scenic standards.

For example, safety features do not have to change the nature of the roadways. Slower speed limits can be imposed, rather than straightening curves; precautionary messages can be used, rather than widening shoulders or removing trees or buildings; one-lane signal controls can be installed to avoid replacement of old, narrow bridges.

The scenic byways program will emphasize simple designations, conservation easements, inappropriate sign removal, screening, community pride and tourism. Additionally, local and state governments are encouraged to consider scenic and recreation qualities when highway construction outside of this program is planned.

Partnerships will create networks of scenic byways

The primary emphasis of the scenic byways program is to maintain the quality of rural landscapes along local and state byways. Local support and local land planning guidelines, zoning ordinances and other appropriate approaches should be the basis for nominations and designations.

Private organizations (including auto clubs), local tourism agencies, chambers of commerce, and other groups should help inform the public about scenic byways and where to find them. Signs meeting scenic standards and maps developed by these groups could direct travelers to these special routes.

Local communities should seek the advice and assistance of historic preservation officers, natural heritage program officials, and others, during the inventory and designation process. Highway users are also important partners in creating scenic byway networks.

Local communities and states should determine which roads and routes should be part of the system. The federal government could provide technical assistance upon request and matching grant incentives to encourage designation of scenic routes, rather than mandate program activities. The economic advantages of these designations to local communities will more than offset minimal costs of designated scenic byways.

Examples of scenic byways

○ Blue Ridge Parkway, Virginia (America's most visited national park, 19 million visitors in 1985)

○ State Highway 1 (the Coast Highway), California

○ Going to the Sun Highway, Montana

○ Route 100, Vermont

○ Natchez Trace Parkway, Mississippi

○ Saw Mill River, Taconic, and Long Island Parkways, New York

---

. . . .

We Must Protect and Enhance Recreation Opportunities on Federal Lands and Waters

We recommend

● An annual report, "State of the Federal Estate: Resources and Recreation," be developed from reports prepared by the seven principal federal land managing agencies and be submitted to the President and the Congress.

● Federal agencies and the Congress place greater emphasis on long-term conservation of natural, cultural and historic resources and the quality of recreation opportunities and experiences. The federal multiple use agencies should assure that recreation is an equal partner with other uses in budgets, staffing and planning.

● Federal land management agencies embrace opportunities for partnerships with other government agencies, and with for-profit businesses and not-for-profit organizations.

● Federal land management agencies encourage and stimulate innovation and experimentation.

● Congressionally-authorized land acquisitions be expedited, making full use of alternative land protection techniques, and exchange procedures be streamlined.

● Review of existing laws and regulations to monitor visitor needs and satisfaction; improve public participation in the planning process; effectively utilize volunteers; facilitate acceptance of donations of real property and easements; collect recreation fees; and stimulate regional ecosystem planning.

● A periodic review of federal lands management.

Federal lands and waters serve Americans in many ways

Federal lands and waters encompass nearly one-third of the country's surface area. They are economic and social forces that begin in the towns, cities, and states where federal lands are local assets and agency personnel are productive citizens. These lands are national treasures of inestimable value, the fruits of our ancestors' foresight and an irreplaceable heritage for generations to come.

Today, our priorities for the public estate continue to evolve in response to changes in our values, as social, economic, and technological conditions change. New pressures on the land base, from development, pollution, and increased demand for outdoor recreation, have created new challenges for management.

After listening to thousands of Americans over the course of our study, we believe these points reflect their priorities for the use of their federal estate:

○ We must, above all, protect the integrity of the natural resource base, which is essential to the future of all uses, including recreation.

○ The importance which the American people attach to recreation must be reflected in agency policies, staffing, and budgets. Recreation, as now mandated in most multiple-use law, must receive attention commensurate with other uses and values.

○ Federal lands and waters should be models of the highest quality resource conservation and use. Innovative management of multiple-use areas accommodating both recreation and non-recreation values can be demonstrated on public lands.

○ Strong partnerships with the private sector, profit and non-profit, and with other federal, state, and local agencies should be forged, with greater public involvement in agency planning.

○ Resolution of the question of the federal acquisition backlog should be expedited. We consider this an obligation to the American people. Beyond this, federal agencies must develop a vision and a blueprint for meeting future needs.

The Federal Land-Managing Agencies and Their Mandates

Bureau of Land Management (BLM), an agency of the Department of Interior, is responsible for 337.1 million acres of Public Lands concentrated in the 11 western states and Alaska. Under the provisions of the Federal Land Policy and Management Act, the lands are to be managed under principles of multiple use and sustained yield. The BLM's Public Lands include the 12.1 million acre California Desert Conservation Area.

Forest Service, in the Department of Agriculture, manages 190.8 million acres of national forests. While the majority of national forest land is in the West and Alaska, national forests are well distributed in the East as well. The Forest Service manages these lands for multiple uses—outdoor recreation, range, timber, watershed, wildlife and fish, and minerals. Included in the National Forest System are several congressionally-designated national recreation areas.

Fish and Wildlife Service, Department of Interior, is responsible for the 90.4 million-acre National Wildlife Refuge System. The system includes wildlife refuges, wildlife ranges, game ranges, wildlife management areas and waterfowl production areas. Management focuses on protection of wildlife habitat. The Refuge Recreation Act of 1962 authorizes recreation use when it does not interfere with a refuge's primary purpose. Hunting is permitted if it is compatible with the major purpose for which a refuge was established.

National Park Service, Department of Interior, manages 76 million acres in the National Park System. The National Park System is the most varied of all the federal land systems, and includes the great national parks like Yellowstone and Yosemite, national monuments which may have either natural or cultural value, a host of historic and prehistoric sites, and national recreation areas in several metropolitan areas. National Park System lands are to be managed "to conserve the scenery and the natural and historic objects and the wildlife therein and to provide for the enjoyment of the same in such a manner and by such means as will leave them unimpaired for future generations."

Army Corps of Engineers, in the Department of Defense, manages 10 million acres of lands and waters at some 460 hydropower, navigation, and flood control projects. The Corps has no explicit recreation mandate, but provides recreation at the reservoirs it manages under provisions of the Flood Control Act of 1944 which authorizes the Corps to operate recreation facilities at its projects, and the Federal Water Project Recreation Act of 1965.

Bureau of Reclamation, Department of Interior, administers six million acres of lands and waters around its dams in the West managed primarily for reservoir storage, water conveyance, flood control, wildlife habitat, agricultural and livestock production, cultural resource protection and public recreational uses. The agency has no legislation that gives it comprehensive recreation authority. However, it manages its lands and waters for recreation under the Reclamation Act of 1902, Federal Water Project Recreation Act of 1965 and the Fish and Wildlife Coordination Act of 1946. In several instances there are specific laws to administer and manage specific recreation areas.

Tennessee Valley Authority (TVA), manages one million acres of lands and waters around its hydropower, flood control and navigation dams. TVA administers the 170,000-acre Land Between the Lakes National Recreation Demonstration Area in Kentucky and Tennessee.

Federal lands meet a variety of needs

The size of federal land systems and their diversity of uses, values, resources, products, and personnel exceed that of any major corporation. They are rich in resources that serve a diverse and complex range of needs for timber, water, fish and wildlife habitat, livestock grazing, energy and minerals, and recreation. They also include important scenic, scientific, and historic resources.

Seven agencies manage most of this diverse public estate in trust for the American people. They are the Department of Agriculture's U.S. Forest Service; the Interior Department's Bureau of Land Management (BLM); National Park Service, Fish and Wildlife Service, and Bureau of Reclamation; the Defense Department's Army Corps of Engineers; and the Tennessee Valley Authority. Each of these agencies has its own unique mix of legislated goals and geography. The role of federal lands in recreation varies tremendously according to type of unit and regional location. The traditional national parks like Yellowstone, Yosemite, and the Grand Canyon hold a special place in the hearts of Americans, to whom a visit may still be a once-in-a-lifetime experience. Other federal parks, forests, and public lands provide more frequent retreats from the pressures of modern life.

Federal lands provide significant natural resource and recreation opportunities in urban areas. Golden Gate (San Francisco), Gateway (New York), Cuyahoga Valley (Cleveland and Akron), and Indiana Dunes (Gary/Chicago) National Recreation Areas are located in and around major metropolitan areas. National forests lie within a short drive of Los Angeles, Portland, Seattle, Salt Lake City, Denver, Albuquerque, and Phoenix; and public lands managed by BLM adjoin Las Vegas, Palm Springs, and Anchorage. While the East has far less federal park and forest acreage than the West, in many states these federal lands provide the only large expanses of land available for general public recreation.

The 708 million acres of federal lands are vital national assets that meet a variety of needs in many different ways.

○ Most of the water for municipal, industrial, and agricultural uses west of the Mississippi originates on or is recharged by snow and rain that falls on federal lands.

○ Salmon, cutthroat trout, elk, waterfowl, bighorn sheep, grizzly bears, bald eagles—all symbols of wild America—are largely dependent on federal lands for their continued existence.

○ Federal lands annually provide hundreds of millions of recreation days and a wide variety of recreation opportunities for the American people.

○ Tourism, recreation jobs, and revenues for hundreds of communities are profoundly affected by the ecological conditions and recreation availability of federal lands and waters.

○ Roughly 50 percent of the nation's softwood timber supply is found on the National Forests and BLM lands.

○ Some 27,000 farmers and ranchers graze cattle and sheep on BLM and national forest rangeland in the West, contributing to the national food supply and regional economies.

○ Minerals and energy sources vital to our domestic economies and national security lie on or under many of these lands.

○ The federal lands contain a wide variety of scientific and cultural resources—ranging from unusual plant communities to the artifacts of aboriginal Indians.

We must take care of what we have, now and for the future

The collection of federal land systems constitutes one of the world's great nature reserve and resource delivery systems. Early in the development of our nation, the outposts of civilization were surrounded by wildlands. We are now experiencing a transformation to the reverse—islands of wild lands, mostly in federal ownership, increasingly surrounded by a sea of civilization.

But no one land or water unit of a federal system is an island unto itself. Every park, forest, grassland, range, refuge, or recreation area affects and is affected by things that occur inside its boundaries and on neighboring lands. As population grows and technology proliferates, the pockets of relatively naturally functioning systems experience still greater pressures. For example:

○ Air pollution is damaging vegetation and affecting visibility on federal lands throughout the nation. Visibility at the Grand Canyon is now noticeably reduced on at least 100 days each year. Acid precipitation damage to historic artifacts at Gettysburg National Military Park will cost $2 million to repair.

○ Wildlife migrate across property boundaries, or are trapped on land surrounded by development. Exotic species alter natural ecosystems. Human activities—including recreational uses—endanger native species.

○ In some areas, oil, gas, mineral, and geothermal resource developments comfortably coexist with recreation and wildlife uses. But in other areas, including some national parks, wilderness areas, and wildlife refuges, these activities can threaten aesthetic values, recreation quality, wildlife, and other resources.

o Diminished quantity and/or degraded quality water flows impair many streams and lakes, and threaten vulnerable ecosystems at Mammoth Cave, Glacier, and the Everglades National Parks, and many other areas.

o Private landowners and public land grazing interests often feed wildlife during critical winter periods. Yet poor range management in some areas has seriously reduced fish and wildlife populations.

Some of these external and internal influences are threats to the purpose of the area or the mission of the agency. These threats are real and need to be resolved. Regional inventories of external threats to federal lands, documenting past and current resource conditions, must be completed. Steps to mitigate these threats should be developed in management plans for each affected federal unit.

We must find ways to assure that actions on lands outside the boundaries of federal areas, and especially protected areas such as national parks, wilderness areas and wildlife refuges, do not adversely affect the resources protected within these areas. Conversely, management of the federal lands can affect adjacent private lands and local communities in ways they may not find desirable.

To document the condition and trends of federal land resources, we recommend that the seven principal federal agencies improve and consolidate their existing reports into a single *State of the Federal Estate: Resources and Recreation* report. This report would be an assessment of recreation-related activities on all federal lands, describing use trends, status of facilities and maintenance, condition of the natural resource base (land, air, water, and wildlife) and budgets and staffing for management.

This annual report should build on the annual or periodic reports already required of most of the seven agencies, such as the annual Report of the Forest Service and its Resources Planning Act Assessment, and the National Park Service's "Fees and Charges" report. The report would serve Congress as a guide to regular oversight hearings on the quality of recreation resources and experiences on the federal estate. It would also be a valuable source of information to encourage interagency cooperation among federal bureaus and public involvement in decision-making.

Recreation must be given greater emphasis on multiple use lands

Historically, some federal lands have been managed primarily for production of certain commodities, such as timber, range forage, and minerals. By law, recreation and wildlife are specifically accorded equal status with other resource values on National Forests and BLM public domain lands, and should be an equal partner with commodity uses in these multiple purpose land systems.

Recreation activities need not threaten or replace other uses. Compatibility is possible when recreation and wildlife interests are considered when land use decisions are made. Greater care must be taken to balance conservation and recreation uses with commodity production when making land use decisions.

We heard a great deal of testimony to the effect that while recreation use is increasing on federal lands, this increased demand is not always fully recognized in agency planning, staffing, and budgets.

One action that Congress can take is to revise the legal mandates of the Bureau of Reclamation and the Corps of Engineers to specifically recognize recreation values as a part of their mission. These agencies also play a major role in providing water-based recreation opportunities. This important role should be written into law to ensure that adequate management resources for recreation remain available.

Recreation on federal lands can and should play an important role in shaping the economic health of communities throughout the country. Agencies should consider the tourism values which accrue to local and regional economies from recreation uses, as well as the direct revenues they receive, along with other values and agency mandates, when developing plans and budgets. Federal agencies should encourage their state, local, and private partners to carry out an aggressive marketing effort to inform people of the values and opportunities for outdoor activities on the federal lands.

Federal agencies need partners

One of the keys to successful management is cooperation. It is difficult for federal officials to carry out agency mandates and protect and manage lands in isolation from surrounding communities. Opportunities for innovation and efficiency are lost when federal agencies do not take advantage of local, state, and private for-profit and nonprofit resources which can assist them in carrying out their objectives.

Recreation and public interest groups, citizens, and local and state officials must be involved in agency planning processes. Early and meaningful involvement forges the ties which can lead to successful partnerships.

All federal agencies are engaged in partnerships with other units of the federal government, with local and state agencies and lands, and with private sector interests. Federal agencies would be hard-pressed to do without the assistance of volunteers to maintain trails and conduct interpretive programs and cooperating associations that publish books and other educational materials.

Other examples include privately run ski areas on the national forests; public, private, and national wildlife refuge lands that jointly support big game herds; private marinas on Corps of Engineers and Bureau of Reclamation reservoirs; lodge and outing concessions in the national parks; and wildlife and fish harvest management by state agencies on federal lands where taking is allowed. Implementation of wildlife management plans under the Sikes Act and expansion of the provisions of the Concessioners' Act to other agencies would provide further opportunities for mutually beneficial partnerships.

Federal lands encompass critical wildlife habitat for hundreds of game and non-game species, and habitat loss continues to be the number one wildlife problem. Thus it is essential that federal agencies work with state agencies to identify and manage critical habitat areas.

Meeting America's outdoor recreation needs on the federal estate requires capital investments in facilities ranging from ski lifts to marinas, campgrounds to grocery stores. The agencies should appraise these needs in their land management planning process to determine what facilities are appropriate and needed, and identify places where privately-operated development can take place without impairing the quality of resources or recreation experiences.

The management of federal lands and waters should be a model for the world

The long-standing role of federal land and water managers in conservation leadership must continue. The federal lands should be models of the highest quality management. Federal land management should include and demonstrate the conservation and restoration of natural diversity in harmony with recreation and other resource management missions.

National leadership by federal managers should extend to experimental recreation management, research, communication, and education. Agencies and managers should form partnerships with scientists, the academic community, and the private sector, both for-profit and non-profit, to utilize expertise from these sectors in land management programs.

Recreation visitor management is critically important to controlling impacts of increasing use on natural and cultural resources. Good visitor management includes guiding and educating visitors, interpreting resources, designing safe facilities that respond to user needs, and enforcing rules. It also means integrating recreation needs into the overall management of resources to reduce the possibilities of misuse, and to balance the demands of the land with the needs of people.

Federal agencies need better tools to find out what visitors want and how satisfied they are with recreation opportunities and services. Current regulations which limit agency-sponsored public opinion surveys should be reviewed and revised if necessary to permit federal providers to gather this information on a regular basis.

Communications with visitors and the general public must be improved. Permitted uses of lands and facilities should be clearly identified through signs, maps, and public service announcements, especially where boundaries include mixes of public and private lands.

While continuing long-term basic research, federal agencies should increase practical problem-solving studies on natural resource management. Scientific studies to determine the effects of visitor use on resources are needed. Field agency personnel and their state, local, and private sector partners should be rewarded for innovative approaches to providing visitor services and identifying and resolving threats to resource quality.

The federal estate includes extraordinary places to teach and demonstrate the values of wild America and give people direct experiences with their natural and cultural heritages. All agencies should develop comprehensive interpretation programs to promote an outdoor ethic emphasizing responsible behavior and personal commitments to stewardship. The Commission applauds the Interior Department's recently inaugurated "Take Pride In America" program as an important contribution.

We must seek creative ways to resolve conflicts among users

Americans desire many things from their public lands. Some want wilderness preserved, others call for more campgrounds and developed recreation sites, others emphasize the importance of commodity production. Agencies are being asked to accommodate an increasing variety of outdoors experiences, some of which are in conflict when pursued at the same time on the same parcel of ground.

Many recreation areas are more crowded today, and the activities users wish to pursue have proliferated both in type and in impact on the resource base. Pressures for consumptive use not necessarily related to recreation have also increased.

An example of the complexity of the issues can be seen in the polarity of sentiments that arise over the use of off-road vehicles (ORVs) on federal lands. ORVs are recognized as legitimate users of some public lands. Two Executive Orders in the early 1970's led to regulations intended to control ORV use, which have been implemented by the agencies with variable success. However, the adequacy of the regulations are differently perceived by different users, and conflicts persist.

There should be places for ORV use on federal lands. But indiscriminate or uncontrolled use of ORVs can harm resources. Continuing consultation with ORV groups, public interest groups, scientific experts, public officials, and others to find ways of monitoring and controlling impacts is necessary.

Recreation activity zones—areas set aside for specific sports or user groups—should be more fully explored. A system such as the Recreation

Opportunity Spectrum (ROS) can be employed to reduce conflicts and enhance efficiency in providing for regionally important multiple uses.

Maintaining the quality of resources and recreation experiences requires a determination of objectives for use and standards to control the adverse impact of visitors. Studies to determine limits of acceptable impact should be carried out for recreation and other uses, and incorporated into visitor management plans. Standards of acceptable limits should be based on credible evidence and scientific theory, and should become management goals, like objectives for grazing and increasing fish and wildlife populations.

Demonstration areas could test new management approaches

At the height of the Depression, the federal government launched a program to demonstrate how depleted farmland could be restored and made available as parkland to increase recreation opportunities near large metropolitan areas. Some 46 areas were designated National Recreation Demonstration Areas.

The Civilian Conservation Corps (CCC) built campgrounds, trails, and other facilities, and planted trees. Most demonstration areas were later turned over to the states and became the nucleus of a number of state park systems. The sensitivity with which the CCC designed facilities in harmony with nature and landscaped natural areas makes the parks where they worked a special heritage today.

In 1960, the Tennessee Valley Authority was given the authority to create a modern-day demonstration area: the 170,000-acre Land Between the Lakes in Kentucky and Tennessee. It was intended to be a demonstration area for resource and wildlife management, outdoor recreation, and education. Land Between the Lakes has become a dynamic field laboratory for innovative resources management involving partnerships between academia, nonprofit organizations, and government.

We urge that the land management agencies be authorized to establish recreation demonstration areas which would emphasize the testing of new approaches to protecting resources and managing visitors.

Acquisition priorities should be established and the process expedited

Over the years, Congress has authorized the acquisition of land for inclusion in the federal systems of national parks, forests, and wildlife refuges. Some of the land Congress clearly intended to be purchased outright—particularly new national parks and wildlife refuges.

In some instances, however, Congress established a boundary within which the managing agency was authorized to acquire land as it felt was appropriate to carry out its mission. The federal government owns only about half the land within the purchase boundaries of national forests in the East, for example, and there was no expectation that all the area, which includes small towns, would be acquired.

While the acquisition of thousands of acres has been authorized, the Congress has not appropriated the money necessary to buy all the land. The gap between authorization and appropriation has been termed the "backlog." Not all of this backlog may need to be purchased; alternatives to fee acquisition, including easements, may fully protect resource values. While there are no definitive estimates, the cost of essential acquisition could easily exceed $5 billion.

There are large areas of private lands within the authorized boundaries of certain federal areas. In the National Park System, for example, there are more than three million acres of privately-owned land within park boundaries. While it is not envisioned that all the private land needs to be or even should be acquired in fee, there is a significant amount of acquisition that remains. Even acquiring less-than-fee interests can be expensive, especially when the land has development potential.

Some parcels within or adjacent to units of the national parks, wilderness, and wildlife refuge systems are faced with the imminent threat of development which could impair the recreation and resource values of the public's land.

Agencies should determine priorities for acquiring authorized lands and waters. Highest priority should be given to parcels where the threat of incompatible development is imminent, which provide essential access or services, to relieve unusual hardships for landowners, or where there are willing sellers. Acquisition of these lands should be accelerated, and the acquisition process streamlined. Methods such as land exchanges and purchase of partial interests should be used when appropriate.

Agencies must have a vision and a plan of action for meeting future needs. A systematic approach to identifying lands which need to be protected and determining priorities for acquisition should be developed. Parcels which are isolated from the main block of federal lands and difficult to manage should be exchanged or sold at fair market value, and the proceeds used to acquire needed land or interests in land or water. Impediments to effective land exchanges in the public interest should be removed.

Finally, the federal government has legal rights to some key outdoors resources, such as abandoned railroad rights of way, which could be converted to trails and greenways. In the West, where the federal government gave the land to the railroads, title reverts to the federal government if it is claimed when the rail line is abandoned. The federal government should assert its rights whenever it has a legitimate claim to physical resources.

Public land policy needs periodic review

The federal estate consists of more than 700 million acres managed by seven different agencies with some overlapping, yet distinctly different mandates. In the late 1960's, a comprehensive review of the nation's public land laws and policies was conducted through the Public Land Law Review Commission (PLLRC).

Since that commission's work, a wide range of new statutes, planning processes, resources, and management practices have been put in place. We now have new national parks in urban areas, millions of acres of wilderness, and federal rivers and trails systems. The Forest Service's Resources Planning Act and the BLM's Public Land Policy and Management Act require complex resources management planning and public involvement in decisionmaking.

The subject of the federal estate and its management for recreation and resources conservation is of such breadth and importance that we believe it deserves periodic assessment. At an appropriate time, a review of PLLRC's recommendations, federal laws, regulations, and policies affecting the management of the federal estate should be undertaken by the Administration and/or Congress. Among the topics which should be addressed are:

○ Equal standing for recreation with other values on federal multiple-use lands in management, planning, programs, budget and staffing;

○ Threats to the natural, cultural, and historic resources of federal land systems;

○ Policies, programs and needs that shape the assets of the major federal resources conservation systems;

○ Methods to reduce conflicts among different recreation activities and between recreation and other uses of the federal lands, including consideration of conflicts in the mandates of the federal agencies;

○ Partnerships between federal land management agencies and the private sector, including nonprofit groups, private landowners and businesses;

○ Coordination among various federal programs, and between federal programs and those of state and local governments, particularly with regard to fish and wildlife management;

○ Information and planning, including the Forest Service's Forest and Rangeland Renewable Resources Planning Act (RPA) program, the Bureau of Land Management's management planning processes under the Federal Land Policy and Management Act (FLPMA), the U.S.D.A. Soil Conservation Service's Soil and Water Resources Conservation Act, the Fish and Wildlife Service and National Park Service surveys, natural heritage inventories, federal and state historic preservation programs, and state outdoor recreation planning efforts;

○ The adequacy of existing organizational structures, including a review of the advisability of consolidating natural resources programs.

We have a responsibility to the future

This generation cannot fix for all time the roles, goals, and uses of federal lands. Such things are evolutionary, not constant. Our federal lands and waters, like our society, are dynamic, and future generations will continue to shape their character. But our actions today will influence the range of choices available to future Americans.

Wildlife and Fisheries: A State-Federal Partnership

A useful model of partnerships occurs in the management of the wildlife and fisheries resources of this country.

Typically a state agency manages the populations of fish and wildlife in trust for the people of a state. Whoever owns the land manages the animals' habitats. Since there cannot be fish and wildlife without productive habitats, partnerships are a way of life. Also, many species, such as migratory waterfowl, salmon and steelhead trout, elk, bears, and songbirds, travel great distances over the course of a year and spend their seasons on many different ownerships and, for some, in many different state jurisdictions.

Were it not for partnerships in management funding, these great natural treasures would have long since perished. Today, for every dire situation in fish and wildlife one can find somewhere a failed partnership, and find at the same time numerous success stories that reflect good partnerships.

Many Agencies and Interests Cooperate in Yellowstone Region

In the Greater Yellowstone Area, three states, two National Parks, six National Forests, two National Wildlife Refuges, Public Lands, and many private interests and rights, are working together to maintain habitat for grizzly bears, vitality of local and regional economies, and continued security of the great natural, cultural, and historic assets of the Yellowstone area. Even a national park as large as Yellowstone cannot fulfill its purpose if treated as an island. Cooperative partnerships among a variety of federal, state, and local agencies, private landowners, and others are essential if the values of the Yellowstone National Park and the surrounding lands are to be maintained.

Our Multiple-Value Lands

The concept of "multiple-value lands" expands the common term of "multiple-use lands" to a breadth that encompasses both the tangible and intangible worth of resources our federal estate provides the American people.

Value means "of merit, a quality considered worthwhile." Use means "to put into service; to consume or expend."

Value, in this context, implies that not all land or resources must be physically used to impart a benefit, and yet it does not exclude use. It in fact embraces benefits, services, and products, and implies equal consideration of each.

Statutes directing the management of lands, particularly those administered by BLM and Forest Service, identify "multiple-uses" as outdoor recreation, range, timber, watershed, wildlife and fish, and minerals. However, it is more appropriate to call them "multiple-value lands." For example, wildlife has existence value and educational value to the viewer, economic value to the property owner and game agency, food and experience value to the hunter, and scientific value to the biologist. Wildlife also has ecological value as a barometer of environmental health such as the relationship of cutthroat trout to water quality.

Similarly, timber has a product and economic value as a raw material, as well as aesthetic and ecological value. A scenic backdrop or landscape provides aesthetic value to the viewer; a potential economic value to the lodge owner with a deck. Wilderness is a composite of many resources and values. Park and wildlife refuges have limited uses, but encompass many values.

Because our federal lands are owned by all Americans, they are therefore held in the public trust. Because they exist in aggregate with vast forests and deserts, refuges and ranges, lakes and rivers, parks and wilderness areas, prehistoric and historic sites, they have immense social value which contributes significantly to our national heritage. Traditions associated with our federal estate are intimately wrapped into America's national character and cultural values.

The philosophical framework which guides federal land policy into the 21st century must provide a bridge between the past and the future.

The time has come to recognize our federal lands as multiple-value lands, versus multiple-use lands. By doing so we can more accurately reflect the diversity of resources and their benefits, capturing the intent of what those who, over the last 100 years, have so diligently pursued as the full purpose of America's federal lands heritage.

SALLY RANNEY
Commissioner

Federal Plans Developed at Local Level

The Forest Service and BLM are developing land and resources management plans at the local level—and with public involvement—which identify needs for increased investments in resources management, rehabilitation and development of facilities, and interpretation and education programs. Recent budgets for recreation on those lands have fallen far short of the identified needs, as noted in the 1986 Report of the Forest Service. At the same time, recreation use has increased and conflict among competing uses has intensified. Dr. John R. Donaldson, former Director of Oregon Department of Fish and Wildlife, told us about the success of Coordinated Resource Management Planning, CRMP in bringing federal and state agencies and private interests together to reconcile potential conflicts and meet mutual goals in wildlife, fisheries, recreation, range, and forestry.

Private Groups Help Federal Agencies

The USDA Forest Service and USDI Bureau of Land Management testified on the use of memoranda of understanding and challenge grants with states and private sector groups. In recent years such memoranda have been initiated with Trout Unlimited, the Rocky Mountain Elk Foundation, the National Wild Turkey Federation, and Ducks Unlimited. Habitat enhancement projects have been accomplished with private monies matching federal investments and volunteered manpower and machinery used alongside state and federal resources.

ORVs: Three Viewpoints

Almost everyone interviewed spoke angrily about the severe damage being caused by the unrestricted and thoughtless use of these vehicles on public and private lands throughout Arizona, pointing out the numerous areas where serious environmental damage already has occurred—places where, said one arid land specialist, it could take a thousand years for the land to recover.

Unrestricted use of such vehicles by children and adults alike has caused severe impacts on wildlife habitat, too. Thoughtless operators have imposed upon other users of the outdoors through careless and noisy intrusion in campgrounds and along trails and back roads normally restricted to hikers and horsemen. They have even managed to wreak havoc in supposedly protected wild areas.

. . . My interviewees' final recommendation is intended for ORV manufacturers and dealers and their advertising and public relations agencies. It is a plea that such firms consciously and conscientiously promote safety and environmental protection in their newspaper and magazine advertisements, promotional books and pamphlets, and (most important of all) television commercials at present often blatantly encourage environmental destruction through dramatic appeals exploiting the Star Trek-like theme, 'Go where no man has gone before.'

RICHARD G. STAHL
Managing Editor, Arizona Highways Magazine

Recreational four-wheeling is one of the fastest growing aspects of the ORV recreational picture in America today. Once unheard of prior to the 1960's today recreational four-wheeling is growing at unprecedented rates. Sales of 4x4 vehicles increased 96 percent from 1975-1979 and sales almost tripled from 1981 to 1984 . . . A conservative estimate today would place the number of primary recreational 4x4 vehicles at nearly 1.8 million. While this reflects only 17 percent of the total 25 percent of the American public involved in ORV recreation, other studies indicate that as much as 40 percent of all ORV use is recreational four-wheeling.

The big difference between ORV recreation and recreational four-wheeling is that recreational four-wheeling off road. The majority of recreational four-wheelers follow existing and designated 4x4 trails and roads. Despite this overwhelming difference and the significance of recreational four-wheeling's increasing numbers, recreational four-wheeling is still being managed as part of the overall ORV recreational scene. Instead of managing recreational four-wheeling as a legitimate separate aspect of multiple-use recreation on Federal lands more and more areas and trails and roads are being closed to all ORV use.

. . . Land doesn't have to be ravaged to be used just as it doesn't have to be locked up to be preserved. Under today's professional multiple-use management there can be both preservation and use. That's true conservation.

Further, most recreational four-wheelers actually request management and are not adverse to logical restrictions and equitable rules and regulations.

Recreational four-wheelers are volunteers freely and unselfishly giving of their time and out-of-pocket expenses to enhance public recreation on public lands.

STU BENGSON
Director
Land-Use United Four-Wheel
Drive Associations

Most people who have had the opportunity to ride off-road on a motorcycle, 3-wheeler, 4-wheel drive pickup or some other type of off-road vehicle enjoy the experience immensely. Many of these people, however, are not aware of the impact their activity can have on the environment. The popularity of ORV's is growing rapidly in New Mexico, but information about responsible use of these vehicles and how to use them safely has been a concern of the ORV Industry, the public, and agencies that administer public lands.

The New Mexico Off-Road Vehicle Education Task Force (ORVETF) was formed to develop a program that would educate off-road vehicle (ORV) users as to the responsibilities they have to protect the environment. That group's only goal is educational. It does not promote or discourage

ORV use. The goal of ORVETF is to help off-roaders understand their obligation to use their vehicles in a way that reflects concern for our resources.

The task force plans to provide off-roaders with as much information as possible about use of ORV's on public lands. Emphasis will be on how to use the areas that are available and why many restricted areas are environmentally sensitive. The group encourages development of special maps, uniform use regulations and a code of ethics to be distributed to ORV users in New Mexico. A brochure is being printed and video spots have been prepared.

NEW MEXICO OFF-ROAD-VEHICLE
EDUCATION TASK FORCE

Effort Underway to Assess Recreational Carrying Capacity

One of the greatest challenges facing recreation managers today is controlling and preventing visitor overuse on recreation lands. One way to attempt to meet this challenge is to identify visitor activities and use levels or "recreational carrying capacities" appropriate for a given recreation area.

In an effort to help the National Park Service meet the 1978 Congressional mandate to set visitor capacities and, more importantly, to protect the parks from visitor overuse, the National Parks and Conservation Association (NPCA) has been studying the carrying capacity question and looking for the most workable strategy for evaluating and preventing visitor-related impacts in the parks. Throughout this project, NPCA has had the cooperation of the National Park Service, the Forest Service and recreation experts from around the country.

From the beginning of this three-year project NPCA believed that it was important that any strategy it developed be scientifically sound. Furthermore, it wanted to integrate resource considerations such as vegetation, soils, water quality and wildlife, with social considerations such as the quality of the visitor experience and user conflicts. A team of scientists from the University of Maryland was enlisted in the effort.

As the NPCA team studied the current theories and research, it became convinced that trying to set one specific visitor number for an entire park would be impossible to define and/or implement. Instead, NPCA decided to focus on developing a planning and management process though which unacceptable impacts to both resources and the visitor experience could be identified and resolved.

The process consists of eight logical steps. In the first three steps, specific management objectives or preferred conditions for an area and its use are defined via measurable indicators. For instance, if it determined that a park trail should provide a solitary wilderness experience with min-

imal signs of human activity, the possible indicators would be the number of encounters a hiker has with other hikers on the trail, the trail width, presence of native rather than exotic plant species, etc.

When discrepancies are found between the preferred and the actual conditions, a range of management strategies, are available. Setting a limit on the number of visitors is only one option available to managers.

To determine if it is on the right track with this process, NPCA is conducting field studies in several parks. Last summer the process was applied to specific visitor use problems at Great Smoky Mountains and Glacier National Parks. In those parks NPCA looked at problem situations in both the frontcountry and backcountry. NPCA is particularly interested in making sure that this process would be useful in frontcountry planning and management because that is where the visitor use levels will continue to increase.

There are several benefits of applying a recreational carrying capacity process such as that being developed by NPCA. It will allow for more cost-effective management of visitors and resources. By identifying and managing for the optimal mix of recreational activities and visitor numbers, problem situations requiring costly resolutions can be avoided. Not only will loss of important resources be largely prevented, but visitor enjoyment of the recreational setting will be preserved.

A possible disadvantage is that visitors may feel that their freedom of choice in certain settings might be infringed upon. The public needs to be involved in the planning for an area and educated as to why certain limits may have to be imposed. Education and involvement will help them understand and support management decisions affecting recreation opportunities.

Possessing the methods and science for preventing visitor abuse of our public recreation areas is not enough. Wise and consistent use of such methods on the part of managers and public understanding of the overuse pressures on recreation lands are absolutely essential in meeting the overuse challenges facing this country's outdoor recreation resources.

CONCEPT PAPER BY THE NATIONAL PARKS
AND CONSERVATION ASSOCIATION

. . . .

Making It Work

We have learned over the course of our study of urgent needs for action to protect our outdoor recreation estate. Preservation of fast-disappearing open space, investment in rehabilitation of deteriorating facilities, getting ahead of urban growth as it races across the land—these are actions which cannot wait, but must be taken now, for tomorrow they will be more expensive, or, in some cases, impossible.

Americans told us they are willing to invest more in outdoor recreation. We believe that we must first turn to the willingness of the public to pay for services received. We can also look to the creative private sector for more imaginative and efficient ways of meeting the costs of protecting outdoor resources and providing recreation opportunities. We encourage all local and state governments to move outdoor recreation higher up their scale of funding priorities.

Then, and only then, do we look to the federal government as a source of funding for outdoor recreation programs. But there is a critical role for the federal government, to challenge and leverage private, local and state investment for recreation, to provide seed money to help spark the prairie fire.

We strongly endorse continuation of the principle of re-investment of some of the proceeds from depletion of the nation's non-renewable natural assets, to endow permanent recreation opportunities for future generations.

A steady, dependable level of funding is essential for program stability. We believe that $1 billion a year, available through a reconstituted Land and Water Conservation Fund, is an absolute minimum *expenditure for meeting current needs.*

We consider it essential that regional differences across our nation be recognized, that programs and funding have the flexibility to respond to a variety of regional needs. Partnerships developed at the local level are our best hope for accurately reflecting widely diversified priorities and conditions. We must look for new ways to build bridges among private for-profit and non-profit groups and governments at all levels to meet common needs.

Private lands, with landowner consent, can represent a significant potential for expansion of our recreation estate, if serious concerns such as liability exposure and vandalism can be effectively addressed. Liability problems restrict a wide range of outdoor recreation opportunities across the nation.

Our communities should be beautiful, attractive places to live, not put together by practices which leave too much concrete, too much noise and visual clutter. We should plan for and get ahead of urban growth, not react to it. The outdoors is too important to be an afterthought.

Well-maintained facilities, appropriately trained personnel, and quality information can open doors for more people to enjoy the outdoors, and ensure better protection of the resource. Greater attention to these topics today is an investment in the future quality of our recreation estate.

Finally, we believe there is a need for national leadership to speak strongly for the importance of outdoor recreation to the American people. We propose a new public-private institution, whose primary function would be to focus the spotlight on leadership activities wherever they occur in the communities of America. We propose encouraging new ideas, fostering partnerships, and rewarding excellence through innovation grants.

Americans have the resources, the creativity, the energy and the commitment to make a permanent difference in the quality of the outdoor recreation estate which we enjoy and pass on to future generations. If we have succeeded, with the proposals and ideas presented in this report, in lighting a spark, Americans will take it from there. Prairie fires start small, gather speed, spread over a wide area, overcoming choking brush, and eventually make the land bloom. Together, we will succeed in preserving what is important to us, taking care of what we have, and passing opportunities for recreation in the Great Outdoors on undiminished to future Americans. This is our responsibility and our legacy.

. . . .

Chapter 1

Partnerships Will Help Us Achieve Our Goals

We recommend

● Partnerships be formed among private for-profit and non-profit entities and public agencies to enhance recreation resources, services and facilities.

● Public policy and planning actions consider, where appropriate, private recreation investments at public places.

● Communities study the development of desirable support services in areas adjacent to public recreation resources, balancing conservation and economic needs.

● Private developers, in cooperation with public agencies, plan for and include recreation space and outdoor amenities in capital projects, with particular attention to connecting their projects to recreation areas through greenways.

A teamwork spirit makes partnerships work

We believe the future of the outdoors and people's full enjoyment of it depends on a variety of dynamic partnerships. People enjoy diverse outdoor activities. At times, this diversity can only be matched through the resources, expertise, and skills of a variety of players.

We heard from at least one hundred individuals about partnerships they have formed that increased outdoor opportunities. Businesses, non-profit organizations, public agencies and individuals have different resources. The key to successful partnerships is to match resources to achieve mutual goals.

The private sector can do more

Involving private enterprise can ease public expenditures in recreation, and the two can work together. We can build on a history of public and private partnerships—ski areas in national forests, outfitters and guides on public lands and waters, for instance. Private sector concessioners, in partnership with the National Park Service, have successfully provided visitor facilities and services to the public in our National Parks for more than six decades.

In Columbus, Nebraska, a local business' need for fire protection provided recreation for handicapped adults. The company built a fire reservoir, which doubles as a swimming pool. The pool adjoins a regional service center for adults with mental handicaps. The center revised its programs to include use of the pool.

In Connecticut, a water utility's private land holdings (19,600 acres) total ten percent of Connecticut's state forests, parks and wildlife acreage.

Nonprofit organizations have many new ideas

Land trusts are nonprofit organizations that work within a local community, state, or regional area to protect lands with open space, recreation, or ecological importance. In 1950, just over fifty land trusts operated in 26 states, primarily in New England and Mid-Atlantic states. By 1985, a total of 535 local land trusts have been instrumental in preserving over 700,000 acres of our natural heritage.

American Youth Hostels convert old buildings in public parks and recreation areas to provide low-cost travel accommodations. The organization expands its market, and the provider of the building saves the cost of maintenance, renovation, or demolition.

Local hiking clubs maintain much of the Appalachian National Scenic Trail, the famous ridgeline trail stretching from Georgia to Maine. The Potomac Appalachian Trail Club maintains the entire northeastern section of the Trail in a cooperative arrangement with the National Park Service. This partnership saves the federal government money and ensures loving care by the hikers themselves.

Local snowmobile clubs work with private landowners to develop trails. In return, the snowmobile community has been instrumental in supporting recreation use statutes providing liability protection for landowners. They have also promoted registration programs which yield the funds needed to maintain the trails.

Corporate America: a giant partner

Corporations and industry are generally recognized for the charitable donations they make. Yet, corporate America has an enormous array of skills and resources that can be tapped for protection and use of the outdoors. Public service agencies that want to benefit from these resources must look to corporate America as a partner, not simply a source of hand-outs.

Public agencies form partnerships to enhance services

Most public recreation and park agencies have experienced budget cuts which have hampered the quality of services. One way these agencies have survived is through development of partnerships. Local park and recreation agencies report that 60 to 80 percent of their program and service functions are under contract to private partners.

The National Park Service has more than 400 agreements with private businesses, nonprofit groups, individuals, and other public bodies. They help maintain the National Park System and serve the user through resource planning and protection, research, training, and other services. In addition, the Service has approximately 500 contracts and permits with concessioners to provide visitor food and lodging, transportation, recreation services and other functions.

The Agricultural Extension Service has an office in nearly every county of the United States. These offices have great potential for reaching rural landowners and as a source of technical information. Extension officers may be successful partners in helping private landowners, including farmers, learn recreation management skills.

Many agencies whose primary mission is not land management use recreation to achieve their objectives, or create recreation opportunities as a consequence of their activities. At a special listening session, 27 federal agencies told us how their programs affect outdoor recreation. We should seek their help.

Partnerships renew vitality in cities

Communities and business leaders recognize the value of outdoor recreation places to revitalize waterfronts and downtown areas. Efforts typically involve many different groups—cultural and historical associations, banks, small businesses, religious organizations, recreation groups, and a myriad of city services, including schools, transportation, and public works.

In Tulsa, Oklahoma, the partnership of city agencies, realty investors and civic groups resulted in the development of public recreation opportunities, including "Williams Green," a recreation complex capping off a parking authority facility. A central city "low water dam" on the Arkansas River features a floating stage and amphitheater built by public agencies, with private sector investments of more than $10 million.

We can promote partnerships in areas adjacent to public recreation resources

We have learned of many settings where actions outside the boundaries of a recreation area negatively affect the public resources or experience. The location, design and scale of private capital investments near public resources present important opportunities to achieve mutually desirable public and private goals.

Public recreation resources often attract specific types of investments, such as food, lodging and recreation services. The creation of local, state and national authorities to encourage appropriate investments near public recreation resources can enhance recreation services and protect the environment.

We can achieve our goals for the outdoors through partnerships

A network of greenways is an important vision for outdoor America. To develop a greenway, a community must draw on the talents of a wide range of people to succeed. To achieve a network of greenways, communities will have to work together.

For example, the Rails to Trails Conservancy helps to assure availability of abandoned railroad rights of way for public recreation. A river that traverses the grounds of a factory could not be considered part of a greenway corridor if public access were not secured from the factory owners. Maintenance of a greenway trail would cost public funds if volunteer groups were not sought.

Achieving the goals we set forth in this report—a network of greenways, community assessments, greater investment of private capital, equitable access to recreation for all citizens—will require innovative forms of mutual cooperation. The roots of achievement in American life are based in competition. We can turn our best competitive instincts to making our partnerships work in order to always have places to enjoy the outdoors.

The most successful partnerships involve mutual self-interest, not charity. Cities must set their own goals for what they want to achieve, rather than simply reacting to private initiatives.

THE HONORABLE WILLIAM COLLINS
Mayor of Norwalk, Connecticut
"Recreation and the American City" Conference
Baltimore, Maryland

With state parks controlling some of New Hampshire's most attractive landscapes and outstanding natural features, the opportunities for partner-

ships with private enterprise are extensive and the potential for saving tax dollars is enormous. Partnerships offer an entirely new way of delivering the same (or better) services to the public while . . . making a major shift in park management toward better resource stewardship, protection, and interpretation, all at no increase in cost!

THIS PARK CALLED NEW HAMPSHIRE
A Comprehensive Development
Plan for New Hampshire State
Parks

Many Federal Agencies Are Potential Partners

The *Department of Defense* operates more than 1,000 military installations in the continental U.S. Many of these facilities offer recreation programs to military families and retirees. About 24 million acres of U.S. land are under military stewardship. The public can hunt and fish on 11 million of these acres.

The *Interstate Commerce Commission* has responsibility under the National Trails System Act to convert abandoned railroad rights-of-way into recreational trails. An estimated 145,000 miles of railroad line have been abandoned since 1920. These railroad corridors have great potential as greenways.

The *Bureau of Indian Affairs* (BIA) administers more than 50 million acres of land scattered throughout the U.S., generally concentrated in western states. For many years this land was essentially closed to non-Indian use; however, over the past ten years, these lands have become more accessible. The general public spends 8.5 million recreation days on BIA lands.

The *Federal Highway Administration*, as overseer of our nation's roadways, has the authority to develop boat ramps, playgrounds, bicycle trails, scenic overlooks, improved access to recreation sites, recreational facilities at safety rest areas, and other amenities in association with highway projects.

The *Department of Housing and Urban Development* (HUD) is mandated to develop housing and improve community life. During fiscal year 1985, HUD spent $70 million on parks and recreation, $25 million on neighborhood facilities, and $17 million on senior centers under the Community Development Block Grant entitlement program.

The *Economic Development Administration* provides funding for recreational or tourism development activities if the activities create jobs or diversify an area's economy.

The *U.S. Travel and Tourism Administration* encourages foreign travelers to visit America's outdoor areas. To help promote the development of an appropriate conservation ethic, promotional brochures and programs could include messages on proper care of these outdoor areas.

The *Minerals Management Service* is working to encourage the conversion of non-working oil rigs to artificial reefs. These rigs are attractive habitats for a variety of sport and tropical fish. Fishing around the 3,600 rigs in the Gulf of Mexico contributes more than $200 million a year to the Louisiana economy.

VISTA (Volunteers In Service To America), the oldest program in ACTION, has worked with volunteers since 1964. ACTION, the national volunteer agency, provides grants, technical assistance and knowledge of volunteer resources to community and neighborhood volunteer groups.

The *U.S. Office of Special Education and Rehabilitative Services* supports training, research and services in recreation for disabled adults and handicapped children and youth. One program within the agency trains personnel in recreation to work with handicapped people, especially in outdoor recreation and education programs.

The *Federal Aviation Administration* has regulations that require the consideration of the impacts of overflights on recreational areas.

The *Labor Department* supplies employment and training funds to support state and local conservation corps.

The *National Marine Fisheries Service* promotes commercial and recreational fishing.

The *Agricultural Stabilization and Conservation Service* provides cost-sharing with farmers and ranchers to carry out conservation and environmental protection practices, including wildlife habitat enhancement, on agricultural lands. The Water Bank Program offers payments to private owners of inland wetlands to maintain their property for migratory waterfowl.

The *President's Council on Physical Fitness and Sports* establish awards and other incentive programs to promote fitness in youth and adults. The Council stretches its $1 million budget by forming partnerships with corporate America, schools, and other entities to inform the public about fitness and sports programs.

Many federal agencies support outdoor recreation, and the potential for further support is great. Parallel agencies at the state and local levels can play similar roles. By creating partnerships that accomplish participating agency's goals, we come closer to reaching our recreation goals.

Corporate Recreation Programs Benefit Local Parks

A few (19.9 percent) of National Employment Services and Recreation Association (NESRA) members provide ball diamond(s) for their employees while 64.5 percent of those same companies have softball teams or leagues. There is indeed a disparity between facilities owned and programs offered by these corporate recreation providers. The solution for the vast majority of companies is to look to community resources (e.g., local park and recreation agencies and for profit agencies). In fact, the sharing of facilities (synergistic programming) has become a necessity for corporate recreation programs to survive; and many communities have profited in some ways from this relationship.

Two cities, Rochester, New York and Schaumburg, Illinois directly benefited from their synergistic relationship with local corporations sponsoring employee recreation programs.

Corporations in these cities donated either funds and/or facilities to local parks and recreation agencies in exchange for their employee program utilization.

CRAIG FINNEY
University of California, Davis

The Point Sur Light Station, Monterey County, California was transferred to the California state park system in 1984 under the federal government's surplus real property disposal program. The 340 acre property is becoming a multi-use recreation complex for day use activities, as well as limited public overnight use in cooperation with a private non-profit group. The state will invest about $750,000 to restore the property and aid public access. The property, formerly managed by the U.S. Coast Guard, is on the National Register of Historic Places. It is a prime location point for observing seasonal whale migrations.

LEE WARREN
California Department of Parks
and Recreation

The Lincoln Home National Historic Site in Springfield, Illinois is one of more than 100 National Park System sites where visitor experiences are enhanced by the Eastern National Park and Monument Association, a private nonprofit group. Sixty-seven cooperating associations function at more than 300 sites in the system. They aid public understanding of the parks through research, education, interpretation and conservation. Since its creation in 1947 Eastern National's cumulative fiscal donations to National Park Service research and education exceed $8 million.

GEORGE MINNUCI
President, Eastern National Park
and Monument Association

The University of Colorado's Rural Recreation Development Project's success in assisting citizens and civic leaders in Colorado's small communities to use local resources for recreation has encouraged expansion to six other Western states with many communities with 300 to 2,500 residents. Since 1981, 65 Colorado towns have participated, raising over $600,000 to support community recreation. The program helps small communities identify potential recreation resources and activities, then work out ways to make them available to residents. Towns provide fiscal support and insurance; statewide recreation and cultural groups provide technical leadership; federal support comes from the Job Training Partnership Act, and extra fiscal resources are from the Mountain Bell Foundation.

PATRICK LONG
University of Colorado

In the past 25 years since the original ORRR Commission made its recommendations, there have been some major changes in the conservation landscape, one of which is in the nonprofit sector. We've seen the growth of nonprofit organizations throughout the country, and we've seen nonprofits take a major role in the conservation business.

195

In fact, 25 years ago *The Nature Conservancy almost didn't exist. There were virtually no land trusts in existence. Now The Nature Conservancy has 275,000 members, 550 staff people, and we acquire approximately a hundred million dollars worth of prime habitat around the country each year.*

This is a major change in the outlook of conservation, and what I want to say to you is the Conservancy and the nonprofit sector is poised and ready to take a major and leading role in conservation throughout this country. We want to do it in partnership with the federal government, state government, and private business. We're ready in a way that we were not ready 25 years ago.

JOHN FLICKER
The Nature Conservancy
Minneapolis Hearing

States Seek Private Sector Partnerships

Public-private partnership opportunities were highlighted in more than half the submissions. Problems and recommendations in this area fall into four main categories:

○ *Encouraging private landowners to open or reopen their lands for dispersed recreation uses (hunting, hiking, nature study);*

○ *Providing mechanisms and incentives for greater private involvement in protection of open spaces, scenic and natural areas from unsuitable or destructive development (land trusts, agriculture and open space tax districts, coordinated development and zoning plans);*

○ *Increasing incentives and/or reducing disincentives (public liability requirements, short lease periods) for entrepreneurial investments in recreation facilities on private lands or in public recreation areas (e.g., skiing, boating, campground and resort developments);*

○ *Working more systematically with nonprofit user and conservation groups to provide facilities and services on public lands (see also "Volunteers" under* Recreation Workforce).

ANALYSIS OF STATE ASSESSMENTS

The use of the Community Schools program is one of the most effective tools available to local governments for the provision of parks and recreation. It provides an effective use of tax dollars and is of great benefit to local communities.

Participants felt that the Community Schools program must be strengthened and maintained.

NORTH CAROLINA GOVERNOR'S
CONFERENCE ON AMERICANS OUTDOORS
February 1986

A Corporation Donates Wetlands

In 1984 the Prudential Insurance Company of America, assisted by The Nature Conservancy, donated nearly 120,000 acres of prime wetlands and forest land in North Carolina, valued at over $50 million, to the U.S. government for preservation in the National Wildlife Refuge System. This three-way transaction, the largest known corporate conservation gift in American history, involved the corporate, nonprofit, and government sectors.

The Good Sam Club

The Good Sam Club has some 500,000 family memberships, including a large number of retired couples. In 1985, the Good Sam Club decided to help the Volunteers in the Parks program in a big way. It became a clearinghouse for matching up national park campgrounds in need of a "volunteer host" with qualified volunteers. Using its magazine to explain the program and its computer to sort through volunteers for match dates and locations, the Good Sam Club placed 500 couples in campground host positions, mostly for three month assignments. The hosts provide campground users with information and assistance with problems 24 hours a day in return for a free campsite in the park. The program was a great success—except that literally hundreds of would-be volunteers couldn't be put to work in 1986. The Good Sam Club will now expand its efforts, locating volunteers for campground hosts in several states for 1987 and offering similar support to other federal agencies, including the Forest Service.

Protect Our Resource

There is no greater responsibility that faces this Commission than to try to set into motion the protection of zones of land for natural recreation uses in the future. There are continuing pressures on both private and public lands for non-recreation uses. We have seen numbers of camps whose undeveloped lands have been open spaces and natural recreation resources be lost to non-recreation use in the last decade. The land has become so valuable that the sponsoring organization has sold the valuable camp property to maintain its own financial stability, or the private individual has seen no way to get his investment back except to sell the valuable land.

There must be some imaginative way in which the public and private sector could join together to provide corridors of recreation land regionally across the country. Some cooperative effort on the part of adjoining states in providing some breaks to private landowners and cooperative planning between the public and private sector could insure that future generations would not lose the sense of vastness as well as natural resources that are part of our heritage. In whatever sort of zoning or corridor plan that is developed, we would urge that consideration be given to linking compatible uses in certain areas. Though certainly the natural resource recreation area would have to have multiple uses, it would seem that it could be planned in such a way that compatible uses are grouped and linked and non-compatible uses are separated.

. . . .

Chapter 2

Private Landowners Have Opportunities and Needs

We recommend

● Private landowners recognize the opportunity to provide expanded recreation resources and services to the public.

● Local, state and federal governments consider incentives to private landowners to increase public access, and review existing statutes, policies, regulations and practices to assure that impediments to providing public recreation on private lands are removed.

● Recreation organizations actively encourage respect for private property rights and assist in managing use of private lands.

Private landowners: important partners for recreation supply

Private lands constitute nearly two-thirds of our nation's land base, and host many recreational activities. The potential for private lands to provide even more recreation opportunities is great. Yet, many landowners have concerns, ranging from liability to vandalism, which prevent them from opening their lands to the public for recreation use.

The pressures on the nation's lands and waters to provide recreation opportunities will continue to grow. Projections of overall recreation demand made in 1962 for the year 2000 were reached in 1980. Present budget limitations at the federal, state and local levels make dramatic increases in public recreational land holdings unlikely.

Today, most of the public lands are in areas of the country where people are not. Conversely, private lands are often located near population centers. This makes private lands especially important in certain regions of the country, notably the East and the South. Some private lands provide the only access to public lands.

Government finally came to the realization that there would never be enough money to purchase, develop and maintain sufficient land and facilities to meet the demand for outdoor recreation. There is a growing recognition that the private sector, owning a majority of the land and resources, must be considered a partner in meeting future recreational needs.

Private lands are integral to meeting future demands for recreation. Whether it be for the production of wildlife, integration of trail systems, provision of support businesses for recreational enterprises, the assurance of solitude or exclusivity or the maintenance of open space near centers of human population, the importance of these lands to the physical and psychological well being of the nation's citizens is indisputable. Recreation planners and supply and demand analysts must take into account the importance of private lands to the spectrum of recreation activity.

HERBERT E. DOIG
Assistant Commissioner
New York Department of
Environmental Conservation

What we must do . . . is create new institutional ways for farmers, foresters and other landowners to be able to deal with the "people" aspects of recreational use. If owners incur costs, and recreation users reap benefits, there has to be a way for the users to repay the owners, or there simply will not be the amount of recreation that would otherwise be possible. We pride ourselves in this country on our ability to let the free market regulate most of our activities, but this is one where we have not yet invented a market mechanism in many places, and we need to encourage that.

NEIL SAMPSON
Executive Vice President
American Forestry Association

The system we have is not working, and the problems of creating quality sometimes seem insurmountable. If we are to save our wildlife and add new dimensions to recreational programs, we must turn to the private sector for answers. But, unfortunately, we are creating problems in this area faster than we can solve them.

DAYTON O. HYDE
National Cattlemen's Association
Oregon

While we recognize the extent and the seriousness of the challenges to opening and reopening private lands to recreation, we also recognize opportunities to do so. Farming, ranching, timber production and other resource industries are experiencing difficult economic times. Adversity has prompted many in these industries to consider moving from single-purpose land management to multiple use management—from farming alone to farming and wildlife management, for example. As one witness told us, some landowners have arrived at a new view of recreation: "If it pays, it stays."

How recreation "pays" can vary. It can pay in community appreciation for the landowner, especially a corporate landowner. It can pay through reduced tax property payments, where a local jurisdiction provides credit for allowing public recreation access, or in reduced federal taxes resulting from donation of a public recreation easement. It can pay though a recreational use lease, typically entered into by a club or a unit of government. Or, it can pay through individual fees charged for services or facilities. Successful efforts to maximize recreational access to private lands must be voluntary and not coercive and originate at the state and local levels, because of the importance of state liability and trespass laws and local taxing practices.

Landowners have legitimate concerns about opening their lands

We participated in a workshop about recreation on private lands, convened by Senator Wallop, which revealed several reasons why private landowners are hesitant to provide public access.

○ Managing land for public recreation is primarily managing for people. Many private landowners have neither the training nor the desire to manage visitors.

○ Recreation use is sometimes not compatible with the main uses of land.

○ Acts of trespass, vandalism and litter are reportedly increasing. "Willful trespass with firearm" is troublesome to many owners.

○ Owners fear liability if people get injured on their property.

○ Personal reasons for owning lands are changing. Many people seek privacy and discourage use by others.

○ Incentives for the landowner are often lacking. In many cases, the landowner is unable to receive any compensation for public recreation uses.

For these and other reasons, substantial portions of the private lands may never be available for general public recreation use.

Land ownership patterns influence recreation opportunities

Patterns and structures of land ownership in this country are changing, especially in rural areas, and these changes affect public access. Much of the change results from uncertain economies for agriculture and forest products, two principal uses of rural, private land with multiple recreation values.

The number of small farms and forests is growing. Owners of small tracts often acquire them for personal recreation space and are less inclined to open their lands to other people. Smaller tracts often preclude certain types of recreation.

The number and size of larger farms and forests are also growing. These larger tracts generally are managed for maximum income production. While the majority of industrial forest land is open for some recreation, restrictions on access are increasing due to concerns over vandalism, liability, and costs.

The future availability of private lands for recreation is difficult to predict because of the lack of consistent information over time to determine these trends.

We must remove disincentives for public access

Some forty-six states have statutes protecting private landowners from liability suits when they provide free public access, except in cases of gross negligence. Legal experts believe these recreation use statutes provide substantial protection to owners; however, the laws have seldom been tested. The costs of successful defenses can be substantial in time and dollars. Some liability concerns in the future may be resolved by amending state and federal liability laws.

However, these statutes can also inhibit private landowners from providing recreation access. The economic costs of maintaining open lands are high, and many landowners must seek financial return for recreation access. But charging fees for access and use generally eliminates the landowners' legal liability protection. Recreation is a valuable commodity, and landowners should receive fair economic value for recreation access.

The Florida liability law provides continuing protection, even when a fee is charged, providing the landowner meets certain criteria for wildlife habitat management. Other states should consider similar expansion of protection.

Trespass is another challenge. Local enforcement officials generally look upon trespass as a nuisance and are reluctant to investigate and to prosecute offenses. In a number of cases, recreation groups have aided landowners through peer pressure, posting of signs and other means. Landowners, enforcement officials and enthusiasts need to develop local strategies for confronting and controlling recreation trespass.

● Recreation organizations should actively encourage respect for private property rights and assist in managing use of private lands.

We must establish incentives for private landowners

Several states encourage private landowners to plan for multiple uses of their lands. Wisconsin rewards land conservation by providing landowners with tax incentives to manage lands for forests. New Jersey gives grants to landowners to develop recreation facilities. Virginia develops agricultural and forestry districts which provide tax benefits and some protection from development to landowners. Many states reduce or postpone property taxes for certain open space purposes, including recreation.

A number of Internal Revenue Service policies and regulations significantly affect potential donors' willingness to consider making a gift of land or conservation easements. An example is the current requirement that donors assume the cost of a private appraisal of the value of a donated easement. These policies and their effects on conservation and recreation philanthropy should be examined.

Private lands have recreation value: make landowners aware

Often landowners do not realize the potential value of their land for recreation. Landowners need to understand how they can increase the value of their lands by providing public recreation access.

In times of economic pressure for agricultural uses, recreation may offer a way for private landowners to remain economically viable.

● States should create statewide councils of private landowners and recreation users to define mutual goals for conservation of private resources, enhancement of recreation access, and monitoring conditions of use.

● Extension agents and soil conservation districts should help landowners expand recreation access through technical assistance programs.

● A clearinghouse should be established to more efficiently monitor, assemble and distribute legal, regulatory and other technical information and advice about recreation on private lands.

The farm bill: potential to improve quality and quantity of land for recreation

The 1985 Omnibus Food Security Act will expand recreation opportunity on private lands. The Act creates two programs, "Conservation Reserves" and "Easements for Credit Exchange," that remove large amounts of land from annual crop production and dedicate them for an interim period to conservation, recreation, and wildlife purposes.

The law authorizes up to 45 million acres to be placed in conservation reserves and removed from farm production for ten to fifty years. Soil, water and vegetation quality are improved when these lands are withdrawn from production. This potentially improves recreation beyond the reserved area as well.

As of October 1986, the U.S. Department of Agriculture had enrolled 9.1 million acres in this program. Much of the reserved land is in the more sparsely populated Plains states. The Easements for Credit program is not yet operational.

The effects of conservation reserves on the supply of publicly available recreation lands is uncertain. The economic distress in agriculture which stimulated enactment of this statute also motivates some farm owners to allow access only to persons or organizations able and willing to pay substantial fees for recreation.

Presently, billions of dollars are paid to agricultural interests in price supports for surplus crops. If equivalent dollars were paid to the same interests for wildlife habitat and recreation access improvement, extraordinary changes might occur in access to private lands.

Coordination of government actions would help

Public actions to expand recreation use on private land are likely to involve coordinated efforts by different agencies—agriculture, parks and recreation, and fish and wildlife, for example. Several people have suggested to us that interagency cooperation is difficult to achieve, and even harder to maintain. For example, fisheries policy, research and management—an area of significant interest to recreationists—is fragmented, and at times contradictory.

● The secretaries of the U.S. Departments of Agriculture and the Interior should jointly create a special *ad hoc* task force to focus attention and make detailed recommendations on issues involving public recreation access to private lands.

Dialogue stimulates recreation on private lands

Landowners have experienced vandalism and other malicious behavior on their lands. This disregard for private property by some individuals can be quite costly to private landowners.

A timber company in Virginia threatened to close its lands for recreation. The Izaak Walton League provided a forum where company representatives and recreation users discussed their problems. As a result, the company decided against closing their lands to the public. The hunters, anglers, hikers and birdwatchers who enjoyed the land agreed to adhere to a code of behavior developed by the landowner and themselves.

Several states have followed this model and officially adopted councils of landowners and users to prevent unnecessary closures and provide a forum to voice concerns.

● A broad coalition of recreation users and private landowners should adopt codes of ethics describing acceptable behavior on all private lands.

In those few instances where landowners know about the law there is a perception that recreational use statutes do not provide sufficient immunity to act as an incentive for public access. Private landowners do not want to know if they will have a successful defense to a recreational injury lawsuit. Their concern is much more basic; they want to know: "Can I be sued?" . . . Unfortunately, the answer invariably is 'yes' with or without limited immunity recreational use statutes . . . Whether you win or lose, it has been said that a lawsuit is the worst thing that can happen to an individual with the exception of death or serious illness. The challenge to encouraging public recreation access to private lands is to somehow insulate the private landowner from the costs attendant to a lawsuit . . . Absent a coordinated institutionalized approach to the issue of recreational injury liability, twenty years from now we will be back once again to explore the challenge, including public recreation access to private lands.

JAMES C. KOZLOWSKI, ESQ.
Springfield, Virginia

So why do we keep our lands open to the public? Because we still feel that the goodwill we generate is worth the trouble. And because we have some concern that if the private sector withdraws its lands entirely, it will necessitate expanded government ownership to meet the demands of the public.

CLARENCE STREETMAN
Bowater Southern Paper
Company

A concern voiced by college students that visit our ranch on field trips is about our rates. Wouldn't hunting get so expensive that the poor man will not be able to afford to hunt. My answer is, "If you give me one coke and one pack of cigarettes a day for a year I will give you a good hunt." It depends on where the priorities are.

HENRY LOUIS WELGE
Doss, Texas

*In the nine Virginia counties served by the Piedmont Environmental
Council, 14 percent of all private lands have been dedicated by their
owners to continued rural use, at least in the short term. This represents
protection of 300,000 acres—one and one half times the area of Shenan-
doah National Park. These lands have been protected through landowner
response to incentives offered by government, primarily Virginia's agricultural and forestry district program, but including conservation easement
provisions of the Federal tax code.*

ROBERT T. DENNIS
President, Piedmont
Environmental Council

How Three States Help Private Landowners

Wisconsin. Wisconsin's 'Managed Forest Law' provides a creative way to directly reward landowners for land conservation. The law encourages the management of private forest lands for commercial use, while recognizing the objective of individual property owners, compatible recreation uses, watershed protection, wildlife habitat and public access. The act provides lower taxes to owners of 10 acres or more who adopt and use an acceptable forest management plan. The plan may include approved, but not mandatory, actions to enhance wildlife, watershed or aesthetic values. The landowners may leave all or some of the area open to public hunting, fishing, hiking, skiing, sight-seeing or other recreation pursuits. Unauthorized access by motorized vehicles is prohibited.

Through 1992 the owner pays a fixed annual tax of $.74 per acre on open lands. On lands closed to the public the owner pays $.74 per acre, plus an additional annual tax of $1.00 per acre. Present taxes on forest land are about $2.00 per acre, so the economic benefits to landowners are especially high for open lands. Participants may not charge a user fee or lease managed lands. In 1992 and every fifth year, tax rates for open and closed areas will be adjusted.

The state pays local governments $.20 per acre in lieu of taxes from a state forestry fund. Participation in the 1987 signup, the state's first, encourages state officials. About 150,000 acres were designated for forest plans, with more than half of the owners choosing to keep lands open to the public.

New Jersey. New Jersey's 1984 'Open Lands Management Act' provides financial assistance to aid the development and maintenance of private property for public recreation. The Act was adapted from authority used by the Countryside Commission for England and Wales where a strategy of aiding private landowners is long-standing.

In New Jersey private landowners are given grants to make lands available to the public. Emphasis is on developing modest facilities to support passive recreation. Funding is also available for repair or replacement of damaged facilities and properties of the landowner or adjacent owners due to public use. Maximum grants are $10,000. Purchase of liability insurance by the landowner is an eligible expense for the length of the agreement.

Funds are used to open up new areas or provide added recreation activities that had not previously existed. Owners agree to a participate for a fixed period, not less than one year. The program guarantees public access for the full term, even with change of ownership. Fees can be charged for use of facilities, but only to cover costs of maintenance and repair.

Participants may be private individuals, businesses or organizations. Landowners benefiting the most from the program to date are nonprofit organizations. Farmland is poorly represented. Agreements with 17 owners have opened about 2,200 acres. The average cost of access covenants is $75 per acre for an average agreement of 5.3 years. Thus, the annual cost per acre is about $14. In the future program managers propose to 'take it to the cities and suburbs' and direct the program to newer private residential developments as well as vacant lands and waterfronts in economic transition.

Virginia. Virginia's authority to create local agricultural and forestry districts has resulted in about one-half million acres of private land voluntarily reserved as open space. About two-thirds of the acreage and perhaps 80 percent of the easements are in the nine counties organized by the Piedmont Environmental Council, a private nonprofit group. Public recreation access is not required, but is usually granted by landowners for hiking, horseback riding and cross-country skiing. "Firearms use is watched very closely," according to local officials, as is use of motorized vehicles.

The creation of districts is locally initiated by landowners and counties and is administered by the State Department of Agriculture and Consumer Services. Landowners, through county officials, generally determine the length of the agreements; 4 to 8 years is the present range. A proposal to amend state law to lengthen the contract term to 25 years will be advanced this year.

There are basically two incentives to landowners: districting "guarantees what the neighborhood will look like", and it provides for use value taxation, as opposed to potential development or market value tax rates. It is also more difficult procedurally to condemn reserved land for other purposes—roads, for example—so officials tend to give greater attention to proposed public projects.

Outdoor Recreation on Indian Lands

Native Americans have developed life-styles, cultures, religious beliefs and customs around fish, wildlife and other outdoor resources. These resources continue to provide sustenance, cultural enrichment and economic development for many tribes.

Native Americans own approximately 90 million acres of land. Native American lands are regarded as private lands, and decisions to develop public facilities rest exclusively with the tribe or pueblo. The opening of reservation lands for tourism and public access is relatively recent. However, these lands support approximately 10.5 million recreation days a year, including 8.5 million days of public use. Most of this recreation activity is water-based, especially fishing.

Reservation lands also provide critical wildlife habitat for endangered species, such as the bald eagle, as well as conservation of other plants and animals. Indian tribes are one of the nation's largest employers of fish and wildlife biologists.

As the population grows in the West, pressures on tribal lands for public recreation increase. As Mr. Cecil Antone from the Gila River Indian Community testified, "The public must be aware Indian lands are not public lands . . . Recreation on Indian lands is a privilege accorded to respectful guests, not a right that comes with American citizenship."

Access is a supply factor that might influence huntling participation at least as much as wildlife abundance. If wildlife is available but hunting is restricted, then there is no recreation provided. Factors related to the willingness of private landowners to permit hunting access have been studied by several researchers. These studies repeatedly show that the primary reason for posting of a land is for protection of property and control of trespass. About 62% of the variance in posting rates in New York was accounted for by three variables: percentage of permanent residents among property owners, educational level of landowners, and property value. These authors felt that a key factor involved with posting was prior experience of property owners with recreationists. Those who had negative experiences with hunters were more likely to post their land, compared to landowners that had not had conflicts with hunters.

The posting of land does not necessarily preclude hunting. Many private lands are intensively hunted by landowners, relatives, neighbors and friends. In fact, about 68 percent of the hunting effort in the United States during 1980 took place on private land. Hunters spent $36.7 million that year for fees to hunt on private land.

ED LANGENAU

. . . .

Chapter 3

The Liability Crisis Threatens Outdoor Opportunities

We recommend

• Recreation providers (both public and private entities) improve risk management practices through better training and sharing of information.

• Federal and state governments enact or improve recreational use statutes to provide greater protection to governmental entities and private providers who allow the public to use their land for recreation.

What is the problem?

Throughout our history, self-reliance has been an American hallmark. From the pilgrims of New England to the pioneers of westward expansion to the pilots of air and space, Americans always have been willing to accept risk in the hope of greater rewards. However, the year of 1986 marked a time of fundamental debate over who is responsible when someone is injured—who pays when something goes wrong.

Day care centers, skating rinks and beaches are being closed because liability insurance is either unavailable or too expensive. From airlines to zoos, all segments of our society are affected. As we held public hearings across the country, we heard time and again about the liability crisis. In 1985-1986, liability insurance premiums for recreation providers skyrocketed 200-300 percent—sometimes more.

In response, some cities cut back on recreation programs: Chicago removed playground equipment, Wheeling, West Virginia, stopped renting horses, Denver refused to let kids sled in the parks. Private recreation providers were also threatened—Seven Springs Mountain Resort in Champion, Pennsylvania, raised the price of ski-lift tickets an average of 25 percent last season to compensate for a sixfold premium increase.

What is tort liability?

Black's Law Dictionary defines a tort as a: "private or civil wrong or injury, other than breach of contract, for which the court will provide a remedy in the form of an action for damages." Three elements of a tort action are (1) existence of legal duty from defendant to plaintiff; (2) breach of duty; and (3) damage as proximate result.

To illustrate, the following case was settled out of court and resulted in the city of Chicago removing some of its parks' playground equipment. A two year old child fell off an eleven-foot slide. The city of Chicago owes that child a duty of reasonable care to provide safe equipment and a safe environment in which to play (1st element). The child's attorney claimed that this duty was violated by putting a playground on asphalt, instead of a softer surface (2nd element). The child was severely injured when he fell and he was injured because the City had violated its duty of reasonable care by putting a playground on asphalt (3rd element).

There are many causes of the liability crisis

In the summer of 1972, neighborhood children were playing on a swing set in the backyard of Morris and Rosalyn Friedman. One of the children—9-year-old Sylvia Ashwal—was being pushed on a swing by playmates Deborah and Lisa Rosenberg when she somehow broke her leg. Rosalyn Friedman took Sylvia to the hospital and assumed that the matter would be forgotten.

But three years later the Friedmans were sued by Sylvia and her parents when Sylvia's fractured leg stopped growing. Her parents also sued the Rosenberg children, Sears and Roebuck (which sold the swing) and Turco Manufacturing Company (which made the swing). A jury awarded Sylvia $2.5 million, but only Turco and Sears were held to be negligent.

This suit shows a willingness of the American public to seek compensation for accidents which used to be viewed as part of life. But at the same time that people are more willing to sue, they are also more willing to participate in high-risk sports. Recreational activities with greater risk, such as hang-gliding, rock climbing, and whitewater rafting, are increasing in popularity. While there are more risks that people are willing to "take", there are fewer risks that they are willing to "accept."

Unprofitable investment practices by the insurance industry during the late seventies and early eighties also helped contribute to the liability crisis by causing an increase in the price of premiums. Another factor is that insurance companies and others are increasingly willing to settle cases out of court to save time and money. This encourages frivolous lawsuits.

What can be done?

The general liability crisis is beyond the scope of this Commission's mandate. Some reforms being considered by others addressing the problem include caps on damages, changes in joint and several liability, and decreasing contingency fees. However, there are some specific actions which could be taken by providers and governments to minimize the impact on recreation opportunities.

Frivolous cases are being presented to insurance companies who are reluctant to bring a case to court at a high cost to the company. These cases are then settled out of court to save time and money, resulting in situations where innocent defendants lose untried cases and they lose their insurance coverage.

KATHERINE BALLIN
Boston hearing

What providers can do: risk management

One positive outgrowth of the liability crisis is increased emphasis on *safety* in the outdoors. Advances have been made in safety procedures, equipment, and guidelines—though room for improvement always exists. Although most recreation involves an element of risk, strict risk management practices can lower the possibility of injury and lawsuit. In one of our public hearings, the manager of two ski areas described risk management this way:

A lot of people don't want to hear it. But we solved it [the liability problem] eight years ago. We started a very, very strict policy of training of our personnel, our working people, our principal owners of ski areas. A lot of this was with the Forest Service cooperation. Safety programs, safety programs, safety programs.

NICK BADAMI
San Francisco hearing

Self-insurance is an option

Some recreation providers have either been unable to acquire insurance or to afford it. Hennepin Parks, an independent special district providing regional parks and trails for Suburban Hennepin County in Minnesota, decided to self-insure after its liability insurance premiums more than doubled from 1984 to 1985. To finance this program, Hennepin Parks set aside $175,000 for claim settlements. This amount compares with a 1985 premium for general liability of $99,000.

However, establishment of a self-insurance pool is not enough. Hennepin Parks also hired a professional independent risk manager to administer the self-insurance program, handle claims, coordinate and strengthen their safety program, conduct risk management training programs, and serve as a liaison to insurance companies.

While self-insurance is not a solution for everyone, it is a viable alternative for entities that can create a sufficient self-insurance pool (either alone or in conjuction with other similarly situated groups) and for entities who will aggressively pursue techniques to lower their exposure to liability.

Better information is needed

There is little hard data on the number of lawsuits, amount of damages, numbers of cases settled out of court, reasons for liability, and other factors. Without information, providers and insurers of recreation make poor decisions.

Kirk Bauer, executive director of the National Handicapped Sports and Recreation Association, told us about a state-owned ski area in New Hampshire where new devices have been used that allow paraplegics and quadraplegics to "sit-ski." However, sit-skiing has been banned because insurance companies will not cover sit-skiers. But Baur provided results of one study which showed that disabled skiers are 50 percent less likely to suffer injury than non-disabled skiers. Presumably, if the insurance company had the proper information, it would cover sit-skiers.

A recreational law institute could be created to provide a clearinghouse for information on risk management and defense of liability claims. A nonprofit institute could be housed at a university and could be self-supporting by charging for the information that it disseminates.

What states can do: recreation use statutes

A recreational use statute provides protection to someone—a private individual, organization, or government—who allows people to use his or her land for recreation without charge. This is done by shifting the standard of care from mere negligence to gross negligence. *Mere negligence* is defined as failure to use such care as a reasonably prudent and careful person would use under similar circumstances. *Gross negligence*, on the other hand, goes beyond mere carelessness; it is outrageous behavior which demonstrates an utter disregard for the physical well-being of others.

The justification for altering the standard of care is that the recreation provider is making his or her land available for little benefit to himself; and since the outdoors contains natural hazards, the person receiving the greatest benefit should accept the greatest amount of responsibility.

In addition, it is impossible to protect people from all natural hazards in the outdoors. A national forest is not Disneyland. The dangers are real. While the government should make the experience as safe as possible, visitors must accept responsibility for their own safety.

Approximately 47 states have recreational use statutes which provide protection for private landowners when the public uses their land for recreation. Lease agreements between the landowners and a public agency may also help to relieve private landowners of exposure to liability. Some states also have recreational use statutes which protect public entities that provide recreation.

We recommend that states enact recreational use statutes to protect volunteers as well, by making them liable only for gross negligence and not mere negligence. Volunteers involved in activities where injuries are likely to happen should be required to know first aid techniques.

Another tort reform recommendation is recreational responsibility statutes. These are similar to recreational use statutes, but they list the responsibilities of both the recreation provider and the recreation user. For example, Colorado has a skier responsibility statute, which defines the responsibilities of the ski resort and the skier. If the ski resort has fulfilled its responsibilities, then there is a presumption that the resort was not negligent. Many user groups support this type of legislation in an effort to create more opportunities to enjoy the particular sport.

What the federal government can do

We recommend that Congress amend the Federal Tort Claims Act to include a recreational use statute that would alter the standard of care for the federal government to gross negligence. We also recommend that entrance and user fees not constitute consideration. In the typical recreational use statute, the requirement of no consideration is inserted to prevent a for-profit operation from enjoying greater protection. However, the federal government does not make a profit on user fees and should not be held to the higher standard.

This amendment will not alter the federal government's responsibility in many states. Under the FTCA, the federal government is treated as an individual in the state where the accident occurred. Many courts have found that if the state has a recreational use statute protecting the private landowner, the federal government is protected under that statute.

How will the crisis be resolved?

As recreational law attorney Jim Kozlowski says, "There is no silver bullet which will bring the crisis to an end." The problem has many causes and will require the exploration of many remedies. Risk management, tort reform, and insurance reform are just a few.

Recreation providers should also look to others affected outside the recreation field. Only through a comprehensive approach will a long-term solution be found.

Kansas Recreational Use Statute

Kansas and Virginia, among other states, have implemented recreational use statutes. The Kansas Statute section 75-6104 (n) reads as follows:

"A governmental entity or employee acting within the scope of the employee's employment shall not be liable for damages resulting from . . . (n) any claim for injuries resulting from the use of any public property intended or permitted to be used as a park, playground or open area for recreational purposes, unless the governmental entity or an employee thereof is guilty of gross and wanton negligence proximately causing such injury."

This law was applied in the case of *Lee v. City of Fort Scott*, 710 P.2d 689 (Kan. 1985). The plaintiffs, Frank and Mary Lee, sued the City of Fort Scott after their son, Frank Lee, Jr., died of injuries received when their son's motorcycle struck steel cables strung between trees in Gunn Park.

The cables had been in place for seven years to keep vehicles off of the golf course. At the time of the accident there was no sign warning of the cables and there was no history of any prior accidents caused by the cables. The lower court and the Kansas Supreme Court both agreed that the City's conduct did not constitute gross negligence and therefore the City was not held responsible for the accident.

The Issue

Liability issues are causing recreation opportunities to be lost or diminished.

The Options

● Strengthen the laws which limit the liability of recreational land owners, administrators and providers.

● Establish a public relations program to recognize private and corporate efforts which allow public use of private property.

● Pass legislation and funding for recreational use easements.

COLORADO OUTDOOR RECREATION
RESOURCES AND ISSUES

. . . .

We Can Keep Our Communities Attractive Places to Live, Work and Play, and Maintain Open Space

We recommend

● Communities target key parts of their local heritage, including open space and natural, cultural, scenic and wildlife resources, and build prairie fires of action to encourage that growth occur in appropriate areas and away from sensitive resources.

● All governments and the private sector make imaginative use of a wide range of growth-shaping tools to identify and protect prime assets in growth planning processes, which also define areas most appropriate for more intensive development.

● States help lead the way by establishing registries of outdoor resources with statewide significance, such as rivers, wildlife areas, historic sites, unique ecological areas, coastal lands, and scenic countrysides; and assist localities to develop and implement growth-shaping plans and policies.

● The federal government coordinate its public investment decisions with state recreation priorities and local growth plans to avoid conflicts and encourage private-public partnerships in protecting key areas.

The choice is ours

We each have the choice of whether we want our communities as they grow to become a jumble of unsightly development and noisy concrete deserts, or whether we will preserve fresh, green pockets and corridors of living open space that cleanse our air and waters and refresh our populations. We have the responsibility and the capacity to choose, for ourselves, our neighbors, and for future generations.

Growth is a reality and can be a positive force in our nation. As new areas are constructed, we must look for ways to produce the parks and paths we need along with the new homes and offices. The alternative is a costly catch-up game of acquiring the last remnants of open spaces in developed areas.

But the time to make rational growth decisions is running out.

Many experts have told us that the next five to fifteen years will be a critical time for preservation decisions in America. The time remaining to protect key open space and other resources is very limited. Robert Bendick, Director of the Rhode Island Department of Environmental Management, told us that his state has five years left to make all the important land use decisions they face.

Decisions made between now and the year 2000 will determine the fate of much of America's remaining land and water resources all across the nation, especially in urban and suburban areas.

In most regions of the country—in newly resurgent areas of the northeast, along coastlines everywhere, and in the rapidly growing "sunbelt" states—open lands are increasingly threatened by residential, commercial, or resort developments. Growth pressures are no longer limited to metropolitan areas; they affect rural environments as well.

Extensive urban highway networks, and the major shift from a manufacturing to a service economy, have encouraged development of "urban villages" of high-rise office complexes surrounded by shopping, service and residential facilities. This trend has intensified pressures for roads, sewers, schools and other services on rural and suburban governments which are frequently not prepared to cope with such rapid growth. Such urban outposts are rapidly consuming farms, forests and other metropolitan open space.

Owners of private open lands, which serve as important environmental buffers and potential recreation resources, are faced with the dual realities of rising taxes and escalating real estate values. Many privately-owned recreation areas, including farm and hunting lands, golf courses, summer camps, and boating marinas now available to the general public are being converted to residential and other exclusive uses.

The response to such pressures cannot be exclusion of all new development. But growth can be planned for and designed to help meet community needs.

Wise development cannot be dictated from a national plan, but must happen due to the actions of thousands of local governments. Local coalitions, community by community, are our best way to address the widely varying wants and needs of Americans across the country.

Communities must get ahead of urban growth, not react to it

Growth is necessary to accommodate our increasing population and expanding economic base. But many communities and states have successfully used a variety of growth-shaping tools to direct new developments into areas that are best suited for development, where the fewest burdens will be imposed on local infrastructure or the natural environment.

We cannot protect all threatened open space, wetlands, agricultural lands, wildlife habitats, or scenic countrysides through direct purchase. While funding for land acquisition is an essential protection tool, particularly for the most sensitive environmental areas, there will never be enough money to address all threats from inappropriate or misplaced development.

Communities can identify key parts of their recreation, natural and cultural heritage. Prairie fires of local action can direct growth to enhance rather than harm them.

How communities can begin

Those with experience in land protection programs now functioning around the country outline several steps that communities and states can take to get ahead of growth.

o The most important lesson is: "You can't protect everything." The first step, therefore, is to identify community or regional features that are *prime assets*—setting goals to protect and enhance those natural, historic, scenic or economic resources that make each area unique.

o Also identify those areas where growth is possible without damaging prime assets. Growth must happen somewhere, and many regulatory tools cannot be enforced unless alternatives to accommodate development exist.

o Identify assets and growth areas as part of a public planning process that involves all interested citizens, interest groups and landowners. A public process increases community recognition and understanding of key assets and benefits and documents alternatives.

o Work with local officials to use growth shaping tools to direct growth away from prime assets and toward appropriate growth areas. Available tools include:

—Development, floodplain, wetland, land dedication, impact fee and agricultural open space ordinances;

—Funding for acquisition of core recreation or conservation lands or easements, including creation of nonprofit land trusts to facilitate acquisition and to respond to emergency protection needs;

—Voluntary management agreements between private landowners and non-profit organizations or government agencies designed to protect the recreation or resource values of the property while allowing the owner continued use;

217

—Tax preferences and development rights transfers to compensate owners of land where growth is restricted.

There are few single-method solutions. Successful programs use all of these tools in a combined, pragmatic way to achieve their goals. Strong commitments to funding of key land acquisitions are essential for areas needing full protection or where private development rights are substantially affected.

Good planning and strong regulatory options are usually necessary to channel growth effectively. They make possible creative negotiations with the private sector that involve trade-offs among needs for development and resource protection.

Making many of these tools work requires foresight, flexibility and the will to use existing government powers. One key to successful application is emphasizing the positive value of enhancing assets rather than simple opposition to change.

Private sector partners must be encouraged and challenged

In many cases, wise development forsakes equal density across a community and permits higher density in some areas, limited or no density in others. Creative cluster development of housing, with community open space and greenway trail links to other recreation areas, is a good way to build recreation into the environment.

Yet many developers continue to build subdivisions on a rigid grid pattern, and many communities continue to approve such plans. The Urban Land Institute, the National Association of Home Builders, and professional planning groups have long endorsed more creative approaches like cluster and planned unit developments, which improve the quality of urban life and reduce public maintenance costs. We can think of better ways to build our communities. How can we make those ideas work?

Private entrepreneurs must rise to this challenge. They must take the time to produce quality designs and sell them to community residents and planners. In the long run quality development pays off for both the developer and the community.

Local governments must encourage rather than hinder creative designs. Development requirements should allow appropriate tradeoffs of greater development density for provision of open space and recreation amenities. The review process for creative development plans should not be more lengthy than that of traditional plans.

Flexible partnerships in planning and development, backed by adequate funding and protection of recognized assets, can pay dividends for all. Citizens will gain land, water, recreation and cultural amenities that help define the places where they live. Governments will save through private provision of some public recreation opportunities. The private sector will benefit through higher profits for quality developments and better relations with governments and community residents.

There is a need for a state role

Natural systems and resources, like air, rivers, soil, mountains and deserts, cross local boundaries. Growth shaping programs in any one community almost always affect and are affected by conditions in the surrounding region.

Because natural resources are often spread over many jurisdictions, states have a necessary role in protecting environmental quality. States can encourage multi-jurisdictional actions to identify and protect common resources.

Most states have assumed coordinating and support roles in education, transportation, law enforcement, and economic regulation. In recent years, more states have begun to adopt greater roles in environmental protection. The natural heritage inventory programs instituted by almost all states over the last decade are excellent examples of what states can do to support community actions to protect key natural resources.

States can help communities shape growth by

● identifying critical outdoor resources that are unique in the state or of greater-than-local significance;

● making sure that localities have adequate enabling authority to deal with growth;

● assisting communities to identify and plan for protection of regional or local assets, particularly where such assets are of statewide value, and making sure that they have enough technical and financial resources to implement growth plans;

● coordinating use of state funding for land protection, and for development of roads, schools and other infrastructure, with local growth schemes.

States seldom control community decisions on growth, but they can provide the vision, the tools and some financial resources to guide and assist many local growth-shaping efforts.

Managing growth is a local and state responsibility; but many federal programs influence growth decisions

The federal government influences state and local development decisions in many ways. Federal grant, subsidy and tax preference programs should be focused to support community growth-shaping objectives.

○ Federal subsidies for agriculture can, through vehicles such as the 1985 Farm Act, be used to encourage land conservation and improvement programs in partnership with landowners, localities, and states.

○ Grants for highways, housing, sewers and other facilities can be keyed to growth and non-growth areas identified by local and state plans. The 1982 Coastal Barriers Resource Act is a model for eliminating federal subsidies of development in critical resource areas.

○ Federal tax policies (e.g., credits for historic preservation, deductibility of land donations) can provide major incentives or disincentives for private-public partnerships to protect key resources.

○ Coordinated Resource Management Programs now operating in some western states have proven to be useful tools for linking federal, state and local open space and recreation objectives. These efforts involve coordinated planning among land managing agencies and identification of goals for management of adjacent lands. They should be mandated in all regions where federal lands are key components of overall open space systems.

Americans have the right to expect that our communities will be the kinds of places where we want to live, work and play. And we have the responsibility to take action, in our own communities, to see this.

Around the metropolitan areas where most of us live, and near the oceans, lakes and mountains where we go to relax, the countryside is being consumed by urban sprawl and by second homes and resort town houses that only a few can afford. Fueled by a growing national population, the decentralization of economic activity and increasing affluence, these development trends will continue until, in many parts of the country, there will be far too little open land for far too many people.

ROBERT L. BENDICK
Director
Rhode Island Department of
Environmental Management

We're Losing Open Lands and Key Private Facilities

The U.S. Department of Agriculture reports that 1.3 million acres of rural land are converted yearly to 'urban' uses. This total includes substantial amounts of prime farmland, key wildlife habitat, woodlands and other open lands. The U.S. Fish and Wildlife Service estimates that an average of 458,000 acres of wetlands are lost each year.

The private marina industry along Cape Cod's rapidly developing shoreline is endangered by rising land values and property taxes. Some experts expect 20 to 30 percent of existing private marinas to be converted to residential uses within the next five years. Many marina owners feel that they are in the same position as farmers in developing areas: despite their desire to continue lifelong boating businesses, they are operating at a loss and can get a good return on their investments only by selling their land for more intensive development.

The Tool Box For Shaping Growth

● *Identification* of critical open spaces, unique habitats, and sensitive areas so that both private and public sectors can make informed decisions about where growth should occur. This critical first step may be accomplished under local planning programs or state programs for specific resources, like rivers, historic sites, wetlands, or coastal zones. Natural heritage programs in 44 states identify unique biological resources such as the habitats of rare and endangered plants and wildlife.

● *Zoning* and other regulations that limit development in hazardous or environmentally sensitive areas. Such actions are particularly critical to protect key water supplies from degradation, to let prime farmlands, estuaries and wetlands continue to produce food and wildlife, to prevent the huge dollar and human costs caused by developments in areas subject to frequent flooding, hurricanes or other natural disasters, and to protect rare or endangered plants and animals.

● *Acquisition* of critical lands and waters which need complete protection, including purchase of development or use rights in lieu of full fee-simple acquisitions, where such less-than-fee approaches are beneficial to both the public and private property owners.

● *Land Trusts* that can employ the full range of land protection tools, including acquisition of land, rights, or easements, voluntary landowner agreements, monitoring and stewardship. Local trusts are nonprofit groups which often have greater flexibility than do government agencies in working with landowners to identify mutually acceptable protection options, and can act more swiftly if acquisition is required. They often have expertise in tax law, making them successful in encouraging donations of land or sales at less than full market value, with landowners gaining tax benefits as a result.

● *Preferential Taxation* to owners of private farm and forest lands when they commit to keeping their lands free of development. California's Williamson Act of 1965 enrolled over 14 million acres of open farmland in its first ten years of operation. Most preferential taxation schemes provide only interim protection; landowners can later opt for more intensive development if they are willing to pay previously "forgiven" taxes. More recent tax programs like Wisconsin's attempt to tie farmland protection more closely to long-term community growth strategies.

● *Impact Fees and Mandatory Dedication Ordinances* which require developers of land to provide for recreation and other facilities essentially linked to new residential, commercial or industrial developments. In the past 20 years, mandatory dedications of land for parks by subdivision developers has been one of the major sources of protected open space in new suburbs.

More recently, the concept of mandatory dedication has been extended in some areas to cover a variety of more flexible, negotiated approaches to providing for essential public resources and facilities associated with new developments.

● *Transfers of Development Rights (TDRs)* are a relatively new tool based on the concept of land ownership as a complex bundle of rights including personal use, physical access, minerals, and the right to further development. Communities in New York, Maryland and New Jersey have successfully promoted programs to allow transfers of development rights from areas of low growth to areas of more intensive development, providing landowners in restricted growth areas with compensation for developments which are prohibited. TDR programs work well only in conjunction with strong growth planning and zoning. Their usefulness may also be enhanced by establishment of TDR "banks" to buy, sell and broker transfers between landowners and developers.

We have in the past decades made remarkable progress in planning communities. We have found many ways to ask more questions about development and ensure greater sensitivity to environmental planning. Many impacts of projects that used to be accepted as unfortunate or inevitable are now being avoided. Yet, despite these gains, more people are asking if we are making our communities better, more humane places to live. And their answer is no. Despite all our efforts there is a steady, perceptible degradation of the countryside—an erosion of the distinctive qualities that differentiate one place from another. As they confront piecemeal urbanization, people all over the country are asking, how can we save our special places?

WILLIAM K. REILLY
President
World Wildlife Fund and the Conservation Foundation

Urban Partnerships Protect Valuable Resources

Concerns about open and natural lands are not limited to undeveloped areas or the urban fringe; there are many valuable resources within cities too.

In Cincinnati, city government works in partnership with a nonprofit Hillsides Design Trust to preserve scenic and natural features along the Ohio River. Special development requirements and technical assistance for private developers promote balanced development and protect historic features on the hillsides that help preserve the community.

An exceptionally successful partnership with private sector investors was the key to converting abandoned buildings and rotting piers on Baltimore's Inner Harbor into a major economic asset and outstanding scenic and recreation amenity. Harborplace is now one of the most popular tourist and convention centers in the country.

Seattle; Portland, Maine; Jacksonville; Indianapolis; Pittsburgh; and Norfolk are just a few of the many communities that have rediscovered the importance of natural shoreline assets. Each has combined private developments with public park and cultural features to emphasize access to natural waters—in oceans, rivers, lakes and bays.

Identifying Priorities for Conservation

The Nature Conservancy now has computerized inventories in 43 states that systematically identify and map the natural areas of greatest significance, thereby setting a system of priorities for future protection. These can serve as models for local inventories to channel growth away from critical areas. Such inventories allow communities to focus resources on the most important priorities, so that conservation can come first rather than last in America's plans for growth.

The Arkansas Natural Heritage Program, for example, conducts research, performs natural area inventories, maintains maps and an electronic data base of all key sites in the state with unique or endangered plant and animal habitats, identifies priority sites for protection, acquires real property, designs and implements natural area stewardship plans. Arkansas has one of the nation's most successful programs for sharing information and consulting with federal, state and local land managers. The state reviews more than 200 proposed actions by various agencies each year in efforts to protect unique natural environments. Because of the ready availability of information, unnecessary damage to the environment is often avoided through advance cooperation on alternatives to development or mitigating measures.

Coastal Conservancy Works with Local Groups

California's Coastal Conservancy has developed a remarkable working relationship with community nonprofit groups to help implement the state's Coastal Plan. In Trinidad, a small town on the northern coast, a partnership agreement has helped to preserve a valuable scenic area and increase access trails to the beaches. With innovative acquisition techniques and partial funding from the Coastal Conservancy, the Trinidad group was able to protect a scenic area twice the size of that proposed for purchase by the State Department of Recreation and Parks at a cost less than one-tenth of what the State estimated.

Maryland Protects Critical Areas

The Maryland General Assembly enacted a Critical Area Act in 1984 to help communities along the Chesapeake Bay accommodate growth while protecting water quality and fish, plant, and wildlife habitat in what has been called the nation's most productive ecosystem. The Act created a Critical Area Commission with representatives from affected jurisdictions and private interests, which has just completed development of criteria for development and conservation areas within 1,000 feet of the edge of the bay and associated wetlands. In 1987, local governments will respond to the criteria by developing local programs for resource use and protection in the critical shoreline areas.

Wisconsin Preserves Farmland

The Wisconsin Farmland Preservation Act of 1977 (FPA) is considered one of the more successful and foolproof of the many state programs aimed at reducing conversions of prime farmlands and protecting rural landscapes. By the end of 1985 over 6.5 million acres of farmland, about 39 percent of the eligible farmland in the state, was enrolled in the program, and enrollments are still growing rapidly.

The FPA program has three primary objectives: preservation of prime agricultural lands; property tax relief for active farmers; and soil conservation.

The program is based on statewide resource protection goals that are implemented through county plans, with support from state tax incentives. This combination is a key to its success. Under the FPA, counties are authorized to offer farmland owners tax advantages in exchange for restrictive use agreements on those lands. In return, farm owners must agree to minimum restrictive use contracts of 10 years.

Incentives for farmers are in the form of state income tax credits or rebates rather than reductions in local property taxes. Because of this, there is no direct loss of tax revenue to local governments. Also, state income tax credits and rebates are tied directly to household income and level of property tax assessment, giving the greatest incentives to smaller farmers on the urban fringes most likely to be susceptible to development pressures. Wisconsin counties were required to develop and enact comprehensive land use plans, including their own provisions for the preservation of prime farmlands. During the initial five-year enrollment period individual landowners could enter the program in any county. But if after five years a county failed to enact a plan, all its contracts were terminated and any credits or rebates to farmers had to be refunded. This created a community of interest among landowners, counties and their subdivisions to develop workable protection plans.

State funding assistance was made available to counties for the development of required plans, to ensure that localities would not be deterred from participation because of lack of expertise or resources. Plans have been enacted by all but two counties in the state.

State officials feel that the main reasons for the success of the Wisconsin program are the state's requirement for county comprehensive plans, and its assumption of most incentive costs through state income tax credits.

· · · · · · · · · · ·

Chapter 5

We Should Protect Our Investment in Public Recreation Facilities

We recommend

● Local, state and federal officials plan and budget for systematic renovation and replacement of existing recreation facilities.

● Older facilities where practical be redesigned and adapted to allow access by people with physical disabilities.

● Local, state and federal governments include recreation facilities in any overall considerations of their public works improvement needs.

● People and private organizations that benefit from public recreation facilities be encouraged to volunteer their labor and dollars to help maintain and repair them.

America's built recreation environment is endangered

In the past century, Americans have invested billions of dollars in public recreation facilities. These facilities, which often are essential to people's use and enjoyment of the outdoors, are now showing their age. That deterioration is a major problem in recreation areas is not surprising. Much of the nation's non-recreation "infrastructure" is also showing wear and tear from decades of heavy use.

Many community parks were first established between 1880 and 1940. Facilities constructed during that period are now fifty to a hundred years old or more. State and national forest and park systems also began to grow in the first part of this century, and facilities within these areas are experiencing similar aging problems. Even suburban and county parks, which experienced a boom after World War II, have older parks in need of redesign or rehabilitation.

A large majority of older recreation facilities block access by people with physical disabilities. Redesign and adaptation to accommodate them should be one of our major rehabilitation priorities.

A growing, changing population creates new demands that cannot always be met by facilities designed in another era. An auto campground designed in the 1950s, when most campers used on-the-ground tents, may no longer meet the demands of a population that uses recreational vehicles. A playground developed during the baby boom years to meet the needs of young children in a residential neighborhood may be obsolete twenty years later if the neighborhood consists primarily of older residents. Creative solutions to the problem of obsolescence require continuous planning processes to keep decision makers informed about changes in recreation demands as well as the condition of recreation facilities.

Well-designed and functional facilities are not only essential to public enjoyment of recreation opportunities, they also protect the environment of recreation areas. They minimize the destructive effects of heavy use on natural resources and help ensure the health and safety of park visitors.

Existing facilities may be forgotten as we acquire and develop new areas. While they try to respond to newly identified needs, elected officials and managers may forget older attractions which are the hearts of many recreation systems, both as popular recreation amenities and as symbols that unite the community's citizens.

Some decay is caused by lack of proper maintenance. But most jurisdictions distinguish between routine maintenance and capital rehabilitation needs. For example, flushing and winter-proofing a hot water heating system every year is routine maintenance that extends a system's life. Such maintenance should be part of annual operating budgets. Eventually, however, boilers burn out, pipes and pumps corrode and systems need complete replacement. This involves new capital investment that needs to be planned as part of long-term development and rehabilitation budgets.

Private businesses, universities, and other nonprofit organizations often create "sinking funds" to lay away dollars to finance future renovation. State and federal governments encourage such private planning by offering tax deductions for depreciation. But most government agencies do not follow this example. They tend to wait for a replacement crisis to occur, instead of allocating funds every year for future needs.

• Government agencies should consider establishment of "sinking funds" that reserve portions of every annual budget to cover future rehabilitation of recreation facilities.

What Are Recreation Facilities and Why Are They Endangered?

Residential communities usually have the greatest needs for developed recreation facilities, including swimming pools, playing fields, picnic areas, streets, paths, nature centers, zoos, and lakes. More intensive developments in urban areas respond to use by larger numbers of people on a daily or weekly basis. State and national recreation areas also have major structural features—roads, trails, campgrounds, visitor centers and sewers—that make these more rural environments accessible to growing numbers of visitors.

As with other types of facilities, age is the primary cause of deterioration in recreation areas. City park systems had their genesis in America with the development of New York's Central Park in the 1850s. The first national park was established in 1872, and a national forest system was created in 1905. State park and forest systems were well underway by the 1920s.

Under the Works Progress Administration (WPA) and Civilian Conservation Corps (CCC) public works programs of the 1930s, thousands of cabins, group camps, trails, shelters, and other facilities were built in local, state, and federal recreation areas. Over time, the number of visitors to these areas has far exceeded the original designers' expectations. Continuous and heavy use has taken its toll, not only in older city, state and national areas but even in suburban parks founded during the last quarter century.

Some factors that have contributed to this crisis of deterioration include:

○ Greater use, fueled by rapid population growth;

○ Changing population demands and technology that make some older recreation area designs obsolete;

○ The politics of capital fund allocations, which favor new construction over rehabilitation;

○ Failure to follow systematic preventive maintenance procedures;

○ Vandalism and destruction of recreational properties, which become worse when decayed or damaged facilities are not quickly restored;

○ Increasing costs for labor, materials, and financing, which can make renovation of older areas much more expensive than initial development;

○ Periods of public resistance to bond issues and higher taxes, resulting in overall declines in real capital budgets.

The scale of rehabilitation needs measures in billions of dollars

In 1978, a national Urban Park and Recreation Recovery Program (UPRRP) was enacted in response to rehabilitation needs identified in the *National Urban Recreation Study*. It provided $150 million in matching grants between 1979 and 1984 for renovation, redesign, and improvements in existing local parks. More than 850 sites in 350 communities were renovated with UPRRP matching grants.

But available funds lag far behind estimated needs. A 1981 survey by the National Park and Recreation Association estimated local park rehabilitation requirements for the next five years at $4.3 billion.

A 1986 survey indicates that a similar crisis affects state parks:

> *Apart from funding, what do [state] park directors see as their greatest needs? For most, the highest priority is the existing system, especially fixing up neglected or obsolete facilities. . . . Although a number of states report spending more money on facilities in recent years, and funding for maintenance has fared better than that for acquisition or development, the need evidently far outstrips spending.*
> PHYLLIS MYERS and ANN C. REID
> *State Parks in a New Era: A Survey of Issues and Innovations*
> Conservation Foundation
> Research Paper, 1986

For federal facilities, the Park Restoration and Improvement Program (PRIP), was initiated in 1982 to arrest the decay of many facilities in the national park system. It provided $1 billion for capital rehabilitation over four years, but the National Park Service estimates a continuing need of $75 million every year simply to maintain the status quo.

In its ten-year Renewable Resources Program plan submitted to Congress in 1985, the Forest Service indicated a $400 million facilities backlog, including $100 million for trails renovation alone.

Systematic planning is needed to support renovation efforts

Public agencies must improve their budgeting practices to allow for capital rehabilitations. But efforts to protect existing public recreation facilities should go beyond one-time funding, and address the more fundamental problem of failure to recognize the value of existing investments.

Under the Urban Park and Recreation Recovery Program, 350 communities prepared Recovery Action Plans. These plans were aimed at making local rehabilitation and maintenance efforts more systematic and efficient. They provided management-oriented models for other system-wide restorations.

Systematic planning helps increase awareness by citizens and public officials, and identifies and prioritizes capital projects to restore and revitalize parks. Then, it is up to citizens and public officials to follow through by funding such projects.

In addition to capital planning, an increasing number of communities, states, and federal agencies are discovering the value of management assessments to improve the efficiency of their maintenance operations. Annual facility maintenance costs, over time, far exceed capital investments. Therefore, management planning that improves work patterns, equipment availability and scheduling for maintenance tasks can produce large savings. Maintenance plans can effectively *expand operating budgets* by reallocating dollars and staff time saved to more critical tasks.

From Manchester, New Hampshire, to Pueblo, Colorado, over one hundred communities have reported success with systematic maintenance programs. The State of New York and the National Park Service are also beginning to implement maintenance management programs for their larger recreation systems.

● Public agencies need to develop and implement maintenance management plans that identify priorities for cyclical maintenance tasks and make optimum use of available dollars and staff.

Recreation should be included in all public works programs

In recent years, concern has grown nationally about the survival of our "infrastructure," the public works which make possible every government or private facility and service and provide an underlying base for all economic development. Since 1983, Washington, Oregon, New Jersey, Connecticut, Georgia and other states have conducted special public works studies and created new grant and loan programs to support cyclical renovation of basic transportation, health and safety facilities.

A National Council on Public Works Improvement was created in 1984 by Public Law 98-501. The Council is studying the nationwide problem of deterioration in highways, transportation, water and sewer systems, and other facilities.

To date, none of these state or national programs has considered recreation facilities. In light of the close ties between recreation, transportation, economic development and the environment, we urge the National Council and the various state and local public works programs to study the needs and values of recreation infrastructure.

● The National Council on Public Works Improvement should incorporate an assessment of park and recreation deterioration problems in its final report to the President and Congress, now scheduled for late 1987.

People start restoration action

Thousands of parks throughout the country are a half-century or more old, and include features of unique historic or architectural interest. They include landscape parks such as those identified by the National Association of Olmsted Parks, larger scale designs produced by the "City Beautiful" movement of the early 1900s, and early state and national areas. These cultural assets often require extraordinary efforts—for instance, estimates for restoration of New York's Central Park exceed $100 million.

Such special projects are not included in the general estimates of rehabilitations needs above. People's willingness to commit large amounts of private and public funds to restore these historic recreation areas shows how important parks can be to communities and the people who use them.

People are proud of their parks, and become attached to their favorite recreation facilities. Recreation and conservation advocates must learn to build on such pride and affection to help increase resources for the preservation of existing parks. Citizens can insist that public agencies include priorities for recreation renovation in annual budgets and provide enough staffing for maintenance.

Park visitors or community residents can contribute through volunteer work projects, and local businesses may "adopt" nearby recreation areas by providing funds and volunteer labor for cleanup and beautification. Some areas have found "Gift Catalogues" that solicit contributions of equipment or volunteers effective in encouraging community involvement. People must speak out—through planning processes and with their own personal contributions—about which recreation areas are important to them and how they should be protected and enhanced.

The time to address the problem of deterioration is now, before it worsens. Continued decay becomes more difficult and more costly to remedy. By neglecting our existing parks and recreation areas, we rob future generations of their use.

Like everything else in this country, our park and recreation systems are part of our national epidemic of infrastructure disease. Facilities are old. They are getting frail. Good, sound management demands attention to current facility needs and proper maintenance, and I hope that you would comment on those.

PAUL GUTHRIE
Minnesota hearing

Rock Bottom: Dealing with All the Nation's Public Facilities

Deterioration of recreation facilities is only part of a much larger national problem. This problem affects highways, schools, jails, public trans-

portation, water, sewer, and power systems, railroads, and indeed almost all public facilities.

The Council of State Planning Agencies estimates "Costs of Maintaining and Repairing Public Services Until 1990":

Facility Type	Cost In $Billions
Highways & Bridges Outside of Urban Areas	$1,000
City Streets	600
Municipal Water Systems	125
Ports and Inland Waterways	40
Water Pollution Controls to Meet Current Standards	15
Construction/Renovation of Prisons and Jails	100

In 1981, a "Futures Group" of the American Council of Life Insurance identified the decay of physical infrastructure as one of five potential worldwide crises. The group's report noted that "approximately one-fourth of the U.S. interstate highway system is worn out or needs resurfacing. Twenty percent of bridges are in such a sad state that they are either restricted or totally closed. . . . Almost one-half of all the communities in the U.S. cannot expand because water and sewer systems are at or near capacity.

THE FUTURIST

Maintenance Planning: The Philadelphia Story

The Fairmount Park Commission in Philadelphia oversees a 120-year-old system with 8,000 acres of parkland. Until five years ago, complaints about the poor condition of grounds and facilities were common. The Commission developed a systematic maintenance management plan. This involved preparing detailed inventories of maintenance tasks—locations, equipment used, travel routes and employees involved—as well as developing job standards and systematic work schedules.

The plan has been a success. It has substantially increased productivity and improved the quality of maintenance. The Commission saved $180,000 per year on lawn mowing alone. Despite budget reductions, greater productivity enabled the Commission to keep up with its workload. In 1985, the Commission was cited as "the most improved department" in Philadelphia.

Chapter 6

Well-Trained Staff Expand Outdoor Recreation Opportunities

We recommend

• A national recreation resources futures workshop be convened to assess professional outdoor recreation education and training needs.

• Partnerships be formed between the private sector and local, state, and federal agencies to ensure college curricula requirements match professional skills needed in the field and are reflected in current accreditation evaluations.

Recreation professionals must have knowledge of people and natural resources

People trained for the leisure industry work in a variety of settings: country clubs, city and national parks, zoos, resorts, cruise ships, ski lifts, campgrounds, nature preserves, amusement parks, youth camps, ball fields and many others. People who manage these resources impact the public's use of the outdoors.

Regardless of the physical site managed or used by recreation professionals, they must understand 1) people and their recreation behavior and 2) natural resources and people's impact on the resource in recreational activity. Ski lift operators must locate ski trails in places that are exciting to skiers, yet not destroy the natural environment on which their business depends. Park rangers are knowledgeable about natural phenomena, yet to ensure its protection they need to inform visitors about entertaining and enjoyable ways to use the area with sensitivity.

Well-trained and dedicated recreation and natural resource personnel are as critical as the availability of physical resources. These professionals manage complex programs which require a balance between what people want to do on a resource and what the resource will sustain.

College curricula should reflect job requirements

According to a 1986 national survey of recreation, sports and leisure personnel, 80 percent learned their skills through a college education, in more than a hundred different disciplines. The variety of disciplines matches the variety of settings these people find themselves managing. Over half received their degrees in physical education, health, recreation and parks, but other fields—tourism, planning, biology, business, zoology, child development, forestry—illustrate the variety in the field.

Since many professionals in the leisure industry receive college degrees, college curricula must reflect the needs of the job market. The education must include training about people *and* natural resources. A curriculum in tourism management needs to include courses on natural resources protection. A curriculum in wildlife management must incorporate principles of people's recreation behavior.

For some managers, skills required in the job market are changing. For example, because of reduced government funding, public park and recreation professionals are asked to charge fees, market their services, and evaluate their programs based on profitability. Business and management skills have become essential to managers of public recreation. In some cases, the application of business principles have kept public recreation services open.

Accreditation of college curricula is one way to ensure that college graduates receive adequate job training. The National Recreation and Park Association, the American Alliance for Leisure and Recreation, the Society of American Foresters, and the American Society of Landscape Architects all have college curricula accreditation programs.

On-going training is necessary for dealing with change in a vital, dynamic profession

Managerial needs shift in response to changes in population, roles of government, and technology. Skills learned in college may need to be improved, refreshed or expanded. Those workers who did not go to college have different training needs.

Many recreation and resources personnel are in a transition from "doers" to "facilitators." Recreation personnel find they need skills to make partnerships with other agencies work. In addition, many local, state, and federal statutes require public participation in major decisions, and managers must have the skills to manage effectively public input.

Recreation industry personnel stay in their jobs, on the average, for fourteen years. The average worker in the field is 41 years old. The industry is retaining employees who have greater experience and knowledge rather than hiring new employees with modern training.

However, in 1985 only 7.8 percent of the recreation employers in private and public sectors required continuing education; 41.2 percent did not require formal training but encouraged it. More than half neither required nor encouraged on-the-job training. This lack of interest or resources by employers hampers the ability of the work force to keep up with population trends or innovations in the field.

Trade and professional organizations and employers offer education, training, and technical skills development: Resort and Commercial Recreation Association; National Recreation and Park Association; National Campground Owners Association; Society of American Foresters; Association of Interpretive Naturalists; Disney University; National Park Service.

Most public agencies and many private organizations face a severely limited training budget, yet we find a disturbing lack of coordination between agencies and organizations in providing continuing education. Typically, these programs are available only to members or employees. However, partnerships among these organizations offer opportunities to invigorate the work force with different approaches and refreshing ways to handle problems. Sharing resources, such as instructors, video courses, written texts, physical sites, and seminars, also promotes an exchange of ideas. Trail club representatives teach ski lift operators techniques of trail construction. Amusement park operators share crowd control strategies with national park superintendents.

Training programs offer an opportunity for the development of professional ethics—toward people and natural resources. Stewardship of outdoor recreation resources should be emphasized. Use of new technologies, like the computer, for solving specific recreation management problems, such as facilities maintenance, environmental conditions monitoring, and project evaluation, is also important. There is an increasing need to strengthen professionals' abilities in working with the public and involve them in resource planning and management decisions.

One of the barriers to the use of these training courses by nonmembers of each particular organization is lack of information. There is no central repository of training programs in each of the different professions in the leisure industry.

We must attract and reward leaders

We have heard across the country that protection of the outdoors depends on leadership. Champions of the outdoors need to be recognized. Typically, the people who greet the public and introduce them to the importance of resource protection are among the lowest paid of recreation professionals. We must find ways to reward dedication, spur innovation, and acknowledge commitment.

We must develop career ladders for technical experts and professional managers to attract innovative people and encourage them to keep their skills up to date. We must ensure that each professional knows skills that encourage and allow people to enjoy themselves as well as skills that protect our outdoor heritage.

Fewer students are entering the field of recreation and parks. For baccalaureate programs, the number of entering students declined 20 percent between 1980 and 1982, and an additional 11 percent between 1982 and 1984 (Henkel, 1985). The supply of professionally-trained activity leaders is decreasing while demand is increasing. It is unknown if the same relationship is true in the other disciplines related to the management of the outdoors. It does appear that salaries in both private and public agencies have barely kept up with inflation.

One way to promote innovation and employee development is through personnel exchanges. For public agencies, the Intergovernmental Personnel Act allows the interchange of employees among public agencies. Exchanges with nonprofit organizations are not permitted by the Act. This provision defeats many of the benefits of employee exchanges in the outdoor recreation field. Trading employees among outdoor recreation providers fosters innovation and exchanges of ideas.

Professional and trade associations offer a wide range of services to their membership, including awards for outstanding service, training, and the latest developments in their field. Affiliation with some associations enhances professional growth and development.

We urge strong support for national certification programs which require both quality academic preparation from accredited curricula, plus continuing education for retention of certification status.

The management of recreation systems at all levels of government should be more professional. Government policy should encourage professionalism in management. Economically disadvantaged areas should not be penalized for their inability to afford professionally managed recreation systems. Government should encourage educational institutions, training parks and recreational professionals to place more emphasis on business management. These professionals need to communicate better with government officials to insure that quality of life issues in America receive the attention they deserve. By sound business management and clear channels of communication, the most efficient use of funding can be achieved.

MAYOR STEPHEN J. DAILY
City of Kokomo, Indiana

One option: a public-private training institute

An institute with basic and specialized training courses for professionals is one option to provide the needed crossover between the private sector and local, state and federal agencies. It could be an impetus for expanded cooperation, and serve as a clearinghouse for information concerning education and training opportunities.

Such an institute could become self-supporting through service charges, grants, university consortium arrangements, corporate sponsorships, and donations. It could establish contracts with recognized institutions to provide needed continuing education and training, and work to develop demonstration training areas using the latest technologies.

The work force can help spread the prairie fire

As we traveled across the country and heard from various people within the recreation profession, we grew confident that our natural heritage lies in competent and dedicated hands. We must ensure that these people are given the tools to perform their jobs.

Therefore, we recommend a conference representing the variety of recreation, travel, and leisure professionals to study these issues and provide specific direction. The conference should focus on incentives for providers to exchange ideas, through training programs and personnel.

The protection of our natural heritage depends in part on the professionals involved in the field. The energy and abilities of our outdoor work force will help support the prairie fire.

Central to any organization are people in executive positions who can give direction to the agency, protect it in political storms, nurture it, monitor its environment and adjust its programs to maintain congruence, anticipate the need for change and initiate it before crises occur, develop a network of supporting agencies, monitor the agency's internal functioning and guide it to a state of organizational health. The short term for this kind of leadership is "pathfinding". The more dynamic the environment and the higher the ambiguity in which an organization must operate, the greater becomes the need for pathfinding. Pathfinders are in short supply.
DAVID GRAY

Park and Recreation Gets Official Accreditation Program

On October 3, 1986, the Council on Postsecondary Accreditation granted the first official recognition to the specialized park and recreation accreditation program sponsored by the National Recreation and Park Association and the American Association for Leisure and Recreation. Recognition follows 20 years of citizen and professional efforts. Today more than 30,000 students—from associate to doctoral candidates—in 500 educational institutions study parks, recreation, and leisure services planning and management.

Project Life (Leisure Is For Everyone) at the University of North Carolina at Chapel Hill has developed training materials encouraging inclusion and choice for the disabled for use at local and state recreation agencies. LIFE provides a cost effective training program that facilitates organizational change that precludes the overlooking of needs of the disabled.

CHARLES BULLOCK
testimony, Washington D.C.

The search for qualified personnel continues to be of great concern in outdoor adventure programming. Typically, an outdoor instructor/leader becomes proficient after the second year of employment. Unfortunately because of relatively low salaries, job-related hardships such as the lack of a stable home environment, or limited career potential, many highly valued personnel leave the profession within three to four years of employment to pursue other endeavors.

Training personnel has generally been accomplished through two mechanisms: intra-training opportunities offered through the hiring agency and programs specifically designed to train outdoor leaders/instructors. Various certification schemes have evolved to help ensure a minimum level of instructor competencies and to offer some mechanism by which there is some transferability of instructor skills from one agency to another. Because of its regulatory aspects, certification has become a hotly debated issue in the field, with a variety of certifying mechanisms discussed and analyzed. To date, there does not exist a nationally recognized certification program similar to that employed by Great Britain or other countries.

ALAN EWERT

Park and recreation maintenance has grown beyond the need for just a "mop and bucket" janitor. Maintenance, in general, has become a complex, year-round operation dependent on efficient and knowledgeable management practices. . . .

As in all other industries in both the public and private sectors, natural resource managers are faced with new problems and new challenges. Answers to these modern dilemmas are to be found in new techniques and technologies as well as creative and professional application of time-tested management practices. Regardless of the approach, training personnel to keep up with the times is essential. There must be commitments at all levels of government to maintaining staff levels in our park and recreation departments.

DELAWARE REPORT TO THE PRESIDENT'S
COMMISSION ON AMERICANS OUTDOORS

Parks and recreation is a composite occupational category. It is a field of work, not a unique occupational group such as medicine. Practitioners trained in such related and unrelated professions and disciplines as landscape architecture, forestry, public administration, physical education, music, adult education, social work as well as recreation and parks are employed by park and recreation agencies. This is due in part to the variety of agencies and organizations providing park, recreation and leisure services. There are health spas, amusement centers, regional park systems, municipal and county departments of parks and recreation, the National Park Service, private sporting clubs, campgrounds, youth serving organizations and human service and health related agencies. All are a part of the leisure service delivery system of which parks and recreation is a part.

H. DOUGLAS SESSOMS

· · · · · · · · · · ·
Decision Makers Need Sound Information

We recommend

● States and the federal government compile and publish annual reports on the State of the Outdoors that describe the condition of our natural resources for recreation.

● Private sector, government and academic interests work jointly to establish a National Recreation Accounts network to facilitate collection, analysis and sharing of statistical data and information.

● A uniform system of National Biological Accounts be established, which compiles, analyzes and disseminates data on critical natural areas, plant and animal species, key geological features, and threats to these resources, utilizing existing information sources such as the state heritage programs where appropriate.

Why we need better information systems

The 1980s are said to be "the dawn of the information age," an era when acquiring, maintaining and using the proper data are more critical to the success of every enterprise than at any time in our history. Yet hundreds of public and private recreation providers, managers, community planners, developers, and manufacturers have told us that they lack the reliable data on outdoor recreation resources and trends they need to guide their investments and policy decisions.

We have also heard that one of the principal causes of poor decision-making about natural resource and outdoor recreation issues is inadequate recognition of values—economic, social and environmental.

Despite hundreds of inventories, surveys, and market analyses prepared for national, state, local and private planning in the 25 years since ORRRC, it is still difficult to find comprehensive, reliable data on what resources are available, on who benefits from these resources, and how much.

Many local, state and federal agencies have good data about their own lands, but wide disparities in methods for collection and analysis exist. Existing efforts to coordinate data nationwide, such as the U.S. Forest Service's Resource Planning Act data base, have helped, but these efforts lack the authority and resources to fill gaps between the various systems.

It is difficult, for example, for one state to know how recreation visitation and the tourist economy are affected by what is available in the next state. Loss of significant wetlands in one county may have serious consequences on water quality, flooding problems, and wildlife populations in a much wider region. Recreation manufacturers and other private entrepreneurs find it difficult to assess market demand for their products and services without good regional and national information.

Many recreation providers have strong convictions about the social and health benefits of their programs, but lack sufficient long-term data to conclusively confirm these intuitive insights. We lose valuable natural resources to development when we cannot show that recreation use creates jobs, produces tax revenue, and accounts for other economic benefits in an area.

● We must improve information about the economic, social, and environmental values of outdoor recreation programs and resources.

Better information leads to better decisions

There are few mechanisms in place for cooperative collection and sharing of key information. Consequently, research, planning and decision-making are performed in isolation, often with duplicative, incompatible, and incomplete results.

These shortfalls are not academic; they have direct impacts on the lives of our citizens every day. When providers do not have good information on what people want or on what is currently available, they fail to provide the quantity or quality of resources and experiences sought by visitors. Spending for capital investments and services based on poor information may be inefficient. The private sector hesitates to make investments because of uncertainty about what markets exist for goods and services.

When unique biological or cultural resources are not identified in advance of planning for development, they may be inadvertently lost simply because we did not realize they were there, or that they were important. Recreation resources are also lost or damaged when threats to them are not identified or are poorly understood.

Good decisions about outdoor resources rely on both comprehensive information about current situations and data on trends in supply and demand. Accurate trends identification is essential to guide future actions.

Trends analysis compares present information with the past and with surrounding areas. Such statistically reliable and comparable data for other times and places is frequently lacking in the natural resources and recreation fields.

Research: foundation for good decisionmaking

A frequent complaint of recreation and natural resource practitioners is that research does not help them make decisions in the field. Practitioners often do not understand the language of the research or how to apply a study's results.

As in any social science, research findings are difficult to apply comprehensively. For example, research about a particular method of informing people in backcountry wilderness may not be appropriate in county parks. Several research agendas have been developed in the past ten years to identify research gaps, but they have not been funded. Knowledge about current research findings are often dispersed and difficult to find.

● We recommend that researchers and practitioners meet to discuss how to direct research talents towards needed management information and how to support these efforts.

Quality recreation depends on the state of the outdoors

A basic premise guiding our work as a Commission is that all outdoor recreation ultimately depends on the quality of the natural resource base. What good is recreation amid unhealthy air, unswimmable waters, inedible fish, or landscapes downgraded and wetlands dried up? Our care of the environment also requires current and accurate information on status, trends, and threats.

We recommend that all states and the federal government annually compile and publish reports on the State of the Outdoors, which describe and analyze the condition of our natural resources. Information contained in the National Recreation Accounts and the National Biological Accounts, and other sources as well, should be useful in undertaking these annual assessments.

Recreation accounts measure the health of the outdoors

Recreation accounts are indicators, much like the economic indicators that measure the health of our nation's economy. A network of these indicators could measure the strength of our country's support for recreation and the outdoors.

We may need new data, or we may simply need to supplement or package existing data. A network of national recreation accounts is one way to recognize existing data sources and identify gaps. We need to develop incentives to private data collectors to share some of their market research results. We also need to develop incentives for public agencies to share data and work together as partners.

A recreation accounts network can be built by combining the recreation research and information of the fifty states, major universities, recreation managers, and private marketing and manufacturing associations. The network's goal should be to provide continuing, comparative data bases of outdoor recreation resources, demand, values, visitation, and market trends over time and across geographic regions.

The network may consist of data from Statewide Outdoor Recreation Plans (SORPs), periodic National Recreation Surveys (National Park Service & Forest Service), market surveys of private firms and other willing partners. The expertise of the Census Bureau, the Bureau of Labor Statistics, and private manufacturers and service providers should be tapped to help determine key indicators and economic benefits of public and private recreation activities.

A biological data base could identify important resources and threats

Attempts to develop a National Biological Survey (NBS) have occurred sporadically over the past half century. There are a number of natural resources inventories of limited scope operated by the state and federal governments.

Forty-four states have natural heritage inventory programs that identify key natural lands or biological habitats that need special management or protection. These inventories are launched and informally coordinated by The Nature Conservancy, a private organization. The Nature Conservancy also maintains a national biological data base used in conjunction with the network of state heritage data centers.

Under the 1976 Resources Planning Act, the U.S. Forest Service has undertaken a major inventory of public and private recreation areas. The U.S. Fish and Wildlife Service operates a National Wetlands Inventory program, and the Environmental Protection Agency sponsors BIO-STORET, a data base on environmental resources and conditions. The data bases contain information each agency needs.

A number of biologists and others have recommended to us that a National Biological Accounts program be created, to coordinate all biological, geological and natural areas information. A national biological data base would help standardize information over time and among agencies, fill the gaps in existing systems, and promote the sharing of information about natural resources and the threats to them. The data base would begin by linking existing biological and natural heritage information systems.

Information systems require long-term maintenance and attention

Powerful, reasonably priced computer hardware and software have made easier the job of coordinating data programs. However, technological improvements cannot replace the need for stable, long-term institutional arrangements that provide adequate personnel for data collection, analysis, and sharing of information among all providers.

• We recommend that all private and public interests in recreation data and information come together to examine existing information and data gaps and determine what needs to be done by whom.

Success of information systems depends on partnerships

National electronic access to a standard data base by any user on a cost-recovery fee basis should be an ultimate goal, but the benefits of the National Accounts Network should not be limited to statistical experts or researchers with computers. The data collected and analyzed should be a key ingredient of the annually published state and national reports on the State of the American Outdoors.

Coordination of the networks must be vested in a single, public or quasi-public office or institution with sufficient dollar and manpower resources to operate national, on-line, computerized data bases along the lines of existing national systems, like those for agriculture.

The primary goals of national programs should be not collection of new information, but standardization, compilation and sharing of efforts by local, state, federal and academic researchers. Special efforts to fill the gaps in existing inventory and survey programs may be needed.

National Accounts should impose the minimum possible numbers of restrictions on researchers, but standard definitions and measurements for a minimum core of information types must be a priority. A consensus on such standards should not be imposed by any single entity but rather developed by managers and planners.

The existing chaos in outdoor recreation information management requires strong measures. National Recreation Accounts and National Biological Accounts systems are badly needed and can be accomplished with modest support from a national coordinating institution and the many existing data collecting agencies.

Failure to collect usable biological and recreation data, or to preserve current data for future reference, make adequate projection of trends in resources and demand speculative at best. To ensure realistic decisions and avoid wasteful errors in the future, we must begin to collect compatible information, to store and maintain it carefully and to share it with the widest possible audience.

What Kinds of Information Are Needed?

Values of Recreation

○ Economic impacts—revenues and benefits from employment, equipment sales, tourism services, related tax revenues from sales and employment

○ Social and health impacts—statistics and case studies on medical benefits of recreation, impacts on community pride, cohesiveness, crime prevention

○ Data on environmental benefits of recreation resources, including values of maintaining natural productivity of farmlands, wetlands and other open areas

Environmental/biological quality

○ Condition of and threats to natural resources, such as air and water quality

○ Status, locations, and condition of endangered species, special ecosystems and habitats

○ Status and condition of existing biological reserves, such as International Biosphere Reserves, Research Natural Areas, state reserves, private preserves

○ Land ownership information on key tracts meriting conservation attention

○ Sources of information such as museums, libraries, and other repositories where biological and ecological data may be obtained

○ Standardized classifications and inventories of biological community types and their best extant examples

○ Baseline ecological information on biological communities

Supply of recreation areas and facilities—private and public

○ Numbers and types of facilities and programs

○ Annual amounts of capital invested

○ Indices of critical resources lost and of the condition of both natural and built resources in recreation areas.

Demand/participation data

○ Visitation data for public and private areas

○ Trends in popularity of recreation activities

○ Market demand surveys

○ User satisfaction with facilities and programs

○ Indicators of awareness of recreation opportunities

○ Special needs of people with disabilities

○ Demographic and economic changes that will affect participation, such as leisure time and discretionary dollars

Marketplace Indexes (like those for inflation, GNP)
○ Measurements of average costs for recreation

○ Increases/decreases, sales of recreation equipment and stocks ("Dow-Jones Recreationals")

○ Amounts of operating costs recovered by public agencies.

The Pacific Northwest Recreation Data Committee

State and federal agencies in the Pacific Northwest (Idaho, Oregon and Washington with NPS, USFS, COE, BuRec, BLM, SCS) have established a shared data base of recreation and water resources information. The Pacific Northwest Recreation Data Committee was initiated in 1975 to conduct joint activity surveys using standard definitions and measurements. Sharing the costs of data collection and management has brought substantial savings to all participants. The common data base has proven cost effective and ensures valid planning, management and development decisions for participants' distinct recreation programs.

Data Bases and Their Management Grow in Importance

One such effort, discussed for some time, is a national data center for recreation. Such a center could provide leadership . . . by keeping abreast of developments in information management in general and within recreation in particular. The center could serve as a clearinghouse for this information, could research technological issues, standardization, collection methodologies and costs, and especially serve to encourage technology transfer and information utilization. The center could interact with providers, the recreation industry and the computer centers of our universities to develop information generation and dissemination capabilities comparable to those utilized in other fields.

EDWARD L. HOFFMAN
Illinois Dept. of Conservation

It should be noted that ample precedent exists for federal support of an industry's data collection and management program. The Agricultural Statistical Reporting Service, the Censuses of Agriculture, Mining and Manufacturing, and the Waterborne Commerce Statistics and Lock Performance Monitoring System are all examples of substantial federal investments in data collection and management for other industries.

WILLIAM J. HANSEN
U.S. Army Engineer Institute for
Water Resources

Computers, particularly microcomputers, are here to stay. A 1983 study by Stuyt and Siderelis (1984) found that more than one-third of the park and recreation agencies nationwide use microcomputers as opposed to less than 10 percent in 1979. At the same time, information for planning about consumers and their desires, supply of opportunities, land suitability and capability, conflicting resource uses, and other situational planning variables are increasingly becoming integral parts of recreation planning. Much of this information and its use are already mandated by legislation, policy or administrative guidelines.

These two phenomena mean that data bases and their management and analysis will grow in importance. Accuracy, reliability, ability to update, and spatial and non-spatial data analysis capabilities will be prerequisites for recreation planning of the future.

WILLIAM J. MCLAUGHLIN
and CHARLES C. HARRIS

Effective management of existing resources, and planning for resource expansion, require the ready availability of knowledge about resource capacities, trends in use, access, resource conditions. Investors and agencies find such information with great difficulty or not at all.

NO ACCIDENTAL SUCCESSES: REPORT OF
THE 1986 GOVERNOR'S CONFERENCE ON
NEW HAMPSHIRE'S OUTDOOR RECREATION FUTURE

Direction cannot be given without the necessary information on making decisions. Louisiana conducts very little research in the field of outdoor recreation. More research in this field is needed if Louisiana's outdoors is to survive the challenges of the future. The decisions of the '90s will be based on the information gathering of the '80s.

LOUISIANA'S OUTDOORS: ISSUES CRITICAL
TO OUTDOOR RECREATION IN LOUISIANA

Users Need Information

Cyclists need to know where to ride, how to find a local bike club, how to ride to local and national parks, and how to get safety training. Although there are more than 270 cross-country, regional and local bike maps available, most cyclists are not aware of them or do not know how to get them. State tourist offices are frequently unaware of the bicycling opportunities in the state and therefore cannot respond to requests for bicycling information. Most people in a state are likely not to know their state has a bike coordinator. This lack of information means that existing resources are not fully utilized.

CATHERINE G. MORAN
WILLIAM C. WILKINSON III
and JAMES FREMONT

Chapter 8

We Need a New Institution for Leadership

We recommend

• A Congressionally-authorized, private, non-profit outdoor institution, to stimulate grassroots leadership and promote innovation and excellence.

• Each state establish an entity to encourage innovation and investment in outdoor recreation.

• Congress and the Executive branch develop mechanisms to facilitate discussion and planning of national outdoor policy, such as a Congressional caucus and a presidential sub-cabinet council.

Who says we need a new recreation institution?

All across America, people told us that recreation is a critical part of their lives. Yet our actions do not seem to reflect the premiere importance which Americans of all ages in all parts of the country attach to recreation.

○ Fewer than ten percent of American cities have a policy statement recognizing recreation as being necessary for the public good.

○ Less than one cent of the federal dollar is spent on parks and recreation.

○ Less than one percent of the estimated $80 billion given away as charitable contributions in 1986 in this country was for conservation programs.

We believe there is a clear need for a central organization whose purpose would be to elevate the importance of recreation and the outdoors. We heard broad agreement that we do *not* want a new layer of bureaucracy, federal or otherwise. But a national level leadership institution could help promote recreation in public and private actions at all levels.

What is the new institution for?

The purpose of the institution would be to stimulate leadership, encourage innovation, and reward excellence in recreation delivery across the nation. It would help build partnerships, and stimulate investment in the outdoors. The institution would promote the importance of caring for our outdoor heritage. The institution could help spark the prairie fire.

We envision a decentralized and flexible organization. It would focus the spotlight on leadership, wherever it occurs, in communities across America. "America works community by community," says Commission Chairman Governor Lamar Alexander, "and from that emerges a national consensus."

The institution would facilitate and celebrate the actions of Americans all across the country, in geographic communities and organized communities of interest. By drawing attention to creative local action, the institution could help build a national consensus about the importance of the outdoors.

How will the institution spark the prairie fire?

The institution would encourage leadership, innovation and excellence primarily through two means: awarding grants and sharing information. A central purpose of the new institution must be to spotlight and spread exciting projects and fresh approaches.

The institution would award innovation grants to spark new ideas and promote building of partnerships. It would share these ideas with communities across the nation. If the citizens of Cripple Creek, Colorado, want to build a greenway, they can learn from the experiences of Jackson, Tennessee, on the South Fork of the Forked Deer River. If Revere, Massachusetts, has found a new way to build public/private partnerships to tend city parks, Newport, Oregon, should hear about it.

The institution would have a critical role in promoting an outdoor ethic. Through publications, forums, and other educational activities, the institution could help spread the word about the need to value and care for our outdoor resources. With grants and technical assistance, the national institution would help encourage communities to develop and promote their own outdoor code of ethics.

How would the grants program work?

Advisory citizens panels would ensure a grassroots orientation to the institution's programs. Grants could be awarded to government agencies (local, state, or federal), private non-profit organizations, or to private individuals.

There should be only two criteria for a government agency or non-profit organization: 1) the grant must be for a project related to outdoor recreation which is innovative and promotes excellence; and 2) the grant must be matched on at least a one-for-one basis.

By requiring a match, the institution would serve as a catalyst leveraging greater investment in the outdoors. Further, the recipient would be encouraged to form new partnerships with other agencies and the private sector. By making regional coalitions eligible for matching grants, the institution could encourage partnerships for regional planning and action for recreation and land conservation. Individuals would be eligible for awards for innovative projects already implemented.

What kinds of programs would receive grants?

There are many definitions of the term "innovation." For purposes of illustration, here are two innovative ideas which have been successful.

In Revere, Massachusetts, an elderly gentleman volunteered to maintain a ballfield. The mayor noticed that because the volunteer had a real sense of pride in his work, the ballfield was always in great condition. So the mayor proposed to form a Senior Citizens Park Maintenance Corps to maintain many of the city's parks.

The city applied for and received a matching grant from the federal government to implement the program. Twenty-five senior citizens were selected by lottery from a pool of 150 applicants. Each corps member was assigned to a specific park, for litter pick-up, weeding, planting, mowing the grass, and general maintenance work. The corps members worked four hours per weekday for 25 weeks and were paid $6 per hour.

After the federal grant was exhausted, the city continued to fund the entire program. The mayor told us at our Boston hearing that he believes the Senior Citizens Park Maintenance Corps is the most cost effective way of maintaining the "millions and millions of dollars that have been poured into our parks; and I think [it] probably could be transferred as a model to other communities throughout America."

In Portland, Oregon, citizens wanted to renovate a public square in the middle of town. They formed an organization called "Friends of Pioneer Square," to raise money from private sources for land acquisition and development.

"Friends" sold thousands of bricks which were personalized with the name of the donor, a relative, a friend, a pet or a business. The organization also "sold" major architectural features of the square, ranging from the amphitheater to drinking fountains, trees, and trash receptacles.

Today a non-profit corporation manages the square and has managers onsite. Use permits and concession agreements provide major sources of continuing revenue. On an average day thirty-five thousand people use the square—sitting, strolling, talking, eating, seeing and being seen. The square provides the opportunity for people in the center of a major city to enjoy the outdoors—and all of this was accomplished by the ingenuity and creative thinking of private citizens.

What will this institution look like?

A new national leadership institution for outdoor recreation should be a non-profit corporation chartered by Congress. It should be governed by a board of directors, appointed by the President of the United States, which has an appropriate and bipartisan membership reflecting the diversity of Americans Outdoors. Membership of the board should rotate frequently.

The board should appoint citizens advisory panels, whose function is to review grant proposals and make recommendations to the board for project funding. Membership of the advisory panels should also rotate frequently.

The institution should be funded by a ten percent allotment from the Land and Water Conservation Fund or its successor. Most of this money should go to innovation grants and awards, with administrative expenses held to a strict minimum.

What should states and others do?

The national institution should serve as a partner with other new and existing institutions in this field.

● We encourage all states to create an entity which would also stimulate innovation and the sharing of information about outdoor recreation. Each state should determine the institutional structure best suited to its needs. Minnesota, for instance, has established a 14-member bipartisan standing council of state legislators which recommends grants for innovative projects related to Minnesota's natural resources. Other states have established permanent outdoor commissions, for ongoing review of the state's outdoor recreation needs.

● Other existing institutions should become partners in an information network. The Soil Conservation Service and the Agricultural Extension Service, for example, both address problems in the outdoors in communities across America. These organizations, and others, represent a vast untapped resource for the preservation of outdoor recreation opportunities.

Here's what we think the federal government should do

● The responsibilities of outdoor policy are separated among several congressional committees. We recommend that a forum be established for discussion and opportunities for coordination of our national outdoors policy.

● There is a similar need for outdoors policy coordination within the executive branch. We recommend that the President establish a recreation sub-cabinet council, to provide the opportunity for the various agencies to discuss and plan actions that affect outdoors policy.

The new institution must spark creative local leadership, promote partnerships, and educate the public about the values of recreation and the outdoors. Its greatest challenge will be, according to Sheldon Coleman, "to develop living programs of sufficient flexibility to successfully cope with change. Its ultimate goal will be to promote or provide opportunities for all Americans to have meaningful experiences in the great outdoors, which will improve the quality of their lives."

The continued absence of a federal agency whose primary mission is provision of quality outdoor recreation nationwide is inconsistent with the national importance of recreation. There are several existing models for creating such an agency that will not require substantial new funding or establishment of a major new federal bureaucracy.

ED HOFFMAN
Office of the Governor
State of Illinois

While local initiative and decision-making will play an increasingly critical role in the conservation and enhancement of America's outdoors, a coherent national voice is needed to provide continuity and comprehension to the total effort. A national focus is needed to mobilize and channel public and private sentiment and support for the stewardship task ahead. . . .

As the President's Commission on Americans Outdoors faces the challenge at hand, we must ask ourselves if the future can allow the continued fragmented approach to meeting the recreation, open space, and visual resource needs of our people.

Isn't it time to search for a new and innovative leadership model? Isn't it time for a leadership model capable of directing not mandating, of sponsoring not enforcing, and capable of cooperation rather than stifling initiatives? Isn't it time to look for a new leadership model devoted to facilititating local initiative rather than creating bureaucratic power?

We think the Commission will agree that the answer to these questions is a resounding yes!

LANE L. MARSHALL
Chair, American Society of
Landscape Architects Task Force
on Americans Outdoors

Needed—A Single Voice for Common Concerns

The many and varied recreation interests in this country are fragmented and lack a single effective voice for common concerns. . . .

In a rapidly changing society, it is insufficient to assemble a national commission every twenty years to take up the cause of recreation for a brief period. The vital work of the President's Commission on Americans Outdoors should serve as the first step in an ongoing commitment to meeting the recreation needs of the nation.

The most appropriate entity for carrying this commitment forward into the future would be a congressionally-chartered, citizen-based organization open to citizens, professionals, associations and private sector interests. [It] would be charged with the following responsibilities:

1. Provide a unified voice to make a case for recreation and environmental values in the public marketplace of ideas.

2. Serve as a centralized information crossroads for reliable data about recreation needs and resources. An information barter system catering to the data needs of both private, commercial interests and government planners may be the best method to develop, expand and keep current such an information system.

3. Offer the public a simple, centralized source for detailed information about recreation opportunities. . . .

4. Coordinate the nation's many recreation-oriented agencies, organizations and interests into a cooperative network.

5. Provide an institutional memory to reinforce long-term consensus goals against threats from short-sighted public policy changes.

REPORT TO THE PRESIDENT'S COMMISSION
ON AMERICANS OUTDOORS
The Governor's Commission on
Tennesseans Outdoors

. . . .

Chapter 9

Strategies for Funding: Paying the Bills

We recommend

● Local, state and federal recreation and resources management agencies charge visitors fees to supplement regular appropriations, with the objective of recovering a reasonable portion of operations and maintenance costs.

● Congress strengthen existing laws which contribute to outdoor recreation in order to increase opportunities available to the public.

● The Land and Water Conservation Fund be succeeded by a dedicated trust—providing a minimum of $1 billion a year—to help pay for federal, state, and local land acquisition, and state and local facility development and rehabilitation.* Congress should consider creating an endowed trust which, over time, would be self-sustaining.

● States establish similar dedicated trusts to help meet their recreation and open space needs.

All across America, they told us: more money is needed—and Americans are willing to pay

From Orlando to Seattle, from Boston to Tempe, private citizens and public officials told us that *more* and *dependable* funding is necessary to maintain existing recreation facilities and programs and to meet stewardship commitments. Current available funds are inadequate to maintain existing program levels, and yearly fluctuations in funding levels create problems in planning and implementation.

---

* Commissioners Wallop and Vucanovich will not support any fixed level of federal funding, given the state of the federal deficit; funding and the method of funding, they feel, should be justified in the annual budget process.

Americans value the outdoors, and are willing to pay to use it. Evidence of the willingness to pay can be plainly seen in the dramatic expansion of private campgrounds, resorts, amusement parks, health clubs, and other enterprises over the last two decades.

The Market Opinion Research poll found that Americans also are willing to pay fees and taxes dedicated to outdoor recreation. But the public feels strongly that money collected for recreation fees should be returned to increase outdoor opportunities, not sent to the general treasury.

In virtually every city we visited, park and recreation officials and citizens told us that current funding is not adequate. Some examples:

○ William S. Briner, director, California State Parks: "Local government spending, particularly for parks and recreation, is at its lowest level in many years . . . The state government alone cannot shoulder this burden. It can, however, share the burden if the federal government can help."

○ The Commission on Minnesotans Outdoors: "In 1985, some 200 local park and recreation agencies competed for $457,000 in grants from the Legislative Commission on Minnesota Resources; funds were sufficient to fund only 15 projects."

○ Gerald F. Guidroz, assistant secretary, Louisiana Office of State Parks: "Louisiana has a $14 million backlog in local or regional park and recreation projects."

○ Jon P. Soderberg, Monterey County, California, parks director: Monterey County has a $2.5 million recreation facilities maintenance backlog, and "there's no funding source on the horizon to recover this backlog."

○ Margaret Gorski, private citizen: "Facilities managed by all federal agencies responsible for recreation management are rapidly deteriorating due [in part] to inadequate levels of maintenance dollars and support."

I think politicians sometimes badly underestimate the true feelings that Americans have for the land.

REPRESENTATIVE MORRIS UDALL

Providing outdoor recreation costs money

In 1985, local and state parks and recreation departments and federal land managing agencies spent $10.7 billion specifically on recreation. Most of that was for operations and facilities maintenance; smaller portions were for acquisition and facilities development and rehabilitation.

This, however, is not the whole spending picture. State fish and game agencies, and a host of other state and federal agencies, also spent money on the outdoors. In the case of fish and wildlife expenditures, a significant portion was contributed by hunters and fishermen in license fees, wildlife stamps, donations, and excise taxes on their equipment.

Other agencies also helped provide recreation opportunities. Departments of transportation built boat ramps; the National Oceanic and Atmospheric Administration managed marine and estuarine sanctuaries; environmental agencies worked at maintaining air and water quality, benefiting fishing, swimming and outdoor enjoyment in general.

Spending strictly for parks and recreation nationwide, however, amounts to less than one percent of total annual government outlays. We believe that local and state governments and Congress must acknowledge their investments and stewardship responsibilities by providing the money, or exploring reasonable alternatives, to adequately maintain recreation facilities and resources.

How will we pay the bill?

In looking for money to increase opportunities, a good place to start is with the user.

In our hearings across the country, people said they were willing to pay more for recreation on public lands. If recreation is to have the management attention it deserves, recreationists will have to pay more for the benefits they receive. Currently much of the costs of providing recreation on federal lands is borne by all taxpayers, not just the beneficiaries.

Americans are willing to pay to enjoy the outdoors. But they want their dollars spent on the sites and resources they use. Fees collected at recreation areas should supplement regular appropriations for maintenance, and perhaps operations. In this way, money collected from visitors is returned to them in the form of better facilities and services.

A number of local and state recreation agencies, in part because of voter-mandated restrictions on taxes and spending, are increasing the portion of their budgets financed from recreationist sources. Certain state and local recreation and park agencies—the New Hampshire state park system; the Ventura County, California, park department; the City of Kettering, Ohio, parks and recreation department, among others—are approaching self-sufficiency in their operations through politically pragmatic and well-articulated fee policies.

Hunters and fishermen serve as an example of how it can work. For more than 50 years they have contributed directly to the costs of providing game and fish through license fees, excise taxes, use stamps, and access fees. In New Mexico, for example, hunters, fishermen, and trappers who pursue their activities on the Lincoln National Forest and adjacent BLM lands purchase a $5.50 stamp, proceeds from which go to manage habitat on the federal lands.

It is appropriate for public providers to develop sensible, locally-determined fee policies aimed at recovering a percentage of operations and maintenance costs. For some states and local units of government, self-sufficiency will not be achievable. Individual decisionmakers, including Congress, should determine reasonable objectives and aggressively seek means to reach them. Innovative mechanisms for fee collection linking the for-profit and nonprofit sectors, volunteers, and a variety of direct user sources with regular appropriations could accomplish the task at hand.

Fees for entrance to and use of federal areas have been controversial. Given the federal budget deficit and user willingness to pay, Congress should enact legislation allowing the federal land managing agencies to collect reasonable entrance and recreation fees to supplement regular appropriations; offsetting increasing operations and maintenance costs.

Recreation fees should be initiated to partially offset the costs of providing recreation opportunities where the uses are costly to provide and demand exceeds supply. Examples include campground occupancy fees, white-water rafting permits, and hunting and fishing stamps. Existing recreation fee structures should be examined for comparability with other local providers.

We support legislation returning all fees to the collecting agency. Some fees should be available agency-wide, with a portion to be used at the area where the fees were collected.

A distinctive auto sticker or shoulder patch might also be sold to the public. This would give the public an opportunity to demonstrate with their pocketbooks their support for outdoor programs. The federal duck stamp program illustrates this concept—many non-hunters purchase stamps.

In addition to fees for entering and using federal lands, agencies also . receive money in return for use of the land or other resources through leases, licenses, permits, and concessions. These receipts should be returned to the agency managing the land that is impacted, and used for resources management projects.

Needed: an array of programs and money

Meeting the diverse needs of Americans will require a number of creative programs. No one program will be sufficient to meet these needs.

As the commission looked at outdoor recreation programs across the nation, we found a variety of imaginative programs paired with equally imaginative sources of special funding. Some were applied narrowly, to fund a single program; others provided general support for programs and facilities. One state, Minnesota, has a wide-ranging grant program designed to encourage innovation and experimentation by state, local and private recreation providers, largely funded by state cigarette taxes.

This type of responsiveness to special needs and employing sources of revenue deemed appropriate at the local, state and federal levels must continue and expand. It is clear that flexibility is needed to cope with regional differences. What works in Seattle may not work in Austin.

Existing laws should be examined

There are existing laws that, upon implementation, modification or renewal, could make substantial contributions to the provision of outdoor recreation opportunities. They include:

The Wallop-Breaux Amendments to the Federal Aid in Sport Fish Restoration Act—presently, federal and state motorfuel taxes are paid on fuel used for a variety of non-highway recreational purposes: 1.08 percent of all federal motorfuel tax receipts are now transferred from the Highway Trust Fund to the Wallop-Breaux Trust Fund to aid fishing and boating. This provision, due to expire in Fiscal Year 1989, should be reauthorized.

Further, federal motorfuel taxes collected on fuel used for other non-highway recreation purposes, including those paid by snowmobilers and ORV enthusiasts, should be quantified and then made available for recreation purposes. Most states already earmark motorboat fuel taxes and many earmark other non-highway recreation fuel collections; we believe all should.

The Sikes Act—enacted to promote hunting, wildlife and recreation programs on military, National Forest and Public Lands. Full implementation could spur provision of access for the public to these lands.

The Urban Park and Recreation Recovery Program (UPRRP)—established in 1978 to assist local governments in restoring dilapidated or outdated recreation facilities and provide innovation grants to stimulate new ideas. An exciting concept, it was never fully funded.

The Reclamation Act of 1902—receipts from public land sales, mineral leases and oil and gas royalties go to irrigation projects. Funds could be authorized to provide access, fish, wildlife and resource management, and recreation in the western United States.

The Highway Trust Fund—excise taxes on motor fuels and lubricants support highway system repair and expansion. Funds could also promote scenic byways, bike trails and repair of park and forest system roads.

The Historic Preservation Fund—enacted to protect and enhance historic resources. Recreation and cultural and historic preservation share many of the same sites and resources. Consideration could also be given to converting this fund to a trust.

To provide for the future: improve the land and water conservation fund

Since its inception in 1965, the Land and Water Conservation Fund (LWCF) has enabled localities and states to acquire 2.8 million acres of recreation lands and waters. Some $3 billion in federal LWCF funds has been matched by local and state money and private sector contributions.

Another 2.9 million acres were added to national parks, forests, wildernesses, refuges, and BLM recreation areas.

Initially authorized at $100 million annually, the LWCF reached its highest level of funding in 1978, when Congress increased the authorization to $900 million annually and appropriated $805 million for the year.

Since 1978, LWCF appropriations have been on a sharp decline. Beginning in 1982, most of the money has gone to additions to the federal lands and waters systems. In 1986, localities and states received just one-sixth of 1978 funding levels.

The Land and Water Conservation Fund is based on a simple principle: reinvestment. A portion of the receipts from the sale of a nonrenewable resource owned by all Americans—oil and gas from the Outer Continental Shelf—is reinvested in permanent assets for future generations.

The LWCF expires in 1989. It is time to consider changes in the fund that will assure a dependable source of money for localities, states, and federal agencies to meet the nation's outdoor needs into the next century.

The changes should be based on the following principles.

● At an *absolute minimum*, the fund should generate $1 billion a year.

● It should be a *dedicated* trust—an identified, dependable source of money (available until expended) reserved specifically for meeting the nation's outdoors needs.

● Revenues from the trust could come from a variety of sources, beginning with a fixed percentage of offshore oil receipts.

● The trust should retain the basic purposes of the LWCF—federal land acquisition and state and local acquisition and facility development. It should also be extended to support state and local facilities rehabilitation.

● Local and state governments should be required to match the federal contribution. The federal share might be adjusted to encourage states and localities to form partnerships to implement some special programs, such as greenways, growth-shaping achievements or stream protection.

● Congress should establish a low- or no-interest revolving loan program available to states and localities.

● The trust should fund the new outdoor recreation institution through a ten percent allotment of its yearly income. Most of this money should be for innovation grants and awards, with administrative expenses held to a strict minimum.

● In order to maximize the potential of a national trust and to accomplish their own individual outdoor goals, states should create dedicated trusts.

Toward an endowment

Once the dedicated trust is in place and functioning, we urge Congress to consider the creation of an endowed trust for the outdoors, sufficiently capitalized to return the minimum of $1 billion annually. An endowed fund would earn its own revenue from interest on investment. A large principal, inviolate except for reinvestment, could generate sufficient interest to sustain a substantial program base and still perpetuate itself. In a budget context, an endowment has two advantages:

○ Revenues tapped to create the principal could have a provision for sunset after a predetermined period, or be diverted to other uses;

○ There would be no need to continually replenish a fund from general revenues to maintain a level of available assets.

Funds for the endowment could come from a variety of sources, with Outer Continental Shelf receipts being the primary source.

A List of Potential Funding Sources

We now tap many sources to help pay the nation's outdoor recreation bill. In addition, the Commission received many suggestions for potential new sources at the local, state, and national levels. Following is a partial list of present sources of funding and some potential new sources which might be considered by Americans to support programs for the outdoors at the local, state, and federal levels.

○ General appropriations. This is the traditional way of funding public programs. General tax revenues are allocated to specific activities.

○ Outer Continental Shelf revenues. Most of the money for the Land and Water Conservation Fund now comes from revenues from production of oil and gas on federally-owned areas on the Outer Continental Shelf. This source, and severance taxes in particular, support the concept of reinvesting non-renewable resources in permanent assets for future generations.

○ Dedication of existing revenues and revenues from new mineral development. Fees on new development of non-renewable resources such as oil and gas, minerals, and geothermal energy could help finance recreation opportunities. Eleven states have successfully used such taxes for recreation and conservation purposes.

○ Sale of surplus federal property. The Land and Water Conservation Fund currently receives proceeds from sales of surplus federal property and land, which pay for creation of recreation opportunities.

○ Excise taxes modeled on the Pittman-Robertson and Dingell-Johnson programs. Money collected from excise taxes on sporting arms and ammunition under the 1937 Federal Aid in

Wildlife Restoration Act—more commonly known after its authors as Pittman-Robertson—pays for wildlife restoration programs. Dingell-Johnson does the same for fisheries and boating programs. Similar taxes might be feasible for other activities.

○ Recreation enhancement taxes. Based on the principle of agricultural marketing orders, manufacturers of different kinds of recreation equipment might contribute voluntarily to a fund that benefits the activity for which the equipment is used.

○ Summer gasoline tax. A modest tax on gasoline sold during the months when most recreational travel occurs could be applied to enhance pleasure driving, our most popular outdoor activity.

○ Highway Trust Fund appropriations. As the Interstate Highway system is completed, money from the Highway Trust Fund might be used to maintain existing scenic highways. This might include better directional and information signs and development of scenic vista and interpretive turnouts.

○ Revenue bonds. Now used locally, a national bond issue would give Americans the opportunity to invest in the future of the nation's outdoor estate.

○ Rechannel or support existing sources. Examples include the Sikes Act and Reclamation Act.

○ Recreation fees. Fees for recreation activity are based on the principle that those who benefit directly pay for the activity. The public now pays for many recreation activities, and we were told often that the public is willing to pay for many activities which historically have been provided without charge, if receipts are used to benefit the activity and not simply applied to the general treasury.

○ Public-private partnerships, cooperative agreements, challenge grants, expanded concession agreements. There are examples by the hundreds where people and their governments have entered into agreements which blend public and private profit and nonprofit money and muscle to achieve results quickly and efficiently.

○ Volunteers. Individual citizen volunteers build and maintain trails, conduct interpretive programs, and provide many other services which supplement the paid staff at many recreation areas. With a modest investment in supervision, volunteers can enhance recreation programs and opportunities at low cost.

○ Donations. Communities and people from all walks of life have responded with generosity to support worthy projects. A number of agencies and parks have successfully solicited donations of money and equipment.

○ Development/Impact Fees. San Francisco's Downtown Plan requires that developers provide public open space with new construction and adds a fee of $2 per developed foot for park acquisition.

○ Land Transfer Taxes. The State of Maryland assesses a 1/2 of one percent transfer tax on all new real estate sales which generates approximately $50 million annually for open space acquisition.

○ Mandatory Land Dedication. California cities can require developers to dedicate three to five acres of open space for every 1,000 people the development will accommodate.

○ Billboard laws. The state of Tennessee uses billboard permit fees to acquire scenic easements along highways.

○ Non-road fuel funds. Eleven states channel a portion of the state's gasoline taxes to snowmobile programs.

○ Dedicated sales taxes. Citizens of Missouri voted to devote one-tenth of one percent of the state sales tax to support the state park system.

○ Special recreation taxing districts. In Illinois, special park and recreation districts provide a voter-supported tax base for recreation.

○ Registration fees. Through California's Green Sticker program, off-highway vehicle area access, maintenance and information publications are supported in part by fees paid for off-highway vehicle registration.

○ Lotteries. Colorado city and state parks receive $14^{1}/_2$ cents of each dollar spent on the state lottery.

○ Cigarette/liquor/accommodations taxes. Minnesota funds innovative resources programs from a 2 cents per pack tax on cigarettes.

○ Income tax checkoffs. Some 31 states permit voluntary contributions to support non-game wildlife programs.

○ Bottle bills. Nine states have reduced litter by passing bottle deposit laws.

○ Surcharge on license fees. New Hampshire asks its hunters and fishermen to become "Super Sportsmen" and voluntarily contribute to state fish and game programs by paying a surcharge on the basic license fee.

Trends and Estimates

○ In real dollars, direct government spending for parks and recreation has increased moderately since 1977. However, an analysis by the Conservation Foundation of state park and recreation budgets indicated that after adjustment for inflation, state spending for parks and recreation decreased 17 per cent from 1980 to 1983. By contrast, state spending for all programs, after adjustment for inflation, fell only 0.4 per cent.

○ The federal budget's Natural Resources and Environment Account, which includes land, air, water, and recreation programs, nearly doubled in actual dollars—from $7.3 billion to $13.3 billion—between 1975 and 1985. When adjusted for inflation, however, the account actually lost ground.

○ The U.S. Forest Service reports a sharp decline—from 74 to 29 percent—from 1978 to 1985 in the percent of recreation facilities at the standard level of maintenance, while the dollar amount of deferred maintenance has more than doubled, to $297 million.

○ A coalition of conservation organizations identified a need of $326.7 million for federal acquisition of critical wildlife habitat, lands previously authorized for acquisition where there are willing sellers, and lands where owners are entitled to court-established payments.

○ The National Recreation and Park Association estimated local parks facilities rehabilitation needs from 1981 to 1985 to be $4.26 billion.

○ State recreation officials responding to a 1986 survey estimated their needs for federal Land and Water Conservation Fund assistance for the next three years at $1.7 billion. This sum was predicated on the availability of state and local matching money.

○ The Fish and Wildlife Service estimates that the nation will need to spend $500 million within the U.S. over the next 15 years to meet the terms of a recently-signed U.S.-Canada wetlands protection pact.

○ The state of New Jersey, which has acquired 330,000 acres of open space in the last 20 years under its Green Acres program, says it still has a deficit of 400,000 acres.

○ The National Park Service and U.S. Forest Service report a $1 billion backlog in facilities rehabilitation. The Park Service needs $75 million a year for maintenance to stem deterioration.

○ Fairfax County, Virginia, reports that it will have to spend $55 million for parkland to keep up with population growth through the rest of this century.

○ The cost of acquiring two ranches that could serve as the core of the proposed Tallgrass Prairie Park in Oklahoma is estimated at $15 million to $30 million.

It was impossible in the short time of our studies to arrive at an exact figure of what is needed for outdoor recreation at the local, state, and federal levels. In fact, the exact amount probably is incalculable, given a growing demand and increased expectations. But it is, in the words of Commissioner Stuart Northrop, "tremendous."

Agricultural Marketing Orders

In the agricultural and tourism fields, federal and state governments have helped producers of goods and providers of services generate monies to support legitimate programs affecting those industries. Dozens of Agricultural Marketing Orders, for commodities as diverse as oranges and wheat, and hundreds of room tax assessments, exist across the nation because of voluntary industry actions. Typically, a majority or super-majority of those potentially affected by the tax must agree to its imposition, at which point the tax becomes binding on all business of that type.

Enabling legislation along the lines of the Agricultural Marketing Orders Act for recreation industries would stimulate public-private partnerships and offer new flexibility in pursuing the strategy of increased financial reliance upon those who are direct beneficiaries of services and facilities. Moreover, such an option would encourage manufacturers of recreational products to understand the needs and use patterns of those ultimately using those products. Finally, the program could produce new revenues to help public agencies meet new recreational needs; a tax on a new, fast-growing activity, such as off-road bicycling, could help manage the new activity and be used for developing trails and other facilities.

LWCF Support and Leveraging Principle

The mere fact of having federal money available enticed the State of Minnesota to put up significant amounts of money in addition to the federal money. The Land and Water Conservation Fund made it easier for the State to provide additional money for both state and local facilities . . . by providing state and local facilities, we provide a stimulus to local economies.

REPRESENTATIVE DOUGLAS CARLSON
Minnesota

The Land and Water Conservation Fund has been a catalyst in promoting State and local government in dealing with growth and development impacts as they relate to recreation and other natural resources. The integration of recreational services into the growing communities of Utah helps to insure the quality of life that Utah citizens see.

UTAH ANNUAL REPORT, 1981

Reinvestment in Resources

I believe it is our obligation to offer future generations tangible benefits from the sale of . . . one-time oil and gas revenues.

FORMER ARIZONA GOVERNOR BRUCE BABBITT

Beginning in 1965, Congress saw the gradual deterioration of such facilities and the threatened loss of State and local parks as a national problem. Through the Federal Land and Water Conservation Fund, the Urban Park Recovery Act and other programs, Congress met this problem head-on. The most useful of the Federal park programs, it should be emphasized, derived their revenues not from income taxes but rather from the sale of leases to oil companies for offshore drilling. Congress set this

*money aside, mostly for parks because it felt that the American people,
in trading off a valued asset, were entitled to one of equal value in return.*
ORIN LEHMAN
New York Commissioner of Parks
and Recreation
New York Times, 1981

The Arkansas Experience

These passages are extracts from an Executive Update, 1985, prepared by the Arkansas Department of Parks and Tourism for the Governor.

o To set the stage, in the past few years the Arkansas State Parks System has seen:

o The Corps of Engineers close selected recreation areas and open others only on weekends.

o The National Park Service and U.S. Forest Service reduce the number of personnel and services offered to the public.

o Many county and city recreation departments reduce programs and services due to budget cutbacks.

o The effect of inflation on family income and high gasoline prices causing people to stay closer to home for recreation.

o In the last 10 years, visitation increased 156%, to 6.1 million; in the last 40 years, the park land base only expanded from 9,000 to 43,000 acres, not quite a five-fold increase.

These factors have placed even greater demands on an already overused State Parks System. Visitors demand clean, comfortable, safe park experiences, complete with the necessary facilities and services. We cannot just shut our doors when we have inadequate funding.

o Inadequate funding for operations and maintenance may be the most critical issue facing Arkansas State Parks today. Appropriations for operations and maintenance, 1979-1985, remained relatively constant, but when adjusted for inflation, have actually declined nearly 30 percent.

o Commitments to revenue generation resulted in a system that earned $7 million in 1985 (nearly nine times the 1972 collections). Since 1979, total revenues increased 167 percent and now amount to 49.9 percent of the operating budget (9th nationally in money generated in a system that ranks 39th in total acreage).

o Renovation which maintains the integrity and style of the facilities, while improving visitor flow and service, is sorely needed. Regular maintenance is being done, but cyclic maintenance, such as road repair or sewage system maintenance, is being postponed due to lack of funding.

o The Capital Improvements Program Budget was essentially not funded for 1983-85. Federal funding through matching grants for park acquisition and development is extremely limited. Even this limited amount cannot be used by State Parks because of lack of state funds to match it.

o Federal funding played a major role in the overall development of the present Parks System. The total contribution over the last ten years from federal sources was $7.65 million, or 40 percent of our total construction budget. In short, without federal assistance, [Arkansas] would never have been able to develop the present system, one of the best in the country.

o [We propose] a six-year, $47.8 million improvements program—

"Is it worth investing $47.8 million in the State Parks System? What has been proposed here will not get any cheaper in the future. Funds appropriated now will buy us far more in thea next six years than funds appropriated ten years from now the needs will still remain."
One recommendation to meet these needs is to investigate alternative funding sources (other than [general funds]) in order to provide an adequate budget, including:

—State Parks Foundation;

—Surcharges on Recreation Equipment and/or Recreation Vehicle Registrations;

—Environmental Taxes;

—Excise Tax on Solid Mineral and Liquid Fuels;

—Sales Tax; and,

—Bond Program.

Appendixes

. . . .

Summary of Key Issues and Recommendations from State Assessments and Reports Prepared for The Commission and from Current Statewide Comprehensive Outdoor Recreation Plans

Issues identified in state assessments

In August 1985, Commission Chairman, Governor Lamar Alexander, called for the governors of all states to form commissions or advisory groups to examine their own outdoor recreation needs, opportunities and problems. This call was aimed primarily at stimulating direct action at the state and local levels, but it also provided invaluable insights on state, local and private concerns for the President's Commission. Twenty-five states responded by establishing commissions or holding governor's forums in response to this call; at least 2,000 individuals testified at hearings or participated in meetings and conferences sponsored by the states in 1986. Another seven states had such groups already in existence or had held conferences in 1984 or 1985 in anticipation.

A total of 32 states submitted reports from their commissions, surveys or forums to aid in the preparation of this report. Under the auspices of the National Association of State Outdoor Recreation Liaison Officers (NASORLO), all 50 states also submitted summaries of priority needs and problems identified in their latest Statewide Recreation Plans (SCORPs). This information was compiled for NASORLO by the Green Acres Program office of the New Jersey Department of Environmental Protection and received by the Commission in May 1986.

The focus of state and local assessment materials covered the major issues addressed in the Commission's report: funding, roles of public and private recreation providers; protecting outdoor resources and environmental quality, land acquisition, recreation facility and service needs, problems of special populations, needs for better planning, research and information management, public and private partnerships, public ethics and stewardship and liability concerns.

The hundreds of pages of State Assessment materials are not published in their entirety. The following overview of State Assessments is a summary of narrative submissions, not a strict statistical analysis. Therefore, numeric data on the number of states dealing with the major issues are provided only as indicators of relative frequency of mention in the various state submissions and do not necessarily reflect all priorities of the states.

Funding recreation resources

To continue to meet the growing needs at the state and local level, Louisiana must have a stable, recurring, long-term funding source such as the Land and Water Conservation Fund Program to assure that the concept of a nationwide network of parks will continue to flourish. The provision of a national-state-local system of park acquisition and development has been a success where many other programs have failed. To discontinue such a successful program of benefit to so many will negate the positive strides in recreation increase made over the past 20 years.

LOUISIANA OUTDOORS: ISSUES CRITICAL
TO OUTDOOR
RECREATION IN LOUISIANA
June 1986

The Land and Water Conservation Fund, scheduled to end in 1989, has been critical to development of an outdoor recreation system. Our future financing needs will be as vital as those of the past: the LWCF program should be continued.

RECOMMIT TO RECREATION: A REPORT
ON MINNESOTA'S FUTURE OUTDOOR
RECREATION NEEDS
June 1986

North Dakota is trying to make progress at a time when the availability of funds to meet our recreational needs is limited. There is a need for increasing numbers of well-qualified recreation and park personnel and for better dissemination and distribution of technical information and assistance to local communities. Our financial needs in outdoor recreation are significant, and we recommend development of a federal matching grant program to provide an incentive for cooperative efforts and to provide outdoor recreation opportunities by both state and local agencies.

GOVERNOR'S REPORT ON NORTH DAKOTA
RECREATION
April 1986

The Land and Water Conservation Fund (LWCF) should be either maintained or replaced by a similar program such as a Natural Assets Trust Fund. Proceeds generated from such a fund should be used for the maintenance and development of recreational opportunities. The current policy of diverting LWCF monies to the General Fund is unacceptable.

Many embraced the concept of user fees. User fees administered at the state or local level could take the form of an annual pass. Additional user fees could also be charged for specific recreational opportunities provided that revenues were returned to benefit that same opportunity. User fees must not be set so high as to discriminate against the poor. Low cost opportunities should continue to be available.

REPORT ON GOVERNOR'S FORUM ON
MONTANANS OUTDOORS
February 1986

The most frequently mentioned problem at the Public Workshops was the need for more money for various recreational purposes. Both recreation providers and users expressed the concern that without a constant and stable flow of dollars, recreation managers could not maintain the quality of existing recreation facilities and services, much less try to expand to address unmet and/or future needs.

PENNSYLVANIA'S OUTDOORS: CRITICAL
RECREATION ISSUES IN THE KEYSTONE STATE
Report to PCAO
July 1986

The most frequently mentioned concern (48 states) was for establishment of continuing, stable sources of funding to support recreation programs:

o "rehabilitation, operation and maintenance" were the most frequently identified funding needs followed closely by new development. More than half the states, however, cited major needs for protection of open space, natural lands or historic areas that could involve funding of land acquisition as one protection measure.

o two-thirds of state assessments say that federal matching funds for land acquisition, development, rehabilitation and planning are essential components of continued, stable funding sources. Most praise the accomplishments of earlier federal recreation grant programs (LWCF and UPARR) and imply that these successful federal commitments have been curtailed prematurely.

More than half the state submissions support the notion of a national trust fund to guarantee funding availability on a year-to-year basis. Others call for multi-year appropriations under existing (LWCF and UPARR) authorities to let states and localities plan their expenditures systematically and reduce the uncertainty currently caused by large fluctuations in annual appropriations. Many assessments also recommend state trusts or other dedicated state funding sources for both state areas and assistance to local parks.

By government level, local or "close-to-home" recreation funding needs were most frequently identified as critical. Rehabilitation of older local parks is a top priority.

The need for equitable increases in fees for park visitors was specifically emphasized by more than half the states; this point was usually tied to findings of "user willingness to pay" when entrance and user fees are visibly used for park operations, maintenance or improvement.

Many western states and others with large federal land holdings complained about recent cutbacks in management funds for recreation in these areas.

Institutions and partnerships

The many and varied recreation interests in this country are fragmented and lack a single effective voice for common concerns. . . .

In a rapidly changing society, it is insufficient to assemble a national commission every twenty years to take up the cause of recreation for a brief period. The vital work of the President's Commission on Americans Outdoors should serve as the first step in an ongoing commitment to meeting the recreation needs of the nation.

The most appropriate entity for carrying this commitment forward into the future would be a congressionally-chartered, citizen-based organization open to citizens, professionals, associations, and private sector interests. [It] would be charged with the following responsibilities:

1. Provide a unified voice to make a case for recreation and environmental values in the public marketplace of ideas.

2. Serve as a centralized information crossroads for reliable data about recreation needs and resources. An information barter system catering to the data needs of both private, commercial interests and government planners may be the best method to develop, expand and keep current such an information system.

3. Offer the public a simple, centralized source for detailed information about recreation opportunities. . . .

4. Coordinate the nation's many recreation-oriented agencies, organizations and interests into a cooperative network.

5. Provide an institutional memory to reinforce long-term consensus goals against threats from short-sighted public policy changes.

REPORT TO THE PRESIDENT'S COMMISSION
ON AMERICANS OUTDOORS
The Governor's Commission on
Tennesseans Outdoors
April 1986

The use of the Community Schools program is one of the most effective tools available to local governments for the provision of parks and recreation. It provides an effective use of tax dollars and is of great benefit to local communities.

Participants felt that the Community Schools program must be strengthened and maintained.

NORTH CAROLINA GOVERNOR'S
CONFERENCE ON AMERICANS OUTDOORS
February 1986

The commission recommends legislation to establish, in the Executive Branch, a permanent Maine Advisory Commission on Outdoor Recreation (MACOR), comprised of eminent Maine citizens appointed by the Governor, subject to approval of the legislature.

REPORT OF FINDINGS AND
RECOMMENDATIONS
Maine
Governor's Commission on
Outdoor Recreation
August 1986

Generally, the respondents felt that more cooperation and coordination must exist on all levels of government regarding outdoor recreation opportunities. The implementation of more joint-use agreements could be considered. This would include better use of schools by the general public.

RESULTS OF SURVEY ON RECREATION
ISSUES
Florida Park and
Recreation Association,
1986

It is in the public interest for agencies to cooperatively work together to promote efficiency and economy. Unfortunately, this does not always occur. Agency directives and goals sometimes conflict, a bit like neighbors who can't decide on the kind of fence to build. . . .

The President's Commission should:

○ Recommend that the President appoint a special local, state, federal, private review team to sort out roles, identify overlaps in responsibilities and suggest guidelines to promote efficiency and economy in the nation's outdoor recreation system.

○ Reaffirm that the federal government has a clear role in outdoor recreation that goes beyond property ownerships and includes research and data gathering; coordination of recreation providers; establishment and maintenance of environmental standards; and technical assistance and support.

> o *Reaffirm the importance of the federal government in maintain-*
> *ing, developing and protecting recreation resources of regional and na-*
> *tional significance.*
>
> RESULTS OF OREGONIANS OUTDOORS
> CONFERENCE
> February 1986

Forty-six states identified needs for better cooperation among public agencies in resource planning, in providing recreation areas and services.

The majority of assessments call for an increased federal role in recreation advocacy, technical assistance, data collection and sharing efforts. Proposed mechanisms vary:

o A new, national institution (public or quasi-public) with authority to promote recreation and resource goals, assist state and local recreation efforts and coordinate the programs of federal land managers and non-recreation managers (like Housing and Urban Development, Defense, Transportation and the Interstate Commerce Commission) to ensure maximum efficiency and recreation benefits from their programs.

o A national information clearinghouse to give states, localities and federal agencies active technical assistance through shared data on recreation supply, demand and benefits of outdoor recreation as well as to share information on ways to solve common management problems.

o A return, at a minimum, to a federal agency like the old Bureau of Outdoor Recreation, which served as a national focal point for recreation policy, planning, financial and technical assistance.

o Increased federal technical assistance, particularly on state and local programs to establish scenic rivers and trails.

Almost half the states identify cooperation between local recreation agencies and independent school authorities as a priority partnership objective because of extraordinary opportunities for shared facilities and programs.

A third of the states supported the idea of state institutions (coordinating councils, advisory groups, reorganized agencies) to improve promotion of recreation values and intergovernmental cooperation at the state and local levels.

Western and mountain states are particularly concerned about failure of federal land managers to coordinate recreation and tourism policies with state concerns in these areas. These complaints are often linked to explicit or implicit perceptions that the National Forests, Bureau of Land Management areas and other multiple-use public lands give too low a priority to recreation in their policies and management actions. These states frequently call for better mechanisms to ensure involvement in recreation and tourism-related decisions on the public lands.

States also point to critical needs for better partnerships among all levels of government in planning for lands and developments of regional significance, particularly those affecting recreation resources that cross political and land ownership boundaries. Emphasis on regional planning needs is sometimes on the need for interlocal efforts to control development impacts and sometimes on state and federal cooperation in resource management.

Public-private partnership opportunities were highlighted in more than half the submissions. Problems and recommendations in this area fall into four main categories:

○ Encouraging private landowners to open or reopen their lands for dispersed recreation uses (hunting, hiking, nature study);

○ Providing mechanisms and incentives for greater private involvement in protection of open spaces, scenic and natural areas from unsuitable or destructive development (land trusts, agriculture and open space tax districts, coordinated development and zoning plans);

○ Increasing incentives and/or reducing disincentives (public liability requirements, short lease periods) for entrepreneurial investments in recreation facilities on private lands or in public recreation areas (e.g., skiing, boating, campground and resort developments);

○ Working more systematically with non-profit user and conservation groups to provide facilities and services on public lands (see also "Volunteers" under *Recreation Workforce*).

Protecting natural systems/reducing threats to parks

We must preserve and manage the "wild" and natural areas still available to us, including our Natural and Scenic rivers, our wetlands, our prairies, and other critical environments. This management should strive to maintain a balance between development of resources for current economic demands and the preservation of critical environmental resources.

ARKANSANS OUTDOORS: ISSUES CRITICAL
TO RECREATION IN THE NATURAL STATE
REPORT TO ARKANSAS GOVERNOR AND
PCAO
February 1986

The only component of the federal Wild and Scenic River System in Arizona is a 39.5 mile segment of the Verde River between Camp Verde and Horseshoe Dam, designated in 1984. Many other stretches of streams in Arizona qualify under the Act. . . . Generally, federal agencies and the Administration have been slow to formulate recommendations for additions to the system, although the Forest Service has recommended the upper Salt for inclusion.

The Wild and Scenic Rivers Act also allows states to designate and protect rivers as wild, scenic or recreational under state law. . . . Arizona has no state wild and scenic river system to date.

"Recommendations. . . .

(32) The State should press vigorously for congressional designation of all additional qualifying Arizona rivers into the National Wild and Scenic River System.

(33) The Governor should propose legislation to create a state wild and scenic river system. State Parks should conduct a rivers study of freeflowing stretches in the state, including both those nominated by the Heritage Conservation and Recreation Service and any others that have not been identified to date for inclusion in a state wild and scenic river system."

ARIZONANS' RECREATION NEEDS ON
FEDERAL LANDS
Governor's Task Force on
Recreation on Federal Lands
June 1986

More than forty states indicated that protecting specific natural resources or resource systems is a pressing need.

Concerns about water access and protection are common to "wet" eastern and midwestern states as well as arid western ones. Needs and recommendations to control development of scenic rivers, coastal shorelines, lakes and wetlands and reduce pollution of lakes and streams were expressed by some 30 states.

Natural heritage programs for maintenance of ecological (biological) diversity were often discussed. A number of states cited specific needs for inventories and studies of natural systems to improve decision-making on their protection.

Thirty-five states indicate needs for additional land and water acquisitions to meet current or anticipated recreation needs. The most common resource acquisition concern (29 states) is for increasing public access to rivers and other water areas for swimming, boating and fishing. Increased hunting lands, expansions of existing park areas to reduce overcrowding and acquisitions to reduce threats to recreation resources also get frequent mention.

Protecting resources is frequently related to public education about the importance and values of natural systems. Techniques to increase public awareness include school and media campaigns and improving public access to such resources, especially lakes, streams and beaches.

Fifteen states express concerns about user-resource and user-user conflicts on existing recreation lands or waters. Conflicts between canoes and power boats or between hikers and motorized trail vehicles are the most frequently-cited visitor problems. Other conflicts mentioned are:

o conflicts between recreation and extractive uses on multiple-value lands;

o conflicts between private landowners and river users;

o safety and resource problems due to deficiency of special areas for "high-risk" activities like rockclimbing;

o lack of adequate law enforcement authority or resources.

Facility development needs

Development of much of the existing outdoor recreation land in Illinois is required to fully realize its recreation potential. Some of the land in the state acquired during the last 20 years has been intentionally left undeveloped, such as natural areas and habitat for threatened and endangered species. Other parcels remain undeveloped or underdeveloped due to a lack of sufficient funds despite the increasing demands for their use. Development needs include access (roads, parking, trails, etc.), basic facilities (water, sanitary, picnic areas), a variety of specialized facilities (campgrounds, athletic fields, etc.) and establishment or improvement of wildlife habitat.

REPORT OF THE ILLINOIS ADVISORY
COMMITTEE ON AMERICANS OUTDOORS
May 1986

Respondents to the Pennsylvania Needs Survey indicated that picnic areas were most in need of rehabilitation statewide, followed closely by playgrounds. However, the most significant fact regarding this list is . . . the fact that the top ten choices ranked so closely together. . . .

. . . the Pennsylvania Needs Survey asked respondents to indicate what types of facilities needed to be acquired and/or developed. Tabulation of the responses indicated that the facilities in most need are bicycle paths, followed by hiking trails, picnic areas, playgrounds and community centers. It is significant to note that all but three of the facilities identified on the top ten list of facilities which need to be acquired or

developed are also on the top ten list of facilities that should be rehabil-itated.

PENNSYLVANIANS OUTDOORS
CRITICAL RECREATION ISSUES IN
THE KEYSTONE STATE
July 1986

Opportunities for outdoor recreation should be available to every-one, regardless of age, income, physical or mental limitations. In some instances, the solution may be as simple as installing ramps or proper "cuts" in a curb, while in other cases the issue becomes more complex as administrators look to relieving budget problems with increased user fees.

Federal and state laws prohibit architectural barriers in public rec-reation areas. The extra costs associated with making most structures fully accessible are so small as to be negligible if provisions are in-cluded in the planning stages. However, "retro-fitting" facilities can be very costly.

ARKANSANS OUTDOORS
February 1986

In facility needs statements, trails of all types were the most frequently cited deficiency (30 states).

Close-to-home facilities, especially neighborhood parks and play-grounds were next, followed by access to and availability of water for activ-ities like fishing, swimming and boating. The large majority of states also emphasize the importance of making facilities physically accessible to people with handicaps.

About half the states made general statements about critical needs for greater development at existing recreation sites. Other frequently men-tioned needs were for: tennis and basketball courts, ballfields, swimming pools, hunting areas, and target shooting facilities.

Complementary Issue: There was near unanimity among state submis-sions on the critical problem of rehabilitation, operation and maintenance of existing facilitie.s. Deficits in transportation access were also frequently cited. The principal cause of facility problems identified by states was lack of adequate financing, including reduced availability of federal and state grants.

Special population needs

There is a need for all agencies which are responsible for providing park, recreation and leisure services to the general populace to re-value the participation of disabled, urban and aged citizens and up-grade the level of service delivery. Education and training of existing staff, and, in some instances, the hiring of specialized staff is necessary.

Physical accessibility of sites and facilities and transportation meth-
ods need to be increased and improved. Increased state funding is nec-
essary for these purposes, and a more proportionate use of existing
agency funds must be allocated for services and programs for these pop-
ulations. Urban recreation centers have suffered decline and deteriora-
tion that parallels urban decay, depriving urban citizens of their right
to appropriate recreational resources.

CONFERENCE REPORT, NEW JERSEY
GOVERNOR'S CONFERENCE ON
RECREATIONAL RESOURCES
June 1985

In its recreation-related programs, [the Michigan] Department of
Natural Resources will continue to emphasize those improvements in
recreation opportunity which are in and near the state's population cen-
ters. Much of the recreation land purchased, and most facilities devel-
oped for recreation use, will be near these population centers.

BUILDING MICHIGAN'S RECREATION FUTURE:
THE 1985-90 MICHIGAN RECREATION PLAN
1986

Several participants felt that the handicapped, together with the
aged and very young, are not adequately accommodated by outdoor
recreational opportunities in Montana. Improved wheelchair access to
rest areas and controlled road hunting were among some of the recrea-
tional improvements suggested for the handicapped.

Additional emphasis on the development of inner city recreation
was felt to be especially important for the young, the aged and the poor.

REPORT ON GOVERNOR'S FORUM ON
MONTANANS OUTDOORS
February 1986

People with disabilities comprise 10-15 percent of our popula-
tion. . . . It goes without saying that each of these groups are made
up of individuals with their own particular needs. When planning for
the needs of our communities, we must also remember such human
concern groups as child abuse, alcohol abuse and drug addiction, and
other special interests such as minorities, single-parent families and the
temporarily disabled population. Several recent studies . . . indicate
that when given a choice, mentally-retarded individuals prefer commu-
nity-oriented activities and in general that their leisure recreation inter-
ests are much more similar than dissimilar to those of the non-disabled
population.

RECREATION AND LEISURE:
WISCONSIN'S CHALLENGE
Summary Conference Proceedings
June 1985

Forty assessments mentioned the need to expand recreation opportunities for special populations. "Special populations" includes urban residents, the very young, the elderly, people with mental or physical disabilities, the poor, troubled youth, and single-parent families.

The issues generally center on improved access to areas, programs and facilities. Elements of access specifically addressed include public transportation, physical improvements for the disabled (e.g., ramps), specially-targeted outreach and service programs and more resource-based recreation opportunities near to urban populations.

Publicizing accessible areas to various special populations was mentioned by several states. Several states offered specific suggestions on how to expand these opportunities—training workshops for state and local park personnel, targeted marketing, and conformance with nationally-approved (ANSI) physical standards.

Better public planning and information management; greater recognition of recreation values in public policies

Park and recreation facilities contribute significantly to the economic well-being of the state. The availability of developed park and recreational facilities plays a major role in the overall economic development of the state by contributing heavily to the $3.9 billion travel/tourism industry and by encouraging industrial and manufacturing expansion or relocation decisions.

Long-range planning is essential for the most effective use of our park and recreation resources. The systematic acquisition, development and management of recreation resources should be key functions of a statewide park and recreation program. Interagency cooperation is necessary for long-range planning at the State level.

FINAL REPORT AND RECOMMENDATIONS:
GOVERNOR'S TASK FORCE ON PARKS AND
RECREATION IN ARIZONA
1982

The Department of Conservation should continue the State's Comprehensive Recreation Planning process, regardless of the future status of the Land and Water Conservation Fund.

The work of this Commission has drawn heavily on information from the 1984 Tennessee Recreation Planning Report, *which is the most recent version of a statewide recreation planning study done every five years as a prerequisite for the State to receive federal Land and Water Conservation Fund grants. The currently authorized dissolution of that fund in 1989 would mean an end to federal incentives for undertaking the ongoing statewide recreation planning process. The Commission feels, however, that this process is important and should be continued. . . .*

Such studies give the State important information about the real recreation needs of its citizens and provide reliable methods of deciding which publicly funded recreation projects meet such needs and which do not.

TENNESSEANS OUTDOORS:
A QUALITY OF LIFE FOR THE FUTURE
November 1986

Effective management of existing resources, and planning for resource expansion, require the ready availability of knowledge about resource capacities, trends in use, access, resource conditions. Investors and agencies find such information with great difficulty or not at all.

NO ACCIDENTAL SUCCESSES: REPORT OF
THE 1986 GOVERNOR'S CONFERENCE ON
NEW HAMPSHIRE'S OUTDOOR RECREATION FUTURE
April 1986

Direction cannot be given without the necessary information on making decisions. Louisiana conducts very little research in the field of outdoor recreation. More research in this field is needed if Louisiana's outdoors is to survive the challenges of the future. The decisions of the '90s will be based on the information gathering of the '80s.

One agency/office/division should be given the responsibility of coordinating the assimilation and retrieval of recreation information, economic impact studies, technical assistance and information clearinghouse responsibilities to prevent duplication and fragmentation of information services.

LOUISIANANS OUTDOORS: ISSUES
CRITICAL TO OUTDOOR RECREATION IN
LOUISIANA
June 1986

About half the states specifically note the contributions nof existing statewide outdoor recreation planning (SCORP) processes to good decision-making, and call for the continuation of such efforts. They identify needs for improved state and local planning in several areas:

o greater emphasis on management problems as well as acquisition and development needs in areas such as stewardship and protection of existing public areas, operational efficiency, carrying capacity standards, and provision of specific opportunities (trails, boating access);

o improved information collection and analysis to provide a better base for decisions;

o better coordination of policies and projects in all state agency programs that affect recreation resources;

○ better identification of values to help justify actions recommended;

○ better state assistance to local recreation planning and a reaffirmation of federal support for state efforts.

Greater citizen participation in state and local planning is seen by many states as a key to increasing understanding and support of recreation values.

At least ten states recommend new statewide mechanisms to focus greater attention on meeting outdoor needs (e.g., interagency coordinating councils, annual reports to governor and legislature, or legislative councils).

Most state assessments reference the values of recreation and the outdoors. These concerns about values are often closely related to overall planning and research needs. They encompass three primary areas:

○ better recognition by and communication to the public about recreation values;

○ need for more research and documentation of quantitative benefits of recreation to the economy, physical and mental health, and other "larger" concerns;

○ greater overall commitments to environmental quality as a requisite for recreation.

Most states see recreation as a producer of economic and social values, but are concerned that these values are little considered in decision-making.

Few states offer comprehensive solutions to the problem of poor recognition of recreation values, but several mention better organizational advocacy or more aggressive identification and "marketing" of recreation benefits (e.g., to economy and health) as tools to increase public awareness.

Recreation visitor services and opportunity information

Adequate information on the location and availability of outdoor recreation facilities is critical to achieving optimal use of existing recreation resources. Members felt that current highway maps are difficult to read and do not always identify recreation sites. Highway directional signs to many private recreation areas are non-existent. Finally, informa-

tional and interpretive materials either do not exist, or are improperly distributed for certain types of popular recreation activities.

REPORT OF THE GOVERNOR'S COMMISSION
ON WEST VIRGINIANS OUTDOORS
May 1986

Issue:

○ *The public has difficulty obtaining information about recreation opportunities in a timely manner.*

Options:

○ *Recreation Providers should work together to systematically develop and publicize user information.*

○ *Publicity efforts at all levels of government should be expanded.*

○ *A centralized information center should be established to coordinate Colorado's outdoor recreation opportunities.*

○ *Non-profit associations should be used to get more information to the public.*

COLORADO OUTDOOR RECREATION
RESOURCES AND ISSUES
1986

Half the states reference recreation service programs, safety, information and other visitor service needs. The need for better information on recreation opportunities is frequently cited, both as an economic marketing tool and as a way to increase citizen awareness of available alternatives.

In ten states, inadequate information on opportunities is cited as a major roadblock to state recreation improvements.

Lack of sufficient onsite staff to provide desired programs and ensure visitor safety is mentioned by a number of states: several raise the problem of poor response to changing population needs (e.g., increasing numbers of elderly visitors; needs of families where both parents work).

Sustaining general environmental quality

While considerable improvement has been made to environmental quality, serious problems still exist. Toxic chemicals which are persistent in the environment pose not only a threat to human health, but also threaten fish and wildlife resources through their persistence in the food chain. In Indiana, as in many other states, health officials have had to issue advisories warning people against eating fish. Contaminants from urban and agricultural runoff and wastewater collection and treatment systems that do not meet water quality standards continue to pose a challenge to water resources. Significant improvements have been

*made in air quality, but the airborne contaminants that remain are
having a long-term impact on forests, streams and lakes.*

*As federal, state, local and private agencies are working to acquire
lands for parks, fish and wildlife areas, nature preserves, etc., for public
outdoor recreation enjoyment, ownership alone will not protect these
areas from degradation and resulting loss of future recreation opportunity due to pollution. In order to ensure that outdoor recreation resources are available to meet future needs, the Commission should
recognize the relationship between environmental quality and outdoor
recreation and the importance of continued support for strict environmental laws and their rigorous enforcement.*

REPORT TO THE PRESIDENT'S COMMISSION
ON AMERICANS OUTDOORS
State of Indiana
June 1986

Twenty-five states note problems with overall environmental quality.
These concerns overlap somewhat with those on specific natural systems,
but are more general in application to all recreation resources in a state.
Specific areas of concern identified include:

o deterioration of recreation facilities and access structures;

o inadequate control of point and non-point pollution sources of water and
air pollution;

o needs for additional hatcheries to sustain fisheries;

o poor reclamation of strip-mined areas;

o scenic impacts of highway billboards;

o soil erosion on public and private lands.

Protecting historic and cultural resources

*Many people find diversion and enjoyment in the cultural and
historical resources of our state. The site may be of special historical
significance, such as a Civil War battlefield, or it may have unknown
or unexplored cultural values, such as an Indian burial mound. Visitors
to many of the state's oldest parks, constructed by the Civilian Conservation Corps, are drawn by the timeless beauty and historical quality of
the old stone walkways and pavilions. All of these areas provide an
important and popular form of recreation.*

*Arkansas' cultural heritage plays an important role in our overall
recreation picture. Programs, such as the Historic Preservation Program,*

which include tax incentives are valuable tools and should be retained. Multiple-use concepts and cooperative efforts such as the proposal for a National Heritage Corridor for the Mississippi River Valley should also be pursued.

ARKANSANS OUTDOORS: ISSUES CRITICAL
TO RECREATION IN THE "NATURAL
STATE"
February 1986

Twenty states emphasize the need for local, state and federal efforts to protect hlilstoric, as well as natural, resources.

Needs cited include better funding for historic acquisitions and restorations, continuation of tax incentives for adaptive reuse of privately-owned historic properties, better public education and outreach on cultural values as a component of recreation programs and more use of public-private partnership mechanisms to protect historic resources as part of development or redevelopment plans.

Conservation ethic

While it is easy to focus on the importance of preserving our land and water resources to meet future recreation needs, it is equally important that present and future generations have an understanding of the importance of wise use, as well as preservation, of our natural resources.

. . . Improving our visitors' understanding of outdoor ethics, as well as the limits of the resources, will allow the public to enjoy their visit more through a greater appreciation of the outdoors. It will also create a more cooperative atmosphere, because people will understand why agencies must place limits on visitor activities.

Promoting hunter education and outdoor ethics programs is essential to maintaining access to private lands.

REPORT TO THE PRESIDENT'S COMMISSION
ON AMERICANS OUTDOORS
State of Indiana
June 1986

Creating awareness and helping Idahoans and out-of-state visitors to understand the many values and recreational uses that underlie the state's recreation/tourism attractions are important. The potential effects of information and education programs should not be underestimated, whether they focus on reducing conflict between recreation users, instilling a land ethic, teaching our youth to appreciate the values of wild-

lands, historical artifacts, and wildlife, or advertising local events, lodging and outfitting and guiding services.

REPORT OF THE COMMISSION ON
IDAHOANS OUTDOORS
June 1986

Eighteen states explicitly call for programs to improve public understanding of and behavior in the outdoors. Ten states call for better environmental and outdoor education programs in elementary or secondary schools, the remainder emphasize efforts to reach the general public in parks and other resource areas. Five states outline programs that involve both school and park locations, like New Mexico's approach to the national "Project Wild" program for fish and wildlife areas and "Project Respect" for private lands.

New Hampshire, Idaho and others relate the lack of an outdoor ethic to specific problems such as littering, vandalism and conflicts between motorized and non-motorized trail users. Some programs call for actions by private user groups, equipment managers and dealers as part of an overall strategy to educate the public.

Liability concerns

Issue:

○ *Liability issues are causing recreation opportunities to be lost or diminished.*

Options:

○ *Strengthen the laws which limit the liability of recreational land owners, administrators and providers.*

○ *Establish a public relations program to recognize private and corporate efforts which allow public use of private property.*

○ *Pass legislation and funding for recreational use easements.*

COLORADO OUTDOOR RECREATION
RESOURCES AND ISSUES
1986

Legal Liability and Insurance:
1. *Develop and implement comprehensive risk management plans. Public, private and independent providers.*
2. *Establish a recreation insurance marketing program. Ohio Department of Insurance.*

3. Support legislation to enable recreation providers to establish insurance pools, joint authorities or other joint risk management systems. [Ohio General Assembly, Ohio Department of Insurance, public, private and independent park and recreation providers].

OUTDOOR RECREATION IN OHIO
A Report to the Governor from
the Commission on Ohioans Outdoors
March 1986

Almost half the states expressed concerns about liability problems that limit recreation opportunities:

o fears about lawsuits reducing the availability of private lands for recreation (e.g., farmlands for hunting).

o unavailability or high cost of liability insurance causing closure of key private facilities or service concessions (horseback stables, river outfitters).

o liability fears closing areas and reducing programs aimed at providing otherwise desirable high-risk recreation opportunities (rock-climbing, wilderness backpacking, sailing, kayaking and other water sports).

Recreation workforce

Park and recreation maintenance has grown beyond the need for just a "mop and bucket" janitor. Maintenance, in general, has become a complex, year-round operation dependent on efficient and knowledgeable management practices. . . .

As in all other industries in both the public and private sectors, natural resource managers are faced with new problems and new challenges. Answers to these modern dilemmas are to be found in new techniques and technologies as well as creative and professional application of time-tested management practices. Regardless of the approach, training personnel to keep up with the times is essential. There must be commitments at all levels of government to maintaining staff levels in our park and recreation departments.

DELAWARE REPORT TO THE PRESIDENT'S
COMMISSION ON AMERICANS OUTDOORS
September 1986

The Tennessee General Assembly should establish a Volunteer Act, as proposed by the interagency Volunteer Committee, to facilitate the use of private citizens in all phases of government.

We need to better recognize our volunteers and the quality and importance of their work by offering them better institutional support from

*the State, including insurance coverage for on-the-job injuries, authority
to drive State cars, and better administrative support.*

TENNESSEEANS OUTDOORS: A QUALITY
OF LIFE FOR THE FUTURE
November 1986

*Today's outdoor users and park visitors expect high quality service
and trained, knowledgeable hosts to help them maximize their recreation time and dollars. Tourist industry labor is characteristically seasonal, poorly trained, low paid, lacking a stake in the business and
increasingly scarce. Labor is often the ultimate constraint.*

RECOMMENDATIONS:

5. . . . Establishment of the New Hampshire Service Corps (NHSC).

*a. Would be a state-supported employment program for 16 to 18
year olds. Enrollees would work for minimum wage, but State would
match earnings from a fund created out of: business profit taxes, endowments; donations; State user fees—to create a trust fund.*

*b. Upon graduation from high school, monies in trust could be
applied to college tuition.*

*c. Upon college graduation, if dollars still owed to the fund, gradu-
ate of NHSC could enroll to contribute 2 years' time at minimum wage
to service work in New Hampshire.*

NO ACCIDENTAL SUCCESSES: REPORT OF
THE 1986 GOVERNOR'S CONFERENCE ON
NEW HAMPSHIRE'S OUTDOOR RECREATION FUTURE
April 1986

Deficiencies in trained, professional recreation leaders and managers
are noted, especially the special problems of small communities that make
investments in capital facilities without providing for skilled management.
This can lead to underuse or misuse of facilities.

Better training, coordination and public recognition of volunteer work
efforts are noted by many states as essential to improve the staffing available in public recreation areas. Such efforts are needed to increase the
numbers of volunteers and their efficiency in accomplishing essential
tasks.

More than a third of the states identify key opportunities for use of
volunteers to meet recreation staffing shortages in areas ranging from construction of trails to guiding and assisting the public in parks.

List of participating states

States that submitted issue-specific reports to the President's Commission (State Commission, Conference or Forum reports, work group analyses or surveys directly related to Commission objectives):

Arizona (2 reports)
Arkansas
Colorado
Delaware
Florida
Georgia
Idaho
Illinois
Indiana
Kentucky
Louisiana
Maine
Minnesota
Montana
Nevada
New Hampshire

New Jersey
New Mexico
New York
North Carolina
North Dakota
Ohio
Oregon
Pennsylvania
South Carolina
South Dakota
Tennessee (2 reports)
Utah
Vermont
Washington
West Virginia
Wisconsin

States that cooperated in NASORLO effort to compile summary recreation need and problem information from current Statewide Comprehensive Outdoor Recreation Plans (SCORPs): all 50 states, the District of Columbia, American Samoa.

States represented in testimony at Commission hearings and meetings: all 50 states.

. . . .
National Conference on Recreation and the American City Baltimore, Maryland May 28-30, 1986

General overview

On May 28-30, 1986, the City of Baltimore, the President's Commission on Americans Outdoors, and the U.S. Conference of Mayors cosponsored the National Conference on Recreation and the American City in Baltimore, Maryland.

More than 120 people participated in the conference's plenary and roundtable sessions. Participants included mayors, local park and recreation administrators and planners, community development officials, State park and natural resource executives, citizens' groups and other private sector interests.

Eight groups focused 3-hour discussions on specific themes, as follows: Finance (2 sessions); Recreation Space; Economics of Amenity; Citizenship and Sociology; Human Condition; Roles, Relationships and Institutions; and Managing Urban Recreation Systems. Delegates self-selected for groups. Group moderators gave an overview of each discussion, highlighting points and recommendations of each group.

The group recommendations address six overall themes:

1. Perceived differences between urban and non-urban recreation resources and public values should be minimized. The national network of public and private recreation places is a continuum of natural and cultural resources and experiences. Often cities contain lands and waters ecologically important to broad resource protection goals. The attitudes and views of urban residents about recreation and resource stewardship are heavily influenced in these local settings.

2. A more adequate level of capital funding for acquiring, developing and rehabilitating public recreation resources and facilities is imperative if existing resources are to be protected, future recreation space reserved now, and special natural or cultural sites preserved. A national trust fund, derived from several sources, flexible in eligibility and use, and equitable in distribution is critical to future public and private partnerships.

3. Increased recognition—political, social and ecological—of recreation values and land and water needs is imperative if recreation resource goals, plans and protection strategies are to be implemented and sustained. Recreation and open space goals must be a major focus of comprehensive urban planning. Better and more innovative citizen involvement efforts, including programs that give opportunities for citizen stewardship roles in neighborhood and community parks are a critical adjunct of improved plans.

4. Present research and technical communication processes are inadequate. "Clearinghouse" functions—data collection and dissemination, management and technology sharing, opportunity for civic and professional contact, research—are critical to more efficient public services, resource protection and general support for recreation and park objectives. The nation would benefit significantly from new federal initiatives in this area and should initiate or actively support national partnerships.

5. More effective interagency and intergovernmental cooperation is essential to enhance public and private recreation opportunities and should be pursued at all levels. The broad public interest in recreation opportunity, protection of natural resources, and management and fiscal efficiency demand better cooperation and coordination of policies, investments and management strategies.

6. Civic activists, professional recreation and park managers, planners and others must be more aware of and responsive to rapid demographic, social and economic change. "Awareness" includes a technical understanding of specific trends, the interpretation of trends to produce relevant resource protection and management strategies, and initiation of appropriate education and training opportunities.

A more detailed discussion of these elements is included in the summary of proceedings.

SUMMARY OF PROCEEDINGS

Background presentations

Three background presentations under the heading, "City Futures: Critical Elements," set the stage for roundtable discussions. Highlights are noted below:

Emerging demographics of urban places

Dr. John G. Keane, Director of the U.S. Census Bureau, presented trend information on the changing demographics of urban areas, as revealed by 1985 surveys and estimates.

o Prospective changes include rapid growth in elderly, immigrant and school age children populations over the next 15 years. These changes will occur predominantly in metropolitan centers.

o The increasing number of single family households, most headed by women, is expected to increase demand for recreation and other city services.

o The most interesting finding from 1985 surveys was that central cities may be staging a comeback after almost 20 years of rapid decline. New data indicate a possible reversal in the rapid population declines noted for big cities in the 1970 and 1980 censuses. Many older metropolitan areas are growing again or declining at much slower rates. While population shifts from frostbelt to sunbelt communities continue, the rate of this migration has slowed substantially and notable exceptions are occurring in resurging areas like Boston and New York.

The physical environment and resources of cities

Peter Stein, urban land program director of the Trust for Public Land (TPL), presented a slide show on the Staten Island Greenway in New York City and emphasized the importance of grassroots neighborhood involvement in identifying, protecting and improving urban recreation resources.

o Open spaces and recreation areas "close-to-home," at the community and neighborhood levels, are a key to improving appreciation and understanding of nature among urban residents. If we are seriously concerned about improving the behavior of visitors to state and federal areas or about building support for broader environmental and resource protection measures, urban areas, where 80 percent of the people live, are the best place to start.

o Programs that give urban residents a stewardship role in planning, development and management of neighborhood parks and community gardens are very effective means to create a "land ethic." Citizen action projects supported by TPL have demonstrated this from "bombed out" areas in New York to the well-to-do Telegraph Hill neighborhood in San Francisco.

o Parks in urban places are more than an aesthetic frill. The larger environmental benefits of open spaces, for example, in reducing air and water pollution, preventing floods, and recharging aquifers critical for city water supplies, are increasingly recognized. The Staten Island Greenway example illustrates both the fragility of urban natural spaces in the face of constant development pressures (e.g., a proposed freeway that would have bisected the Greenway) and the constant vigilance of community residents in protecting these precious remnants. The Greenway's environmental integrity has been protected by citizen action.

o There is an amazing variety of natural and naturalistic areas still coexist-ing with urban developments, as well as vast amounts of abandoned land in cities which can be reclaimed as recreation spaces from earlier develop-ments that have been abandoned (e.g., Platte River Greenway in Denver, Baltimore's Inner Harbor).

o Creative ways to involve citizens in park stewardship are needed. TPL has had several successes in "selling" square inches of threatened open space areas to demonstrate community support for their protection. While the sums raised have been significant as matching sources for public grants or other commitments, these efforts were not aimed at "privatizing" parks but at demonstrating to local, State and Federal officials the support of hundreds of thousands of people for public protection of in-city open spaces.

Politics and partnerships

William Collins, Mayor of Norwalk, Connecticut, discussed his city's experiences with public-private partnerships.

o The most successful partnerships involve mutual self-interest, not char-ity. Cities must set their own goals for what they want to achieve, rather than simply reacting to private initiatives.

o It is better to appeal to corporate needs for improved image than to philanthropy alone. Public relations and advertising budgets are usually larger than philanthropy budgets.

o Cities should look for companies that need to improve their image and match them to a particular public need through image-building projects, such as adopting of park areas near their offices or joint purchase and park development of adjacent land. Corporations with a "sense of guilt" about their products or processes are good candidates. Norwalk has been suc-cessful with paper and beverage container manufacturers.

o Once a few partnerships have been developed, a systematic "get on the bandwagon" campaign should be developed to recruit new private partners by citing the activities of their peers or competitors.

o Public decisions on development rights and infrastructure development are very valuable commodities, and should be "sold" for top benefits to the community. This must be recognized through careful negotiations with private developers to provide the best possible public amenities.

o Public-private partnerships cannot substitute for local partnerships with state and Federal governments; there are not enough private resources available to replace existing support from higher levels of government. But successful partnerships with the private sector make good arguments for greater support from the State or national government because they reflect grassroots commitments to recreation values.

Roundtable conclusions & recommendations

The heart of the conference was its series of roundtables. These smaller focus groups on specific topics ran for three hours. Each group agreed upon a short list of priority problems and proposed solutions in its subject area. Major conclusions are summarized below.

Better capital funding is critical

o Cutbacks in Federal funding for recreation space and park development were deplored as a "cop-out." The large majority of U.S. citizens live in urban areas and the national government must bear some responsibility for redressing imbalances created by changing conditions (e.g., population shifts and industrial disinvestments) that are national in scope and greatly influenced by Federal policies and programs.

o Cities have always committed the greatest portion of fiscal resources for operating recreation programs and services and for managing their systems to ensure maximum protection of resources and productivity. But they need outside help in the form of seed money to acquire parks and otherwise protect threatened open space, to reclaim vacant lands, to develop new facilities and to rehabilitate old ones.

o A national trust fund supporting the same objectives as LWCF and UPARR programs (or a straight reauthorization of those programs with adequate annual funding) were recommended in two Finance Roundtables, as well as in sessions on Recreation Space, Managing Urban Recreation Systems, Economics of Amenity and Roles/Responsibilities.

o The principle of reinvesting revenues from exploitation of natural assets, like receipts from Outer Continental Shelf oil and gas or other Federal mineral leasing, in the natural "capital" of parks and recreation areas was endorsed by conference participants. Grants to state and local governments for park acquisition and recreation development or rehabilitation are considered highly effective vehicles for equitable national distribution of such reinvestments.

o A parallel State role in funding assistance to localities was also called for. There was a strong consensus that renewed Federal parks funding would help to stimulate more State financial and technical assistance to communities.

Decision makers must give greater recognition to urban recreation and open space values

○ Public and private decision-makers must place a higher priority on recreation and open space in urban areas, which means recognizing and marketing the economic, social and environmental values which make recreation a basic part of the urban infrastructure.

○ There is a particular need to quantify the economic and social values of community parks and recreation programs to facilitate better integration of recreation into urban planning and development decisions. Better data on economic benefits is a key to promoting public-private development partnerships. For example, improved awareness by private developers about the value of recreation and open space amenities gives public agencies a stronger negotiating position when dealing with private proposals. Likewise, there is evidence that recreation could play a much greater role in sustaining family values through improved emphasis on play that joins rather than separates parents and children.

○ State and local planning and development requirements should give increased recognition to the place of parks and recreation in the overall urban fabric of economic development, housing, health, crime prevention, environmental improvement, and other concerns. One exciting suggestion was to regard "The City as a Park," a unique environment which is part of both human culture and the natural world and which provides a vital link between them. Examples cited were Urban Cultural Parks in Massachusetts (Lowell) and New York (Hudson-Mohawk). Participants also emphasized the value of strong and innovative citizen involvement in recreation planning and management as a vehicle for bolstering people's appreciation of park values.

○ Financially-strained communities, under pressure to cut operating costs, tend to react to "brushfires," instead of planning systematically to meet present and future needs. One participant stated: "You can't improve the transportation system if you're too busy driving the bus!" Communities must overcome these reactive tendencies through systematic planning programs.

○ Financial and technical incentives from Federal and State governments for good local planning will improve targeting of resources, increase productivity and encourage better partnerships among public and private institutions. Such incentives include financial assistance for systematic resource and management studies and enforcement of parallel planning requirements as a condition for other assistance.

○ Broader and more intensive educational efforts involving both children and adults are needed to increase awareness of the environmental values of parks and open space and improve prospects for better long-term decision-making about natural resources and the environment.

A national research and information clearinghouse program would do much to improve consideration of recreation values

○ Seven of the eight roundtables gave priority to establishment of better national research and data collection efforts to aid public and private decision-making on park and recreation issues. The availability of current data and projections on levels of recreation supply and use from many areas around the country would provide comparative guidelines to stimulate public and private actions at the local level. Basic research on the economic and social benefits of recreation would help local advocates and providers to quantify working assumptions on the types and amounts of commitments that their communities should make.

○ A national clearinghouse could also form the nucleus of a management information network to broadly share technical approaches, success stories, and "how to" information. Models for such a network already exist in the fields of law enforcement and agriculture.

Better interagency cooperation needed at all levels

○ Local elected officials and managers must recognize that park and recreation resources can and should be linked to other local resource and service functions. Particularly noted was the importance of better coordination between municipal or county recreation agencies and independent school boards. While many communities recognize the value of school grounds and facilities as a component of the overall recreation system, there is virtually no use of expensive school properties for general public recreation in others. These situations can be remedied by improving working coordination between recreation, education and other agencies and by identifying sources for the relatively small budget amounts needed for supervision and maintenance of school facilities during non-school hours.

o Similar cost-savings and improvements in service can be obtained through coordination in the planning and implementation of community housing, law enforcement, and social welfare programs.

o Greater cooperation between public park and recreation agencies and non-profit or neighborhood volunteer programs is also a critical step in eliminating gaps in services and duplication of efforts.

o State and local planning and action to meet recreation and park needs should be well coordinated. State recommendations and/or financial support for cooperation among local jurisdictions can, for example, improve prospects for better park and recreation use of multi-jurisdictional coastal, river and trail corridors.

o State and Federal assistance programs for education, housing and urban development, law enforcement and other local programs should recognize the increased cost-savings and improved effectiveness inherent in local coordination between these programs and recreation by providing financial incentives and technical assistance to encourage joint efforts. Earlier Federal incentives of this type (e.g., Education's Community Schools and Environmental Education programs) have unfortunately been abandoned, in many instances before they got beyond the "pilot" stage.

Park and recreation administrators and planners must adapt to changing demands and conditions

o Park and recreation planners and managers need initial and continuing career education programs which provide skills in business management as well as traditional resource and program management disciplines.

o Park professionals and advocates must increase their skills as advocates and educators to promote and defend their goals in the political arena. This means developing university and continuing training to teach professionals the best ways to analyze and articulate the values of recreation programs in terms of the economic, cultural, environmental and personal well-being of citizens.

o Public and private recreation managers should keep up to date on changing population characteristics and adapt their programs to meet the evolving needs of new population mixes, including the foreign-born, active seniors, latchkey children, mentally and physically disabled people, and family groups.

○ Public program managers must better understand how private investment and development decisions are made and develop greater skills as facilitators of public-private partnerships in the public interest. These strategies must include both for-profit and non-profit actions.

National Conference on Recreation and the American City
Finance Roundtable Number One

HARRIET SAPERSTEIN,
Moderator

Participants in this roundtable session included local government officials, representatives of recreation industries, non-profit groups and individual advocates. The moderator was amazed at the many innovative local responses to ameliorate conditions brought on by local financing cutbacks. Despite these innovations, however, localities are left with the basic problem of sustaining and improving recreation infrastructure in the face of pullbacks of support by Federal and State levels.

To aid the President's Commission, the group decided to concentrate on a single, priority recommendation, which is listed below with background and elaboration.

Conclusions & Recommendations
○ The Federal government must have a continuing role in supporting recreation, especially urban recreation, and should not either "opt out" or "dump down" this responsibility to lower levels of government.

○ Urban communities need a continuing source of long-term, stable funding for capital park and recreation purposes.

1. The national government should create a true Recreation Trust Fund large enough so that income from the trust can provide grants and low-interest loans to State and local governments for parkland acquisition, recreation development and rehabilitation of existing recreation infrastructure. (New Jersey Open Space loans and Michigan Trust program could be models.)

2. The Trust should combine Land & Water Conservation Fund and Urban Park and Recreation Recovery grant approaches in terms of what they do and who they serve. That is, the program could rely on State administration, but should include some national criteria to target an equitable portion of funds to those localities with the greatest needs. Some such criteria might include amounts of poverty, population density and composition and local tax base available (a measure of current investment/disinvestment by the private sector), as well as special conservation opportunities.

3. The Trust Fund should be set at a minimum of $6 billion.

a. The source for this amount could be the $6 billion in authorized but unappropriated LWCF funds projected to be available at the end of Fiscal 1989.

b. Since this amount will need to grow in the long term, to keep pace with growing needs, Federal and State governments should be examining other revenue sources that could be dedicated to recreation purposes, such as:

○ land transfer fees or taxes
○ excise taxes on recreation equipment and services
○ taxes on litter
○ taxes on accomodations and entertainment
○ "sin" taxes on cigarettes, liquor, etc.
○ taxes on extraction of non-renewable resources
○ a national lottery
○ Federal and State income tax checkoffs.

In determining additional sources of revenue for the trust fund, it will be important to keep in mind the principle established by the LWCF Act use of OCS mineral leasing and royalty revenues—that income from a non-renewable natural resource should be reinvested in the earth to provide an environmental balance to resource consumption.

National Conference on Recreation and the American City
Finance Roundtable Number Two

ROBERT THOMAS,
Moderator

The moderator noted general agreement with many of the points made by the concurrent finance group (Finance Roundtable No. 1). However, this roundtable reached consensus on its own set of issues, as listed below.

Conclusions & Recommendations

1. *National Trust Fund*

○ A national trust fund for park acquisition, development and rehabilitation should be established to provide a long-term stable source of funding to continue the tradition of the Land and Water Conservation Fund.

○ The Urban Park and Recreation Recovery (UPARR) program or a similar effort should be continued to target financial and technical resources to the special management, renovation and service needs of major urban communities.

○ States should be encouraged, possibly through incentives under a national trust, to establish their own trust programs (along lines of Michigan Land Trust) to support both State and local park projects. States should also explore low-interest loan programs like New Jersey's Green Trust.

2. *National Research and Technical Assistance*

○ Tremendous amounts of local effort are now wasted in basic justification of local budgets because there is no good national data on the values of good park programs. A Federal Office of Parks/Recreation Research and Technology should be created to do studies and surveys and to collect and disseminate information from around the country on the human, economic and natural resource values of parks and recreation. Such a national center should also provide information on better planning and management approaches.

○ A modest Federal investment in such an institution would likely save millions of dollars in overlapping local and State research efforts, thus freeing up local resources that could be redirected to pro-active management and service functions.

3. *More Flexibility in Conversion or Adaptation of Recreation Facilities in Federally-Assisted Parks*

○ The Land and Water Conservation Fund (LWCF) Act contains stringent provisions (Sec.6[f][3]) requiring maintenance in perpetuity of grant-assisted State and local recreation areas. The Roundtable fully supports perpetual maintenance of park *lands* assisted by LWCF grants. However, the consensus is that this or a successor program should give grantees more leeway in adapting, redesigning, or even demolishing obsolete park facilities that have served their useful life, particularly when costs of maintenance or renovation are disproportionate to the services provided.

○ Requirements for local planning and commitment to maintain overall levels of service within the local recreation system (c.f., UPARR Recovery Action Plans) might be instituted in lieu of facility-by-facility protection.

4. *Public and Private Policy on Recreation*

○ National, State and local policies should formally recognize the value of direct public investments in recreation resources as well as indirect investments through tax incentives for public-private partnerships.

○ In the area of tax policy, private contributions of land to the public estate should be made deductible, even when such donations are mandatory under local ordinances or development guidelines. Recognition that such mandatory dedications contribute to recreation policy goals as much as do direct purchases of land or public developments would give localities greater leverage in negotiating with private developers for land and other recreation amenities.

5. *Funding for the Arts and Humanities*
   o Public funding for arts and humanities programs contributes substantially to local conservation and recreation programs. Further cutbacks in Federal or State funding for these activities would have serious, negative impacts on recreation budgets. Therefore, the Roundtable urges that arts and humanities funding be protected at current or enhanced levels.

6. *National Recreation Assistance Programs for Localities*
   o The Federal government should continue to provide and encourage States to provide staffing and other resources to support financial and technical assistance to local governments. The Land and Water Conservation Fund program once involved a very effective State-Federal partnership in grants administration, but recent cutbacks in grants money available to States and in Federal guidance to the States has led to reductions in State monitoring and technical assistance efforts as well. Adequate administrative resources in a grant program are the key to prevention of fraud, waste and abuse. But a pro-active, positive approach involving advice to grantees in planning and project implementation is much more effective than simply catching grantee errors after the fact.
   o Current and future national grant programs should include sufficient administrative resources to ensure that Federal field staff and cooperating State offices are able to perform such vital planning and technical assistance functions.

National Conference on Recreation and the American City
Recreation Space Roundtable

MARION CLAWSON,
Moderator

Conclusions & Recommendations

1. *Improve Recognition of Values of Recreation Spaces in Urban Areas.*
City decision-makers must put parks and open space areas on a higher priority level. They must recognize that open space is more than a frill, it is part of basic urban infrastructure just like roads, sewers and water lines.
   o There needs to be more research on economic, environmental and social values of parks/open space in terms that elected officials and developers can understand. There is evidence that recreation space improves property values, that areas of natural vegetation can help improve

air and water quality, that human beings need open spaces to compensate for urban congestion and stress. But such tentative indications should be explored in greater depth to provide solid arguments for equal consideration of open space needs in urban development.

○ Broader and more intensive environmental education programs are needed for both children and adults to increase awareness of the values of recreation space and, thus, improve prospects for better long-term decision-making by an active and committed citizenry. The national government should play some role in expanded environmental awareness programs.

○ Education about open space values should not be limited to schools and books. A major tool to improve citizen awareness is increased volunteer involvement in neighborhood and community parks. Local governments must increase the participation of individual citizens in park and open space design, use and maintenance to assure voter and taxpayer support for open space initiatives. Partnerships with non-profit recreation and conservation groups and with community businesses have long-term educational benefits in addition to their immediate impacts on the amount and quality of recreation space.

2. *Improve Planning and Development Guidelines to Better Recognize Value of Parks and Open Space.*

○ States, counties and cities must increase the amount and quality of comprehensive planning to include consideration of recreation and open space value AND relate them to other major concerns such as economic development, housing, crime prevention, health, safety and overall environmental improvement.

○ Local governments should inventory *all* vacant lands, including abandoned or underutilized industrial or commercial areas, waterfronts, vacant or soon to be cleared areas, etc., to be sure that recreation space opportunities are not missed because of ignorance of alternatives. *The definition of open space must be broad and all-inclusive:*
— remaining natural areas
— once developed, but now vacant lands
— waterfronts and riverbanks
— downtown plazas
— existing parks/playgrounds
— adaptive reuse of streets, other rights-of-way
— temporary use of transitional building sites
— rooftops and other unconventional spaces

○ Recreation space amenities should be included in all public developments and negotiated in all private ones. Special attention should be given to maintaining waterfront access for public recreation.

○ Federal and State governments must provide "carrots and sticks" to encourage good local planning, including:

— Requirements for sound planning that consider recreation needs in the context of overall urban development should be maintained or restored in all grants or loans for capital acquisition/development (e.g., LWCF or successor, UPARR, State Bond Issues, HUD CDBGs, housing and infrastructure grants).

— Federal and/or State financing for local parks planning should continue. There are several existing models, such as Federal Urban Parks (UPARR) planning grants, State grants for local planning as in Maryland, California, Wisconsin, Oregon (usually tied to a planning requirement for either LWCF or State grant money), LWCF SCORP grants to States (could be extended to localities).

3. *National Planning, Research, Information and Technical Assistance are Essential to Support Local Efforts.* Local planning cannot occur in a vacuum. There is consensus among local professionals that better national research, data acquisition and coordination are needed to provide key information on national demands, standards for comparison of areas and programs, and answers to basic research questions unlikely to be addressed on a piecemeal basis. The lack of national recreation data comparable to what the Federal government provides for agricultural, commerce, transportation, crime and health is a barrier both to local awareness of recreation space issues and to the efficiency of local planning and research.

○ There should be a national clearinghouse for information on recreation planning and management. This could be run by a Federal agency, a professional group or a quasi-public institution, but it must be assured of continuing dollars and staff at some minimal level to avoid the waste and frustration caused by previous false starts and wasteful restarts that have characterized many previous attempts to coordinate national information on recreation.

○ Comparative national data on what other localities, States national agencies and private entities are doing, what needs they are responding to and how, could provide guidelines and models critically needed to stimulate local planning and commitments to adequate recreation spaces.

4. *Adequate Resources Must Be Made Available to Increase and Protect Urban Recreation Space.* Remaining natural open space in urban areas is a finite resource. Acquisition or other protection of critical natural areas in the path of urban development must be expedited or these areas will be irretrievably lost.

○ Federal, State and local governments should share responsibility for financing critical land acquisitions where no alternatives to fee simple purchase are available. LWCF grants to States and localities have been a major incentive to recreation land acquisition since 1965 and should be continued in some form. State open space bonds and other grant programs (many of them stimulated by Federal matching money) have had impacts at least equal to Federal grants and should be encouraged.

○ While fee purchase of critical lands is a key incentive for land protection by both public agencies and private landowners, better incentives and models for less-than-fee approaches to protection of recreation space are needed. Because such approaches usually involve many local governments, complex land use coordination, substantial needs for seed money, and economic or environmental issues larger than any one locality or region, State and Federal governments should be key actors in developing and promoting more and better demonstrations of less-than-fee protection methods (See Adirondack State Reserve and New Jersey Pinelands National Reserve models).

○ The Federal government, through its own programs and its major influences on State, local, corporate and individual investment decisions, should play a much larger catalytic role in encouraging public-private partnerships to protect recreation space. Possible actions include: better tax treatment of private land donations, investment incentives or disincentives that encourage public and private actors to consider open space values, and proclamation of national goals and policies that educate people about the importance of parks and open space.

National Conference on Recreation and the American City
The Economics of Amenity Roundtable

ROBERT McNULTY
Moderator

Park and recreation amenities are urban necessities that add to the perceived attractiveness of cities and to their human physical functions. Collectively, they are an important resource in attracting investment. The moderator presented a comprehensive definition of amenities which included air and water quality, noise, culture, parks and recreation, animation and design. The group struggled with the assignment of amenity as a definition of recreation services. Some in the group felt that recreation was an essential social service and should be supported from this perspective. This thought led to two levels of amenities—those that provided basic services and those additional services and activities that encouraged investment.

Conclusions and Recommendations

1. *The Economic Value of Parks and Recreation Is Not Readily Known or Quantified.*

○ Provide national support for research and data acquisition about how park and recreation programs contribute to the economy at all levels. Research that helps to quantify recreation benefits is particularly needed. Develop an information network or sharing system that supports the profession similar to the national data base supporting police services.

○ Support and maintain a recreation data base over time to facilitate identification of trends in the interaction of parks, recreation programs and the economy.

2. *Urban Park and Recreation Opportunities Serve 80% of the American Public and Deserve Equal Standing With More Remote, Rural Opportunities in Federal Programs.*

3. *It Is Necessary to Redefine Parks and Recreation as Impacting the Entire Fabric of the City.*

○ Promote the notion that the entire city is a park—a part of the natural environment and the culture heritage.

○ Increase public recognition and support that parks and recreation contributes to economic development, augments other social services, promotes cultural identity, provides learning opportunities, fosters preservation and conservation values, enriches the natural estate, and encourages public health in urban settings.

○ Develop an information system and network that supports this new definition of parks and recreation.

○ Recognize that the changing role of the profession permits new linkages to improve economic and social life in the city.

○ Ensure that this new definition of parks and recreation incorporates all the important social services that ensure quality of life for city residents.

4. *Parks and Recreation Professionals Need Training According to This New Definition of Parks and Recreation Services.*

○ Develop training programs and university curricula that will allow professionals to more fully analyze and articulate the relationships of their service to the local economy, cultural identity, natural environment, and personal health and well-being.

5. *Private Sector Investments Need To Be Encouraged To Maintain, Develop, and Redevelop the City's Recreational and Cultural Assets.*

○ Identify and develop incentives for the private sector at the state, federal and local levels.

○ Encourage investments in the urban neighborhoods as well as in the center city.

○ Take an active role to identify and discourage disincentives for investment and involvement by private-for-profit and nonprofit organizations at the local, state and national levels.

6. *A Substantial National Trust Fund Needs to Be Created for the Acquisition, Development and Redevelopment of Open Space and Recreation Facilities.*

○ Provide funding for projects in urban, suburban and rural areas.
○ Ensure that funds provided under a national trust are equitably distributed to urban areas.

National Conference on Recreation and the American City
Managing Urban Park and Recreation Systems Roundtable

MAYOR WILLIAM COLLINS,
Moderator

The moderator was impressed with the level of professional competence and creativity shown by the members of this roundtable. These attributes are essential for survival in an era of fiscal stringency. Roundtable participants were quick to note that localities themselves must do more to initiate improvements in systematic management, interagency coordination and public-private partnerships. At the same time, there was consensus on the need for greater national leadership in the areas of liability protection, information sharing and incentives for good local planning.

Conclusions and Recommendations

1. *Liability Protection*
   ○ There is a need for better Federal ground rules on tort reform and control of insurance rates. It was recognized that this problem extends to many areas other than recreation and that changes in Federal liability law are now under discussion.
   ○ Model legislation for State and local liability law reform is also needed. Such reforms should recognize that liability problems affect most nonprofit recreation providers as well as public agencies.
   ○ States must gain better control over insurance rate setting through: improved public information on actual awards and settlement costs; better tracking (preferably on a national basis) of legal precedents to help defendants defend against unreasonable suits; more government self-insurance pools to provide alternatives to unreasonable rates and to gain better information on insurance costs.
2. *Professional Development*
   ○ Park and recreation professionals need training beyond standard resource and program management to include business management.
   ○ Park professionals and advocates must increase their skills as advocates/educators to promote and defend recreation programs in the political arena.

○ Program managers also need better skills as enablers of public-private partnerships and as negotiators with private entrepreneurs.

3. *A National Recreation Management Clearinghouse System*

○ A national organization with sufficient resources to collect and disperse management information on a sustained basis is badly needed to share data, provide good management models and reduce inefficient duplications of effort.

○ It should also promote research and demonstration efforts addressed at solutions to common management problems.

○ It should provide both statistical data that can be readily applied to management solutions and "how to" reports on successful management initiatives in the public and private sectors.

4. *Greater Interagency Coordination*

○ Local managers and elected officials must recognize that "no recreation department is an island." Park and recreation departments must be ready and able to link their programs with other local resource and service agencies, particularly with boards of education to make better joint use of vast school recreation facilities that frequently sit idle. At the same time, local executives and councils must be ready to facilitate appropriate coordination efforts by providing the minimal resources needed to facilitate coordination. While this may add to the budgets of individual agencies, it reduces waste and overall costs in the long-term and thus produces savings to the taxpayers of the community.

○ Greater cooperation is also essential between public programs and non-profit or neighborhood recreation providers to improve coverage and eliminate overlaps in the overall, public-private recreation system.

5. *New Incentives for Systematic Local Planning*

○ There is a tendency for cities under pressure to simply react to the most pressing needs of the moment, to react to brushfires, instead of planning systematically to meet present and future needs.

○ It is in the interest of Federal and State governments to provide incentives, through planning grants and planning requirements for other financial assistance, to encourage communities to plan systematically for management of recreation resources. Small investments in planning can produce big dividends by eliminating waste and ensuring the continuity of large investments in land and facilities.

○ UPARR management planning grants provided since 1982 have proven very successful in this area, despite cutbacks in capital funding by the Federal government. This program is an excellent model for future Federal or State assistance.

National Conference on Recreation and the American City
Roles, Relationships and Institutions
Roundtable

Len Simon,
Moderator

The roundtable started with the pretext that nothing existed, and looked at federal, state, local, private and individual roles in the light of what each might ideally do best. The basic conclusion was that all levels of government and the private sector *should* be involved in urban parks and recreation, that things will work best under a scheme of multi-dimensional partnerships that provide stability, continuity, flexibility and diversity.

Conclusions & Recommendations

FEDERAL ROLES: It is appropriate for the national government to have park and recreation responsibilities in urban areas where 80 percent of the population resides. Urban recreation touches on many national concerns including environmental protection, social equity and economic stability. Federal programs should not be dominant in urban park decisions, but rather a functional part of a national-state-local-private partnership in which all members have appropriate responsibilities and commitments.

o *Funding.* Reductions in Federal assistance for State and local parks have created a serious imbalance in what was previously a very effective conservation/recreation partnership. The national government must recommit itself to the objectives of the LWCF and UPARR grant programs through reauthorization of these programs or inclusion of their goals into a new national trust fund for recreation.

o *Data Gathering and Dissemination.* The national level is the most appropriate place to collect certain types of recreation supply, demand, and economic data. Better coordination of the data efforts of many Federal agencies is also more cost-effective than independent collection of the same information by hundreds or thousands of state and local entities. There should be federal support for some type of data collection and dispersion function which would supply basic information to and coordinate the products of all federal, state, local, academic and private research and planning efforts.

o *Training and Demonstration.* The National Park Service, the Forest Service and other federal agencies have employees with unique knowledges and skills which should be shared with lower levels of government through systematic training and education programs. Funding or other encouragement of pilot/model programs in recreation management, re-sources protection and environmental education is one of the most effec-tive ways to transfer successful approaches from one part of the country to another, and the federal government is better qualified than any state, local or private institution to support and report on such model efforts.

o *Unique Urban Resources.* Many cities contain cultural and natural re-sources of national significance; there is a continuing role for the Na-tional Park Service and other land managers in direct management of such resources. Further, such "urban outposts" provide an on-site pres-ence which is valuable in support of technology transfer and informa-tional functions mentioned above.

STATE ROLES: In our federal system, States have major responsibilities for domestic well-being which extends to urban residents. State responsi-bilities for the economic and environmental welfare of urban areas are preeminent and have in some cases been overdelegated to local govern-ments which lack the authority and resources to control land use and eco-nomic forces extending beyond their boundaries.

o *Funding.* States have clearly-defined responsibilities for financial as-sistance to communities which include funding of some urban park and recreation programs. State funding functions best in partnership with fed-eral and local matching efforts.

o *Planning.* Most urban open space and natural resources conservation efforts occur in a regional context, involving coastlines, rivers, trans-portation corridors and tracts of land that extend beyond any one local-ity. States are the logical source for planning and direction of most environmental and economic decisions within and between multi-juris-dictional urban regions, and should assume greater responsibility for guiding and assisting individual localities in such decisions. State coast-al management, water pollution control and river protection activities have increased substantially in the last decade and provide many good examples of the benefits to regions and localities of greater State involve-ment.

o *Technical and Information Assistance.* Just as the Federal agencies have unique skills and information at the national level, States are better equipped than most localities to note statewide trends and supply tech-nical information critical to local decision-makers. State park, natural re-sources and environmental agencies, along with State land grant univer-sities, should be full partners in national-state-local information networks that do research, collect data and provide practical planning and man-agement information on recreation topics.

LOCAL ROLES: Local governments are the ultimate supplier of most park and recreation opportunities. They are at the "end of the funnel" which channels national, state and private programs and resources into urban areas. As such, they are responsible not only for direct provision of recreation space, facilities and services, but also for coordinating a wide range of basic delivery systems from public safety and law enforcement to housing, education and environmental control. They are responsible for putting the products of federal, state, local and private programs and actions into a coherent package that includes recreation and relates it to all other functions in a way that maximizes its social, economic and environmental benefits.

Cities have not always placed parks and recreation in such a broad context, but there is increasing realization, in the parks and recreation profession as well as among elected officials and other urban decision-makers, that recreation needs and opportunities cannot and should not be considered apart from all other goals and functions of urban government.

○ *Local Control and Stewardship.* As local governments have the right to control most recreation resources and investments within their jurisdictions, so they have a primary and inescapable duty to maintain those resources, to operate recreation programs in efficient ways and to respond equitably to the recreation needs of their citizens. Localities can and should receive assistance in these efforts from state and national governments, from the private sector and from individual citizens, but they can never "opt out" or delegate their ulimate responsibility to make local recreation systems work.

○ *Entrepreneurial Recreation.* In a rapidly changing world, local recreation professionals must be more than good resource and people managers, and more even than effective advocates for recreation programs and values. They must follow the lead of economic development and transportation officials, for example, by becoming "entrepreneurs of recreation." This means that they must do more than simply deliver a service; they must actively market their recreation goods: to citizens, to private developers, to other government departments, to non-profit and community groups and to potential private benefactors.

○ *Critical Potential of School Resources.* In many communities, school recreation facilities are a major potential resource for general recreation now being neglected because city officials and independent school boards cannot agree on who will pay for what. Joint school-recreation programs have been successful in U.S. cities since the 19th century, and some outstanding model programs continue to deliver maximum recreation benefits from both general and education tax dollars. But fiscal stresses in many communities have caused such cooperative efforts to be reduced or eliminated in recent decades. Curtailing school-recreation programs to save the modest funds needed for utilities and building overhead is a false economy and a terrible waste of facilities sitting idle while needs go unmet.

○ *Cultivating the Private Sector.* Today, park and recreation functions must compete with many other worthy causes for limited private resources, charitable and corporate. Nevertheless, local recreation advocates must be aggressive in soliciting donations. Such solicitations should go beyond the standard environmental and open space arguments to include justifications based on the economic and social values of recreation.

o *Local Colleges and Universities.* Institutions of higher learning are anxious to be good members of their communities. This provides an opportunity to take advantage of unique academic resources by using professors and students for research, planning and management consultations necessary to justify and implement good recreation systems.

o *Volunteers.* Park and recreation departments should systematically cultivate, coordinate and support volunteer activities by individuals and community service groups. This means developing volunteer projects, selling them to the appropriate groups, training volunteers as needed, providing adequate guidance and supervision. For city councils and executives, it means recognizing that volunteer efforts are a supplement to, not a substitute, for public commitments. Sufficient public dollars and staff must be made available in the local budget to make volunteer programs work. An important benefit of volunteer programs is the further creation of constituency groups with active commitments which can support overall park and recreation programs in the political arena.

o *Private Sector Recognition of and Active Support for Recreation.* The private sector is a source of recreation amenities and funding for many communities. Because of its great diversity and complexity, the Roundtable did not attempt to define specific roles for the private sector, but recognized several principles which guide public and private interactions. *The first condition of good private involvement remains a public commitment by the community to recognize, market and realize recreation values.* Responsibilities of private citizens and organizations for recreation programs, as for other functions, encompass a clear understanding of public needs and constraints, awareness of park and recreation values and a willingness to support efforts of mutual interest. The products of interactions range from reservation of parklands and recreation facilities in private developments to direct provision of recreation services by private groups to donations of dollars, goods or labor to public programs.

National Conference on Recreation and the American City
The Human Condition Roundtable

JILL DISKAN,
Moderator

The discussion focused on the contribution of urban parks and recreation in nonrecreational fields and how to capitalize on and promote these contributions. The economic contributions included the number of business decisions made in recreational settings; the amount of money generated in recreation activities; and the cost consequences of people not having the opportunity to engage in recreation pursuits. Social contributions included park and recreation settings as a first point of acculturation for many ethnic groups; socialization opportunities; and creation of individual self confidence and self esteem. It was decided that recreation is important to the social, moral, environmental, and economic fabric of the nation—a part of the nation's infrastructure.

Conclusions and Recommendations

1. *Growth of Special Populations, Such as Elderly, Foreign Born, Disabled, Place Stress on Recreation Systems.*
   ○ Develop a data base on recreational needs and preferences of these special populations and, most importantly, disseminate this information.
   ○ Provide special training to professionals to adequately serve these groups.
   ○ Recruit people from these groups into the profession of recreation and parks.
2. *The General Public Needs to Be More Informed About the Values of Recreation and the Opportunities Available to Them.*
   ○ Use the mass media to improve marketing of recreation services.
   ○ Sensitize government agencies, especially the U.S. Department of Education and the U.S. Department of Health and Human Services, about the benefits of recreation for inclusion in their program guidelines.
   ○ Market parks and recreation as an essential public service.
   ○ Encourage the development of an organized constituency for parks and recreation services.
3. *The Provision of Recreation Services Needs To Recognize the New Configurations of and Pressures on the American Family.*
   ○ Encourage recreation providers to provide services and programs that promote family recreation.
   ○ Continue to supply healthful recreation opportunities for children and youth, recognizing the changing roles of the family.
4. *The Provision of Close-to-Home Recreation Opportunities is Critically Important and Must Continue.*
   ○ Create incentives for other community services, such as schools, to allow or provide additional recreational opportunities.
5. *It Is the Responsibility of the Parks and Recreation Profession To Promote the Worthy Use of Leisure Time.*
   ○ Continue physical education as an educational requirement.
   ○ Continue or institute better environmental education programs.
   used throughout life.

o Educate the recreation consumer so that she or he can make informed recreation decisions throughout adult life.
o Create a strong, central, national voice advocating the values of recreation.

National Conference on Recreation and the American City Citizenship and Sociology Roundtable

RALPH W. E. JONES, JR.,
Moderator

The objective of this roundtable was to discuss the relationship between park and recreation opportunities and individual and group behavior. This relationship potentially has various aspects, among them: recreation which reinforces positive social behavior; recreation which aids socialization in many settings and under many conditions; and recreation as a potential influence to change antisocial behavior.

Observations and Conclusions

The group tended to assume the recreation/citizenship/socialization relationship, then focus on actions which might reasonably result in progressive policies and additional recreation resources or program opportunities. It observed that there should be sustained efforts by "providers" to communicate more effectively with the public, especially youth, about parks and recreation values. This would likely involve elementary and secondary educational resources and processes, increased public knowledge about the high public cost of incarceration (which might ultimately occur if positive personal values are not stressed); research (and dissemination) directed to recreation and behavior relationships; and institutional and program leadership.

The group expressed concern that the President's Commission on Americans Outdoors might be taking a too-narrow approach to its work by concentrating too heavily on the physical resource base for recreation. Appointment of a "task force" to produce a "supplemental report" on social aspects was suggested.

Recommendations

1. *Take Concerted Actions to Increase Public Awareness of Broad Park and Recreation Values, Especially Those Positive Contributions of Quality Recreation Experiences That Address the Needs and Problems of Youth*
   o The group observed that a lack of recreation opportunity is perceived as directly proportional to a high incidence of youth crime, and that cer-

tain conditions in urban places might further contribute to antisocial behavior. Recreation services and resources often help to ameliorate such difficult conditions. Development of a "social ethic" about recreation, as well as an "environmental ethic," was suggested. The group tended to agree that while recreation may "cost a lot of money, a lack of recreation (ultimately) costs more." "Recreate rather than incarcerate" was one popular expression of this view.

o All recreation providers should reassess public communication themes and outreach actions and opportunities. For example, the group observed that shopping centers and malls were extremely popular congregation places for youth and many older persons, and that these sites themselves served recreation purposes. There should be appropriate public incentives to private interests involved in the development and management of shopping centers, and/or the co-location of public recreation sites and services in these private settings.

o The group favored public incentives for the private sector to provide or allow public access to recreation lands and other spaces, especially in urban areas. Recreation program opportunities, as well as space, should be provided. Education opportunities, from early childhood and continuing through life, directed to the development of a leisure ethic and recreation knowledge should be a matter of public policy and practice.

2. *Leadership by National and State Institutions on Recreation Policy, Research and Allied Functions Must Be Expanded. National Institutional Leadership Is Defined in Terms of an Organization At or Above the Cabinet Secretary Level or, At Least, Equal to the Role of the Department of the Interior Through the 1970's.*

o The group observed that no national public entity presently deals comprehensively with parks and recreation, and that a similar situation apparently exists among the majority of the states. Thus, the social values of recreation, as opposed to the consideration of physical resources, receive little focused attention in public policy actions. Advocacy of recreation values, in terms of policy initiatives and reviews and technical assistance functions appear to be especially lacking. Absent national and state leadership opportunities to develop or enhance recreation experiences as a part of *other* public policies, resources or investments opportunities are usually "lost." National and state institutional leadership should directly influence many public agencies and policies, including those dealing with the courts and juvenile justice, the family, housing, health and welfare, education, drugs, transportation, and other matters.

Roundtable participants suggested numerous specific actions which, individually or collectively, might contribute to the recommendations stated above.

o Leisure education should be a mandated component of public education. Education agencies should develop "modules" of learning to instill a recreation ethic through a) physical, b) environmental or c) human wellness themes and actions which will bring about positive individual actions and community change;

o Initiate actions to minimize or eliminate legal and other barriers to shared use of public and private property for recreation, e.g., access to undeveloped urban land for community gardens or recreation use of abandoned railroad or utility rights-of-way;

o Actively promote the benefits (personal and social) of park and recreation volunteerism to the public and decisionmakers;

o Substantially improve the analytical capability of the parks and recreation field through increased research and dissemination of findings and information;

o Require the National Endowment for the Arts to set aside a portion of funds for long term art programs as a component of urban recreation;

o Support the establishment of a parallel National Endowment for Parks and Recreation;

o Expand recognition programs that focus on positive citizenship, including State and local conservation corps programs, a National Service Corps and the Congressional Award Program;

o "Target" public recreation investments to "high crime" areas;

o Support "Olmsted Heritage" legislation which would contribute to urban park restorations and likely encourage broader restoration efforts in the vicinity;

o Initiate and promote public "marketing" or communication efforts to improve the understanding of recreation values and recreation for "play's sake."

. . . .
List of Contributors to the Commission's Work

Listed below are the hundreds of individuals who spoke at one of the 18 public hearings held across the country, prepared literature papers, wrote concept papers, organized field trips, participated in strategic planning sessions, or assisted in other ways.

While they are not a scientific sampling of the country, they do represent the opinions of a substantial cross section and thus are of great value when considering what this Nation should pursue in its outdoor policies and programs.

Gordon Abbott, Jr. ○ Bob Abby ○ Joe Abrahams ○ Steve Adams ○ David Adamson ○ Landis Aden ○ Donna Aegerer ○ Keith H. Ainsworth ○ Beth Alafat ○ Richard Albert ○ Arnold J. Albrecht ○ Karen Allen Albright ○ Bill Alderich ○ Barbara Alderman ○ George Alderson ○ Richard Alesch ○ Susan Alexander ○ Sam S. Alfano ○ Charles Allen ○ Lawrence Allen ○ Robert Allen ○ Lucy Ann Aloi ○ Stephen A. Altieri ○ Gregory Alward ○ John Amodio ○ Anthony F. Amos ○ Beverly Anderson ○ Bill Anderson ○ Bob Anderson ○ Gary Anderson ○ John Anderson ○ Judy Anderson ○ Lois Anderson ○ Mark Anderson ○ Robert O. Anderson ○ Joseph Anthony ○ Cecil Antone ○ Dale J. Antonich ○ Robert K. Antozzi ○ Donald B. Ardell ○ Keith A. Argow ○ Robert Arkins ○ Mary Arman ○ Dede Armentrout ○ Robert C. Arnold ○ Ron Arnold ○ Ross Arnold ○ Jeff Arthur ○ William Ashley ○ George S. Asmus ○ Phil Auerenheimer ○ Michael Aune ○ Robert Augsburger ○ David R. Austin ○ Grant Avery ○ David Axtell

Gov. Bruce Babbitt ○ Edmund H. Baca ○ Don Bachman ○ Adela Backiel ○ Nick Badami ○ Howard Bahar ○ Susan Bahr ○ Guy Baier ○ Bill Bailey ○ Rod Bairo ○ Bryan Baker ○ James Jay Baker ○ James M. Baker ○ Karen Baker ○ Roger Baker ○ William C. Baker ○ Margit Baldivid ○ Malcolm Baldwin ○ Armand Ball ○ Katherine Ballin ○ Gary Ballman ○ Dick Barbar ○ Melissa Barker ○ John Barnes ○ Glenda Barrett ○ Pope Barrow ○ Cameron Barrows ○ David Barrows ○ Dan Bassler ○ Alvin Bastron ○ Nanci Bateman ○ Rick Bates ○ Joan Batory ○ Charles M. Bauer ○ Don R. Bauer ○ Kirk Bauer ○ Jasper N. Baum ○ Barbara Baynes ○ Mollie H. Beattie ○ Leslie F. Beaty

○ Jim Beck ○ Bob Becker ○ William H. Becker ○ Bill Beckner ○ Katherine Beebe ○ Charles Beeman ○ Tony Bevinetto ○ Jean C. Behrens-Tepper ○ Cong. Anthony Beilenson ○ Larry Belknap ○ Robert L. Bendick ○ Stu Bengson ○ Richard Benjamin ○ Betty Bennett-Talbot ○ Ben Bennion ○ Delwyn E. Benson ○ Norm Berg ○ Jim Berger ○ Stu Bergson ○ Dennis Bergstad ○ Alfred Berner ○ Donald Bessler ○ Robert Beymer ○ Dean Bibles ○ Walter Bickford ○ Lillian Bieber ○ Judith S. Bishop ○ Mike Bishop ○ Sarah G. Bishop ○ Sharon Bishop ○ Hon. W. Louis Bissette ○ Malcolm I. Bivins ○ Maleese Black ○ John Blackwell ○ William O. Blair, Jr. ○ Charlie Blatchford ○ Dana Blatt ○ Ethyle R. Bloch ○ Ed Bloedel ○ Charles Bloomquist ○ Mark Blosser ○ James L. Blue ○ Kent J. Blumenthal ○ Walter Boardman ○ Major Boddicker ○ Wayne A. Boden ○ Margaret Bohannon, Jr. ○ Robert R. Bonczek ○ Dale Bondurant ○ Shirley Bonine ○ Bonnie Bonneau ○ James L. Boone ○ Charles J. Borawa ○ George Borozan ○ Michael Bosanko ○ Joni Bosh ○ Phillip Bosserman ○ James E. Bossi ○ Diane Bostow ○ Larry Bourret ○ Leonard Bower ○ Wallace Bowman ○ Thadis W. Box ○ Hon. Brian Boyle ○ John Boyle ○ Francis J. Bradac ○ Darby Bradley ○ Ronald L. Bradsby ○ Bill Brakken ○ Jim Branch ○ Wendy Brand ○ Donald E. Brannon ○ Robert M. Brantley ○ H. Marie Brashear ○ Richard Brass ○ Paul M. Bray ○ Sue Bray ○ Cong. John Breaux ○ Cindy Bricker ○ Bill Briggle ○ Bill Briner ○ Preston Bristow ○ Al Brodie ○ Alan Brohn ○ Christopher Brong ○ Richard Brook ○ Hooper L. Brooks ○ Julie Brooks ○ Bettye Daniel Brown ○ Bruce Brown ○ David Brown ○ Karen Brown ○ Perry Brown ○ Thomas K. Brown ○ Tommy Brown ○ Torrey Brown ○ Willard W. Brown ○ Kingsbury Browne ○ Patrick J. Broyles ○ Barbara Bryant ○ John L. Bryant, Jr. ○ Hon. Angela Bay Buchanan ○ Janis Budge ○ Robert Buell ○ Leon J. Buist ○ Charles Bullock ○ David A. Burack ○ Si Burch ○ William R. Burch ○ Bob Burdette ○ Robert Burford ○ Becky Burgess ○ Peter Burk ○ Steven F. Burke ○ Robert Burkhardt ○ Bob Burns ○ Eric Burr ○ Lynn C. Burris ○ Leon J. Burst ○ John Burton ○ David Burwell ○ Raymond L. Busbee ○ Frank E. Busby ○ Bob Bushnell ○ Russell D. Butcher ○ Col. D. Fred Butler ○ Rod Byers

Jim Cain ○ Edwin Cake, Jr. ○ Lynton K. Caldwell ○ Tim Caldwell ○ Ruston Calisch ○ William C. Calkins ○ Hon. Howard H. "Bo" Callaway ○ Jimmy Calloway ○ Larry Calvert ○ Benella Caminiti ○ Lynn Campbell ○ Richard W. Carbin ○ George H. Cardinet ○ Timothy Carey ○ Frederick G. Carlson ○ Rep. Doug Carlson ○ Kim Carlson ○ Chris Carpenter ○ Forrest A. Carpen-ter ○ Jorge Carrasco ○ Marcia Jean Carter ○ Lisa Cashdan ○ Christine Cashel ○ Robert J. Cassity ○ Bill Cecil ○ Sen. John H. Chafee ○ Robert D. Chamberlain ○ Wesley T. Chambers ○ Don Chance ○ Rod Chandler ○ Helen Chapman ○ Cong. Bill Chappell ○ Cheryl Charles ○ Don Charpio ○ Ronald Chase ○ Lee Chauvet ○ Davis Cherington ○ Gordon Chernae ○ Wally Chesbro ○ Alan Christensen ○ Eugene Christensen ○ Harriet H. Christensen ○ Robert Christie-Mill ○ William T. Civish ○ A. Ludlow Clark ○ Orlin Clark ○ Roger N. Clark ○ Susan Clark ○ Toby Clark ○ Ladd G. Colston ○ Clark S.

Colvin ○ Edwin Colvin ○ James Cone ○ James A. Conforti ○ Clare Conley ○ James E. Conley ○ Tom Conley ○ Cal Conniff ○ Phillip Cook ○ William J. Cook ○ Hon. Frank Cooksey ○ Gerald Coop ○ Ken Cooper ○ Ken Cordell ○ Frank Cosgrove ○ John Cossaboom ○ Walter H. Costa ○ Laurie E. Coughlan ○ Victor G. Counts ○ Gerald Coutant ○ Jerry Covault ○ Anne Cox ○ Randy Cox ○ Mike Craden ○ M. K. "Dutch" Cragun ○ Pamela Crespi ○ John L. Crompton ○ Richard Cronin ○ John Crossley ○ Edward Crozier ○ Ralph Cryder ○ Richard A. Crysdale ○ Pamela Cuiklo ○ Matt Cuney ○ Dan Cunningham ○ Kirk Cunningham ○ Laura C. Curran ○ Donald M. Currie ○ Steve Currier ○ Richard Curtin ○ Joseph E. Curtis ○ Charles S. Cushman ○ M. Rupert Cutler

William Daehler ○ Mayor Stephen J. Daly ○ John Dane ○ Mary Danielak ○ Ronald R. Darner ○ John Dattilo ○ Rick Davidge ○ Dennis Davidson ○ Don Davis ○ Donald L. Davis ○ John Davis ○ Sara H. Davis ○ Wes Davis ○ Patrice Davison ○ Pat Dawres ○ John Day ○ Donald Dayton ○ Paul De Angura ○ Freed De Bloois ○ Thomas Deans ○ Roger Deaver ○ John deBessonet ○ Richard Decabooter ○ Lester A. Decoster ○ Mary Dedecker ○ Kevin Delaney ○ Chris T. Delaporte ○ Ed Delate ○ Stanley Dempsey ○ John G. Dennis ○ Michael Dennis ○ Robert Dennis ○ William C. Dennis ○ Maria Dennison ○ Jack Denton ○ Dan Derbes ○ Marilyn M. Desborough ○ B Deveny ○ Henry Diamond, Esq. ○ Wright Dickinson ○ M. A. "Skipper" Dickson ○ Holly Dill ○ Reed Dils ○ Pat DiMatteo-Knobloch ○ N. R. Van Dinter ○ Bonnie Direnfeld-Michael ○ Jill Diskin ○ Robert P. Dlugolenski ○ Rebecca Doby ○ Herbert Doig ○ Ernest Doiron ○ Richard J. Dolesh ○ John R. Donaldson ○ Michael W. Donelly ○ Paul Donheffner ○ Dominic Dottavio ○ Pat Downes ○ Joseph Downs ○ Wena Dows ○ John Doyle ○ Thomas B. Doyle ○ K. D. Drachand ○ Bob Drake ○ B. L. Driver ○ Phil Driver ○ Sue Drummond ○ Chris Duerksen ○ Dalton DuLac ○ Bob Dulli ○ Harvey Duncan ○ Diana Dunn ○ Hampton Dunn ○ Kate DuPont ○ Forrest V. Durand ○ Sen. David Durenberger ○ Jean Durning ○ Hon. Gary Van Dusen ○ Bill Dvorak ○ Polly Dyer

Ted Earl ○ A. H. Early ○ Paula P. Easley ○ Will Eason ○ Paul W. Eastman ○ William A. Eastman ○ Julie A. Eaton ○ Herbert E. Echelberger ○ Nathan Edelson ○ Wayne Edgerton ○ Christopher Edginton ○ Theodore M. Edison ○ Bevla Edmiston ○ James Edmonson ○ Beverly Edwards ○ Frank Ehret ○ Bill Eichenberry ○ Yvonne B. Eider ○ Douglas Eiken ○ Kay Ellis ○ Gary Ellis ○ Joan T. Ellis ○ Sabrina Ellis ○ Robert Ellsworth ○ Anna Elsing ○ Gary Elsner ○ Malcolm L. Ely ○ Nord Embordin ○ Steve Emmons ○ Benjamin R. Emory ○ Jean Englert ○ Donald English ○ Amos Eno ○ Nancy Eppley ○ Wayne B. Erickson ○ Dennis Eshelman ○ Fred L. Eskew ○ Robert D. Espeseth ○ Bill Estes ○ C. E. Eubanks ○ Bob Eury ○ Dave Evans ○ Gov. John V. Evans ○ Keith Evans ○ Gary Everhardt ○ Alan Ewert ○ Charles Exley ○ Jim Eychaner ○ Mark M. Eynatten

Lloyd Fagerland ○ Edward F. Fairbanks ○ Edward J. Fanning ○ Andrea Farbman ○ Virginia Farley ○ Tom Farnsworth ○ H. E. "Bud" Farnum ○

Sandra Fecht ○ John Fedkiw ○ Arthur Feinstien ○ David Fell ○ Michael D. Fenderson ○ Carolyn Fennell ○ Helen C. Fenske ○ Carlos M. Fetterolf ○ Roy Feuchter ○ David Field ○ Donald R. Field ○ Elliot Field ○ Elliot Field ○ Donald L. Fife ○ Maureen Fennerty ○ Craig Finney ○ S. Michael Finney ○ Mike Finnigan ○ Nancy Fischer ○ Gail Fischmann ○ John Fisher ○ Mary Betty Fisher ○ Hilton Fitt-Peaster ○ Joyce L. Fitzgerald ○ Jeannette Fitzwilliams ○ Katherine M. Flaherty ○ Richard Flannelly ○ Lorraine Fleming ○ John Flicker ○ Theodore Flickinger ○ Larry Flint ○ Dave Flipp ○ Christi Flood ○ Sonny Flores ○ Norman Fluegel ○ Peter Foley ○ Kathleen A. Foote ○ Linda Forbes ○ Rosemary Forehand ○ Douglas Forrest ○ William Forrey ○ Gerald Forsman ○ Charles H. W. Foster ○ Roger Fournier ○ Robin Fowke ○ Don D. Fowler ○ Dale G. Fox ○ Kevin Fox ○ Maggie Fox ○ Tom Fox ○ Sheri Fraker ○ Ronald Franceschi ○ Henry S. Francis, Jr ○ Rollie Franzen ○ Douglas Frechtling ○ Wayne Frederich ○ Robert Freedman ○ Doug Freeman ○ Larry Freeman ○ Zussman Freeman ○ Charlotte Fremaux ○ James Fremont ○ Cliff French ○ Lex Friedan ○ Anne Frondorf ○ Alan Front ○ Tom Frostman ○ David W. Fruge ○ Roger Fuehrer

Larry Gadt ○ Sherwood Gagliano ○ Wally Gallagher ○ Pat Gallavan ○ Dennis Galvin ○ John Gans ○ Steve Garret ○ Tom Garrison ○ William C. Gartner ○ Jan Garton ○ Gudy Gaskill ○ Ed Gasser ○ Walt Gasson ○ Madge Gatlin ○ Lawrence Gaydeski ○ David Van Gekler ○ Billie Axline Gentry ○ Jennie Gerard ○ Jeff Gerbino ○ Bill Gerhardt ○ Randy Gerke ○ David Getches ○ Navaz Ghaswala ○ Richard G. Gibbons ○ Bil Gilbert ○ Bob Gillies ○ Daniel Gilligan ○ Glenda Gilmore ○ James Glass ○ Tom Glass ○ Joe Glasscock ○ Geoffrey Godbey ○ Charles R. Goeldner ○ Marcy Golde ○ Bob Golden ○ Albert J. Gomes, Esq. ○ J. C. Good ○ Sid Goodloe ○ Vickie Goodwin ○ Wendy Gordon ○ Leon Gorman ○ Margaret Gorski ○ Alan R. Graefe ○ Gregg Grange ○ Rebecca Grant ○ Ed Grasser ○ Jim Green ○ Terrell Green ○ Pamela Greenberg ○ Bill Greene ○ Gordon K. Greene ○ Robert E. Greengo ○ Mike Di Gregorio ○ Peter Grenell ○ Leo Griego ○ Martin J. Griffith ○ Sheri Griffith ○ Harold K. Grimmett ○ Sterling Grogan ○ Daylon E. Gronewald ○ Geoff Gross ○ Ralph Grossi ○ R. E. Grossman ○ Luverne D. Grussing ○ Paul Guest ○ Gerald F. Guidroz ○ Palmer Van Gundy ○ Clare A. Gunn ○ Steve Gunzel ○ Larry Gustke ○ James Gutensohn ○ Paul Guthrie ○ Wayne N. Guthrie

Glen Haas ○ Gordon Haaland ○ Peggy Hackett ○ Tom Hager ○ Bart Hague ○ Byron Haley ○ Sam Hall ○ Gary L. Haller ○ Robert Ham ○ Sam Ham ○ Russell Hamerly ○ Sarah Hamill ○ Edward Hamilton ○ George T. Hamilton ○ Geri Hamilton ○ John Hamilton ○ Larry E. Hamilton ○ Tom Hamilton ○ Michael Hammer ○ Laurie Hammil ○ Rick Hammil ○ David A. Hammond ○ Dave Hampton ○ Cathy Hands ○ Richard Hankin ○ Stephanie Hanna ○ David Hannah ○ David F. Hannum ○ David Hansen ○ Kate Hansen ○ William J. Hansen ○ Garner B. Hanson ○ Greg Hanson ○ Allan Hanssen ○ Rose Hanzlicek ○ Warren Harang, Jr. ○ Ben Harding ○ Charles Harris ○ Don Harris ○ Edward Harris ○ David Harrison ○ James P. Harrison ○ Eric

Hartfelder ○ David Hartman ○ Paul H. Hartman ○ Lawrence Hartmann ○ Ann Harvey ○ Mike Harvey ○ Harry Haskell ○ Ed Hastey ○ Don Hatch ○ Bob Hathoy ○ J. David Hause ○ Bill Havert ○ Fred Hawkins ○ Keith Hay ○ Robert M. Healy, Jr. ○ Edward N. Heck ○ E. M. Hedrick ○ Paul Don Heffner ○ Robert W. Heidermann ○ Donald S. Heintzelman ○ Dan Heinz ○ Marge B. Heiss ○ Bette Heller ○ Bill Helmke ○ Pat Helton ○ Steven A. Hemmat ○ Stan Hemphill ○ Carol L. Henderson ○ Glen Henderson ○ Jean Hennen ○ Jean Hennessey ○ Robert A. Henning ○ Gordon Henry ○ Vernon Henry ○ Wesley Henry ○ Hon. Robert L. Herbst ○ Norm Herkenham ○ Gov. Ed Herschler ○ David M. Hess ○ Jack Hession ○ John Heywood ○ Jerry Hill ○ Gerald E. Hillier ○ Saunders Hillyer ○ Jim Hinds ○ Lucy Hirsch ○ Richard F. Hite ○ Glenn D. Hoagland ○ J. Anthony Hoare ○ Jean Hocker ○ Secretary Donald Hodel ○ Dave Hodgdon ○ Harry G. Hodgdon ○ Jack V. Hoene ○ Douglas Hofer ○ Edward L. Hoffman ○ Wendy Hoffman ○ Alan K. Hogenauer ○ Terry Holcolm ○ Ron G. Holiday ○ Arthur J. Holland ○ Dennis F. Holland ○ Gordon Holland ○ Steve Holland ○ Eric Holle ○ Bill Holman ○ Dell M. Holmes ○ Shirley Holmes ○ Ruby Holmquist ○ Marlene Howladel ○ David Hood ○ David L. Hook ○ Bud Hooker ○ Hern Hoops ○ James E. Horan ○ Ken Hornback ○ Hewlett C. Hornbeck ○ Peter J. Horvath ○ Alexander P. Hoskins ○ Oliver Houck ○ Rep. Charles Hover ○ J. Russell Hoverman ○ Charles "Bud" Hover, Jr. ○ Deborah V. Howard ○ Dennis Howard ○ Wayne Howard ○ Charles A. Howell, III ○ Bruce Hronek ○ James L. Huckabay ○ Mayor William Hudnut ○ P. B. Huff ○ Margaret Huffman ○ Elden Hughes ○ John Hughes ○ John Hultsman ○ Wendy Hultsman ○ J. Kip Hulvershorn ○ Don Hummel ○ Fred Humphrey ○ David Humphreys ○ Eldridge G. Hunt ○ John D. Hunt ○ Marc Hunt ○ Verne Huser ○ Ira Hutchinson ○ Andrew E. Hutchison ○ Dayton D. Hyde

Douglas B. Inkley ○ Ruth Ittner

Leonard B. Jackson ○ Gerald Jacob ○ Jafar Jafari ○ E. P. "Jeff" Jaffarian ○ Sybil Jaffy ○ Lynn Jamieson ○ Roy Jansen ○ Christopher K. Jarvi ○ T. Destry Jarvis ○ Jerry Javne ○ Barbara Jankins ○ Rhonda L. Jennings ○ Carol Jensen ○ Dennis B. Jensen ○ Janice Jensen ○ Roy Jensen ○ Cynthia Johnson ○ David A. Johnson ○ George Johnson ○ Ken Johnson ○ Lieut. Gov. Marlene Johnson ○ Lynn Johnson ○ Norman Johnson ○ Offut Johnson ○ Robert B. Johnson ○ Wayne Johnson ○ Dave Jolly ○ Jack Jonas ○ David Jones ○ D. R. Jones ○ Jerry Jones ○ Richard Jones ○ Gilbert Jones, Sr. ○ Charles R. Joy ○ John Joyner ○ Gary King, Jr. ○ Martha T. Judge ○ Arnold Julin

Charlotte Kahn ○ Paul Kaiser ○ Larry Kajdan ○ Keith Kambak ○ Max Kaplan ○ David O. Karraker ○ Stanley Karson ○ Jane Kaufman ○ Matt Kaufman ○ Jchn Kaufmann ○ Robert Kaufmann ○ Jean Kavanagh ○ James Kearn ○ Kevin B. Kearney ○ Bruce E. Keeler ○ Mary Beth Keller ○ Donald Kellerstrass ○ Brig. Gen. Patrick J. Kelly ○ John R. Kelly ○ Joyce Kelly ○ William Kemsley, Jr. ○ Bruce Kennedy ○ Dan W. Kennedy ○ Michael Kenney ○ Mary

M. Kenny ○ William Kepner ○ Craig Kesselheim ○ Don Kesselheim ○ Jim Kimball ○ Kenneth Kimball ○ Thomas Kincaid ○ Charles King ○ Don King ○ Gary King, Jr. ○ Cathryn B. Kinser ○ Mike Kirkoff ○ Sandra Kirsch ○ Ray L. Kisiah ○ Bruce Kistler ○ Julie Kitka ○ Larry Kitto ○ Lawrence T. Klar ○ L. S. Kliman ○ Gary Klingman ○ Jeanne Klobnak ○ Robert Klos ○ James E. Knight ○ Timothy B. Knopp ○ John Knorr ○ Bob Knous ○ Hon. Tony Knowles ○ Chresten Knudsen ○ Dan Knuffke ○ Edward J. Koenemann ○ Jan Konigsberg ○ Carol Ann Koski ○ James Kozlowski ○ Alfred H. Kramm ○ Richard Kraus ○ Ray Kreig ○ Paul J. Kress ○ Daniel H. Krichbaum ○ Karlissa Krombein ○ Edwin E. Krumpe ○ Richard A. Kuehner ○ Christen Kundsen ○ Robin Kunstler ○ David Kuntz

Michael LaBaire ○ Robert J. Labar ○ Jahn Lacey ○ Mac Lacy ○ Nancy Lakner ○ Al Lalim ○ Jim Lambert ○ Randy Lanctot ○ Tom Landis ○ Ney C. Landrum ○ Ed Langenau ○ Wayne Lapierre ○ Lori A. Larson ○ Ron R. Larson ○ June Latting ○ David Latvaaho ○ Jean Lauder ○ Curtis S. Lawson ○ Berman Layer ○ Eric Leaper ○ Stan Leaphart ○ John Lear ○ Naomi Lede ○ De Ann Lee ○ Evelyn Lee ○ Larry L. Lee ○ Steve Lee ○ Daniel L. Leedy ○ Henlen Leemkuil ○ Orin Lehman ○ William Leinesch ○ Jennifer Leipold ○ Renee Leiter ○ Clement LeMire ○ Christopher K. Lenaan ○ Joanna Lennon ○ Thomas P. Lennon ○ Toni Lenz ○ Shereen Lerner ○ Dave Leshuk ○ Robert Leslie ○ Hon. Bob Lessard ○ Vanessa Lester ○ Judy Levine ○ Charles H. Lewis ○ Darrell Lewis ○ Hon. Drew Lewis ○ Cong. Jerry Lewis ○ Nancy Lewis ○ Vivien Li ○ Pete Libby ○ Steven Liebig ○ Paul Light ○ Joe Lightfoot ○ David Lime ○ Keith E. Limnell ○ Richard H. Lincoln ○ Michael Lindberg ○ Hon. Jon Lindsay ○ Jerry A. Lineback ○ Dick Linford ○ Les Lingscheit ○ E. M. Liska ○ Kay Lloyd ○ Claude A. Look ○ Judith Locke ○ Steve Loe ○ Karen L. Loechler ○ Gary D. Long ○ Hon. Cathy S. Long ○ John Loomis ○ Jack Lorenz ○ Rick Lowe ○ Dan Love ○ James Lowrey ○ David Lucas ○ Robert Lucas ○ Dan W. Lufkin ○ Robert Lund ○ Stephen Lundy ○ Donnabelle Lush ○ Loren Lutz

June MacArtor, Esq. ○ Earl F. Machart ○ Gary E. Machlis ○ Steven MacKay ○ Albert Mackie ○ Phoebe MacRae ○ Carolyn Maddick ○ Edward M. Mahoney ○ Joseph Mailander ○ Fran Mainella ○ Jerry Mallett ○ Amanda Malmberg ○ J. Paul Malmberg ○ E. L. Maner ○ Michael Manfredo ○ David F. Mangels ○ Barry Mangum ○ Bill Mangun ○ Albert M. Manville, II ○ Dave Markett ○ Rosemary Marple ○ Debbie K. Marquez ○ Suzanne Gall Marsh ○ Greg Marshall ○ Lane L. Marshall ○ Louise Marshall ○ George Marsik ○ Eric Mart ○ Marlys Martin ○ Mary Martin ○ Mary Jo Martin ○ Terri Martin ○ James Mason ○ Tom Matney ○ Jim Matson ○ Bill Maxwell ○ Ernie Maxwell ○ Ronald C. Maynock ○ Cong. John McCain ○ James A. McCarthy ○ Jerry McCarthy ○ Joseph McCartin ○ Gina K. McClellan ○ Rosalind McClellan ○ Bethlyn J. McCloskey ○ Beau McClure ○ Charles E. McConnell ○ Grant McConnell ○ Steve McCormick ○ Christine McCoy ○ Jerry McCoy ○ Robert R. McCoy ○ William D. McCoy ○ David L. McCraney ○ John McCrone ○ Jessyna

McDonald ○ Kwame J. C. McDonald ○ Maureen H. McDonough ○ Sam E. McDowel ○ Bob McDuffie ○ Paul R. McEncroe ○ Douglas McEwen ○ Pat McGee ○ Kayo McGillvray ○ William McGinnis ○ Mary G. McGown ○ James McGuffey ○ Charles McIlwaine ○ Louis McKey ○ Dennis McLane ○ Jo McLaughlin ○ Sylvia McLaughlin ○ William McLaughlin ○ Dan McLean ○ Fred S. McLean ○ Edward T. McMahon ○ Patrick McMahon ○ Molly McNamee ○ Ronald McNay ○ C. M. V. McRae ○ L. David Mech ○ John Mechler ○ Rick Medrick ○ Robert L. Meinen ○ Charles E. Mender ○ Dee Merriam ○ Tom Merriman ○ James D. Mertes ○ Delores Mescher ○ Larry D. Meser ○ Steve Messerli ○ Philip Metzger ○ Amy Meyer ○ Steven Meyer ○ Don Meyers ○ Eric J. Meyers ○ Bob Michaels ○ Richard M. Milanovich ○ Charles Milham ○ Bruce Miller ○ C. Richard Miller ○ Jennifer Miller ○ Margaret Miller ○ Mark Miller ○ Marvin D. Miller ○ Nancy Miller ○ Charles Millham ○ Lorraine Mintzmyer ○ John Mitchell ○ W. Mitchell ○ Arthur H. Mittelstaedt, Jr. ○ John W. Mixon ○ Kenneth Mobily ○ William A. Molini ○ Matt Montagne ○ Jim Montgomerie ○ John Montgomery ○ Linn Montgomery ○ Robert Montgomery ○ Roy T. Montgomery ○ Bob Moore ○ David Moore ○ Roger L. Moore ○ Susan Moore ○ Thomas Moore ○ Catherine G. Moran ○ Thomas More ○ William Morgan ○ John C. Morgenroth ○ William J. Moriarity ○ David Morine ○ William Morrill ○ Virginia Morrison ○ Steve Mosow ○ William Penn Mott ○ Sue Mottinger ○ Mac F. Moulden ○ Ray Murray ○ Jim Murphy ○ Barbara Musgrove ○ Roy W. Muth ○ Phyllis Myers ○ Judith L. Myers-Marx

Doug Nadeau ○ Jeff W. Napier ○ Roderick Nash ○ John A. Nattinger ○ Penny Naumhoff ○ Jack Nawrot ○ James Nelson ○ Robert E. Nelson ○ Robert H. Nelson ○ Susan Nelson ○ John A. Nesbitt ○ Lloyd Nesseth ○ Beverly Nester ○ Rodney Newcomb ○ George Nez ○ Boje Nielsen ○ Stephanie Nona ○ Paul Nordstrom ○ James Norton ○ Steve Nottonson ○ Stephanie Nova ○ Richard A. Nunis ○ Glenn A. Nyquist

Valerie Oberle ○ Vie Obern ○ Charles H. Odegaard ○ Peter N. Odell ○ Jeanne Off ○ Tom Offutt ○ Neil Ofsthun ○ Gerry Ognibene ○ Marvin Olinsky ○ Gina Oliva ○ John C. Oliver III ○ Donald G. Olson ○ Richard J. Olson ○ Warren E. Olson ○ W. Kent Olson ○ Brian O'Neil ○ Ann Orr ○ Gov. Bob Orr ○ Robert Oset ○ Tony Ostos ○ Steve Otis ○ Steve Over ○ Carlton N. Olen ○ Kevin M. O'Brien ○ Pat O'Brien ○ Phyllis O'Connell ○ Glenn O'Dell ○ Joseph T. O'Leary ○ Terry O'Sullivan

David L. Pack ○ Edwin Page ○ Leonard F. Pampel ○ Carolyn Pareneaut ○ John Parish ○ John L. Parish ○ David C. Park ○ Don Parmeter ○ Donald R. Parrish ○ John D. Parsons ○ William Partington ○ Shannon Pater ○ Eva Patton ○ Wilbur Paul ○ Neil Paulson ○ Joe Payne ○ M. L. Payne ○ William Pearson ○ Lee Peart ○ John D. Peine ○ Roger Pelletier ○ Gerald W. Pelton ○ Hon. Federico Pena ○ Perry Pendley ○ Mike Penfold ○ Russell Pengelly ○ Steven Pennoyer ○ Don Perkins ○ J. R. "Bob" Perkins ○ Robert Perkins ○ Elliott Perovich ○ Kate Perry ○ Dave Pesonen ○ Steve Peters ○ Eric C. Peterson ○ Gene Peterson ○ George L. Peterson ○ Jack Peterson ○ James

A. Peterson ○ Katrina Peterson ○ Mark R. Peterson ○ Michael Peterson ○ R. Max Peterson ○ Susan Peterson ○ Joseph E. Petrillo ○ Marc Petty ○ John R. Phares ○ Christopher Phelps ○ Lawrence Phelps ○ John Picher ○ Clifton Pierce ○ Reuel H. Pietz ○ Dan Pike ○ Karen Piontek ○ Michael J. Pisansky ○ Barry Pitegoff ○ Alex Plaisance ○ Chris Plakos ○ A. J. Planche ○ Clarence Planthaber ○ Ron Plapp ○ George E. Plumb ○ Janet Poage ○ Rich Poelker ○ Rich Poirot ○ Joe Pollini ○ John Pollock ○ Ronald L. Polteck ○ Janet Pomeroy ○ Daniel A. Poole ○ Dan Pope ○ Michael J. Porter ○ Russell Porter ○ Maryann Potteiger ○ Dale`Potter ○ Jeff Powell ○ Herb Pownell ○ Thomas P. Pratte ○ Robert L. Prausa ○ Beverly B. Price ○ Harry S. Price ○ Hugh C. Price ○ Patricia Doyle Price ○ Paul C. Pritchard ○ Norville S. Prosser ○ Richard Pruett ○ Jeff Pryor ○ Paul S. Purifoy ○ Carse Pustmueller

Craig Rademacher ○ Helen Radke ○ Gilbert Radonski ○ Richard Ragatz ○ Sharon Randall ○ Janna Rankin ○ Jay Scott Raphael ○ Robert Raschke ○ Robert Rasor ○ Frederick L. Rath, Jr. ○ Jim Ratz ○ Charlotte J. Read ○ Rick Recht ○ Charlie Recker ○ Clayton A. Record, Jr. ○ Lee Redding ○ Charles Redman ○ Neal Redmon ○ Clyde Reed ○ Matthews Reed ○ Hon. Nathaniel P. Reed ○ Wyn Reeves ○ Villere Reggio ○ Debbie Regnone ○ James Reichwein ○ Ann Christine Reid ○ N. R. Reid ○ Betsy Reifsnider ○ William K. Reilly ○ Kathleen M. Reinburg ○ Jim Reinhart ○ Jeff Rennicke ○ Peter Reshetniak ○ Carter Revard ○ Reid Reynolds ○ Catherine Rezabeck ○ Judy Rice ○ Kannon Richards ○ John Richardson ○ Dan Riche ○ Bill Richwine ○ William Rickards ○ James M. Ridenour ○ Louis Ritrovato ○ Frances Land Ritter ○ Gary M. Robb ○ Robert O. Robertson ○ Renee Robin ○ Doug Robinson ○ Jack W. Robinson ○ James Robinson ○ John P. Robinson ○ Mark H. Robinson ○ Joseph Rodota ○ William G. Roe ○ John M. Rogers ○ Warren Rogers ○ Joseph Roggenbuck ○ James P. Roles ○ Holmes Rolston, III ○ Jack Romanek ○ Richard Rome ○ David Romero ○ Paul Romero ○ Hon. John Rose ○ Martin Rosen ○ Margaret Rosenberry ○ Bob Ross ○ I. M. Ross ○ Molly Ross ○ Neil Ross ○ S. Ross ○ J. E. Rowe ○ Mayor Charles Royer ○ James B. Ruch ○ Hon. William D. Ruckelhaus ○ B. Suzi Ruhl ○ Paul Rundquist ○ Ford Runge ○ David C. Russell ○ Evan Russell ○ John L. Ruthven

Sharon Saare ○ Cong. Martin O. Sabo ○ Louise E. Sagalyn ○ Betsy Sale ○ Charles Salkin ○ Dotti Salmon-Baker ○ Stephen Salta ○ Neil Sampson ○ Roger Sanborn ○ Duane Sand ○ Vicki Jo Sandstead ○ Andrew Sansom ○ State Sen. H. Tati Santiesteban ○ Frank Sargeant ○ Mark S. Sargent ○ Paul R. Saunders ○ Eric Sawtelle ○ Hugh J. Saynor, Sr. ○ David Schaenen ○ Virginia R. Scharf ○ Ralph Schell ○ Larry Schenk ○ William W. Schenk ○ C. W. Schert ○ Bill Schilling ○ Dave Schilperoort ○ Karen Schirm ○ Marsha Schlosser ○ Donald Schmidt ○ Jerry Schneider ○ Jerry Schnepf ○ Donna Schober ○ E. A. Scholer ○ Col. Wayne Scholl ○ John Schreiber ○ Richard Schreyer ○ Otto Schults ○ Jack Schuster ○ Nancy Schuster ○ Paul Schwieger ○ Marvin Schwilling ○ Gov. Ted Schwinden ○ Dave Scott ○ Dick Scott ○ Donald Scott ○ Joseph C. Scott ○ Cecil Searle ○ Naomi Searle ○ Walllace

Sears ○ Joe Seavey ○ Mike Segrest ○ John R. Seibold ○ Helen A. Selleck ○ Jon Wesley Sering ○ H. Douglas Sessoms ○ William R. Seymour ○ Kathy Sferra ○ Elwood L. Shafer ○ Will Shafrath ○ Bill Sharp ○ Harold Shefler ○ Bo Shelby ○ Bernice Sheldon ○ Jim Shepard ○ R. G. Shepard ○ Roger Shepherd ○ Hon. Barbara Shinpock ○ Jay S. Shivers ○ Donna J. Shober ○ Charles C. Shockley ○ Joan B. Shorey ○ Milo J. Shult ○ Otto Shults ○ Terri Shuman ○ Wayne Shuyler ○ Chrystos Siderelis ○ Leroy C. Siler, III ○ Clay Simon ○ Lieut. Gov. Marlene Simmons ○ Ovalene Simmons ○ Al Simon ○ Scott Simons ○ Al Simpson ○ Julie Simpson ○ John Skibinski ○ Steve Skold ○ Peggy Skonecki ○ Ronald Skoog ○ Stephenie Slahr ○ Ken Sleight ○ Gordon H. Small ○ Glenn Smart ○ Betty van der Smissen ○ Ben Smith ○ Bill Smith ○ Charles Smith ○ Chris Smith ○ Conrad Smith ○ Dan Smith ○ John A. Smith ○ Peter Smith ○ Ralph Smith ○ Roger T. Smith ○ Ron Smith ○ Steve Smith ○ Wally Smith ○ Warren Smith ○ William Smith ○ Zane Smith ○ Walter H. Snyder ○ Dennis L. Soden ○ Peter Soderberg ○ John R. Sokol ○ Susan Soloman ○ Ron Somerville ○ Joseph Sommer ○ Martin Sorensen ○ David Spain ○ J. Spansail ○ Helen A. Spencer ○ John R. Spencer ○ Karlton Spindle ○ William T. Spitzer ○ Ira Spring ○ Wayne C. Srapf ○ Richard G. Stahl ○ George H. Stankey ○ Kirk W. Stanley ○ Jeff Stant ○ Kelly Starsa ○ Dick Stauber ○ Gaylord L. Staveley ○ George Steele ○ Brian Steen ○ Gene Steffen ○ Joseph W. Stehn ○ Walter O. Steiglitz ○ Peter R. Stein ○ Brock E. Stenman ○ Press Stephens ○ M. Sterkel ○ William Stevens ○ Sid Stevenson ○ Ronald K. Stewart ○ Michael Stewart ○ Clarence Stiard ○ Robert Stignani ○ Robert Stilson ○ Roger Stilson ○ Judith Stockdale ○ Ron Stockman ○ Charles Stoddard ○ Gerald L. Stokes ○ Robert Stokes ○ Turner Stokes ○ John R. Stoll ○ Gregory Stone ○ Ron Stone ○ David Stoner ○ Marie Stoner ○ Martha Stough ○ Donna E. Stout ○ Michael Stratton ○ Dick Strauber ○ Jim Stray ○ Clarence Streetman ○ Jeremiah Stromberg ○ Franz Arthur Strong ○ Don Stroud ○ Sen. George Stuart, Jr. ○ Wally Stuckney ○ Thad Studstill ○ John L. Sturgeon ○ Doss Sturse ○ Odin Stutrud ○ Geoffrey Styles ○ Daniel J. Stynes ○ G. H. Suderman ○ Barbara Sudler ○ Carl R. Sullivan ○ Sidney Summers ○ Rep. Kathleen Sun ○ Rudolph Sun ○ Susan Sutro ○ David Sutton ○ Ronald D. Sutton ○ Vicki S. Sutton ○ Eugene Swan ○ Lee Swanberg ○ James A. Swanke, Jr. ○ John R. Swanson ○ Jean Swartz ○ Lorin Swinehart

Don Tahkeal ○ David G. Talbot ○ Thomas W. Talbott ○ Lawrence J. Taylor ○ Lyle A. Taylor ○ Tom Taylor ○ Walter Taylor ○ Michael L. Teague ○ Robert W. Teater ○ James G. Teer ○ Jim Tellerico ○ Jerry Terstiege ○ Elizabeth E. Thach ○ Bud Thies ○ Jack Ward Thomas ○ Robert Thomas ○ Claude Thompson ○ D. C. Thompson ○ Ed Thompson ○ Gov. James R. Thompson ○ Tommy Thompson ○ Burch Thomsen ○ Gregory S. Thomson ○ Margaret Thomsen ○ S. Thornberry ○ Jer Thornton ○ William T. Thornton ○ R. Dean Tice ○ Anne Tidwell ○ John Tidwell ○ Pat Tierney ○ Bill Tilden ○ Howard E. A. Tinsley ○ Sherri Tippie ○ Bill Tischer ○ John Titre, Jr. ○ Elizabeth Titus ○ John Toenes ○ Marilyn Tomasi ○ Tom Tsongas ○ Ann

Toole ○ Thomas C. Tougas ○ David L. Towne ○ Raymond Traut ○ Mark Trautwein ○ Charles D. Travis ○ William E. Trout, III ○ Richard C. Trudeau ○ James Truncer ○ John Tunberg ○ Ted Turner ○ Jackie Tuxill ○ Mary Ann Twyford

Mark Udall ○ Hon. Stewart Udall ○ A. H. Underhill

Banning Vail ○ Carlton Van Doren ○ Laurence R. Van Meter ○ Lloyd Van Sickle ○ John Vanderwalker ○ Jay Andrew Vasenden ○ Donna Veno ○ Cong. Bruce Vento ○ George Ververis ○ Joseph I. Vincent ○ Ronald A. Vine ○ Mary Violett ○ Vern Vivian ○ Herbert Vogelman ○ Michael Voiland ○ Bob Volpert ○ Joe Voskerchian

James Wacker ○ Bill Wade ○ Ian Wade ○ Randall A. Wagner ○ Phil Wagoner ○ Teri Waivada ○ Frances Wallach ○ Richard Walsh ○ Jack Walter ○ William C. Walters ○ Emma Walton ○ Murray Walton ○ Tom Walton ○ Elaine Warren ○ Nan Warren ○ Roger Warren ○ Ronald Warren ○ Wayne Warren ○ Alan Watson ○ Charles Watson ○ Roland H. Wauer ○ William Weare ○ Bruce F. Weaver ○ Tad Weaver ○ John Webley ○ Henry Webster ○ Burt Weerts ○ Roger Wehling ○ Frank J. Weiler ○ William Weiner ○ Paul D. Weingart ○ Henry Welge ○ Annette T. Wendel ○ Gary Werner ○ Robert Werner ○ Linda K. West ○ Patrick C. West ○ Casey Westell ○ Edward Whalley ○ Douglas Wheeler ○ Jim Whelan ○ John C. Whitaker ○ Charles W. Whitcomb ○ Bill White ○ Gordon E. White ○ Debi Whitmire ○ Sandra Whitmore ○ Hon. John C. Whitaker ○ Jim Whitney ○ Pam Whittaker ○ Roger L. Whyte ○ William H. Whyte ○ Jack Widmeyer ○ Frank J. Wieiler ○ Carl Wiese ○ Andy Wiessner ○ Tamara Wiggins ○ Vernon R. Wiggins ○ Steven Wigray ○ Ken Wilcox ○ Mayor Evelyn Wilcox ○ William Wilcox ○ Robert L. Wilder ○ Leslie Wildesen ○ Bill Wildt ○ Bill Wilen ○ Gerold W. Wilkin ○ Bruce T. Wilkins ○ Bill Wilkinson ○ Daniel Williams ○ Don Williams ○ Donald V. Williams ○ James Williams ○ John Williams ○ Tom Williams ○ Jed Williamson ○ LTC Edward Willis ○ Ted Willis ○ H. G. Wilshire ○ Ellen Wilson ○ Georgia Wilson ○ Jo Luck Wilson ○ Larry Wilson ○ Orlando Wilson ○ Steve N. Wilson ○ Willard A. Wilson ○ Peter G. Wingle ○ Ira I. Winn ○ Darrell Winslow ○ Cong. Timothy E. Wirth ○ Donald E. Wirth ○ George Wislocki ○ Peter Witt ○ Robert Wohlers ○ James R. Wolf ○ Gary Wolfe ○ Jerry Wood ○ Ronald Wood ○ Scott Wood ○ Richard Woodrow ○ Mark Worcester ○ William Worf ○ Randolph Worls ○ Patricia Worthington ○ Ann Wright ○ David G. Wright ○ Esther C. Wunnicke

Steven L. Yaffee ○ Hank Yake ○ Todd Yann ○ Tom M. Yates ○ Ed Yeager ○ Mike Yeager ○ Ed Young ○ Nancy Yust

Gus Zaso ○ Michael D. Zagata ○ Art Zeiger ○ John Zeliff ○ Barbara Zell ○ Milburn Zell ○ Marty Zeller ○ Dave Zentner ○ Kent Zimmerman ○ Jody Zoeller ○ Betty Van Zonneveld ○ Elizabth Zuidema

Federal Register
Vol. 50. No. 21
Thursday, January 31, 1985

Presidential Documents

Executive Order 12503 of January 28, 1985

Presidential Commission on Outdoor Recreation Resources Review

By the authority vested in me a President by the Constitution and statutes of the United States of America, including the Federal Advisory Committee Act, as amended (5 U.S.C. App. I), and in order to create an advisory commission to review outdoor recreation resources, it is hereby ordered as follows:

Section 1 *Establishment.* (a) There is hereby established the Presidential Commission on Outdoor Recreation Resources Review.

(b) The Commission shall be composed of not more than 15 members appointed or designated by the President from among the private sector, the Legislative branch of the Federal government, recreational and other service organizations, and State and local governments. The President shall designate a Chairman and Vice Chairman from among the members of the Commission.

Sec. 2 *Functions.* (a) The Commission shall review existing public outdoor recreation policies, programs, and opportunities provided by the Federal government, State and local governments, and private organizations and entities and shall review privately provided outdoor recreation resources to the extent that they affect the demand for public outdoor recreation resources. The Commission shall, consistent with the need for fiscal economy at all levels of government, make recommendations to the President concerning the outdoor recreation resources, programs, and opportunities that will ensure the future availability of outdoor recreation for the American people. In making its recommendations, the Commission shall assess the budgetary and regulatory cost increases or cost savings of its proposals, and shall, to the extent possible, utilize such studies, data, and reports previously prepared or under preparation by Federal agencies, States, private organizations or other entities.

(b) In conducting its review, the Commission shall examine:

(1) existing outdoor recreation lands and resources and the land and resource base necessary for future outdoor recreation;

(2) the roles of the Federal, State, county, and municipal governments in providing outdoor recreation opportunities, protecting outdoor recreation resources, and meeting anticipated outdoor recreation conditions;

(3) the role of the private sector in meeting present and future outdoor recreation needs, and assess the potential for cooperation between the private sector and government in providing outdoor recreation opportunities and protecting outdoor recreation resources;

(4) the relationship between outdoor recreation and personal and public health, the economy, and the environment;

(5) the future needs of outdoor recreation management systems, including qualified personnel, technical information, and anticipated financial needs;

(6) the relationship of outdoor recreation to the broader range of recreation pursuits and its implications for the supply of and demand for outdoor recreation resources and opportunities;

(7) underlying social, economic, and technological factors that are likely to affect the demand for and supply of outdoor recreation resources, including trends in disposable income and demographic characteristics of the United States;

(8) the findings and recommendations of the National Urban Recreation Study (1978), the Third Nationwide Outdoor Recreation Plan (1979), the Forest and Rangeland Renewable Resources Planning Act-Assessment Supplement (1984), and other relevant Federal survey and planning activities.

(c) The Commission may conduct public hearings and otherwise secure information and expressions of public opinion on recreation issues, policies and programs, and anticipated national, regional, State, and local recreation needs and concerns.

(d) The Commission shall submit its report and recommendations to the President not later than twelve months after the date of this Order.

Sec. 3. *Administration.* (a) The heads of Executive agencies shall, to the extent permitted by law, provide the Commission with such information as may be necessary for the effective performance of its functions.

(b) Members of the Commission shall serve without compensation for their work on the Commission. Members appointed from among private citizens of the United States may be allowed travel expenses, including per diem in lieu of subsistence, as authorized by law for persons serving intermittently in the government service (5 U.S.C. 5701-5707).

(c) The Secretary of the Interior shall, to the extent permitted by law, provide the Commission with such administrative services, facilities, staff, and other support services as may be necessary for the effective performance of its functions.

Sec. 4. *General.* (a) Notwithstanding any other Executive order, the functions of the President under the Federal Advisory Committee Act, as amended, which are applicable to the Commission, except that of reporting annually to the Congress, shall be performed by the Secretary of the Interior, in accordance with guidelines and procedures established by the Administrator of General Services.

(b) The Commission shall terminate 30 days after submission of its report, or March 1, 1986, whichever sooner occurs.*

Ronald Reagan

THE WHITE HOUSE.
January 28, 1985.

---

*Amended by Executive Order on August 15, 1985

(1) The title of the Commission is changed to the "President's Commission on Americans Outdoors."

(2) The Commission should submit its report to the President no later than December 31, 1986.

Editor's Note

As part of its research, the President's Commission on Americans Outdoors solicited a number of case studies on how recreation resource and visitor service problems were being addressed at the local level. These were intended, in the words of the Commission staff, "to provide specific examples of policy, planning, and management approaches that might be generally applicable to a wide range of local, state, federal or private activities across the country." ISLAND PRESS has selected for publication 12 of the studies which describe innovative approaches to solving problems and capturing opportunities to protect resources and expand recreation opportunities.

. . . .

Open Space Preservation in the 31-County New York Urban Region from 1960 to the 21st Century—A Midpoint Review

HOOPER BROOKS
Open Space Director
Regional Plan Association

I. Introduction

The Regional Plan Association has launched its most ambitious look at the tri-state (New York, New Jersey, Connecticut) Region's environmental and recreational needs and resources since *The Race for Open Space* was published in 1960. At the same time, the President's Commission on Americans Outdoors has been set up in Washington to examine similar issues at the national level.

Regional Plan's new program is a response to severe open space management and preservation problems throughout the Region, as well as to the consequences of large reductions in federal spending for parks since 1979. Lands used for outdoor recreation are not the only concern; also at stake are lands which conserve natural resources, especially water, and those which produce food and timber. The program has three main components:

1. A survey of what is already known about the status of open space in the Region today, looking toward tomorrow, with targeted research to fill in any gaps.

2. A leadership group from the public and private sectors to forge a strategy with specific recommendations for the protection and maintenance of open space in the Region.

3. An energetic public awareness campaign to communicate the program's findings and recommendations and to help spread the open space ethic.

The project will take three years and has a budget of nearly a million dollars which is being provided from foundation, corporate, and government sources.

In order to focus public attention on significant preliminary findings of the Regional Open Space Program, this case study has been prepared for submission to the President's Commission on Americans Outdoors. It examines progress made since 1960 in the New York Urban Region to reserve open space and park lands for the future, the problems being encountered today, and what is needed, particularly in terms of federal leadership and partnership with other levels of government, the non-profit and private sectors, to address future needs.

II. Background

The first Outdoor Recreation Resources Review Commission (ORRRC I) and Regional Plan Association's (RPA) 1960 Race for Open Space occurred just in time for the 31-county New York Tri-state Region. The ratio of population to public open space was increasing at a great rate and—especially after World War II—rapid land development was removing options for additional open space preservation. Land and Water Conservation Fund stateside grants of over $177 million, protection of the Appalachian Trail, Fire Island National Seashore and Gateway National Recreation Area were among ORRRC I's dramatic legacies to the Region. *The Race for Open Space* complemented national actions, touching off such far-reaching programs as New Jersey's Green Acres Program and other preservation actions in such fast-developing areas as mid-Long Island.

The thousands of acres set aside for outdoor recreation represent a great achievement, yet major challenges remain. Renewed growth in the Region is causing new urban sprawl and consequent pressure for development of remaining open spaces, private recreation areas, farmlands, large estates, critical natural areas, urban waterfronts and inner urban vacant land. An enormous preservation agenda remains, while dollars available for acquisition dwindle. Moreover, what has been preserved is not being given adequate care or used to its fullest advantage.

Dramatic action is needed if today's open space challenge is to be met. Without stable funding, strong leadership, and a good blueprint of what is needed, the more sophisticated preservation techniques now available cannot be fully or wisely implemented; the trend toward resourcefulness will translate into being penny wise and pound foolish.

III. What Should Happen Next

Good open space management is a shared responsibility of every level of government, the non-profit and the private sectors. Why? Because healthy open space benefits all levels of the Region's economy and its entire population. The multi-billion-dollar tourism and recreation goods and services industries are the most obvious beneficiaries of accessible, attractive open spaces. Public health benefits and a high quality of life are more intangible results of preserved open spaces, but benefit people and influence location and investment decisions in the Region.

Improved coordination and stronger partnerships among all levels of government and private agencies would enhance the value of everyone's contribution. To foster that objective, Regional Plan Association makes the following recommendations to the President's Commission:

1. A stable, permanent source of funds should be established at the federal level with sufficient flexibility to provide catalytic leadership in meeting diverse needs including those of non-profit trusts, conservancies, and volunteer groups.

2. Where possible, the funding should be derived from non-income tax sources.

3. Distribution of these funds should be based on a formula which takes into account population densities, and which allows regional, state and local and non-profit and private sector entities to set their own funding agendas.

4. Federal leadership should provide incentives to put preservation funds to better use:

○ incentives should be used as the carrot to stimulate local planning approaches;

○ seed money for operations and maintenance endowments should accompany acquisition dollars to encourage long-range resource stability;

○ incentives should be established to improve public administration standards for park and recreation administrators to generate better open space management;

○ incentives and standards for public/private partnerships in resource management planning, agency management, and use of volunteers should be developed to stretch the value of all resources;

○ clearer, more lenient income-tax policies should be developed to encourage low cost preservation techniques such as easements.

5. As the preservation challenge shifts emphasis from protecting individual parcels to protecting systems, the federal government should play an important role in testing, explaining, and encouraging use of the sophisticated techniques and approaches which have become available.

6. Stronger guidelines and incentives are needed to facilitate the outdoor recreation uses of all lands, including private, institutional, and government properties not protected as open space, a process which the federal government should share.

7. Better data management, surveys, and research are needed to build the quantitative and qualitative rationale for open space which clearly

exists,but which needs to be updated and documented. Federal stimulation of coordination, establishment of uniform collection standards, and custodianship is essential.

A common theme underlying these recommendations is the federal government's role as catalyst, stimulating maximum participation from regional, state, and local public, non-profit, and private sector entities. Outdoor recreation and public open space have had a positive impact on the economy which deserves more recognition. Enormous public investment in land, facilities and programs has enriched the nation and its people and protected its natural resources. Improved real estate values, increased recreation equipment sales, and higher demand for recreation services are all by-products. And where natural resources preservation has been successful, infrastructure investment to control flooding, erosion or water quality has been reduced. The beneficiaries of these open space investments are capable of sharing more in their funding, maintenance and preservation, but it is the federal government which must make this happen.

Why a stable source of funds?

Most federal funding for state and local open space has terminated. Despite its obvious success, Land and Water Conservation Fund appropriations have been greatly reduced and Congressional authority for this program does not extend beyond 1989. This has exacerbated an already unstable funding situation. Every other level of government and the non-profit and private sectors have stretched to fill the gap, but even if they stretch more, they will be unable to keep up with the need. It is impossible to properly plan for and manage the Region's open space—and especially difficult to reach out for private sector assistance—under these conditions.

For example, the corporate and business communities have found open space preservation to be in their own best interests, and have confirmed this by protecting their own resources and by matching government and non-profit efforts. With increased, dependable government-dollar participation the private sector interest can be encouraged to expand.

How can funds be derived from non-income tax sources?

The success of the Land and Water Conservation Fund (LWCF) as a non-tax revenue funding catalyst has paved the way for establishment of a "natural assets trust fund." Such a fund would be geared to reinvesting revenues from the depletion of nonrenewable resources to preserve open space resources important to the country's natural and cultural heritage. Possibly the unappropriated LWCF funds estimated at $6 billion could be used to start the trust.

There are many promising ways to build a trust fund by indexing a revenue stream to private sector forces which affect open space. Real estate transfer taxes are gaining in popularity and, as long as claims of special recreation privilege are not indulged, there is a potential for more dollars to flow annually from taxes on sales of recreation goods and services. Additional dollars could be raised by providing an optional checkoff on income tax returns to send a dollar to help with preservation of the nation's open space resources or by creating a special savings bond to preserve open space resources. Even a modest share of federal tax revenues would be appropriate, when the payoff is a much better yield of matching dollars from all other possible sources.

Stretching the value of the federal contribution is as important as the source of revenues. In addition to stimulating direct and indirect matching dollars, techniques such as the Green Trust, a low interest revolving loan fund established in New Jersey, should be evaluated as a model for distribution of a portion of federal dollars. To better protect the investment, dollars raised from taxes on recreation goods and services could be used to create companion maintenance grants for each new land acquisition in the form of seed money for maintenance endowments or to encourage public/private cooperation in resource management.

How to guarantee fair distribution of funds?

Forty percent of the LWCF dollars were originally allocated equally among the states. This percentage should be reduced, and the balance allocated better to reflect population densities and, if possible, the cost of land. Otherwise the Region's funding share will not adequately reflect its needs, or the cost of meeting them.

One way to guarantee better regional representation and guarantee more local self-determination without compromising accountability would be to establish a separate agency to manage funding, much as the Bureau of Outdoor Recreation did. The governing structure of this new agency could be modeled on successful elements of the National Trust for Historic Preservation and similar agencies, which involve a partnership of all levels of government, the non-profit and private sectors, including developers.

How can leadership provide incentives and why?

For planning—Encouraging local action within the boundary of an important natural or cultural system has led to preservation of watersheds, scenic rivers, and scenic roadways by state, local, and non-profit groups. Federal participation has provided the necessary regional overview and incentives.

For operations and maintenance—In the past, funding acquisitions and capital projects have had obvious political appeal. But support for continued acquisition has been eroded by a lack of visible support for maintaining our existing facilities, many of which are now in disarray. Maintenance stability must be built into future funding for acquisition to gain needed public and legislative approval. The Nature Conservancy suggests that the annual interest on an endowment of 25 percent of the market price of a parcel is a realistic estimate of long-term maintenance and management needs.

For improved public administration—Another reason that public open space facilities have decayed is due to poor administration. The emphasis of professional education needs to encompass not only the specifics of pruning trees and mowing grass, but the broader requirements of good public administration. Each kind of expertise is required to properly manage open space, but they are not necessarily interchangeable, as current practices often assume. Federal leadership is needed to propose standards for appropriate training and hiring.

For better public/private partnerships—Good public administration is knowing how to use and being resourceful in using volunteer, non-profit, and private sector assistance. The track record of programs such as the Urban Parks and Recreation Recovery Program point the way for new federal leadership in this respect.

For clearer tax policies—Clearer Internal Revenue Service policies with respect to easements and elimination of guidelines which hamper non-profit conservancies and land trusts are examples of how small changes in income tax regulations could yield big results.

Testing, seeding and explaining techniques

Local, county and state acceptance and implementation of new techniques is slow. Providing examples of success elsewhere, seed financing, better technical information, model legislation and better education for professionals and local lay decision makers would be quickly repaid by better local stewardship. Federal money and expertise for technical assistance is a strong signal to state and local governments that they should be concerned.

There is an enormous potential for achieving preservation by integrating open space and environmental protection into the development process using techniques which are cost effective for both developer and preservationist. Much more can be accomplished without threatening the tax base, independence and economic potential of local communities. Also, there are better opportunities for tapping the flow of private development dollars more directly in ways that benefit the public more efficiently.

Boosting outdoor recreation uses of all lands

Just addressing the opportunities which now exist on private, institutional, and government properties not protected as open space would add many public outdoor recreation choices. Additionally, defining and facilitating the appropriate private sector role in public open space would be a cost effective move as long as the public purpose is retained.

This job must be shared by everyone, but the federal government can take the lead by making available inventories of government properties where open space opportunities exist by encouraging their use, helping to set guidelines for private sector involvement on public land, supporting measures to reduce the impact of liability costs, and streamlining troublesome federal tax policies which now work at cross purposes with preservation goals.

The need for better basic information

Given that healthy open space is essential to health, welfare, and the economy, we must understand it better. There is a need for better information and understanding of the open space resource, its economic value, and the spending patterns and needs of people who might use it. The federal government should aim, structure, and oversee such an effort. For example, minorities in the tri-state Region have doubled since 1960 and are expected to double again by the year 2000, to 45 percent of the total population. Knowing the needs and trends of this population will be essential to building future open space and to nurturing a constituency for proper management of all open space.

At present, many jurisdictions have no idea who uses or could use their open space facilities. In fact, they lack basic inventories of the extent and condition of lands and facilities they own. When managers do not even have a good profile of what they manage it is difficult to plan for acquisition, capital improvements, programing, operations and maintenance.

IV. A Closer Look at Problems Which Call for New Leadership & Better Partnerships

Open space preservation in the tri-state Region has come a long way since 1960, but the gains of the past two decades must be viewed in light of some alarming trends. The Region's stewards are having a hard time taking care of what has been preserved or making sure that it is used to its best advantage. At the same time, the speed of renewed growth—coupled with inadequate funds, plans or leadership—is making it difficult for all levels of government, non-profits, and even the private sector to address a reasonable land preservation agenda for future outdoor recreation and environmental protection needs.

An operation and maintenance crisis. Parks have suffered the most serious management consequences. Federal funds for parks and recreation assistance to local governments for acquisition, improvements, youth employment, training, planning, and so forth, went from $1.2 billion nationwide in 1976 to some $268 million in 1983—a decrease of 78 percent without even considering inflation.

Virtually every federal program for funding local parks has been eliminated or cut to the bone in anticipation of eventual elimination. Many officials complain that the process to obtain what scarce federal funds remain
has become so unworkable as to discourage them from applying.

Funding cuts have intensified an already severe operations and maintenance crisis at the state and local levels. In New York State, for instance,
park maintenance staffs have shrunk by one-third in the last ten years,
while visitation has remained steady at about 44 million people a year. The
effects are evident in damaged landscapes and crumbling facilities—many
of them built by WPA or CCC in the 1930s. Some areas are overused, others
underused, and others used inappropriately.

Population growth: sprawl and lost opportunities. And while open
space professionals and advocates alike have been scrambling for ways
to meet the operations and management crisis, the population has once
again started to grow, there is a resurgence in the economy. Open space
options are disappearing because of unplanned sprawl. RPA estimates that
there are roughly 3,698 square miles of developed land in the 31-county
Region, an increase of over 934 square miles since 1963. This leaves about
8,579 square miles of vacant land after subtracting 1,500 square miles of
public open space. Using current growth projections, the footprint of new
office and home development could consume an additional 1,000 square
miles of land by the year 2000.

The remaining 8,500 square miles of vacant land are not necessarily
acres which should or could be developed for various reasons; 2,168
square miles are used as farmland, 93 square miles are private preserves,
114 square miles of camps, 93 square miles of golf courses, and 16 square
miles of private campgrounds. Preliminary Regional Plan research suggests
that 20 to 50 percent of the 8,500 square miles which remain vacant have
limited development potential because of bedrock conditions (steep
slopes, shallow depth to bedrock), soil conditions (wet soils, floodplains),
or water supply and quality constraints. Our future research will develop
more reliable data on this matter, but it is clear that the last 8,500 square
miles of vacant land in the Region do not offer the same choices as the
3,698 that have been developed. Open space preservation in the future will
play an important role in shaping development choices for the greatest
long-term public health and economic benefit.

In urban areas, the most significant trade-off between urban open
space and redevelopment is occurring on the waterfronts. And as alternatives run out, even chronically vacant land in blighted areas becomes attractive for investment. In the 1970s, this land was viewed as readily available in abundant quantities to be converted for recreation purposes, but
this may no longer be the case. Economic growth is good for the cities,
but it sharpens the already difficult challenge of providing sufficient urban
open space to make new development livable. In the suburbs, saving key

Table 1: Land Use in the Tri-State Region
PRA 31-County Study Area (NY, NJ, CT)

Square miles

(percent of study area)	1964	1984
Public Open Space	873.5 (6.3%)	1,489.54 (10.8%)
Developed Lands (including roads)	2,763.6 (20.1%)	3,697.9 (26.9%)
Remaining Land	10,129.9 (73.6%)	8,579.54 (62.3%)
Totals	13,767	13,767

Table 2: Open Space Uses of Private Lands (1985)
RPA 31-County Study Area (NY, NJ, CT)

	NY	NJ	CT	Total
Farmland*	784	1,147	237	2,168
Private Camps**	95	13	6	114
Private Preserves/ Protected Open Spaces†	23	27	43	93
Commercial Recreation Facilities††				
a. Golf Courses	58	24	11	93
b. Private Campgrounds	10	5	1	16
Totals	970	1,216	298	2,484

*From 1982 Agricultural Census.
**Includes data on private commercial, private non-profit, girl scout and boy scout camps.
†Including Audubon, Nature Conservancy, Land Trust preserves, plus private nature centers.
††Figures for NJ based on estimate of 50 acres per 9-hole course and 100 acres per 18-hole course.

remaining parcels of land and securing close-to-home opportunities for recreation have become critical.

Here, upzoning, urbanization, and traffic have suddenly made saving more open land necessary to stabilize the suburban quality of life. In the exurbs, large private holdings suffer the most visible impact. The challenge regionwide is to shape the footprint of development to accommodate recreational and environmental needs without threatening economic growth. Familiar scenic vistas, strategic access parcels, hiking and riding trail alignments, aesthetic buffers, and agricultural areas are being lost to development, even when they have been targeted as open space on state, county or municipal plans.

Watershed and aquifer lands and environmental buffers such as wetlands are also being lost. Flooding, poor water quality, and insufficient amounts of drinking water result. New York City officials fear an inadequate future water supply. Long Island's only aquifer is endangered by permanent contamination. New Jersey suffers regular water shortages due to poorly laid out systems. Local surface and ground water quality is a universal concern. Paving and filling steep slopes and wetlands has caused serious cycles of flooding and drought in places where this has never before been a problem. At the Great Swamp National Wildlife Refuge near Morristown, New Jersey, for example, drastic action may be needed to make sure that this magnificent public resource survives the impact of these flood and drought cycles. The consequences of actions well beyond the official Refuge boundaries are effectively eliminating the critical environmental protection function of this vast area and removing its capacity to serve passive outdoor recreation needs.

Existing environmental protection measures, particularly those which affect land, cannot keep up with the protection needs, even in the tri-state area, which is considered to have some of the country's strongest environmental protection programs.

Nationwide, new approaches offer economically responsive open space management tools, but are misunderstood and underutilized. It is possible to link saving land for environmental protection to meeting social needs such as housing. More constructive future dialogues between developers and preservationists are also possible if we can employ natural resource-based zoning techniques. As yet, the possibilities have been only modestly tested.

What makes it most difficult to shape the footprint of future development is rising land values. In some parts of the Region, land values have gone up by almost 50 percent in the past year, sending ripples of price escalation to all corners of the Region. Despite current aspirations in the tri-state area for new open space preservation bond issues and increased non-profit and private sector activity, it is unlikely that funding for the next twenty years from state, county, local, non-profit and private sources will match the dollar totals of the past 25 years. Proposed bond issues and revolving loan capacity right now are probably less than half of what was spent between 1960 and now, and the buying capacity well below that.

Special concerns: privately-owned open space. In the suburban and exurban areas, privately-owned lands have a great potential for satisfying open space needs. Taken as a whole, commercial recreation facilities, non-profit camps, farmland, institutional lands, school properties, large estates, surplus corporate lands and surplus military lands may well total over 3,000 square miles of the 13,000 square mile Region. There are over 90 square miles of golf courses, 109 square miles of commercial facilities, and 114 square miles of private camps, including Boy and Girl Scout camps. But literally dozens of these and other similar lands are being sold for development every year. Church, hospital, military, public, and private school lands are also on the auction block for many of the same reasons. In some instances, even public parkland is being sold to accommodate economic pressures.

Rising land values are only one factor affecting the decision to sell privately-owned recreation lands, although it is the major one. Private commercial facilities, such as stables and ski areas, face astronomical liability premiums and rising taxes. Private and non-profit camps, which may be able to obtain low-cost liability protection through national offices and organizations, face escalating operating costs imposed by state health and other regulations. Camps and non-profit scout operations also face dwindling enrollments at the moment, even though there may be unmet needs in cities or in the future. On Long Island, schools that used to provide enough scouts for four or five troops have been closed. In many cases, conversion of the surrounding land encroaches upon the open space quality or "wilderness" value of an area: a private campground, or a girl scout camp or a stable's trail system may not be a viable commercial enterprise once surrounded by strip developments. This does not mean, however, that its value as open space is negligible.

It is hard to focus preservation efforts to help protect such diverse land types and their owners. Moreover, the parcels are arrayed in piecemeal fashion across the landscape so that rapid conversion occurs without a focused attempt to recognize and address some of these causes. Specific campaigns to protect individual parcels have been mounted, but effectively using the far-reaching alternatives to acquisition requires more coordination than currently is possible. Certainly, the difficulty of protecting private open land seems to contradict arguments touting private sector recreation and private open space stewardship as the wave of the future.

With most of the existing outdoor recreation properties stretched to capacity during the warm months and used throughout the year and with existing conservation areas suffering degradation, there is universal concern about the loss of these privately owned lands. In many cases opportunities for public parkland with pre-existing investment in recreation facilities are being lost.

V. Foundations for New Action—Twenty-Five Years of Accomplishments

While the Region's problems make a compelling case for remedial action that stands on its own, it is the achievements of the past 25 years that will be the foundation on which future action is built and are an important part of the investment which must be protected.

Acquisition and funding sources. Since 1960, public open space increased by almost 65 percent in the 31-county, 13,000 square mile tri-state Region, to almost 1,500 square miles. Federal acreage increased from under 10 square miles to almost 100 square miles, including Fire Island National Seashore, Gateway National Recreation Area, the Delaware Water Gap National Recreation Area, the Upper Delaware Scenic and Recreational River and the Appalachian National Scenic Trail.

The dramatic progress in preservation was due to the catalytic effect of the Land and Water Conservation Fund (LWCF) and other federal land-acquisition and development funding assistance, such as pre-1973 Housing and Urban Development (HUD) Open Space funds and use of Urban Development block grants. Federal dollars served as a catalyst for the allocation of state, county, and local funds—bond issues, general funds, special funds, fees, and concession income. In many cases, one federal dollar sparked the contribution of over 10 state dollars. Without this federal leadership and partnership, many feel that local government plans for acquisition and development would never have gained approval.

The largest acquisitions were made in New Jersey, accounting for over half the Region's increase (324 square miles). New York accounted for over a third of the increase (over 200 square miles). Connecticut, with the smallest area in RPA's tri-state Region and only three percent of the federal lands, accounted for ten percent (44 square miles). It is difficult to assess total public and private dollars spent to acquire and improve these lands. Dollars from the Land and Water Conservation Fund and state bond issues are probably the best indicators.

The LWCF's $177 million in stateside assistance was divided as follows: 36 percent to New Jersey, 53 percent to New York, and 11 percent to Connecticut. They helped with acquisition, development and redevelopment in different ways in each state, with New York and New Jersey having spent over two-thirds of their share on development and redevelopment, and Connecticut spending almost two-thirds on acquisition in earlier years but shifting dramatically in recent years.

In New Jersey, the Green Acres bond issue made the most of the federal initiative and stimulated many additional municipal and county dollars through direct and matching grants: a total federal-state-local impact estimated at $905 million exclusive of the recently established Green Trust, a revolving loan fund. The $83 million Green Trust low-interest revolving loan could result in $300 million in additional acquisition enabled by loans over the next 20 years. An additional $50 million in bond money has been authorized for farmland preservation. Open space leaders have identified a remaining preservation agenda in New Jersey of 400,000 acres.

In the 1960s, New York also did a great deal with $100 million in bond issues and direct appropriations. State assistance sparked certain counties and municipalities to carry out their own ambitious programs. In 1972, $175 million additional bond issue dollars were authorized for acquisition of parks, forests, wildlife habitat and scenic treasures. Virtually all is spent or spoken for. There were also some substantial donations of land, the most recent being 750 acres of the Pocantico estate in Westchester County, which the Rockefeller family recently donated along with a generous maintenance endowment. The proposed 1986 Environmental Bond Act proposed between $250 and $500 million more for acquisition, development and historic preservation statewide. Suffolk County is considering a $30 to $50 million bond act to help save 4,500 additional acres. The currently projected statewide preservation agenda, however, would cost several times the sum of these bond issues.

Connecticut has more or less indexed its yearly authorizations to the rise and fall of Land and Water Conservation Fund dollars, and increasingly, these have gone to state and local capital and redevelopment projects rather than acquisitions, but there are signs of change. Over $22.7 million bond dollars have been approved for acquisition of farmland development rights since 1978 and this year the legislature is being asked to consider bond acts as high as $10 million for acquisition of a broader range of open space types. As in New York State, the acquisition agenda identified by public and private leaders around the state would cost several times the 20-year sum of annual bond act amounts currently being proposed.

Despite great achievements regionwide, open space preservation has made the least progress in urban areas. High urban land values and complex politics stand in the way. Stringent capitalization needs often take precedence. For example, 96 percent of LWCF money in New York City was spent on development and redevelopment. There were hundreds of acres added by portions of Gateway National Recreation Area and 300 more by New York State parks. However, the city's total acreage is still nowhere near accepted national standards for acres per person. Vast areas are still without adequate, close-to-home open space or convenient access to citywide or regional open space resources.

The Urban Park and Recreation Recovery Program (UPARR), which provided some $23 million in the tri-state Region between 1979 and 1984, introduced a promising strategy for bolstering urban parkland. While not for acquisition, these grants for rehabilitation, services and planning

helped localities make more effective use of existing open space where
new acquisition possibilities were scarce and expensive.

*Protection by regulation, cooperation, tax policy and other-than-fee
acquisitions.* All three states have legislation and executive policies that
promote temporary and permanent "other-than-fee" open space preservation, using regulation, tax policy, cooperative arrangements, and other-
than-fee acquisition. Some encourage landowners to trade rights for dollars
or tax abatements (and impose penalties for conversion afterwards). Others
create special districts or critical area designations to establish ingenious
regulatory powers and encourage strong municipal ordinances to help in
implementation. Yet others enable private and non-profit stewardship for
public benefit through contractual and cooperative agreements.

New Jersey has adopted preferential farmland assessment legislation
along with agricultural retention and development areas and an Open
Lands Management Program that encourages public access to certain private lands; New York State has created special designations such as the
14 Urban Cultural Park areas and is advancing the "greenline" park concept pioneered by the Adirondack Park. Also in New York, recent easement
legislation enriches preservation action. Connecticut's inland wetlands legislation provides stringent review of development in many environmentally-
fragile acres, and tidal wetlands legislation actually prohibits development.
Its farmland preservation legislation creates opportunities to remove development potential from hundreds of acres of prime farmland.

Federal programs such as the Wild and Scenic Rivers Act, the Coastal
Zone Management Act, The Barrier Island Protection Act, and the National
Flood Plain Insurance Program complement state efforts. Appalachian Trail
maintenance involves close cooperation between the National Park Service
and volunteer groups.

Innovative management and acquisition strategies such as those introduced in the one-million-acre New Jersey Pinelands National Reserve offer
additional "greenline" principles which could be adopted elsewhere. Here,
one-third of the total acres within the Pinelands are in public ownership
and two-thirds are private. Direct federal and state funds have been used
for acquisition of 42,065 acres. An additional 25,000 acres are in the process of being purchased by the state. Environmental regulations are depended upon to protect river corridors, wetlands, and other sensitive environmental areas. Development right transfers have been used to remove
development rights from sensitive zones to other areas within the Pinelands
where development is encouraged. The important principles used here are:
1) to focus public attention on a particular resource of regional or national
importance by delineating a boundary, be it a river corridor, trail system,
watershed or aquifer; 2) to develop a public policy to protect the resource;
and 3) to craft a protection strategy to fit the particular economic and cultural needs of the constituency as well as the resource to be protected,

usually a combination of acquisition, regulation, cooperation, and tax policy.

Summary data for acreage under easement, farmland protection, wetlands regulation, floodplain designation, and permanent non-profit ownership is incomplete. Rough tri-state estimates show that development rights or other forms of protection affect over 600,000 acres of farmland out of an estimated total of over 1.38 million acres. Data on miles of trails and acres of regulated wetlands, floodplains, and coastal areas is incomplete and not as useful for measuring degrees of preservation. There is no summary data on how much open space is in cluster and similar subdivisions in the tri-state area or how much is associated with corporate campuses and urban plazas.

Private involvement. Non-profit land conservancies and land trusts lead private sector involvement in open space preservation. Very rough estimates show over 70 land trusts and small conservancies in the tri-state Region, owning or protecting over 32 square miles of land, sometimes for a fraction of fair market value. The preserves of larger non-profit organizations, such as The Nature Conservancy and the national and state Audubon Societies, add 37 square miles of protected open space to our Region and private nature centers add another 24 square miles. In urban areas, privately owned and maintained parks and plazas have become part of the landscape on almost every downtown block.

VI. Conclusion

The tone of success suggested by this record of past achievements and current opportunities must not be misinterpreted. It is a strong base from which to build. But the framework in which these successes have occurred has come apart and the rebuilding process has not kept pace with overall growth in the tri-state Region's economy. It is this growth which makes a new framework of leadership and partnership essential—the framework which has been outlined at the beginning of this report and which the President's Commission is strongly urged to consider.

· · · · · · · · · · ·

Natural Areas in the West: Part of the Recreational Continuum

RON G. HOLLIDAY
Director
Division of Parks & Outdoor Recreation
Denver, Colorado

Introduction

Many good reasons exist for protecting "natural areas" in America. Many of America's national and state parks were established as nature preserves—natural areas for the study and enjoyment of wild and outdoor America. Natural areas are set aside as outdoor laboratories—places to conduct scientific research and environmental education. Natural areas provide habitat for threatened or endangered species, preserve biotic or aquatic diversity, protect relics or remnants of pre-European settlement or native ecosystems and protect outstanding scenic grandeur and "sacred space". Natural areas preserve America's natural heritage and protect elements of natural diversity.

Natural areas occupy an important place on the recreational continuum by preserving the best condition areas for scientific research and education. The escalating use of fragile wilderness areas and parks emphasizes another important, but often overlooked, reason for the establishment of natural areas or restricted preserves—to assist resource managers in their land use decisions for wilderness and parks management.

Natural areas are barometers of land health. In evaluating the effects of various uses on America's land base, natural areas provide standards against which other land uses can be measured. Nature reserves and natural areas are islands surrounded by seas of land used intensively for many other purposes, including outdoor recreation. Although natural areas are not large enough to do the job of nature conservation alone, they are baselines for gauging the magnitude of recreational and other impacts, supplying information for managing land to protect the natural inheritance of future generations in America.

Protecting natural areas in western states:
The Colorado experience

Many states have established state natural areas programs to protect natural features and phenomena as an enduring resource for their citizens to use and enjoy. In western states, where much of the land is public land, it makes sense for federal and state agencies to cooperate in protecting unique or exemplary natural features. The federal government owns 36 percent of the land in Colorado. More than 10 percent of the remainder of the land in Colorado is owned by state or local governments. How does a state agency charged with identifying and protecting natural areas succeed in dealing with the myriad of land ownerships and numerous public and private land management agencies which exist in the western United States?

The Colorado Natural Areas Program. The Colorado Natural Areas Program was established by the Colorado Legislature in 1977 to protect special, rare, and threatened natural features in Colorado through a statewide system of designated natural areas. Designated natural areas are formally recognized under the provisions of the Natural Areas Act; a legal agreement exists between the landowners and the State of Colorado for their management. Registered natural areas meet the ecological criteria of the Natural Areas Program, but no legal management agreements exist. The Colorado Natural Areas Program has registered and designated 50 natural areas comprising almost 65,000 acres in Colorado between 1978 and 1986.

The Colorado Natural Areas Program maintains a comprehensive statewide inventory of exemplary, rare, or threatened natural features in Colorado. The Inventory identifies and recommends areas which meet the scientific criteria of the Natural Areas Program for designation as Colorado Natural Areas. The Inventory reviews proposed development projects in Colorado and provides scientific data in response to information requests from public and private developers. The Inventory was maintained by the Nature Conservancy under contract to the Natural Areas Program. Cooperation with the Nature Conservancy was beneficial in standardizing data collection and analytic methods, linking a national network of information on endangered species. The focus on Nature Conservancy national agendas, priorities and methodologies for the Inventory reduced the flexibility of the Natural Areas Program to set data collection priorities and to resolve data management issues peculiar to Colorado. Closer coordination between the Nature Conservancy and the Program has resolved many of these problems.

The Colorado Natural Areas Program was administratively merged into the Colorado Division of Parks and Outdoor Recreation in 1986. Two state parks contain designated state natural areas—Roxborough State Park and East Sand Dunes in the State Forest. Two registered natural areas are in state parks—Bonny Prairie at Bonny Reservoir State Recreation Area and Dome Rock at Mueller Ranch State Park. Natural areas in state parks serve interpretive and educational purposes for parks visitors and can be used effectively to emphasize the natural history, unique natural values, or scenic beauty of the parks. Park managers afford on-site management and protection for natural areas.

During the past eight years the Colorado Natural Areas Program has received a quarter of its annual operating budget from state tax dollars. Federal funds have contributed more than two-thirds of the Program's budget; federal funds are matched with state general funds and cash funds on a 3 (federal): 1 (state) ratio. Currently, three full time professionals are employed in the Program.

Multiple Use: A Management Conundrum. Cooperation with federal land management agencies in identifying and designating special management areas is required by state natural areas programs in the West. The Colorado Natural Areas Program signed cooperative agreements with the Forest Service and BLM to designate certain areas on federal lands as state natural areas. The Colorado Natural Areas Program works with the National Park Service in designating state natural areas in national parks. The Department of Natural Resources (Natural Areas Program) signed a cooperative agreement with the U.S. Fish and Wildlife Service under Section 6 of the Endangered Species Act for the protection of federally listed and candidate plant species in Colorado. Over 60 percent of Colorado's natural areas are on federal land; natural areas on federal land in Colorado comprise 94 percent of the total acreage protected in the Natural Areas Program.

The organic acts of the U.S. Forest Service and the Bureau of Land Management authorize multiple use management for federal lands, including the designation of areas for special management. Federal land management agencies have defined the multiple use guidelines as maximizing the total number of uses available for each acre of federal land, rather than viewing multiple use on a national forest or district-wide basis. This multiple use definition traditionally means land uses such as logging, mining, and grazing, less frequently recreational uses, and rarely special management area designations. Single purpose use in specific areas is the result. Yet, many federal land managers resist special management designations because these designations are viewed as single purpose, violating the spirit of multiple use management.

The prevailing multiple use approach in the West is a management conundrum which is partially resolved by the contributions of individuals in federal or state agencies who believe in the importance of balancing multiple uses with special management applied to appropriate areas.

Although these individuals may be sprinkled throughout the federal or state bureaucracies, the most effective individuals to support specially managed areas are usually located in the field—Forest Service supervisor or district ranger offices, BLM district or resource area offices or national park offices.

A western portfolio: Natural areas in Colorado

Three examples show how the Colorado Natural Areas Program works with the state's scientific research community, environmental organizations, and private citizens in identifying, evaluating, and protecting natural areas in Colorado.

Geologic Advisory Group. No systematic or comprehensive evaluation of geologic areas for significant geologic features used for scientific research and education purposes had occurred in Colorado prior to 1984. The Bureau of Land Management and the Colorado Natural Areas Program agreed to establish a geologic advisory group comprised of professional geologists from the state's colleges and universities, state and federal geologic surveys, and the private sector. The Colorado Natural Areas Program coordinated the geologic advisory group. Members of the geologic advisory group volunteered their time and expertise. The Geologic Advisory Group established guidelines for identifying and evaluating geologic areas used for research and education on public lands in Colorado. Areas were prioritized by need for special management. A two year effort resulted in forty areas evaluated for significant geologic features; twenty-five areas were recommended to BLM for special management. BLM and the Colorado Natural Areas Program benefited from the pool of expertise in the Geologic Advisory Group. Strong links were established between members of Colorado's research community and BLM managers. Better understanding of management needs for BLM lands resulted. An ad hoc paleontological permit review committee provided a forum for reviewing permit applications for research on BLM lands and advising BLM on permitting geologic research. The Geologic Advisory Group continues to advise BLM on significant geological features on public lands.

Roxborough State Park. Roxborough State Park was designated a Colorado Natural Area in 1979. Dominated by massive erosional remnants of Fountain Sandstone, Roxborough State Park is one of Colorado's most spectacular natural areas. Separated by less than a mile, the eastern and western boundaries of the park enclose a geologic span of 500 million years, dating from the Precambrian to the late Mesozoic Era. Unusual hydrologic and topographic characteristics combine to support richly diverse plant and wildlife communities at Roxborough State Park.

The Natural Areas Program provided botanical and geological assistance during the preparation of the management plan for Roxborough State Park. Geologists from the U.S. Geological Survey and the Colorado Geological Survey and from various universities assisted in describing and interpreting the geological history of Roxborough State Park. Botanists and plant ecologists from the Colorado Natural Areas Inventory completed the vegetation inventory and analysis for the park. Staff from the Colorado Natural Areas Program participated on the advisory committee for preparing and implementing the management plan for Roxborough State Park.

The Roxborough State Park Management Plan designates various land use zones within the park. The "protected zone" contains most of the designated natural area and includes the geologic or ecological features of most importance to the park. These areas contain unique rock formations, unusual occurrences of plant species or plant communities, or critical wildlife habitat. These areas are protected because they are unusually fragile and regular use will destroy their unique character. Educational use of these areas is encouraged by interpretive trails. Public off-trail use is allowed for specific educational studies and is carefully monitored. Interpretive trails and descriptive natural area exhibits at the visitors center are the principal educational features of the park.

Recent visitor surveys at Roxborough State Park show that 97 percent of the respondents support zoning to protect fragile resources in the park. Nature study was the reason for visiting Roxborough State Park given by 91 percent of the visitors surveyed (DPOR 1985). Personal service programs, interpretive activities guided by a park naturalist, were requested by 92 percent of the survey respondents. Guided interpretive nature walks are a valuable tool for educating park visitors on the importance of the natural values at Roxborough. Roxborough State Park's proximity to the Denver metropolitan area makes it a popular area for outdoor/environmental education activities. Several school systems integrate Roxborough State Park into their curricula. Field seminars are offered to provide more in-depth study for interested naturalists.

The combination of geography, topography, and proximity to an urban center at Roxborough State Park results in excellent opportunities for environmental and outdoor education. Cooperation between the Natural Areas Program and Division of Parks at this park ensures that the natural area is used to increase public appreciation of the natural history of Colorado while providing adequate resource management and protection.

Boulder Tallgrass Prairie Natural Area. The Colorado Natural Areas Inventory identified several tallgrass prairie remnants containing native grasses in good condition on open space land owned by the City of Boulder. The combined 270 acre tallgrass prairie was designated a Colorado Natural Area during a ceremony in the office of Governor Richard Lamm. The City of Boulder and the Colorado Natural Areas Program agreed to complete a tallgrass prairie management plan for the prairie remnants that were good examples of native ecosystems.

A management advisory committee consisting of range scientists, botanists, wildlife biologists, naturalists, and ranchers was assembled by the City of Boulder and the Colorado Natural Areas Program. The committee was charged with: (1) examining past and current management practices for the prairie relicts; (2) evaluating known prairie management tools used for maintaining tallgrass prairies; and, (3) recommending appropriate tallgrass prairie management practices to the City of Boulder.

Major disagreements existed in the committee on the appropriateness of current management practices on the tallgrass areas, particularly levels of livestock grazing and fire management. The first several meetings were marked by lively debates. Movement toward common ground began slowly. After several meetings the management committee agreed on most management issues. The principal purpose for the tallgrass prairie remnants was to protect them for scientific research and educational use. Subcommittees were appointed to resolve remaining issues and to recommend specific monitoring methods and management practices. Monitoring enclosures were established on the sites and research and educational needs were emphasized for the prairies. The use of fire as a prairie management tool remained a problem as the city representatives worried about burning in semi-urban settings and possible liability for damages caused by prairie management practices. Several prairie management experts met with the management committee to discuss management practices. The committee recommended a management plan for submission to the City of Boulder in 1986.

Lessons from the labors of the tallgrass prairie management committee demonstrate that people with widely divergent views can agree on appropriate management and monitoring practices to accomplish common goals. People involved in the decision process have a vested interest in the success of the project. The biological importance of the tallgrass prairie remnants is better understood and recognized by decision makers and managers. Cooperation between local and state government agencies creates a positive environment for the completion of similar projects which benefit the citizens of Colorado.

Conclusions

Natural areas occupy an important position on the outdoor recreation continuum. Natural areas protect rare natural features for educational use and appreciation by Colorado's citizens. Interpretive natural areas (e.g., Roxborough State Park) provide educational and recreational opportunities for many people. Natural areas are islands which serve as baselines for monitoring the effects of various adjacent land uses, including outdoor recreation. Research natural area designations on U.S. Forest Service and National Park Service lands lag behind designated wilderness areas in Colorado. In 1986, twenty-seven designated wilderness areas containing 2.6 million acres were used by over two million people, one-sixth of the total wilderness use in the United States. At the same time, twelve research natural areas having 30,129 acres were designated by these agencies in Colorado. Special management area designations to assist in recreational and land use management are not keeping pace with recreational area designations. Combined with recreational use areas, natural areas can provide long term evaluation of the magnitude of recreational impacts. Without the ecological standards provided by natural areas, recreation managers will not be able to accurately determine management trends and impacts.

The escalating recreational use of fragile wilderness and park areas requires the establishment of natural areas or preserves to assist resource managers in their land use decisions for wilderness and park management. The experience of the Colorado Natural Areas Program substantiates the usefulness of federal, state, and local government agency cooperation and, in concert with private organizations and interested individuals, of protecting rare and fragile natural features in Colorado.

. . . .

Recreation and Power Production on the Ocoee River, Tennessee

MARC HUNT
President
Sunburst Adventures
Benton, Tennessee

Power versus recreation on a federal water project

Between 1976 and 1983, a public controversy developed about the future uses of the waters of the Ocoee River in southeast Tennessee. The needs of TVA to efficiently generate electricity were in conflict with the desire of the public to use the water of the Ocoee for recreation. In the effort to gain a resolution, impediments arose that nearly caused an end to whitewater recreation on the Ocoee. Those impediments developed as a result of the way federal projects are commonly authorized and managed. The purpose of this analysis is to provide insight to the inherent problems for recreation in such decision-making processes.

The Tennessee Valley Authority (TVA) was created as a federal agency by Congress in 1933. The TVA is governed by a presidentially appointed, three member board of directors. The TVA operates its multi-billion dollar power production program much the way a private company would; the Board of Directors has sole authority, and funding is generated by the sale of electricity. The other programs of TVA, involving maintenance of navigation, flood control, economic development, and recreation, are funded by annual appropriations from Congress. Many TVA water projects were designated and funded at the time of authorization as multiple purpose; others were authorized as single purpose power projects.

At its inception, the TVA purchased the Ocoee #2 hydroelectric system as a single purpose power project from the private Tennessee Electric Power Company. The diversionary system takes advantage of the steep gradient of the Ocoee through the use of a unique 4.7 mile long wooden flume to maintain hydraulic head. The project usurped virtually all of the flow of the Ocoee, rendering the stretch of river paralleling the flume a dry rockbed. The project was taken from service in September of 1976 due to structural deterioration of the flume, which had stood since 1913. Water once again flowed in the riverbed.

Whitewater recreationists in rafts, kayaks, and canoes were quick to discover this "new" whitewater playground. Annual visitation grew at an astounding rate. By 1983, over 90,000 river users and over 50,000 spectators enjoyed the Ocoee, ranking the stream among the five most popular stretches of whitewater in America.

Great public controversy developed as TVA pursued its intentions of rehabilitating the project and returning it to service. Many felt that a future for the Ocoee that would provide for recreational use was in the best interest of the public. The TVA Board, citing legal obligations, took the position that because Ocoee #2 is a single purpose power project, the operational efficiency of the system could not be financially compromised. The agency proposal was to return the project to service and to make scheduled discharges for recreation contingent on financial reimbursements being made to the power program. The reimbursements would represent foregone power revenues. In the fall of 1983, the project rehabilitation was completed and the plant was returned to service. After heated discussions and significant political efforts, the TVA proposal was accepted, and a financial scheme involving an expensive Congressional appropriation was achieved. Under the arrangement, recreational flows are available 116 days annually, and it appears that recreation will continue on the Ocoee well into the future.

The law's inflexibility and recognition of recreation values

Whether or not the TVA Board could have exercised other alternatives, they chose to strictly interpret the TVA Act in regard to future accomodation of recreation on the Ocoee. Because whitewater recreation did not exist at the time, the decision makers did not include it as a project purpose at authorization. The public sentiment regarding the Ocoee issue was clearly in favor of continued recreation, and the TVA board acknowledged it. The resolution of the Ocoee issue, in the end, did not provide for a reorganization of project purposes, but instead, an accomodation of the existing project purpose.

There are no clear provisions in federal laws that allow for simple reorganization of project purposes. Currently, the means to achieve a reassignment of project purposes is by act of Congress. When such efforts have been made, they have usually failed, given the challenge and difficulty of achievement. It seems that Congress chooses to avoid setting precedents about such matters. The result is that many federal water projects are not able to accomodate changed demands and needs as related to recreation, when such accomodations are clearly in the best interest of the public.

Other situations have arisen that presented dilemmas similar to that of the Ocoee. At Summersville Dam, U.S. Army Corps of Engineers project on the Gauley River in West Virginia, annual fall drawdown discharges were being made without regard for the scheduling needs of the 25,000 recreationists who visit the Gauley each year. The Corps' position was that since downstream whitewater recreation was not a project purpose, needs of these recreationists could not be a factor in operation. Congressional action was necessary for the Army Corps to agree with recreationists on an appropriate schedule. Without the authorization related contraints, the task could have been simply resolved.

At Glen Canyon Dam on the Colorado River in Arizona, the Bureau of Reclamation is currently seeking to modify the power generation and discharge capacity of the dam. It has been shown that such modification will have significant negative impacts on downstream river recreation. Downstream recreationists, however, are having a difficult time ensuring that due consideration will be given to their needs. Downstream recreation is not a project purpose of Glen Canyon Dam.

Reservoir recreation is sometimes affected similarly. Some federal dams were authorized with no reservoir recreation purposes included. Recreation has in fact developed on those reservoirs and is sometimes hurt by large changes in water surface elevation.

Another problem encountered on the Ocoee is also common to many federal decision-making processes where multiple demands and needs are present. Power production for TVA generates tangible, quantifiable revenues to the agency. In recent years, TVA has been judged largely by its ability to provide low cost power to the area. There is great public and political pressure on the management of TVA to be economically efficient as a result. Despite their response to real needs, benefits for public recreation opportunities are not so tangible or easily quantifiable as those for power. To provide for whitewater recreation on the Ocoee would add nothing to the financial "bottom line" for TVA. It has clearly been the mandate and mission of TVA to exhibit balanced regard for revenue producing and non-revenue producing factors in decision making. In regard to the Ocoee issue, TVA demonstrated a significant bias in favor of power production from the very start.

The same sort of bias is present in many federal land and water use decisions: timber and mining versus recreation uses in National Forests, power production on many reservoirs and rivers versus recreation, and access and development versus wilderness preservation in National Parks and National Forests are but some areas of decision making affected.

The Ocoee River will be an available and prominent recreation resource well into the future. The efforts required to achieve an acceptable resolution were remarkable, involving heroic efforts by the political leaders of Tennessee. In 1983, Senate Majority Leader Howard Baker spearheaded an effort to gain a $7.4 million continuing-spending amendment for Ocoee recreation under the TVA power appropriation. Many called this a "pork-barrel." But that type of expensive effort and precedent should not have been necessary to achieve a solution that was clearly in the best public interest and should have cost the taxpayer nothing.

Much time has passed since the original authorization of many federal water projects. Recreation demands and needs constantly evolve, and recreation resources are diminishing. Decision-makers need new and more flexible means to enhance recreation opportunities where federal projects are involved.

The New Jersey Pinelands: An Analysis of Our Country's First National Reserve

JOAN BATORY & SUZANNE SUTRO
Division of Park and Resource Planning
National Park Service
Mid-Atlantic Regional Office

The Pinelands: A unique ecosystem

New Jersey's Pinelands, also known as the Pine Barrens, are a unique landscape found in the Atlantic Coastal Plain in the southern part of the state. The Pinelands span approximately 1.1 million acres, nearly 40 percent of the state's entire land mass. The 17 trillion gallon Cohansey aquifer beneath the Pinelands is recharged by precipitation that filters through the predominately sandy sediment layers deposited by the ocean over the past 100 million years. Pitch pine and scrub oak forests dominate the uplands; cedar or hardwood swamps, pitch pine forests, bogs and marshes are found in the lowland areas which constitute nearly 40 percent of the Pinelands. Five hundred and eighty native plant species grow in the Pinelands including 54 species classified as threatened or endangered in the state. The Pinelands provide habitat for 299 bird species, 91 fish species, 59 species of reptiles and amphibians and 35 species of mammals. The bobcat and the black bear formerly inhabitated the Pinelands and the eastern coyote reportedly visits the area.

Development patterns: resource dependent

The Pinelands' timber, water and sand resources attracted primarily English colonists over 300 years ago. A flourishing iron industry, dependent on charcoal made from pitch pine, and natural bog iron deposits found in local streams, manufactured cannon and shot for the revolutionary army.

In the 19th century, iron making gave way to the production of glass, paper, brick and textiles. The native cranberry thrives in the high water table of Pinelands' sandy soils. Today, New Jersey ranks third in the commercial production of cranberries which are produced in the heart of the Pinelands. Elizabeth White's experiments with the native blueberry produced the first cultivated blueberry whose yearly harvest makes New Jersey the second largest commercial producer in the country. Pinelands natives for many generations have practiced a seasonal cycle of subsistence activities such as hunting, trapping, moss-gathering, timber harvesting, shell-fishing, charcoal-making and berry picking.

Historically the Pinelands have provided a safe haven for a variety of groups, including Russians, Blacks, Europeans, Jews, Quakers and Native Americans, each contributing to the "down home" Pinelands culture.

Development pressures and government response

Public interest in the Pinelands was sparked in the 1950's by increasing development pressures on the region's periphery. A regional study in 1956 proposing a major jetport in the central Pinelands generated public opposition and stimulated awareness of the area's importance as a disappearing wilderness that harbored an immense water supply. This underground water supply supports the Pinelands' unique wetlands and has been threatened by withdrawal and exportation schemes to supply adjacent "water poor" areas since the 1850's.

Early New Jersey planning efforts

A Pinelands Environmental Council was appointed by Governor Cahill in 1972 to develop a plan for 340,000 acres of Pinelands forest. The Council's report, released in 1975, was criticized as too development-oriented by many environmental organizations. These organizations joined forces as the Pine Barrens Coalition and began to pressure the state government for a more conservation-oriented policy. Governor Brendan Byrne responded in 1977 with an executive order establishing a new body, the Pinelands Review Committee, to define boundaries for the Pinelands and develop a policy for state actions in the region. The executive order contained some of the principles later embodied in state and federal Pinelands legislation: land use consistent with natural resource protection and limitation of future development to existing developed areas.

Federal role as catalyst to promote a comprehensive planning process

Several National Park Service studies resulted in a 1975 report by the Bureau of Outdoor Recreation which proposed the establishment of a Pine Barrens National Ecological Reserve with a variety of options for acquisition and management by state or federal governments.

In 1977, several concurrent bills calling for varying degrees of state and federal involvement were introduced into the House of Representatives and the Senate. President Carter signed the National Parks and Recreation Act, P.L. 95-625 on October 13, 1978. Section 502 created the Pinelands

National Reserve, the country's first national reserve. The legislation combined major concepts found in the previously introduced bills, particularly legislation introduced by Congressman James J. Florio, (D-N.J.). The state would be responsible for preparing a management plan for the area. The federal government assumed oversight, technical assistance, funding responsibilities and membership on the Pinelands Commission which the governor would appoint to develop and implement the management plan.

To insure the coordination of federal programs affecting the area, the legislation stipulated that the Pinelands Commission would review any application for federal permits, licenses, funding or assistance during the development of the management plan. The Secretary of the Interior would render a final decision on any application that could negatively impact Pinelands resources.

The legislation also authorized $26 million in grants to the state from the Land and Water Conservation Fund to cover 75 percent of the cost of developing the management plan and 75 percent of the cost of state land acquisition. To safeguard this investment, the legislation provided that Secretarial approval would be required for any modification of the plan.

State response to federal initiative

Shortly after the passage of the National Parks and Recreation Act, Governor Byrne took dramatic action by issuing Executive Order No. 71, imposing a moratorium on development in the Pinelands during the preparation of the management plan. The order established a Pinelands Planning Commission to prepare the management plan and review all applications for new development in the Pinelands. The Commission could prohibit any new development that threatened to substantially impair Pinelands' resources.

In response to the executive order and the federal legislation, several bills were introduced in the New Jersey Legislature. Senate Bill 3091, known as the Pinelands Protection Act, was adopted in June, 1979. The act went beyond the federal legislation in specifying the state's roles and responsibilities. It created the Pinelands Commission to prepare and enforce a comprehensive management plan and review all local development applications until local governments brought their master plans and zoning ordinances into conformance with the plan. The act required the Commission to develop a payment-in-lieu-of-taxes plan to pay local governments for revenues lost through state land acquisition and gave legislative sanction to the development moratorium imposed by the executive order.

A notable inconsistency between the state and federal legislation is that the boundaries defined for planning purposes differ. The Pinelands National Reserve (the federal boundary) encompasses 56 municipalities in whole or part while the Pinelands Area (the state boundary) includes 52 municipalities. That portion of the Pinelands National Reserve that overlaps

New Jersey's Coastal Zone is managed by the Division of Coastal Resources
in cooperation with the Pinelands Commission.

Development of the Pinelands
Comprehensive Management Plan

The newly formed Pinelands Commission faced a difficult task in
preparing what is now called the Comprehensive Management Plan (CMP).
The Commission hired staff, contracted for scientific studies and geared
up the mandated public input program to meet the 18 month deadline for
completion of the Plan.

The lack of scientific data on which to base the plan presented an
immediate obstacle to the planning process. The Pinelands Commission
contracted with consultants to prepare more than 20 major studies on every
aspect of the Pinelands. Literature searches, public workshops, field work
and interviews with knowledgeable persons contributed to the pool of
information. A Technical Advisory Committee of Pinelands experts helped
define issues that the plan should address.

The Pinelands Commission held public meetings regularly and formed
a Pinelands Municipal Council composed of the 56 Pinelands mayors to
review the CMP prior to its approval as mandated by state legislation.

Overview of the Pinelands Comprehensive
Management Plan

The emphasis on sharing responsibility for managing Pinelands resources among all levels of government is evident in the development regulations set forth in the CMP. The CMP stipulates that local governments will
administer the regulations through their development review process once
the Pinelands Commission determines that their master plans and zoning
ordinances conform to the CMP's performance standards and regulations.
The Pinelands Commission reserves the right to call up for review any
development application approved locally that does not appear to conform
to the agreed upon development regulations.

State regulations are modified as necessary to implement stricter standards where specified in the CMP. Federal agencies provide technical assistance to the Commission, coordinate the activities of federal installations and agencies within the Pinelands and monitor the implementation
of and amendments to the CMP.

The CMP land use management areas are based on the carrying capacity of the Pinelands resources and existing development patterns. Of the
total 1.1 million acres in the Pinelands National Reserve, state landholdings
comprise nearly one-third of the area, approximately 243,000 acres. Federal
military installations and wildlife refuges total approximately 75,000 acres.
Eight land use management areas were established in the CMP: the Preservation Area (337,000 acres); the Forest Area (420,000 acres); the Rural

Development Area (145,000 acres); the Regional Growth Area (119,000 acres); the Military and Federal Installation Area (48,000 acres); and 65 Pinelands Villages and Towns (15,080 acres assigned to towns and acreage assigned to villages incorporated into the other management areas). The CMP's "Minimum Standards for Land Uses and Intensities" assigned various development densities to each of the management areas to protect essential characteristics of the Pinelands. These performance standards guided the municipal conformance process. For example, the Regional Growth and Towns and Village Areas received the highest average density assignment (one unit per acre with the use of a septic system) while development in the Preservation Area was severely restricted. The CMP recommended the acquisition of 100,000 ecologically sensitive acres to be added to the state's public lands. Congress authorized $23 million for acquisition and $3 million for plan development as part of the 1978 legislation.

Local conformance to the Pinelands Comprehensive Management Plan

Local and county governing bodies were mandated by law to revise their master plans and zoning ordinances to conform to the CMP within a year after the CMP was approved. In the meantime, the Pinelands Commission reviewed and approved all development applications. Predictably, opposition to the temporary loss of local control was extremely strong. However, using a flexible negotiating process with individual towns, the Pinelands Commission has approved nearly all of the municipal master plans and zoning ordinances thereby restoring home rule to 42 of the 52 municipal planning boards in the Pinelands Area. In addition, agreements between the Pinelands Commission and federal and state agencies have been developed to assure intergovernmental conformance to the Commission's program. The Commission projects unanimous compliance by 1987.

Pinelands Commission members

It must be noted that the Pinelands Commission is not an apolitical body. Each of its 15 members represents a specific local or statewide interest as required by the legislation. The governor appoints seven members to represent statewide interests like resource conservation and agriculture; each of the seven Pinelands counties appoints a local representative and the Secretary of the Interior designates a voting representative. Given the diversity of interests, the possibility for conflict within the Commission itself could have negated the mandate to protect the Pinelands' resources. Recognizing this, the Pinelands Commission made a concerted effort to reconcile their differences. The result is a Comprehensive Management Plan that blends the various interests into a program that provides cooperative multi-governmental protection for an ecologically sensitive area.

Effects of the planning process

Many of the fears expressed by local residents and officials regarding the political and economic impact of the management plan have not materialized. For example, some reduction in the tax base has been experienced in the Preservation and Agricultural Areas where development opportunities have been virtually eliminated. Newly adopted state legislation provides compensation to Pinelands municipalities to restore tax receipt losses that are directly attributable to zoning changes that conform to the CMP. The state has also provided funds to develop an infrastructure management plan that will enable Pinelands municipalities to plan for and construct new sewer and water facilities to promote development in those areas designated for growth.

New state legislation supports the Pinelands transfer of development rights program intended to relocate development from sensitive to more suitable Regional Growth Areas by providing $10 million to fund a Pinelands Development Credit Bank to finance the state's purchase of development rights from owners of non-developable land. Additionally, state funds that are passed through the Pinelands Commission to local governments have financed most of their planning efforts.

Growth opportunities are being realized in those areas designated for growth where land values are beginning to increase. Since the CMP took effect in January, 1981, 13,425 new homes have been approved; 7,268 have been denied approval. As of March, 1986, all but 134 of these units have been approved in designated Growth Areas. Farming activities have increased in the Agricultural Area. Currently most Pinelands municipalities review and approve local development applications.

Lessons learned from the Pinelands experience

The effect of the management plan on the Pinelands resource itself has yet to be measured. To do this more complete data needs to be compiled. In addition, it will be several more years before the management plan is fully implemented so that the effects of designated development on the delicately balanced natural system of the Pinelands can be clearly demonstrated and evaluated. The United Nations has designated the New Jersey Pinelands as an international biosphere, a unique ecosystem worthy of scientific research which should add considerably to current Pinelands information.

Judgment on the overall success of the national reserve technique as an experiment in multi-level cooperative regional planning cannot yet be rendered. Nevertheless, it can be said that local awareness of the resource has increased considerably because of the planning process. Formerly hostile local government officials now feel comfortable describing themselves

as "environmentalists" at public meetings and local residents have organized to protect resources of which they were previously unaware.

While it is still too early to say whether the right choices have been
made in the Pinelands, from the federal perspective the national reserve
concept has encouraged the protection of an outstanding resource without
the need for federal acquisition and management and at a much lower
cost. The comparatively small federal investment in the Pinelands has
leveraged protection on a scale which could not have been accomplished
by direct federal intervention. Federal funds have served to support the
state's actions and have preserved home rule. The national reserve concept
has allowed the Pinelands' economy to continue to function and its residents to continue living there. Public involvement in the planning process
has heightened public awareness of the Pinelands' resource.

Current issues which the Pinelands Commission must address
include: development of a more comprehensive data base with which to
compare the cumulative effects of developments on the resource; maintenance of a clearly defined cooperative relationship between government entities; continued regulation of future uses of the Pinelands area and finally,
protection of its vast underground water supply from exportation to outlying
water-poor areas.

The success of the Pinelands National Reserve concept to date can
be attributed to several factors. Congress served as the catalyst by approv-
ing federal legislation to protect the Pinelands by elevating the issue to national importance. Congressional designation of the Pinelands as nationally
significant focused New Jersey's attention on the need to enact comprehensive companion legislation. The unswerving personal commitment of the
New Jersey governor to allow the concept to be tested resulted in the development moratorium and his very visible support against legislative attempts
to weaken the state legislation. The federal and state Pinelands legislation
established clearly defined goals, tasks and mandates which have allowed
it and the CMP to survive numerous court challenges. The Pinelands Commission members have worked tirelessly to represent their various constit-
uents and personalize their relationship with local governments while setting aside differences in order to preserve the Pinelands. Finally, the success of this unique approach to its conservation can be attributed to the
recognition of the Pinelands itself as a truly significant resource.

Pennsylvania's Hiking Trails: The Marvelous Menagerie

JAMES C. NELSON
Assistant State Forester
Pennsylvania Bureau of Forestry
Department of Environmental Resources

Pennsylvania's hiking trails

There are more than 3,800 miles of hiking trails in Pennsylvania, varying from short hikes in city parks to long loop trails for backpacking in remote forest areas. These trails pass through a wide variety of natural, cultural and historic resources. The menagerie, however, is not the trails themselves, but how they came about.

Pennsylvania has a reputation for being a densely-populated, industrialized state. While it *is* industrialized, it is also a heavily-forested state with 60 percent of the land area classified as "forest" and an additional 19 percent in farmland. As the name indicates, "Pennsylvania" is still "Penn's Woods."

In addition to being blessed with a large, undeveloped landscape, Pennsylvania also boasts big amounts of public recreation land, with two million acres in State Forests, 1.2 million acres of State Game Lands, one-half million acres of National Forest land, and 250,000 acres of land in State Parks. The total population is 11.8 million, of which 1.25 million are hikers, 500,000 are backpackers and almost 500,000 are cross-country skiers. These statistics give some background, but let's look at the trail system and how it developed.

The first hiking trail built specifically for recreational purposes was the Appalachian Trail. Pennsylvania's 222 mile link in the Maine-to-Georgia, national trail was completed in the late 1920's by a group of hiking enthusiasts who formed the Appalachian Trail Club. The major emphasis came from people in the Washington, D.C. area. Much of the Trail was located on public land, with "gentlemen's agreements" for sections that crossed private lands.

The Horse-Shoe Trail, developed in 1935, was the second major effort by a private group in the state. This 120 mile trail, located in southeastern Pennsylvania, extended from Valley Forge and connected with the Appalachian Trail near Indiantown Gap. It was intended for both horseback and hiking use, hence the name "Horse-Shoe". Most of this trail is on private land; no formal use agreements exist except where it uses utility rights-of-way and crosses large industrial forest holdings. Many miles are located on old logging trails or early wagon roads.

During this same period of the mid-1930s, the Civilian Conservation Corps built hundreds of miles of trails on State Forest land. Most of these trails were constructed as firebreaks and accesses for fire crews into otherwise roadless areas. Some, however, were developed explicitly as hiking trails. Following Maslow's Law on the hierarchy of needs, little use was made of recreation trails at a time when most people were more concerned with putting food in their stomachs. Recreational trail use was also low during World War II because people did not have time, and many trails lost their identity due to lack of use.

The early 1950s saw a renewed interest in hiking and trail development. The Pittsburgh Council of the American Youth Hostels laid out the 140 mile Baker Trail in western Pennsylvania, while the Williamsport Alpine Club developed the 57 mile Loyalsock Trail in the north-central part of the state. While the Baker Trail followed rural roads, the Loyalsock was primarily on State Forest land. Both trails did cross private lands, but no formal agreements on recreation use were needed in either case.

Up to this time, all the state's major trails had been linear or cross-country. The state's first loop trail was developed in 1966 when the Susquehanna Trail Club developed an 85-mile, circular route within the Susquehanna State Forest.

A renewed interest in hiking led to rapid growth in backpacking during the late 1960s, and this coincided with planned revisions in the management plans for the two million acres of State forest. The first 15-year plan for State Forests had been prepared in 1955. Although it was called a multiple-use Forest Management Plan, it was really a timber management plan which mentioned other uses like recreation, wildlife and water but provided no guidance for management of these resources. Because of increased demands for hiking trails and other forms of forest recreation such as snowmobiling, canoeing and cross-country skiing, as well as for more timber, water and minerals, the 15-year plan developed for 1970 embodied new concepts in a Forest Resource Plan.

The Forest Resource Plan instituted a coordinated management program for all forest resources, which ensured consideration of recreation uses. A major part of the plan's Recreation Section was devoted to trails. Because of potential conflicts, not only between trail and other resource uses, but between different kinds of trail users themselves, the following categories of trail use were defined:

○ Foot (hiking, snowshoeing, cross-country skiing, backpacking)

○ Slow Rider (bicycling, horseback riding)

○ Motorized Rider (snowmobiling, trail biking, ATVs)

○ Water Travel (canoeing, rafting)

○ Handicapped (physically-impaired and blind users)

The likes and dislikes of users and compatible and imcompatible forest resource uses were determined for each category. For example, foot travellers are aware of both mini- and maxi-environments. They are looking for spectacular views, unusual geologic forms, rare vegetation or wildlife, and are conscious of the trees, flowers, birds, animals and sounds of the forest. They don't like to come in close contact with resource development such as timber cutting or gas well drilling, but don't object to such activities off in the distance. They do not like interference from horseback riders or motorized vehicles. These factors were considered during the planning process for hiking trails. In an effort to minimize conflicts, wherever possible trails were located in Natural Areas where no extraction activities are permitted, in Wild Areas (the State Forest version of wilderness) or on lands classified as non-commercial forest because they were too steep, too rocky or otherwise poor sites for timber.

Foot trails were further broken down into: a) cross-country, like the Appalachian; b) long-loop, where one can park a car and walk an entire trail (on to six days) without backtracking; and c) short loop, nature or interpretive trails of one to four miles.

During the inventory phase of the *Forest Resources Plan,* every old logging road, fire trail woods road and abandoned railroad grade was walked and evaluated for its recreational potential.

Since 1970, the Bureau of Forestry has concentrated on long-loop trails using State Forest or other public land as much as possible. Where it was necessary to cross private land, efforts were made to locate trails on larger parcels like forest industry lands where ownerships tend to be stable and trail use is not incompatible with planned future management. Small, private tracts or lands with high development potential are avoided.

Loop trails are preferred over cross-country because they are more convenient for hikers, eliminating the need for backtracking or having two cars for pickup. Such loops can be laid out to avoid or minimize highway and river crossings. As a rule, fewer landowners are encountered per mile of trail. The larger the private tract, the easier it is to get permission to locate a trail. Most landowners have granted free use of their land for trails, but have been reluctant to enter into formal, written agreements.

One of the lessons learned from the first 85 mile loop trail, built in 1966, was that a trail of this length requires too great a commitment of time for most hikers; as a result they are hiked in two or three segments and the advantages of a loop trail are lost. Consequently, loop trails built since 1970 contain cross-overs that form several interconnecting loops. For example, the Quehanna Trail has a 75 mile outer loop with cross-overs that form 14.3 mile, 38.9 mile and 36.8 mile inner loops.

Experience gained from observing use patterns on the Appalachian Trail taught us not to construct trail shelters along the backpacking trails. The Appalachian is the most heavily used trail in Pennsylvania; every hiker wants to do at least one segment of this famous route. Shelters, spaced about one day's hike apart, are marked on trail maps, with the result that tremendous overuse occurs in their vicinity. Our experience has shown that avoiding designation of camping areas helps to disperse campers along the trail so that environmental damage from overuse is less of a problem.

We found after several tries that abandoned railroad rights-of-way may not be all they are cracked up to be. Some "railroad rights-of-way" are strictly that: a right-of-way over which trains can be legally operated. In two cases, railbeds that would have made ideal bicycle trails were lost because the rights-of-way reverted automatically to adjoining landowners as soon as they ceased to be used for railway purposes. The railroad company had legal ownership only of the bridges, tunnels and station sites, and could not convey title to the rest of the right-of-way. Another potential problem with converted railroads is the large number of bridges, trestles and culverts which they bring into a trail system. Bridge painting, trestle maintenance and culvert cleaning can be very, very expensive operating costs that may be hard to justify for trails, which generally have relatively low maintenance costs.

The extensive trail system developed on State Forests since 1970 has been due, in large part, to volunteer efforts and public works programs. Pennsylvania is especially fortunate to have a large number of active trail clubs with enthusiastic, hard-working members. The Keystone Trail Club, an alliance of 41 smaller groups, coordinates the trail activities of many hiking clubs and other outdoor groups in and around the state. It has been responsible not only for developing many of the trails and publishing maps and guide books to them, but for much trail maintenance and relocation when necessary. The Bureau of Forestry's role has been to provide assistance in locating trails, along with tools and materials, while volunteer trail groups supply the labor.

The other major trail efforts have come from employment and public works programs like the Young Adult Conservation Corps, Youth Conservation Corps and Pennsylvania Conservation Corps. Trail construction using hand tools is an activity well suited to the relatively unskilled but enthusiastic young people employed through these programs. In such cases, the

Bureau provides trail location, supervision, tools and materials. One administrative advantage of corps efforts is that they can be directed to development or maintenance projects that respond in a timely manner to priority needs identified in resource and management plans.

Pennsylvania's trail system will continue to expand over the next 15 years, but at a slower rate than during the past 15. Current levels of use are at or below optimums for an enjoyable recreation experience. When use rises above optimum levels, additional trails will be developed.

Maintenance of existing trails is the major concern for the near future. We hope and believe that trail clubs will continue to perform much of this workload. Clubs do an excellent job of maintaining the trails that they have developed themselves, and they contribute substantially to maintenance of other trails as well. In the summer of 1985, for example, the Keystone Trail Club successfully accomplished the almost impossible task of reopening trails closed by a tornado that blew down timber in a one-mile swath for a distance of 60 miles. Because the Bureau of Forestry is fiscally unable to maintain the entire trails system, it is dependent upon youth corps and public works programs for maintenance of those trails not covered by volunteer efforts.

Developing a statewide hiking trail system is easy under the right conditions. My advice is:

○ Pick a state with a large acreage of public land.

○ Import a large number of enthusiastic, hard-working volunteers and youth corps members.

○ Develop a good state economy, but not so good that all public works programs become unnecessary.

The Wisconsin Conservation Corps: Return of a Good Idea

DAVE LESHUK
Publications Editor
Wisconsin Conservation Corps

The Need for a Conservation Corps

In 1983, the year in which the Wisconsin Conservation Corps was created, unemployment among young adults in the United States was estimated to be 22.4 percent for those between ages 16 and 19 and 14.5 percent for those between 20 and 24. By 1985 those numbers had improved only slightly to 18.6 percent and 11.1 percent respectively.

In a seemingly unrelated problem, state and local efforts at resource conservation weren't meeting the demands for conservation work voiced in many sectors of society. Wisconsin's economy depends on its natural resources—on outdoor recreational areas, fisheries and wildlife for tourism; on forests for wood and pulp; on cropland and ground and surface waters for agriculture and recreation; and on all of these for the high quality of life the state offers. Those with a stake in these resources have often pointed out that the absence of significant work to maintain and improve these resources can only lead toward economic decline and a wasted land.

The creation of the Wisconsin Conservation Corps by the state legislature and governor three years ago was aimed at solving both of these problems. By employing young adults between the ages of 18 and 25 for one year at minimum wage and by rewarding them with a $1,000 scholarship or a $500 cash bonus upon completion of that year, the Corps launches unemployed young adults into a brighter future. (They are not eligible for unemployment compensation following Corps service.) By putting Corps members to work on conservation projects around the state, Wisconsin's natural resources are improved and an increased awareness of the value of our natural surroundings is instilled in members.

Yet it was not only unemployment and inadequate conservation efforts that sparked the creation of WCC; equally important were the good reputation of WCC's predecessor, the Depression-era Civilian Conservation Corps, and a deeply ingrained conservation ethic among state residents. Many ideas and events throughout Wisconsin's history have combined to make the state a crucible for thought about how people interact with their natural surroundings: the writings of conservationists like John Muir and Aldo Leopold, rampant forest fires and exploitative logging in the late 1800s and early 1900s, the rich tradition of family farming with its deep respect for the land, persevering Indian culture, and the abundance of lakes and rivers. On the whole that has created a sense of obligation to the land—an awareness that the relation between land and people must be a reciprocal one.

The heritage of the Civilian Conservation Corps, often called "the best government program ever," is especially strong in Wisconsin. The CCC, one of Franklin Roosevelt's New Deal volleys in the battle against unemployment and the crisis state of the nation's natural resources, put 92,000 men to work in Wisconsin, mostly on forestry projects. At the height of CCC activity in 1935, Wisconsin had 103 camps; in the entire history of the CCC only three other states had a greater number of camps. Today's WCC is strongly supported by alumni of the CCC. Many others old enough to remember the good work of the "Tree Army" also find merit in WCC's philosophy and accomplishments.

Several publicly funded work programs have come and gone in the years since the New Deal: the Comprehensive Employment and Training Act (CETA), the Young Adult Conservation Corps (YACC) and the much-trimmed Youth Conservation Corps (YCC) to name a few. But what distinguishes WCC and most other conservation corps from other work training programs like CETA and the Job Partnership Training Act (JPTA), and what in large part accounts for its success to date, is the fact that each WCC crew is a self-reliant group with its own unique identity. Each crew is a team that in most cases sees the job through from beginning to end. And they take a great deal of pride in their projects, which are done in or near their home towns, because they know it will be their neighbors and their children who will benefit from the finished products. Unlike the YACC and YCC, each WCC crew is led by a more experienced crew leader, and each crew is well aware of its membership in the statewide WCC family.

The impetus for the creation of WCC evolved in the state legislature and among environmental, labor and governmental organizations over a period of years. Former state Senator Tom Harnisch, whose father was once a CCC member, was behind the passage of an initial conservation corps bill in 1981. That bill was vetoed by former Governor Lee Dreyfus. The following year a report from a roundtable meeting of environmental, labor and governmental representatives, A CCC for Wisconsin?, was published, and Assembly Speaker Tom Loftus made the passage of another conservation corps bill one of his top priorities. He charged a committee with the task of writing the bill. The committee researched the issue and held public hearings around the state to solicit input and to build public support for the idea. All this was done early in the state's budget-making process, allowing the bill to be included in the 1983-1985 biennial budget bill. Funding for the Corps was convenient because of an available surplus in the state forestry account during what was otherwise a very tight budget year, and Governor Anthony Earl signed the Corps into law as part of the overall state budget.

How the Corps works: A cooperative venture

WCC members know they are doing important work. The WCC Woodland Dunes crew recently wrote, ". . . Our crew portrays a symbol of pride of the past and a dream of hope for the future. We believe in conserving, protecting and enhancing our natural resources. We . . . take action toward the 'making' of our country's heritage and natural resources." In a more practical mood the WCC Douglas County crew wrote, "We . . . constructed the best-looking outhouse in Douglas County for a ski trail, and we built an excellent shelter for a scenic overlook. . . . Like the handbook says, 'You will get tired, sweaty and sore;' we've all had our share of that!"

Project sponsors—the people in the local governmental or non-profit organizations who supply the crews with materials and project direction—believe in the program too. It's not uncommon to hear comments like this one from a city engineer in Waupaca County: "I estimated that it would take the crew a week to do the cross-country ski trail project, based on my experience with city crews over the past 20 years. But this crew is incredible and they finished the project in two days. . . . We are glad to have them working with us."

During WCC's first two years of operation, 69 projects were completed at sites from the northernmost tip of the state in the City of Bayfield to Lake Geneva on the southern border, and from New Richmond on the Mississippi to Sturgeon Bay on Lake Michigan. In April 1986, one-third of the way through its second biennium, WCC had 47 new projects operating around the state, and it planned to finish the biennium with between 70 and 80 completed projects. The variety of work done is too great to be detailed thoroughly here, but here is a sample: building campgrounds; cutting trails and building trail facilities; building log-cabin style and rustic educational and recreational buildings; building and improving beaches, boat landings and piers; planting trees; thinning forests; reconstructing prairies; installing and sampling groundwater testing wells; surveying and controlling soil erosion; controlling non-point water pollution; tagging geese and ducks; expanding fishery facilities; tagging deer during hunting season; restoring abandoned cemeteries; constructing park recreation equipment; reconstructing buildings with historical value; disaster assistance in the wake of tornados; fire fighting and creating or enhancing wildlife habitat.

Those who work in or closely with WCC attribute another part of its success to its unique, three-party cooperative structure. The coordinated efforts of three groups—the WCC Board and staff, the project sponsors and the crew leaders—create a dynamic, constructive venture that is highly cost-efficient, productive and enthusiastically accepted in the communities where crews work.

The WCC Board is a seven-member policy-forming body composed of citizen volunteers who represent regional, environmental and agricultural interests. The Board meets four to five times each year to conduct business and to review and approve applications from sponsors for WCC crew projects. This approval process is highly competitive and helps assure that only dedicated and qualified organizations are chosen as sponsors.

The WCC staff serves the Board and conducts the daily administration of the Corps. This administration was accomplished during the first two-year budget period at a cost of $248,790 or less than 5 percent of WCC's $5 million budget for those two years (an exceptional feat that probably can't be repeated). The staff received some accounting services from other state agencies. Of the remaining expenditures, over 98 percent went directly to crew members in the form of wages, scholarships and cash bonuses. Administrative costs are expected to comprise 11.2 percent of the 1985-1987 biennial budget. With administrative costs so low and with a staff of only seven (full-time positions) administering the up to 700 full-time crew members, WCC depends heavily upon the cooperation of project sponsors and upon the skill and hard work of individual crew leaders.

Daily supervision and direction of each crew is the primary responsibility of the crew leader, who also works side by side with crew members except when she or he is taking care of other duties. These other duties include payroll accounting for the crew, dealing with personnel issues, working with the sponsor in procuring materials and tools, and in setting schedules and ensuring the crew's safety.

In addition, because the crew leader is in the field with few administrative resources, the most successful crew leaders are adaptable and self-reliant in performing other functions that require extra personal dedication and resourcefulness. A crew leader might help a crew member with a drug or alcohol problem. He or she might search out job leads for members or encourage them to use their WCC scholarship at a vocational school or college. Most crew leaders have some special skills such as carpentry or forestry which they can pass on to crew members. When one crew found an owl that had recently died, the crew leader, armed with degrees in biology, led the crew in an after-work dissection of the bird. If a job requires that the crew be trained in skills that the leader does not already have, he or she often must search out and arrange for that training. (Formal crew training sessions, however, are usually minimal. As much as possible, crew members learn by actually doing the work.) Another crew leader responsibility is making the local community aware of the work the crew is doing. This might involve contacting local TV stations and newspapers, helping with the opening ceremony for a new hiking trail or speaking to community volunteer organizations.

Further, to ensure that a project gets off to a good start the crew leader begins work two weeks before a crew is hired. During this time the leader becomes familiar with the sponsoring organization, helps hire crew members and makes sure that plans, materials and safety equipment are ready for the crew.

In doing all this, crew leaders consult WCC staff members and inform them of progress. They submit a short report every two months and are encouraged to call in when they need help. A personnel coordinator, a projects coordinator, and a field support specialist are available to provide support to crew leaders. Among other duties, the personnel coordinator must approve all hiring decisions and terminations, and advises crew leaders on corps member discipline or personal problems. The projects coordinator interacts with crew leaders by arranging special work projects and by dealing with occasional problems, such as sponsors who evade their contractual obligations. (Although this occurs rarely, the effort that goes into correcting the problem is significant.) He also screens, reviews, evaluates and summarizes sponsor project applications for presentation to the WCC Board, and coordinates the writing and completion of the contract that is made between WCC and each sponsor.

Helping with both these positions is the field support specialist. Between these three people, the operations manager and the executive director, every project in the state is visited at least twice a year so that staff members can monitor first-hand what is happening in the field. A final important feature of the relationship between the WCC staff and crew leaders is the fact that the input of crew leaders for the creation of new policies and procedures is highly valued and encouraged. New ideas are bounced off a "Sounding Off Board" of five crew leaders ("SOBs"—that's Wisconsin humor) who are elected to the advisory board by their peers.

Because experienced crew leaders who have proven themselves on the job and who have attended WCC's three-day crew leader training workshop are so important to the smooth operation of the Corps, some efforts are made to keep them on for more than one year. Under current policy crew leaders can work for WCC for up to two years and possibly longer if they prove particularly valuable to the Corps, and project start-up and completion times are scheduled in such a manner as to make it convenient for a crew leader to move on to a new project when a previous project ends. They are paid between $6.00 and $7.42 per hour according to experience and job performance.

Project sponsors, the third party in the three-party partnership, can be governmental bodies, non-profit organizations or combinations of two or more of these. Even very small organizations are able to work with WCC when they sponsor a project in cooperation with one or more other organizations.

All projects must meet certain minimum standards and are selected primarily on their ability to provide meaningful, dynamic and intensive work activities for Corps members, but also on the extent to which the projects result in long-term conservation of natural resources. The work done by Corps members around the state varies widely, of course, but certain types of work are avoided or excluded. WCC avoids projects which involve the use of heavy machinery because its operation is often beyond the skill level of crew members and because the work corps concept entails labor-intensive projects. Projects which include leaf raking, weed hoeing, lawn mowing, toilet maintenance, garbage pickup or similar routine maintenance work are not accepted.

Project work usually must be done on land owned publicly or by non-profit organizations. A project must benefit a large segment of the public, and it should provide a diversity of tasks which will in some way enhance a Corps member's work abilities and experience. Work may be done on private land in cases where it offers significant public benefit, such as water quality improvement projects. Project sponsors must also assure that WCC members do not replace permanent employees.

The Corps members

All three parties—the WCC Board and staff, the crew leaders and the project sponsor—revolve around the central component of the Corps: the corps member. Since the beginning of WCC's second biennium in July of 1985, WCC has employed over 470 young adults in 349 crew member positions. By the end of the biennium in June of 1987 WCC will likely have employed more than a thousand crew members in about 700 positions. During the first biennium some 900 people were employed in almost 570 positions. Crew member profiles have not yet been compiled for the current biennium, but here is what the data from the previous biennium shows: twenty-four percent of all corps members were women. Minorities comprised 25 percent, and 5 percent were handicapped. Two of every five corps members left before their term of enrollment expired, but 48 percent of these people left to take a more permanent or higher-paying position and only 22 percent of those who left were dismissed. According to a survey taken in 1985, 39 percent of all corps members had received some type of government assistance during the year prior to their enrollment.

WCC currently operates exclusively on a non-residential basis. Corps members live at home and work in crews of from seven to ten people (including the crew leader). Wisconsin Job Service screens applicants to make sure that they meet the minimal requirements of being 18 to 25 years old and unemployed. Crew leaders and sponsors together interview applicants and then submit a list of candidates to the WCC personnel coordinator for final approval. WCC is increasingly trying to select Corps members who can make the most of the opportunities which a year in the Corps can offer them.

Crew leaders and sponsors are directed to consider motivation and enthusiasm over prior experience in deciding which of the candidates who meet the minimum qualifications should be hired.

WCC members, like the members of any large group, differ greatly. But here are two who recently took advantage of an opportunity to make their thoughts known about WCC. Alan Valley is 21 years old and married. Laid off last year from his job at a window manufacturer in Stevens Point, he was having trouble finding other employment. Now a member of the WCC University of Wisconsin-Stevens Point Environmental Center crew, he is working with six other people like himself to do many improvements, including constructing two log cabin style dormitories. He said he is learning carpentry and masonry skills which he plans to use in future jobs. "WCC means helping people out that need a start in life—young people like me. Giving them a chance at a job."

Dee Cofer is 23 and the assistant crew leader at WCC's Ashland Lakeshore and historical improvement project. Speaking about WCC she said, "I do love the Conservation Corps. It's going to be a benefit to me in any job. Any place that I go I have to be able to be with people. . . . I like the feeling of accomplishment, of doing the job and looking back and saying, 'I helped do that.' I like knowing that that will be there for a long time and that other people will be able to see it and that it will have lasting benefits for the whole community."

The summing up

Again, it is the cooperative, three-party structure of WCC that makes the organization a success. Each of the three parties retains primary control over certain components of the venture. The WCC Board and staff direct how and where crew members work. The crew leaders are self-reliant (but not completely independent) captains of their crews. The local project sponsors design projects for which they have a need, and they determine how the project will be physically implemented. This division (and the inherent cooperation) results in several important characteristics. First, the fact that the project design originates at the local level assures that the work is needed, wanted and appropriate. Local sponsors tend to know well what their community does and does not need, what local residents will accept, and what will work in their area. Second, money either stays or goes into the community. Crew members are residents of the project locale where they earn and spend their wages, and many of the materials used in the project are bought locally. Third, WCC projects tend to become community efforts. This can happen in many ways, but here is one example. In the building of one log cabin, a WCC crew did the physical work at a community environmental center. Some of the timber for logs was donated by local landowners and the cost of other materials and tools was underwritten by an "adopt-a-log" campaign to solicit individual donations.

WCC Director Bill Brakken singled out what he considers to be four equally important factors in WCC's success. First is the pivotal role crew leaders play and their generally top-notch job performance. The nature of their job requires them to be natural resource experts, personnel managers, politicians, public relations representatives, bureaucrats, engineers, and year-round outdoor workers. Successful coordination of 50 crews scattered around the state could not be accomplished with less-skilled crew supervision. These crew leaders are also integrally involved in forming WCC policies and procedures; the administrative staff strongly encourages their input and often acts on their ideas. This cadre is assembled with targeted recruitment, and training and group interaction enhance their abilities. WCC publicizes crew leader openings among recent natural resource college graduates in the state who are seeking supervisory experience. Intensive orientation and supervisory training sessions help prepare them for the job, and "revival meetings" during the course of the year generate enthusiasm and new ideas and allow crew leaders to get together as a group.

The second is the fact that crew members are able to identify themselves as part of a large group with an important mission. This has come about largely due to the enthusiasm that crew leaders try to pass on to their crews, but also through the publication and distribution of a monthly WCC newsletter. Caps, hardhats, sew-on patches and T-shirts displaying the WCC logo identify crew members, and metal WCC signs identify their projects. Newspaper articles in the few hundred daily and weekly newspapers around the state highlight the local WCC crew members and their projects, as does TV and radio coverage. Project sponsors and other organizations often give awards or otherwise recognize WCC crews. All of this helps instill in crew members a sense of pride and purpose and belonging.

The third factor is the unique administrative structure represented by the citizen-volunteer board. This policy-making board provides for a constructive diversity of opinion and fair representation of statewide interests. It also contributes to the visibility of WCC in state media and in the legislature, in seven disparate areas of the state Board members call attention to issues that affect WCC.

The fourth factor in WCC's success has been its unique identity in Wisconsin. WCC is an independent state agency rather than a branch of another. Thus it avoids the often negative stigmas which may be associated with larger and more established agencies. Other factors that set WCC apart are the citizen-volunteer board structure and the inherent youthfulness of its image, as projected by crew members themselves.

Conservation—conservation of natural resources—is literally WCC's middle name. But corps members are probably the most valuable "resources" in the whole picture, for it is upon them, the people who will be making decisions about natural resources for the next half-century, that future conservation efforts depend. As has been said so many times before, it is a waste to let the energy and potential of youth wither in the face of a future that is jobless and that lacks opportunity. WCC creates opportunity by giving crew members a year of solid job experience. It creates opportunity by letting them learn new skills on the job, and by exposing them to a dynamic work environment and a strong work ethic. It creates opportunity by bringing them into an active role in their community and trying to give them a sense of obligation to society and the land. And finally it creates opportunity in a most concrete way by giving those who complete the year of work a $1,000 scholarship or $500 cash. Over 1,000 young Wisconsin citizens have taken advantage of those opportunities since 1983, and most all of them are proud to have been a part of WCC and the work it has accomplished.

Hundreds of thousands of unemployed young adults around the country need and deserve the kinds of chances WCC offers. They need the chance to do something for their communities—something they can take pride in. Conservation is this country's too-often neglected duty to the rich land which has helped build one of the world's most productive economies. More than 30 state and local conservation and service corps, most of which have only existed since 1983, are addressing these needs with an idea that works well and that works hard. WCC hopes more state and local governments around the country will take advantage of the benefits that this idea can offer them. Because, in the end, conservation and service corps are more than just a stop-gap solution to today's problems; they are highly productive tools to build a heritage—institutions that embody the pride and energy of the youth of our nation.

Total Planning for Park and Recreation Systems: Some Local Experiences

Pat DiMatteo
Grants Administrator
Department of Planning & Development
Cumberland County, New Jersey

Alexander Hoskins
Director
Fairmount Park Commission
Philadelphia, Pennsylvania

The critical role of planning and technical assistance

Is there a need for a federal presence in local park and recreation systems? This question has been the object of much debate, especially in light of the massive budget cuts in domestic programs experienced at the federal level in the past six years. For 20 years the Land and Water Conservation Fund (LWCF) and more recently the Urban Park and Recreation Recovery (UPARR) program have served as major funding sources for the acquisition, development and rehabilitation of both state and local park systems. As the funding levels for these programs have decreased, the level of discussion on redefining the federal role has grown. These dicussions have centered on whether existing programs should be continued as is or reshaped to create a new federal role.

While adequate funding for conservation and development purposes remains essential, it has become increasingly evident that a strong planning and technical assistance component is needed to complement any capital expenditures. One lesson learned from the UPARR program is that there is no substitute for up-to-date technical information and good planning when trying to insure the adequate operation and management of existing resources. It is in the area of technical assistance that the federal government can and should assert a leadership role. And through funding assistance the federal government can serve as a catalyst for improving how park and recreation systems are developed, operated, managed and maintained.

A leadership role at the federal level, in providing planning and technical assistance and in coordinating local and state planning efforts, can insure that the impact of recreation at the state and local level is both strengthened and maximized. The purpose of this paper is to validate this position by relating local experiences of the UPARR program.

Planning for recovery

The Urban Park and Recreation Recovery Act was passed in 1978 to improve recognition of the recreation needs of urban populations, particularly in physically and economically distressed communities. More than 75 percent of our nation's population live within urban areas. Budget cuts over the previous decade had wreaked havoc on urban infrastructure, including park systems. Dwindling staff, aging facilities and lack of funds to operate these facilities contributed to a decaying park environment.

In order to begin to effect recovery, a three-pronged approach was developed that would provide funding for the rehabilitation of neighborhood facilities, innovative approaches to programming, and planning on a systemwide basis. The planning component of the program was designed to assist local communities in focusing on systemwide recovery and maintenance of their park and recreation facilities. A small portion (three percent) of the annual UPARR appropriation was to be available for the preparation of Recovery Action Plans (RAPs).

The RAP consists of a written plan that summarizes the issues, opportunities and needs of the park and recreation system, states specific goals and objectives for the system and then outlines detailed strategies to address the priority issues facing the system. By preparing this plan, localities showed commitment to ongoing planning, rehabilitation, services, operation and maintenance within their whole park and recreation system. It was the intent of the RAP process to lead cities to make systematic changes in how recreation was offered, managed and perceived by their local constituencies. With guidance from the UPARR Act's strong mandate for systematic recovery programs, this change has occurred in many cities.

In tracing the evolutionary process begun by the RAP, it seems clear that UPARR planning created opportunities for problem resolution at all levels of park operation and beyond. Historically, parks and recreation departments have been accorded low priority status within city governments in terms of budget and staffing. Usually the first affected during the time of fiscal crisis, parks departments have traditionally had to "make do with less." The efforts of many departments were focused on responding to crisis situations, precipitated by either pressures from the citizens served or the local political structure. The UPARR planning program gave such communities the first incentive in years to take a step back and analyze their systems in an organized fashion.

Recovery Action Plans also broadened community attitudes toward what planning could really accomplish. This new experience for recreation departments became, over time, a vehicle for park managers to refocus perspectives from a purely physical development or "master plan" approach to a process that addressed management and operation of park systems and services to the public. Many communities had never inventoried and analyzed their park systems before UPARR. These planning processes began with small steps, but evolved into strategic blueprints for change.

Government: A catalyst for change

Key elements in the success of UPARR planning incentives were the availability of adequate dollars, a national overview from the federal level and strong technical support by regional staff of the administering agency. The program's philosophy was that UPARR should avoid being "just another federal grant program" and serve as a catalyst for change in the context of unique local problems and needs. By administering both funding and technical assistance in light of this goal, federal staff were able to convince local officials that achieving maximum value from the program required looking beyond the minimum UPARR requirements to address the total needs of their systems and ensure their survival.

After completion of initial recovery plans, it also became obvious that a more comprehensive approach to overall management planning was needed. By encouraging excellence and adhering to strict standards of performance, the program coached or cajoled local governments into management planning processes that addressed the root causes of capital deterioration and declining programs. "Rubber stamp" approval of plans simply as a way to qualify for capital funding was avoided. Instead, cities were encouraged to embark upon long-term programs of management analysis and implementation that would supply useful answers to basic capital and operating problems.

The Fairmount experience

Philadelphia's Fairmount Park Commission manages one of the largest urban park systems in the world. Comprising over 8,700 acres, the park system contains many premier examples of landscape architecture and park and recreation facilities. Over the last decade, declining personnel levels, diminished resources and severe budget constraints have caused significant deterioration of physical resources and the quality of maintenance in the system. The commission and the city made a commitment to develop a Recovery Action Plan that would address the issue of declining services—a source of constant criticism by the local citizenry.

A UPARR planning grant was obtained to conduct a user analysis, identify problems and develop recommendations on the best ways to improve park operations and management. In addition to the UPARR grant, federal planners on the regional staff provided intensive technical assistance to guide and direct the commission's work. These actions have resulted in a comprehensive management approach to the problems facing Fairmount Park. A use assessment system has been fully incorporated into all park operations so that no redesign or renovation project can be undertaken without a clear understanding of its maintenance and service implications.

In addition, a complete reorganization of the maintenance functions was accomplished. Annual savings of $180,000 in mowing operations alone have been realized through implementation of the plan. The park's first master plan was developed with a city investment of $215,000. The focus of this plan was reshaped to address the management issues facing the system, and a management information system was developed and is now being implemented. An initial federal investment of $85,000 has resulted in a city investment of $250,000 to complete the system. While the Fairmount Park Commission still faces myriad problems in terms of budget and staffing, the RAP process has given local managers a building block to choose and implement priorities and actions.

Second generation planning

The impact of the RAP process in communities like Philadelphia can be seen in changed perceptions about the value of planning among community residents and decision makers. Instead of an onerous distraction, planning is now seen as a strategic working tool by many directors. Once the value of the UPARR planning approach was demonstrated, both federal and local agencies recognized that the planning function had to be expanded so that cities could begin to solve real problems. This dynamic process resulted in a "second generation" of planning efforts and grants, also known informally as Recovery Implementation Grants or RIGs, that were individually designed to address the specific management issues identified in each community's "first generation" plans. Negotiations for a RIG involve an extensive technical assistance effort on the part of federal staff to ensure that the city's proposal will adequately confront and resolve management issues. These grants support more self-sufficient and efficient management through operation and maintenance plans, tapping of private sector resources, system-wide improvements in the organization of services, and information management or computerization efforts.

Erie County's maintenance plan

Recovery implementation planning is distinguished from initial RAP efforts by its emphasis on testing new management approaches within recreation systems. Erie County, New York, provides a second example. It received a grant to explore methods to better utilize existing staff during a severe fiscal crisis. The first Recovery Action Plan identified inadequate levels of maintenance as a major issue in this county which has 3,900 acres of parkland scattered over 1,034 square miles. The county used its RIG grant to develop a management plan to systematically organize and direct its widespread maintenance efforts. Along with a capital improvements schedule, this plan includes clear statements of management objectives, an inventory of park facilities and equipment and a systematic list of related maintenance tasks.

Erie County's management program has substantially improved the department's scheduling ability and increased staff productivity. An unanticipated discovery was that maintenance workers were being constantly diverted from their duties to patrol park grounds and do ad-lib park interpretation. An urban rangers program was developed to address this problem and initiated with a grant from New York State. A thirty-one member urban ranger corps is available to perform patrol functions, resulting in savings of $100,000 that was made available to the maintenance function.

The plan also showed that it was more cost-effective to transfer maintenance of park roads to the Public Works Department which already had trained staff and equipment available. By establishing different levels of maintenance for high-use and low-use areas, changing from metal to wood structures, and prohibiting alcohol in the parks, significant cost savings and an increase in staff efficiency have been realized. In the first year alone over $23,000 was saved and 2 maintenance positions were freed up to perform other tasks.

Conclusions

The history of the UPARR program demonstrates that a strong planning outreach program at the federal level can provide key incentive for improving local park and recreation systems. Most cities are isolated in terms of the information available to them on new ideas and techniques in the field of recreation management. This results in wasteful duplication of efforts to discover already-proven methods and models. State agencies are often unable to respond to these needs because they lack nationwide information on local management approaches or because of their own fiscal constraints. Under the aegis of a federal grant funding program, such parochialism can be reduced through nationwide exchanges of information on park planning and management techniques.

Local comprehensive planning encourages and fosters self-sufficiency on the part of recreation providers and reduces their reliance on outside capital funding. The payback on UPARR planning investments has been very high, with first-year savings often exceeding the total cost of management planning efforts. In addition to dollar savings, such efforts can bring increased support from the local citizenry, improved professionalism and pride among park workers, increased political effectiveness and awareness on the part of parks department and movement from "crisis management" to planned responses. Because of UPARR planning, many communities are using more efficient techniques to bring recreation opportunities to their citizens. Several key elements in this success are:

○ Seed money for recreation planning has laid the groundwork for the more successful rehabilitation, operation, management and maintenance of local park and recreation sytems.

○ Increased perceptions of efficiency have helped to garner more citizen support for recreation programs and improve their status in the eyes of decision-makers.

○ Federal technical assistance efforts have aided creation of vehicles for participation by volunteers and partnerships with private groups.

○ The nationwide perspective from federal involvement has brought about a comparative data base and a system of contacts for gathering and sharing up-to-date ideas on successful management and planning techniques.

Recommendations

Without its national emphasis on technical assistance and planning, the Urban Park and Recreation Recovery program would have been much less successful in improving overall delivery of recreation services. Based on the UPARR experience, the President's Commission on Americans Outdoors is encouraged to include catalytic federal planning and technical assistance components as integral parts of any proposed national funding for capital improvements in recreation. The following recommendations are submitted to support this goal:

○ A funding and technical assistance program should be established at the federal level to incorporate the planning aspects of the UPARR program and the development/rehabilitation aspects of the LWCF.

○ A set-aside percentage of funds should be earmarked specifically for planning by local park and recreation departments.

○ Strong federal leadership should be exerted to assist and encourage local and state recreation planning.

○ A direct program relationship between the federal government and local recreation providers should be maintained, with regional or field staff of the federal agency working to facilitate the flow of ideas and information.

○ Program components and regulations should be sufficiently flexible to encourage creative responses by local, state and private planners.

○ A national information network should be developed to tap the best resources of all levels of government, educational institutions and professional and non-profit recreation organizations.

. . . .
Washington's Winter Recreation Program: A Model Participant-Supported Approach

JAMES E. HORAN
Winter Recreation Administrator
Washington State Parks and Recreation Commission

The winter recreation program today

In recent years winter recreation activities have grown considerably in Washington State. Cross-country skiing, dog sledding, snowshoeing, and snowmobiling increasingly attract many thousands of citizens annually on both public and private lands. Reasons for such participation vary: fun, exhilaration, camaraderie, and health are usually listed as most important by winter recreationists.

In Washington State two specific programs, administered by the Washington State Parks and Recreation Commission, provide a variety of services primarily to cross-country skiers and snowmobilers. Financing of such services results through the sale of approximately 9,000 Sno-Park permits to cross-country skiers, and the registration of over 17,000 snowmobiles. (The snowmobile program also receives a snowmobile fuel tax refund).

Actual participation by cross-country skiers is probably closer to 27,000 individuals since the Sno-Park permit is applied to the windshield of a vehicle and most vehicles carry about three persons.

Over 40 parking lots are annually available for the use of these winter recreationists. Twenty plus trail grooming projects groom over 2,000 miles of trail each year. Safety training, law enforcement, wildlife studies, project surveys, and a variety of other costs are all financed through these twoo programs. Two citizen advisory committees advise and assist Washington State Parks in the administration of the annual $700,000 budget.

User conflicts are identified before they get out of hand and are usually resolved to most people's satisfaction in a timely manner. As the popularity of these winter recreation activities continues to grow the administrative framework is in place to respond easily to both growth and change. Transition from one trend to another can rapidly be reflected in changes in program direction. But it hasn't always been this way. Until recently lack of proper coordination and direction was resulting in limited facility development, an insufficient revenue base, and escalating user conflicts.

Background on the problem

By 1969 in Washington State there was a need for winter recreation facilities and programs. Snowmobiling and cross-country skiing were becoming popular; however, parking, sanitary, and other trail head facilities were almost non-existent. Approximately 10,000 snowmobilers, cross-country skiers, snowshoers, and other (non-downhill ski) winter recreationists were using various public and private lands for outdoor winter recreation activities.

Adequate funding was needed to provide access to these lands, primarily by ensuring parking lot snow removal. Historically winter recreationists just parked their vehicles wherever they could, as close to a point of access as possible. Sometimes highway snow plow operators would make a few extra passes to widen an area for a few extra cars. But the growth of winter recreation activities soon outgrew these extra spaces. Adequate, safe, and dependable parking was necessary to accommodate winter recreationists needs.

Public funds such as general revenue taxes were unavailable for these purposes. Compared to public health, safety, education and transportation, winter recreation was not a priority when it came to spending the public's tax money.

Based on a report resulting from public meetings initiated by the Washington State Parks and Recreation Commission (WSPRC) in 1969, the Washington State Legislature passed the 1971 Snowmobile Act. Though intended to create a reliable source of dedicated funding for snowmobile facility, enforcement, and safety education programs through annual snowmobile registration fees and fuel tax refund, the Act distributed funds to so many state and local agencies that the result was often too little funds for program development by any one agency.

To be sure, some safety training occurred, a few parking lots were plowed, a couple of winter shelters were built, but a considerable amount of funds were spent without knowledge or support from snowmobilers. WSPRC was assigned overall coordination authority under the Act, but, in fact, had no real authority to coordinate other agencies' expenditures. By 1979 over $850,000 dollars had been distributed to four state agencies and up to twenty counties under the Act. Of that amount, approximately $260,000 remained unspent in the snowmobile account in the State General Fund. From 1971-1979 it became evident that greater user participation and assistance in project development and fund distribution was important to gain user support for the snowmobile program.

During the same years, cross-country skiers, snowshoers, and other non-snowmobile winter recreationists realized that they also were going to have to develop a new source of funds to provide for winter parking, safety, and trail head services.

In 1975 therefore, at the request of various mountaineer and cross-country ski groups and individuals, the Washington State Legislature created the Winter Recreation Parking Program commonly referred to as the "Sno-Park" program. The legislation also provided for the establishment of an advisory committee to assist WSPRC in the administration of the program. The makeup of the advisory committee consisted primarily of cross-country skiers and snowshoers, but also included snowmobilers.

The source of funding for the Sno-Park program was the establishment of a Sno-Park permit. Purchasers of the permit were authorized to park in designated Sno-Park lots. Unfortunately, from 1975 to about 1980 insufficient revenues accrued from this source to satisfy growing parking lot, trail grooming, trail signing, trail mapping, and sanitary facility needs.

Problems—Solutions

From 1979 to 1986, a series of legislative actions initiated by various winter recreation groups in concert with WSPRC provided firmer groundwork for ensuring efficient, effective administration and coordination of a statewide winter recreation program, including snowmobile and cross-country ski information, education, enforcement, and facility development and maintenance programs.

Critical to success has been the establishment of dedicated sources of funding (partnerships created between WSPRC, U.S. Forest Service, counties, and various user groups) and a high degree of citizen participation in the administration of the winter recreation program from a statewide basis to volunteer assistance in individual projects.

In 1979 the Washington State Legislature, at the request of the Washington State Snowmobile Association (WSSA) with the support of WSPRC, radically changed the original 1971 Snowmobile Act. The key changes resulted in all snowmobile registration and fuel tax funds being appropriated "only" to WSPRC (rather than 23 other agencies) and creation of a Snowmobile Advisory Committee to assist and advise WSPRC in the administration and implementation of the statewide snowmobile program. The legislation also increased the annual snowmobile registration fee from five dollars to seven dollars and fifty cents per snowmobile. In one fell swoop the remaining critical elements of a successful program fell into place; i.e., effective program coordination authority, a formal avenue for citizen participation, and a funding base consistent with current and projected needs. Added to a user fee registration and fuel tax refund program and the assurance of program funding continuity by earmarking the revenues in a dedicated fund, the snowmobilers and WSPRC now had every opportunity to forge a partnership leading to efficient delivery of needed and requested services.

Since 1979, $900,000 in snowmobile program dollars and $200,000 in Sno-Park program dollars have been distributed through grant-in-aid contracts and equipment to public agencies and private organizations, including the U.S. Forest Service, various state agencies and counties, as well as clubs and individuals. In 1984 for example 74 projects totalling $349,000 were financed. In 1985 $514,000 has been budgeted to fund 88 projects.

Many examples of private and public sponsoring of winter recreation projects exist in the Washington State Parks and Recreation Commission Program. One that stands out is the Apple Country Snowmobile Club. Established many years ago as a group to provide organized social occasions as well as to seek opportunities to enhance the future of snowmobiling in the Wenatchee, Washington area, the club financed the purchase of some used trail grooming equipment. Following the purchase of the equipment the club contracted with the Washington State Parks and Recreation Commission to groom local snowmobile trails. Club members served as volunteer equipment operators, worked to clear and remove brush from overgrown vegetation on trails, annually put up and removed trail signs, and produced and distributed trail maps. Key club members submit the annual project application including reporting forms for the previous seasons performance to the Washington State Parks and Recreation Commission.

The application is somewhat complex in that the burden of obtaining landowner permission, Department of Game support in terms of wildlife concerns, and compliance with the Washington State Environmental Policy Act is placed squarely on the shoulders of the applicant. Some club members participate in a wide variety of fund raising projects to finance club activities and eventual replacement of the grooming equipment.

Another example of a typical project sponsor is the Spokane County Parks Department. In this case WSPRC contracts with the County to provide trail grooming services. WSPRC provides the trail grooming equipment and sufficient annual operating funds plus an assurance the equipment will be replaced when appropriate (usually this type of equipment is scheduled to be replaced when it has 1700-2300 hours on it). The Spokane County Parks Department in turn works with a local Snowmobile Advisory Committee to establish a proposed annual budget, develop a schedule of trail grooming for the season, obtain land owner permission for the project, cooperate with other user groups as needed, sign and brush trails, produce and distribute trails maps, and other activities which develop during the course of the year. The relationship between WSPRC, Spokane County Parks Department, recreationists, and land owners is very positive, is kept up to date, and is effective and efficient.

WSPRC's ability to deliver these services has become dependent on establishing trust between WSPRC and winter recreationists. Trust is essential to citizen participation. It requires always being honest, providing factual information, being willing to recognize that differences in opinion or methods can be modified to suit the objectives. It always requires communication, understanding, and compromise.

Critical participants, from the very start, have been and continue to be the leadership of the organized winter recreation organizations, WSPRC staff assigned to work with these organizations, key staff in agencies and legislative committees affected by this type of program, and individuals able to gain the support of opponents or at least neutralize their opposition.

For credibility and continuity, the original advisory committee appointments needed to be made carefully, giving consideration to the key participants involved in initiating major program change. WSPRC devised criteria which were essentially politically neutral and which emphasized active participation and leadership in the particular sport and involvement in clubs and associations. Snowmobile clubs, cross-country ski clubs, dog sled clubs, mountaineering clubs, and other recreation organizations and associations are invited to participate in the nomination and selection process.

We looked for leaders who demonstrated an ability to work with others toward a common goal, and who could take all available facts of an issue and act on it. The first committee appointments were made largely of persons who had been involved in supporting and initiating the major program changes. They fit our criteria and enjoyed considerable credibility with the user groups they represented. Further, as initiators of change, they had the most complete conceptual understanding of what was intended by the proposed program changes and would work diligently toward successful accomplishment of the intended results of those changes.

Both advisory committees now play a critical role in assisting WSPRC in determining the annual distribution of funds. Each committee has established a process to review and evaluate annual project applications leading to project funding recommendations.

To date little additional staff work has been needed to carry out the committees' recommendations. Furthermore the process is viewed by the public as fair, even handed, and responsible. The advisory committee members take their roles seriously and are very thorough in their preparation for and analysis of issues.

For the future

In 1982 and 1986 at the request of the organized cross-country skiers, snowmobilers and mountaineers. the legislature modified the winter recreation program statutes to allow WSPRC to establish the annual Sno-Park permit and snowmobile registration fees. This action gave WSPRC the ability to respond to increased funding needs more rapidly by not having to wait for the next legislative session for action. Legislative action was by no means guaranteed in any case.

Based on historical expenditures and current program policies models are being developed which predict expenditure growth by area of priority using various fee levels. By combining this information with recreational demand surveys, we can determine what levels of fees and services the public is willing to accept.

As time passes two aspects of the winter recreation program require attention. The continued growth in dispersed outdoor winter recreation activities such as cross-country skiing and snowmobiling have produced additional program revenues and project requests. In 1979 we considered approximately 15 projects; in 1986, over a hundred. The level of detail supporting project applications has lengthened the project review and evaluation process to a point where modifications in that process are needed.

Secondly, most potential nominees to the advisory committees available today were not involved in the major changes which established the current program policies; therefore, a sense of historical perspective is lacking in their judgment. A list of the most important committee actions and the reasons they were taken needs to be compiled for future reference and review.

Lessons learned

A program relying so heavily on citizen participation seems to spend a great amount of time responding to citizen concerns. The geographically dispersed selection of advisory committee members helps to ensure communication at the local level, resulting in concerns needing follow-up being directed back to the program manager in WSPRC. This is not necessarily bad, but does require time to respond.

Advisory committees made up predominantly of laymen require more time to learn and adjust to the bureaucracy. New appointees to well established committees may find it is especially difficult to "get up to speed," until they have mastered the language and processes of the working agency. New appointments to advisory committees need to be made at a time when less than critical recommendations or advice is being sought to give the new members time to adjust to the committee and vice versa.

As the program expands and grows more complex, volunteers, from those on advisory committees helping to set statewide program policies to individual project supporters, need to be encouraged and nurtured. However, certain types of effort such as program administrative needs, some types of ongoing annual project supervision requirements, are not accomplished as effectively if dependent too heavily on volunteer effort.

Under certain conditions, individuals and clubs demonstrate remarkable accomplishments overcoming difficult and complex hurdles, yet a mix of public agency and volunteerism has usually provided the best results in terms of project quality and continuity. A standardized yardstick has not been developed to measure total benefits of volunteerism as it relates to our winter recreation programs. However, depending on the project, we feel it usually ranges from 25-50% of the dollars budgeted for the project.

Because we do not budget based on anticipated receipts, budgeting is not a problem for our Winter Recreation Program. Our annual budget is based upon previous years' revenues plus carry over. Unspent funds are not lost, they carry over to the next year's budget. We therefore do not have to spend funds unwisely in anticipation of losing them and we can plan for major expenditures by saving money until a sufficient balance is built up. This is especially valuable in establishing major equipment replacement schedules and one-time costly construction projects.

Finally, for ongoing annual projects such as snow removal and trail grooming, we actively encourage individual project supervisors not to spend any more funds than necessary. Unspent funds do not mean a lower budget level the next year. There is a tendency in all levels of government to spend to the limit of the budget because the expectation is that next year's budget will likely be decreased to the prior years expenditure level. In our Winter Recreation program, however, for ongoing projects we establish an agreed-upon annual expenditure limit based upon normal expected operating costs. Typically most of our ongoing projects have unspent funds at the end of the project season. By establishing an emergency reserve for unanticipated emergencies we have eliminated any concern that insufficient funds were budgeted for ongoing projects.

. . . .

A New Era For Urban Parks: The "City As A Park"

PAUL M. BRAY
Counsel, Hudson-Mohawk Urban Cultural Park
Founding Director, N.Y. Parks & Conservation Association
Albany, New York

Introduction

The social and economic problems of urban areas are too well documented and well known to require repeating. With respect to parks, urban problems include deteriorating and underfunded traditional facilities and inadequate recreational opportunities. One response to the urban park deficit has been to step beyond the problem and develop new recreational facilities near cities. The problem gets left behind. Another answer is to view entire urban areas as cultural and recreational resources and to expand the accepted definition and approach of urban parks to encompass these resources and provide benefits in response to today's needs and interests.

This case study will review an evolving phenomenon that expands the role and geographical dimensions of the traditional urban park and treats the city as a park. The phenomenon can be found in formal initiatives like New York State's urban cultural park program, Pennsylvania's heritage area program and Massachusetts' state heritage parks. Elements of the phenomenon have occurred in cities throughout the nation in an ad hoc fashion. In *The Politics of Park Design: A History of Urban Parks in America*, Galen Cranz identifies the urban cultural park as a manifestation of the fourth era of urban parks. The first three were the Olmsted pleasure ground, the reform era playground and the recreational facility.

The "city as a park" concept represents both an idea for resource-based urban planning and a pragmatic approach for coalescing residents of an urban community to revitalize neighborhoods, business districts and waterfronts. The brochure for the Massachusetts' Heritage State Parks declares, "Each park reflects the unique character of its city and a renewed sense of pride. Buildings are rejuvenated; the commons and waterways are alive with activity."

It is pragmatic in many respects. Streets, existing parks, public places and architecture are given new life as park resources. "What once seemed dull, ugly or commonplace in our urban landscape appears as a rich tapestry embroidered from the lives and dreams of earlier generations." (*American Land Forum*) A main street in Albany, New York became a ski slope in Ski Albany. ("Skiers head downtown to the slopes," reported the Albany *Times Union*.) In Saratoga Springs, the fountain pavilions in the city's traditional parks were restored as part of their urban cultural park to highlight the city's history as a 19th century Victorian resort. New life was given to the affected city parks. In a description of the urban cultural park idea in *The New Yorker* it was noted that "the conditions of a functioning park, meaning a public place where people can feel at home—safe, at ease, off duty and able to move around at their own pace" can be found in newly restored public areas like South Street Seaport. The city as a park takes advantage of underutilized urban resources.

The pragmatism goes beyond the economy of preserving and finding multiple uses for existing resources. It includes the economy of the partnership of developing and operating these new parks and the economic dividends therefrom. Both formally and informally, the new parks are a product of government at all levels working closely with private entities. Each new park in New York State has an overall plan or blueprint, but it manifests itself as a by-product of numerous projects involving many actors. In the Hudson-Mohawk Urban Cultural Park (Riverspark), the actors include the state transportation agency which provided signage for a heritage trail bikeway and interpretive exhibits for a canal lock park, the U.S. Army that is developing a museum in a historic cast-iron building, R.P.I., an academic institution that is developing a park interpretive facility, the not-for-profit Gateway which undertakes park tours and private developers adaptively reusing historic structures. These and many more actors in Riverspark gel to make a mosaic that is a "live in, learn in park." And the dividends include economic benefits from a city setting that is much more attractive as a place to live and for many other types of activity.

Three examples have been selected to highlight the "city as a park," or urban cultural park approach: Riverspark, the New York State system of urban cultural parks and the Holyoke State Heritage Park.

Riverspark, Hudson and Mohawk Rivers, New York

Riverspark, originally called the Hudson-Mohawk Urban Cultural Park, was created in nineteen hundred seventy-seven by the local legislative bodies of six neighboring municipalities at the confluence of the Hudson and Mohawk Rivers. They ranged in size from the city of Troy with fifty-thousand people to the village of Waterford with less than 3,000 people. These communities shared abundant but underutilized natural resources particularly associated with their rivers. The activities of a local preservation group, The Gateway, had revealed and highlighted their rich and shared cultural heritage as an industrial hub in the nineteenth century. In the early nineteen seventies, that cultural heritage was not viewed as an asset and an alternative to the departed manufacturing economy was not evident. The urban renewal approach showed itself as a failure. A cooperative effort to identify, conserve, develop and use the area's natural and cultural resources came to be perceived as something worth trying.

From its inception, Riverspark has been managed by a commission made up of the chief executive officer of each municipality. Initially, planning and coordinating recreational activities like a marathon through the six cities and towns were done by the planning staff of the two principal municipalities, Troy and Cohoes. Since 1981, Riverspark has had its own administrator and staff underwritten by the park's municipalities.

The nine-year history of Riverspark is complex and the scope of its facilities and programming are still evolving. It is a participatory park with many cooperating actors. A review that just touched upon the hundreds of sites and the multitude of actors and projects that have come under the Riverspark umbrella would stretch this case study beyond its reasonable limits. As an alternative the following highlights are set forth to give a sense of the planning for partnership and fostering of urban recreational resources that has been part of Riverspark's development:

○ The Riverspark municipalities adopted a goals and objectives statement for the park in 1977.

○ The New York State legislature designated the area at the confluence of the Hudson and Mohawk Rivers as the Hudson-Mohawk Urban Cultural Park, declared its natural and cultural resources to be of statewide significance and directed the state office of parks and recreation to prepare a plan for a heritage trail to link the resources of the park.

○ In 1979 consultants completed a plan for a 28-mile Heritage Trail along existing public streets suitable for guided bus tours and self-guided automobile tours. Provision was made for walking tour loops, bicycle trails, boat routes and subsidiary bus and automobile loops. The plan provided an extensive cultural resource inventory and identified 26 major sites because of their strong visitor interest.

○ Through a grant from the state transportation agency matched with local funds the Heritage Trail was posted with signs declaring it both a heritage trail and a bikeway.

○ In 1982, the Heritage Trail was designated a National Recreation Trail. At that time it was the Nation's largest urban trail.

o Many significant historic preservation projects including the adaptive reuse of the Ogden Mills in Cohoes for housing with a public square created adjoining thereto, and the Quay mixed adaptive use of river warehouses in Troy have been undertaken usually with some form of public support. These projects have protected the nineteenth century character of the communities of the park and enriched the visual qualities of the park.

o The Commission has contracted with the nonprofit Gateway to prepare a tourism plan for Riverspark and to carry out a wide variety of tours including an orientation tour, industry tours, walking tours and boat tours.

o A number of action projects including restoration work on historic properties, creation of an open space park and signage have been undertaken with funds generated by the Commission.

o The Commission has developed activities to foster cultural identity like Community Heritage Days, when the public is invited to bring memorabilia to be reviewed by experts in order to create a community archive. The Commission's other programming has been recreational (bike tours, boat races, etc.) and educational (programs for school children and Learning Leisure Weekends for Adults).

o Recently, the Commission, with the assistance of citizens representing business, educational, governmental and civic organizations, completed a comprehensive management plan for Riverspark necessary for inclusion in the statewide urban cultural park system. This plan specifically addressed the state's four goals for UCPs: preservation, recreation, education and economic development. The backbone of Riverspark which includes the entire bounded area of park municipalities is made up of two visitor centers and seven theme attractions. Cooperating partners like the U.S. Army in the case of the Watervliet Arsenal Museum which is a National Historic Landmark will have primary responsibility for many of the theme attractions. A summary of the costs and benefits is attached.

o Riverspark's first visitor center is scheduled to open in Troy, in Spring, 1987. An interpretive audiovisual production for use in the center is about to be completed.
     As these highlights indicate, an approach to six municipalities as a park reveals a reservoir of natural and cultural resources for beneficial use and a great number of potential public and private partners to bring resource based projects to fruition. The Riverspark Commission has so far functioned primarily as a planning entity, a catalyst and coordinator. The role of manager will be added next year as some of the park's primary facilities come on line. Yet, even then, the park's primary benefits will come

from the tapestry of sites and experiences that Riverspark has helped to protect and to make more accessible for public enjoyment.

New York's statewide system of urban cultural parks

New York State's Urban Cultural Parks Program was developed through a planning effort, begun in 1977, that reached a level of fruition in 1982 with the enactment of a law to establish a statewide system of urban cultural parks. As defined in this law, an Urban Cultural Park (UCP) is a "definable urban or settled area of public and private uses ranging in size from a portion of a municipality to a regional area with a special coherence, such area being distinguished by physical and cultural resources (natural and/or man-made including waterways, architecture, or artifacts) which play a vital role in the life of the community and contribute through interpretative, educational and recreational use to the public."

Fourteen geographical areas of the state, ranging in size from portions of New York City associated with the harbor to the Village of Whitehall on Lake Champlain (known to be the birthplace of the U. S. Navy), were designated by the Legislature to be parks within the state system. Two parks, the Susquehanna and the Hudson-Mohawk, comprise a regional grouping of communities. Buffalo, Rochester, Syracuse, Albany, Sackets Harbor, Saratoga Springs, Schenectady, Ossining, Kingston and Seneca Falls—the latter also having a national designation—will make up the remainder of the system.

Each of these areas has a special significance in the historical and cultural evolution of New York State and their place in the state's urban history is evident from their physical landscape.

Administration of the State's role in the system is entrusted to the State Office of Parks, Recreation and Historic Preservation (OPRHP), with the help of an advisory council that includes the Commissioner of Education—to assist in matters of interpretation and educational programs; the Commissioner of Commerce—to assist regarding tourism and economic development; and other representatives of the executive branch of the State government, local government and the public.

A plan for the statewide system of Urban Cultural Parks was prepared by OPRHP before the 1982 law was enacted and this law recognizes that plan as a basis for establishment, development and management of designated Urban Cultural Parks.

To become a formal part of the state system, each designated area must prepare a management plan to be reviewed and approved by the Commissioner of OPRHP. The plan provides a blueprint for: (1) resource management, including an inventory of natural and historic resources and the standards, techniques or means for their protection; (2) the educational and recreational programs that offer the most immediate benefits to the public; (3) for special park facilities; (4) a financial plan; and, (5) the organizational structure for park management. The plan becomes the basis for coordinating State programs that are beneficial to the individual parks and for determining consistency with State plans. It must be a "participatory" document, open and clear to all the affected parties in the community as well as to State agencies that have the power to either support or undermine the implementation of the plans.

The cost of the plan is to be shared equally by the State and local government and the end product is deemed to be the plan for both levels of government. Its approval is to be based on its attainment of resource protection and the provision of educational, recreational, preservation, economic and cultural benefits for the public at large.

Much attention has been given to the costs and benefits of the state system. For benefits, the state points to the revitalization of unused and underutilized buildings in downtowns within UCPs, protection of urban, cultural and natural resources, enhancement of the image of UCP communities and the development of a tourism economy and private investment. The typical UCP is expected to require $4 million in public lands which should generate $24 million in private investments. The state expects to contribute $35 million over the first eight years of the program.

In 1981, OPRHP received the National Outstanding Planning Program Award for the statewide UCP system plan from the American Planning Association. The system approach was recognized for creating an effective partnership between the state and the designated municipalities. As part of a statewide system, local initiatives are to become major features of the state. Municipal and state objectives dovetail very nicely in this system.

Yet, the state's program has not been without its problems. A report of a legislative committee in 1985 declared that "the program is floundering." Despite the substantial efforts of the designated municipalities to prepare the specific park management plans, OPRHP had not started the system management plan. The report stated that: "The localities have had to make decisions assuming an overall system will be in place. OPRHP has been unable to provide guidance as to how the system will function." The report also pointed out the state's failure to live up to its appropriation commitment. Many of the problems can be attributed to the complexity and newness of the urban cultural park program. There are no models to draw from and the program brings the traditional park bureaucrat into an entirely new realm involving cooperative ventures and a recreation estate that encompasses public and private lands. Although state and municipal officials appreciate the benefits of their partnership in this program, each has tried to minimize its costs and has been suspicious of the degree of commitments by the other party.

As of July 1986, prospects for the system look substantially better. Twelve of the fourteen designated UCPs will have their management plan approved by the state before the end of July. That means they will be eligible for state grants and preservation legislation and measures will be in place in each community. A new director of the state's urban cultural park program with experience in local government has been appointed. Core facilities like the city of Albany UCP interpretive center have opened. The state legislature has acted to include urban cultural park projects in the eligibility category for funds from the $250 million land protection/historic preservation part of an environmental bond act to be submitted to the voters in November 1986.

The New York State experience in creating a statewide system of urban cultural parks has shown both the pitfalls and promise of planning for partnerships. This exercise in partnership is not complete, but one can now look at a statewide plan, a statutory framework, a coordinating organization, state preservation standards and many local partnership plans and projects to guide other states and municipalities to make beneficial use of their urban cultural and natural resources.

Holyoke State Heritage Park, Massachusetts

Massachusetts has undertaken the development of Heritage State Parks in a manner consistent with the city as a park idea. But it has followed a different development approach than New York. While New York has focused primarily on planning a resource-based urban park system, Massachusetts jumped into the development of state built and operated core facilities of a more traditional park nature. Community planning and outreach has evolved after the facility is in operation. Although New York State's urban cultural park plan called for a strong system infrastructure that included state facilities in each urban cultural park, the state, until recently, has resisted direct participation in development of facilities like interpretive centers. Legislation passed to implement an Environmental Quality Bond Act of 1986 provides for 100 percent state funded visitor centers in each state designated UCP. It is now clearly recognized in New York that each city designated and managed as a park needs a defined core facility for orientation and interpretation.

Holyoke State Heritage Park offers an excellent model of a core facility. It will be officially open one year in August 1986. The park is intended to celebrate a city that is one of the first planned industrial centers in the nation. The state landscaped a five-acre site that had been a freight yard. On this site is a newly constructed visitor center with exhibitions and a restored railroad train. The cost of the project was $3.4 million and came from the state except for $600,000 from the Land and Water Conservation fund. A second phase is planned that will include site work on additional land and an adjoining canal. The city of Holyoke is undertaking development of a children's museum and a neighboring site.

The visitor center overlooks the mills and canals of Holyoke and linkages with the industrial city are intended by use of an antique railcar and canal boat rides. Further linkages come through programming which includes both community use of the state facility and park initiated activities throughout the community. The former is exemplified by events like Martin Luther King Day activities being held at the park facility. Activities like walking tours and preservation advocacy in the city help make the park encompass the community. In addition, the state's main street preservation assistance program is targeted to Heritage Park communities. Unlike New York's urban cultural park, formal planning of the community was not undertaken to have it part of the park.

An average of 5,000 people visit the park facility in the summer months. In addition to exhibits, recreational activities at the park facility are family oriented and include old fashioned games, winter carnivals and historical pageants. The park now has a three-member program staff.

It is too early to evaluate the full impact of the Holyoke Heritage State Park, but positive signs are evident. Economic revitalization efforts in the city point to the visitor center as the place to gain an introduction to what Holyoke has to offer and the park is viewed as a linchpin for future development. The landscaping and operation of the state facility has set a standard that the city is attempting to match in its older urban parks. Holyoke clearly shows that recreation and heritage interpretation have an important and valuable role in urban places.

Observations

Urban areas are rich in cultural and recreational resources. If properly managed, they can significantly expand the recreational estate in the front yard (streets, public places and waterfronts) of cities.

When density and land prices exclude adequate recreational space, the conditions of a park can be creatively created in projects like South Street Seaport and the Baltimore Inner Harbor as well as in many less dramatic urban settings.

At a time when amusements like media abound, the public becomes selective. Urban cultural parks have shown that the public responds positively to recreational activities in a culturally rich or heritage setting and appreciates an educational element.

The city as a park—a "live in, learn in" environment such as an urban cultural park—helps develop close to home an ethic and respect for cultural and natural values and fosters a local participatory approach to conservation. The United States has reached a point of maturity when a desire for continuity with the past and recognition of the attainments of earlier generations will shape park and recreation demand and services.

Ensuring access to urban recreation resources requires cooperative ventures with complementary roles for federal, state and local governmental entities and private institutions. New partnership and participatory models like the urban cultural park should be recognized and encouraged.

The role of urban parks and recreation must be accepted as much broader than in the past in order to respond to contemporary needs and realities. That broader role both expands upon the social role that began with Olmsted and the reform era playground and embarks on new functions related to urban planning, liveability, cultural identity and economic planning. Existing urban parks can and should be fully integrated into expanded systems and concepts of urban parks.

The alternative to the coordinated, participatory approach of the urban cultural park approach is costly as noted in the following finding in the Rochester urban cultural park management plan: "To not act upon the UCP, thereby maintaining a fragmented policy with respect to the preservation of natural and cultural resources, would represent the eventual loss of these resources and a lost opportunity to achieve a cohesive redevelopment of the area. Continuation of the status quo would result in the inappropriate and inadequate (re)development of resources and further deterioration of the character of significant UCP areas."

Conclusion

The General Overview from the National Conference on Recreation and the American City (May 1986) declared "Often cities contain lands and waters ecologically important to broad resource protection goals." Of course, it should be noted that all cities have cultural or heritage resources that reveal man's attainments. John Messick, architect for the Blair House restoration, called the city "the ultimate artifact of our culture." So it should be evident, as the Conference noted, both that the resources of cities are part of the continuum of the national network of public and private recreation places and that the ethic of stewardship is heavily influenced by and has a place in our cities.

Furthermore, in Gilbert M. Grosvenor's words, "American cities are thrilling, vital places to be." When we recognize and accept the recreational and educational values of the urban landscape we cannot help but protect important urban resources and unlock a treasure house of recreation opportunities. This is clearly the experience from the city as a park phenomenon.

It is timely for the President's Commission to give clear recognition to the "city as a park" or urban cultural park as a valuable model for urban resource protection and beneficial enjoyment and as part of the continuum in the national network of public and private recreational places.

. . . .

New Mexico's Adopt-A-Trail: A Progressive Partnership

KAREN BROWN
Recreation Planner
Division of Resource Management & Development
New Mexico Department of Natural Resources

Background

The New Mexico State Trails Act was passed by the Legislature in 1973. The Act established a system of state trails and provided for a state trails council to oversee the system and work with the State Park and Recreation Commission to administer the system. The State Trails Act contained no funding for the system, however, and no appropriation was forthcoming in the next few years, so, after an initial organizational meeting, the council disbanded.

Ten years later, the idea of a state trails system surfaced again, when input from the public revealed that it was still a priority with a majority of the state's citizens. This time, a series of meetings was held between the land managing agencies, and groups of trail users. Agency representatives quickly realized that their credibility with users had been severely eroded by ten years of inaction. The New Mexico State Trails Taskforce was established to address this issue. This Taskforce was composed of representatives from federal, state and local land managing agencies.

At the same time that the Taskforce was being activated, The Appalachian Mountain Club was initiating its National Volunteer Program (NVP). New Mexico, particularly the Albuquerque area, was selected as a site for an NVP pilot project because of a history of successful volunteer programs including the Wilderness Information Specialist Program instituted by Region Three of the U.S. Forest Service. The new Albuquerque group called itself Volunteers for the Outdoors (VFO), and began actively to pursue projects and sources of funding. The VFO approached the State Natural Resources Department and the State Trails Taskforce for ideas about projects and funding, and the Adopt-a-Trail program was launched.

Adopt-a-Trail programs

In times of budget constraints and shortages, agencies are often forced to curtail or abandon a number of worthwhile programs; staff shortages, lower maintenance budgets and operation shortfalls sometimes necessitate changes in priorities. The State of New Mexico currently has over 3000 miles of trails, mostly on federal land, and some in very remote, inaccessible areas. Such trails are difficult to operate and maintain, and so may become unusable over time. Because certain trails are the favorite haunts of trail users who hike or ride there, these people are often the most willing to help maintain them. This is the concept of the Adopt-a-Trail program. A group or individual will contract with a land managing agency to take on the responsibility of maintenance of a trail or a segment of trail. This commitment usually involves several days a year when the adopter hikes or rides the trail, doing minor maintenance and repairs such as clearing debris, repairing water bars, or cutting back brush. Major problems are also noted and reported to the managing agency.

While agency personnel have always been supportive of volunteer programs, and are usually willing and able to work with volunteers, they had complained that a lack of training and knowledge of trail maintenance among volunteer workers sometimes resulted in improper care of the trail, thus making more work for public maintenance personnel. Adopting groups needed better training and better supervision if agency personnel were to be relieved of the burden of constantly monitoring work groups. If this could be accomplished, agency personnel could concentrate their efforts on major repairs or rebuilding projects.

Approaches

The problem was approached in several different ways. The State Trails Taskforce paved the way for the establishment of a statewide Adopt-a-Trail program by working within their respective agencies to educate field staff in the effective use of volunteers. Meanwhile, Volunteers for the Outdoors contracted with the New Mexico Natural Resources Department for $25,000 to develop the program. The effort was assisted by the Land and Water Conservation Fund through a planning grant, approved by the National Park Service Southwest Regional Office in Santa Fe, New Mexico. The VFO would produce a series of educational and promotional materials to advertise the program and to recruit and train volunteers. The three aspects of the program, promotion, recruitment and training were tied together through a Memorandum of Understanding among the agencies and organizations involved.

The MOU did not involve exchanging funds among agencies, but it did commit eight federal, state and local offices to the sharing of resources and staff time for the program, and provided for the standardization of trail maintenance practices and procedures statewide. Through the MOU, VFO trained volunteers could adopt any trail on any public land in the state. In addition, a volunteer who contacted an agency about the program would not be turned away because a field officer or park manager was not familiar with the program. The MOU was subsequently signed by the Regional Manager or State Director of the U.S. Forest Service, National Park Service, U.S. Fish and Wildlife Service, Bureau of Land Management, and the Army Corps of Engineers at the federal level. The Natural Resources Department and the New Mexico Game and Fish Department signed at the state level, and the City of Albuquerque was the municipal partner. The MOU was written by Forest Service personnel and revised by the Department of Interior Solicitor until it was acceptable to all agencies.

The VFO then went to work to design and publish materials, and plan workshops. A brochure describing the Adopt-A-Trail program was designed first. It contained a history of trails, and some background information about the concept; it also listed who to contact and the dates of the workshops. A detachable form was included for those who might wish to receive more information. The brochures were distributed through sporting goods stores, visitor contact points (e.g., park and forest ranger stations), and at the New Mexico State Fair. Once the brochures had been distributed, the VFO conducted four workshops in Albuquerque, Taos, Las Cruces, and Alamogordo, New Mexico. Attendance at the workshops was low, and some of the volunteers were quite discouraged, but the project continued.

The majority of volunteer time was devoted to the publication of an Adopt-A-Trail Maintenance Manual. This publication was produced at minimal cost to the state and 2000 copies were printed for $3500 through a cooperative effort with the University of New Mexico. The manual was reviewed and revised by each land managing agency, the University Recreation Program coordinator, and Natural Resources Department staff. Revisions made reflected concerns about format as well as actual maintenance practices. The manual was distributed free to all workshop participants, and a $2.00 charge was levied for other interested parties who wanted copies. The proceeds from this charge were deposited in a special VFO fund to defray the cost of reprints. In addition to the VFO produced materials, the Natural Resources Department produced a nine-minute video tape to help promote the program.

One critical element in the operation of the program was the close cooperation among the people involved. Recreation staff in the various agencies had worked closely with each other for several years, not only on the job, but socially and professionally through the New Mexico Recreation and Park Association. New Mexico is a small state and those in the parks and recreation field know each other very well. This type of close cooperation produced a commitment to the project outside the normal demands of the job.

On the ground implementation

In the process of instituting the Adopt-a-Trail program, a number of on-the-ground projects were initiated. Probably the most successful was the rejuvenation of the La Junta Trail. This is one of the most popular trails in the state, but had been closed by the Bureau of Land Management because of extremely hazardous conditions. La Junta Trail, which snakes down a rocky cliff to the confluence of the Rio Grande and Red River about 20 miles north of Taos was in grave need of repair. The BLM wanted to repair the trail, but bids for the project ranged from $85,000 to $105,000. Through a contract with Volunteers for the Outdoors, the project was completed for $22,000: $3,000 for VFO and $19,000 for materials.

During the months of April and May, 1985, nearly 300 volunteers worked on the trail, their only reward a BLM-sponsored white water raft trip on the Rio Grande through the Taos Box. When the project was completed, the trail was once again useable for hiking. The BLM people in Taos are convinced that the project would never have been completed without volunteer assistance, and the project marks the first time that BLM has gotten involved with a volunteer effort on such a grand scale. It will likely not be the last.

A second trail project that was very successful was a cooperative effort between the New Mexico State Park and Recreation Division, VFO and the New Mexico National Guard. While in the process of remodeling Fenton Lake State Park, it was decided that this park was an excellent place for a cross-country ski trail. The park's proximity to Albuquerque, and its excellent winter snow conditions made it an ideal location. VFO was contacted to design and build the trail. In the meantime, discussions were held with the National Guard about the possibility of also building a biathalon trail at Fenton Lake. Eventually, the trail was constructed for both uses, and in such a manner that cross country skiers could observe the biathalon competition safely, and not be restricted from use of the trail during these events.

Planning and promoting trails and trail use in New Mexico is a primary goal of the Natural Resources Department. Jogging, bicycling, hiking and walking are activities engaged in by nearly 60 percent of the state's residents on a regular basis. But trails often get low priority in budgets, so volunteer help in building and maintaining trails is even more vital.

What happens next?

Ideally, with unlimited funding, the program would have a bright future. A full time or part time trails coordinator in the Natural Resources Department could expand the program to reach more people, and to match volunteers to trails on a statewide basis. Numerous promotional materials could be produced which would capitalize on the economic development potential of trails as a tourism resource, and funds could be contracted to the VFO to recruit volunteers, and to educate agency personnel.

In reality, however, funds are limited and staff time is divided among a number of different functions. Therefore, future plans revolve around continued operation of the State Trails Taskforce with more involvement by trail user groups, and possible organization of a State Volunteer Advisory Committee for the development and promotion of outdoor projects. Also planned are a number of trail related publications including a quarterly newsletter to keep trail adopters informed about upcoming projects and activities, and a master list of adopted trails, adopting groups, and trails available for adoption. The Natural Resources Department will function as a clearinghouse to match agencies with interested adopting groups, will publish the newsletters and maintain the master list.

One interesting suggestion which will also be pursued is the establishment of a Trails Foundation to fund trail projects and activities through grants to clubs and groups.

Lessons learned

As in many such ambitious projects, lack of adequate funding had a serious impact on continued implementation of the program. Limited staff in the Natural Resources Department reduces the time that can be spent on the program at the expense of other department priorities. A positive note is the serious commitment by a number of people which has enabled the program to continue despite these problems. Evaluation of the program has revealed only one serious flaw in the way the workshops were conducted. It was determined that attendance was low because the workshops were not adequately advertised, and the purpose was unclear. Very specific notices of the reason for the workshop, and a more detailed agenda may have attracted more people.

There is also the need to broaden criteria for this type of program to allow funds for implementation. Organizations like the VFO frequently struggle for fiscal stability only to run out of money just as the program begins to flourish. Likewise, a program like Adopt-a-Trail organizes, then is unable to continue because of lack of funding. It is not government's responsibility to fund volunteer groups, but a better system of raising funds through industry and business would help. A better definition of roles is also needed in order to avoid duplication of efforts in data collection, public information and planning.

. . . .

The Clinton Community Garden: Citizen Action for Open Space

LISA CASHDAN, EVELYN LEE AND PETER STEIN
The Trust for Public Land
New York, New York

Up from rubble

More than 91,000 acres of America's metropolitan areas are covered by community gardens that provide recreational benefits to hundreds of thousands of residents. These community gardens represent one element of the web of interrelated open space resources which are provided by federal, state, local and nonprofit entities. This combination of resources yields major benefits because of the variety of uses they offer and flexibility to adapt to changing demographic patterns and recreational needs. Community gardens complement and act as a buffer to municipal park systems, providing urban residents with unique horticultural experiences and visual pleasures which may not be available through traditional parks.

The tremendous public support that exists for these gardens, particularly in low-income urban areas, became highly visible a year ago when residents in the Hell's Kitchen neighborhood of New York City turned to the public to preserve an award-winning garden they had carefully tilled for eight years. Review of this historic Clinton Community Garden preservation campaign illustrates the need for cooperative support from all levels of government to ensure the continued existence of community gardens in the urban environment.

For 28 years the Clinton Community Garden was no more than a rubble-strewn lot, one of many thousands that mar New York City's landscape. One day in 1978, to the amazement of community residents, a few people concerned with their neighborhood began to cart away debris and clear the land with the dream of establishing a garden. Over the next few years this dream was fulfilled as a cross section of residents receiving technical assistance from a volunteer organization, the Green Guerillas, worked hand-in-hand to create a neighborhood amenity that includes a splendid garden which won All American Garden Selection honors, a grassy play area, greenhouse and a shade garden for sitting and socializing. Most importantly, the garden became a vibrant focus for a depressed neighborhood—the site for harvest festivals, nursery school classes, out-patient programs from the local hospital and a site for a youth employment program. The garden provided an important cultural and recreational resource in the community.

This story is not unique to Clinton Community Garden. In response to declining Parks Department budgets and the desire for amenities in their own neighborhoods, over 400 community groups in New York City alone have created similar open space areas for residents and visitors to enjoy. These community gardens foster a sense of community pride, contrasting markedly with some city-run parks plagued by vandalism and restricted maintenance budgets. Community gardens represent a very constructive alternative to vacant land. They provide an invaluable contribution to the city's formal park system and produce over $19 million of food value per year nationwide.

Ownership and control

Besides the endless hours of volunteer labor, the creation of the Clinton Community Garden depended on a certain degree of assistance from the City of New York, which owned the property and agreed to lease the site to the community residents on an annual basis. Gaining access to land has become a major issue in the community gardening movement. Gardening groups operating without leases have no protection against the sale and development of "their" lots and loss of their garden sites. One-year leases offer a little more protection but not much. For this reason, an increasing number of garden groups are pursuing longer-term leases with the landowners. But, as the rest of the Clinton Community Garden story reveals, the only means of ensuring long term or permanent protection of community gardens is through site ownership or incorporation of these sites into the established park system.

Leases are simply not sufficient in an atmosphere where housing and economic development projects compete for funds and where real estate deals are a source of phenomenal profits. Between 1980 and 1983 nearly 10% of the community gardens in Manhattan were sold for development by the city or private owners. For many gardeners, the loss of a garden is equivalent to the loss of the neighborhood and physical displacement. Within the boundaries of these garden oases one finds much more than greenery; in an increasing number of neighborhoods they are the heart of the community.

Some cities, such as San Jose, California, have recognized the benefits of community gardens and have incorporated them into the municipal system, and provided long-term leases for individual plots on Park Department property. This, however, is the exception; most community gardens struggle with the difficulties of long-term access and site protection.

By 1981, the area surrounding Clinton Community Garden, like the garden itself, was experiencing extensive development pressures, partly in response to the city's plan to promote growth in that area. This created a serious problem for the gardeners as the already fiscally restricted City of New York found itself in the difficult position of leasing out an extremely valuable piece of Manhattan property for a community garden. In 1981, the city announced plans to auction off the Clinton site. Gardeners immediately inundated the Mayor's office with letters and petitions, giving the first inkling of the extent of support that exists for community-run urban open spaces. In response, the city delayed the auction for one year and then another two years.

"Inch" campaign

During this three-year period, community members, with assistance from larger organizations like The Trust for Public Land, the Green Guerillas and the local housing groups, explored alternative means for garden preservation. In 1984, one of the senior gardeners came up with an innovative preservation strategy that would involve the public. In a grassroots manner mimicking the creation of the garden, neighbors would "sell" square inches of Clinton Community Garden for $5, square feet for $500 and square yards for $5,000. The gardeners would have nine months to raise money to purchase the site in a so-called "restricted auction". Under this type of auction, future use by any owner is restricted to open space purposes. This mechanism, which enables nonprofits to be competitive with developers and usually results in lower sales prices, provides gardeners with a powerful tool to help make their community gardens become a permanent part of the urban environment. In spite of the restricted sale mechanism, the Clinton Garden was priced at an incredible $900,000.

Urban real estate prices, particularly in already developed areas, are a major deterrent to community groups purchasing their garden sites; some sort of public assistance is essential if they are to have a reasonable chance.

Despite these odds, the Clinton gardeners, their supporters and technical advisors launched a major preservation campaign. In the following months, the garden received more support than could ever have been imagined, testimony to the strong national and community support for community gardens. Using slogans such as "It's a cinch to buy an inch", 20,000 inches were sold to city residents and interested persons nationwide and abroad—to transplanted native New Yorkers, garden enthusiasts, people concerned with livability issues, and people who simply wanted a "piece" of the city. Magazines donated ad space, television shows aired public service announcements, advertising firms provided *pro bono* work, local merchants displayed posters, and several publicity events were held. A special "Committee to Save Clinton" was formed, composed of public figures and celebrities, to bring increased recognition to the plight of the garden and urban community gardens in general. The Clinton campaign appealed to an unusually wide audience and was a tremendous success.

The historic square-inch campaign raised over $100,000 but, more importantly, gave a loud and clear signal to city officials that community gardens and open spaces were worth saving. A month shy of the proposed auction date, the city agreed to transfer the property from its Division of Real Property, which is responsible for lot sales, to the Department of Parks and Recreation, under whose auspices it would be leased to the gardeners for continued community open space activities. It was the first time the city had agreed to an interagency transfer of property for this purpose. And all parties benefited from it. The city is providing a badly needed and highly sought after open space resource for its residents without maintenance costs, one of the biggest deterrents to additions to urban park systems; the gardeners and community at large now have a park which meets their needs and which is serving a vital social function in the neighborhood; the area surrounding Clinton Community Garden is benefiting from increased community participation, strength and pride.

Community-City participation

The mechanism by which the Clinton Community Garden was pre-served—interagency transfer—is being pursued as a possibility for saving several other garden sites in the city. To date, support exists from the Parks Department but the city's land sales agency has been uncooperative. Although the Clinton case clearly demonstrates the many benefits of community-managed open spaces and cooperation with municipal agencies, a major concern of cities is the loss of revenue from the sale of the properties and lowered ratables from tax reassessment and property exemption. Although minor steps to incorporate community gardens into the urban open space system are slowly being taken, there still remains a general unwillingness by the city to lend its full support to projects which could result in lost revenue. Only with greater reassurance that the city will not forfeit significant revenue from these transactions, or that any loss will be worth it in terms of providing valuable open space, will the city begin to consider this idea on a broader basis.

Despite its extremely developed and urban nature, New York City has the ability to create one of the best, comprehensive park systems by using existing resources: city-owned land and community groups. Over 3,000 acres of land are owned by the city as a result of tax foreclosures and abandonment. A portion of this acreage presents a tremendous opportunity to develop a well-planned open space system. As noted above, over 400 community groups have developed workable solutions to their open space needs. By working with existing community groups, the city can improve and expand its parks system at a reasonable cost and continue to meet the new recreational needs of city residents.

It is unrealistic to think "inch-by-inch" campaigns can solve the many city open space needs. There are limits to people's energy and generosity. But, it is not unrealistic to believe citizen input can and should be greatly encouraged, both in park planning and maintenance. To optimize this input, city gardeners, government agencies and nonprofit groups, as well as higher level government agencies, must all work together.

The city's recognition and encouragement of community gardens in the urban environment need not be completely without financial compensation, as in the Clinton case. Reasonable restricted sales prices and reasonable terms would be desirable to many city groups and would provide some income to the city.

The Trust for Public Land, a national nonprofit land conservation organization, has recently launched a Garden Preservation Fund to provide incentive grants and loans to groups trying to purchase their garden sites and eliminate the constant fear that leases will run out and their gardens will be developed. Upon repayment of loans by one community group, money will be lent to additional community groups. Quite fittingly, seed money for this innovative fund came from the Clinton Community campaign when site purchase was no longer required for preservation.

Federal or state funding for the remainder of the fund, and for similar funds in other urban areas, would provide hope for many city gardeners and residents who prefer this type of open space alternative and who do not have the means to leave the city and visit traditionally supported rural and suburban parcels. Equally important, a secure source of funding might encourage New York City and other city governments to sell properties to community garden groups.

In the past, Land and Water Conservation Fund monies have been used on an experimental basis to match local resources in support of community garden activities. This type of funding partnership could prove immensely helpful to the protection and enhancement of numerous community gardens which are threatened with imminent loss. Another area in which Federal support would be valuable is that of overall urban open space planning. Without this incentive, city and state agencies will be hardpressed to take a lead.

Supporters of community gardens and urban open spaces in general are hopeful that examples like Clinton Community Garden will persuade government agencies at all levels that:

○ even in an urban setting where demand for housing and jobs presents fierce competition to open space, where real estate values are incredibly high, and where federal and state support has historically been limited, strong support exists for community-managed gardens; and

○ more public-private cooperative efforts like this are needed to create balanced urban park systems through use of limited, existing resources.

. . . .

The California Desert Conservation Area: A Multiple-Use Partnership That Works

WESLEY T. CHAMBERS
Assistant District Manager
California Desert District
Bureau of Land Management

Background

The population of southern California had reached almost 12 million by the early 1970's. Urban development was rapidly filling in the coastal plain between San Diego to the south and Santa Barbara on the north. Here resided a relatively young population eager to enjoy year-round recreation at nearby beaches, mountains, and deserts. At the same time, popularity of 4-wheel drive vehicles and knobby-tired motorcycles provided access to rugged back country, and more and more venturesome individuals began exploring the California Desert. Recreation took many forms from racing to rock collecting, however, the main attraction was escape from the pressures of urban living.

The desert was experiencing rapid growth in other uses, including freeways, utility transmission facilities, agriculture and housing for a resident population based on military employment, tourism, and retirement. It was becoming evident that the very quality that had made the desert so desirable was being threatened by uncontrolled use and development.

A special report was prepared by the Bureau of Land Management (BLM) pointing out the issues and the effect of unconstrained recreation activity on fragile desert resources including wildlife, vegetation, soils and irreplaceable archaeological sites. The report also stressed the need for an intensive resource inventory as a prelude to preparation of a comprehensive management plan; you've got to know what you've got before you can manage it.

The report led to public discussion of the issues and, in 1971, to introduction of legislation in both the House and Senate to create a California Desert Conservation Area (CDCA) and direct the Bureau to prepare a management plan to protect resources for present and future generations. Finally, in 1976, the proposed legislation was incorporated under Section 601 of the Federal Land Policy and Management Act, Public Law 94-579. The Secretary of Interior was directed to complete a plan for management of the public lands in the California Desert by September 30, 1980.

The boundary of the CDCA encompasses 25 million acres of which 12.2 million are managed by BLM. The planning area stretches 500 miles from north of Death Valley National Monument to the Mexico border. It is 200 miles wide, reaching from the Colorado River to the fringes of the Los Angeles metropolitan area. This vast area also includes national monuments and State parks, military reservations, and a substantial amount of private land.

The first two years of the program were devoted to collecting existing resource data, conducting special inventories and, where possible, employing new technology such as analysis of LANDSAT satellite images. The purpose was to determine the characteristics and extent of resources so that their relative values could be mapped. Maps were prepared showing wildlife habitats, sensitive soils, wilderness values, scenic qualities, mineral potential, plant communities, and other data needed to develop the plan and provide measures for appropriate capacity for use. The inventory phase of the program included the mapping of recreation opportunities and current patterns of recreation use, from the most intensive, like organized off-road vehicle (ORV) competitions, to the least intensive, like bird-watching and primitive camping. The management plan obviously had to provide for these and other uses, where appropriate, in a manner that would minimize impact on sensitive areas and reduce conflicts among users.

Unfortunately, the bureau planning system in effect at that time was not appropriate to meet the requirements of the Federal Land Policy and Management Act of 1976 (FLPMA) and the National Environmental Policy Act (NEPA) for an area roughly the size of Ohio.[1] A new approach had to be developed that would carry out the concept of multiple use as defined in the law. The plan also had to attain a reasonable balance between appropriate uses of land by commercial and recreation users and the protection of resources. It was decided that a system of land use zones or classes would be devised to define the types and levels of use permitted, similar to the way cities and counties control development on private land. Zone designations could set the framework for managing public lands through guidelines developed for each class.

For the CDCA, four classes were needed: Class C (controlled use) for wilderness; Class L (limited use) allowing only those users and activities compatible with sensitive resources; Class M (moderate use) for more intensive use; and Class I (intensive use) for the most intensive activity including "open" areas for motorized vehicle play.

Clearly, this approach would further the following program objectives:

o Provide for multiple use while protecting resources.

o Provide a desert-wide framework for managing resources and maintaining consistency.

o Establish a foundation for more detailed planning.

o Provide the public with a clear understanding about how their public lands would be managed.

The Desert Plan was adopted by the Secretary of the Interior in 1980, following public review of a draft plan and related documents. The plan established the multiple use class system throughout the desert and set the stage for implementation·of recreation programs.

Public participation

Public involvement formed the cornerstone of the planning program. Led by a 15-member Citizen Advisory Committee, every effort was made to encourage and elicit public input during the inventory and plan preparation phases of the process. The "public" included organizations representing special interests, other governmental agencies, institutions, corporations, and individuals. Membership on the Committee represented a balanced cross section of interests including wildlife, mining, vegetation, recreation, Native Americans, archaeology, education, conservation, and the general public.

During the inventory phase, efforts were made to identify specific interests, concerns and opportunities. The public was asked to help identify issues and recommend solutions, to review resource findings, and submit information that could be used in the plan. The Advisory Committee conducted panel discussions on topics ranging from Native American concerns to the potential for sources of clean energy on the desert. Interaction also included questionnaire surveys, workshops, and public hearings. Organizations were asked to submit position papers on a range of topics. It was through this early effort that the scope of the plan was determined and alternatives formulated which included public concerns, as well as resource values.

Comparisons of Proposed and Final Desert Use Classes

Multiple Use Classes	Draft Plan Balanced Alternative	Proposed Plan	Final Plan
C	15.1%	17.1%	17.3%
L	43.4	49.0	48.5
M	35.7	27.3	27.5
I	3.4	4.1	4.1
Other	2.4	2.5	2.6
Total	100%	100%	100%
No. of ACECs*	50	73	75

* ACECs—Areas of Critical Environmental Concern established to provide specific measures to protect resource values.

During the planning phase, the final two years of the program, the public was encouraged to attend Advisory Committee meetings and to become familiar with the steps being taken to develop the plan. Ample opportunity was provided for public review of the draft plan in which three alternatives were presented. These alternatives represented the full range of public values, a protection concept at one end of the spectrum and a use/production oriented concept at the other end. A "balanced" or mid-range concept represented compromise. The companion EIS evaluated the effect of each alternative on the environment. It is important to note that all three alternatives met the requirements of FLPMA and NEPA and were implementable.

Following analysis of public input on the draft, staff prepared a "proposed" plan and final EIS and, again, the public was invited to comment. The proposed plan was close to the balanced alternative, as can be seen in the preceding table. A number of formal public hearings were held throughout southern California, and the Advisory Committee conducted a series of open work sessions to put final touches on the plan. Members of the committee, representing a cross-section of interest in the desert, disagreed on many issues. However, at their final workshop, they did agree to support the recommendations and forwarded a resolution to the Secretary of the Interior to that effect.

It was believed by some members of the Advisory Committee that agreement could be reached and that the plan should represent a consensus among competing interests. A special technique was used to resolve conflicts by bringing together the actors to iron out differences and develop support for a balanced approach. Some agreements were reached through this approach. However, the larger issues could not be resolved in this manner. An editorial in the *Los Angeles Times* summed it up this way:

The plan appears to protect the interest of preservationists while recognizing needs of miners, ranchers, and utility companies. It is a balanced plan, no one group will be entirely happy with it, and that's a good sign.

Over time, the plan has gained public acceptance as members of each interest group realize what the plan has provided for them. They are prepared to protect their gains against incursions by opponents.

Plan effectiveness

In the five years since its adoption, the California Desert Plan has withstood a number of legal challenges and a change of administration. The plan can be modified to resolve new issues and to adjust to changing conditions while carrying out its legal mandate. The annual amendment process provides for adjustments to the multiple use classes and other elements of the plan. Amendments can be initiated by members of the public, organizations, other agencies, and local government. The public is involved in all proposed changes.

The plan has provided a framework for management and has been particularly effective in directing the California Desert District's recreation program. However, reduced funding has substantially delayed implementation. Many projects scheduled for completion by this time have been rescheduled. The number of rangers and visitor services specialists envisioned in the plan has not materialized—in fact, there are fewer of these specialists now than when the plan was adopted.

The following recreation activities and programs have been given priority and guidance under the Desert Plan:

o *Routes of Travel Designations*—Routes of travel throughout the desert have been inventoried and analyzed in accordance with provisions of the Desert Plan. This program, when completed, will provide access to recreation areas, as well as cross-country travel. All designated routes will be consistent with multiple use classes. The program includes signing of primary routes and publishing maps for the recreation public.

o *Wilderness Areas*—The plan recommends establishment of 44 wilderness areas (class C) for inclusion by Congress in the wilderness system.

If so designated, 1.9 million acres of desert landscape will be set aside for hiking, primitive camping, and other contemplative forms of recreation. In the interim, until Congress acts, these areas will be managed to protect their wilderness values.

o *ORV Areas*—The plan identifies a number of designated "open" areas to accommodate motorized vehicle use. Opportunities include including hills, dunes, lake beds, as well as open country. Providing these areas for off-road vehicles and restricting their access to others has effectively reduced impacts on sensitive resources and conflicts with other forms of recreation.

o *Competitive Events*—The plan establishes three popular point-to-point race courses for off-road competition. These courses are designed to avoid sensitive areas.

o *Special Areas*—The public is attracted to many outstanding desert features including scenic vistas, unique land forms and geology, historic and prehistoric sites, and unusual displays of plants and habitats.

o *Recreation Projects*—Recreation improvements include camp site development, purchase of access across private property and trash pick up. Related facilities are being developed in the intensive ORV-use areas and will be financed with State off-highway vehicle funds. The desert plan has given BLM a foundation for assuring the State that these funds are being expended in appropriate areas for maximum benefit of the user public.

Lessons learned

There are three important lessons to be learned from the California Desert experience; the need for recognition, the importance of involving the public in the planning process, and the potential for strengthening the concept of multiple use.

Importance of recognition

Public lands have often been viewed as leftovers available for sale or trade or for eventual annexation to other agencies. In this light, the Bureau is considered by many, including some members of Congress, as caretaker of these lands with limited need for funds to carry out custodial responsibilities. There are no official boundaries, no recognized management entities, and no formal status such as you find with national parks and forests.

The California Desert experience with the concept of National Conservation Areas (NCAs) is useful and important. The public lands need greater identity and visibility. Such recognition brings improved standards of behavior and caring about the resources. There is a perception, even following FLPMA's effort to define systematic management of BLM's public lands, that they are not part of a managed "system" with stature equal to those of the National Forest System.

The boundaries of the CDCA are signed along major highways in the same manner as national forest lands and national monuments. This has had a positive payoff by increasing people's recognition of the distinct values of public lands. Is the concept applicable elsewhere?

BLM manages other NCAs—the King Range in northern California near Eureka and the Steese Mountain in Alaska. In these other cases, the regions are remote and not often visited by the traveling public; thus, the identity and visibility of BLM-administered public lands are not greatly enhanced. In other states, BLM is considering using the NCA concept to identify areas which need special management attention and protection. The idea is to give special areas visibility, management priority, and raise public consciousness. But the areas being considered are relatively small areas, usually less than 100,000 acres of public lands.

The California Desert experience and success would lead one to conclude that the National Conservation Area concept could be used to identify large areas of public land elsewhere and give them a better identity as *managed systems*. But they need to be large enough to be traversed by common travel routes.

Of major importance, though, areas designated as National Conservation Areas must be large enough to allow a broad spectrum of activities and planned to provide a balance between protection and active use. People entering the CDCA know that some areas are wilderness and some are ORV-play areas. If all other NCAs were protection or preservation areas, this balance might be lost, and the public uncertain of what to expect. BLM's job is multiple-use resource management, like the Forest Service. The CDCA experience would lead one to conclude, that, perhaps, National Conservation Areas should be equal to national forests as BLM's counterpart "system."

A partnership with the public

The Desert Plan represents a partnership between the public and the Bureau. It strikes a balance between use and protection of resources and sets the stage for a continuing dialogue with those interested in the desert. The Advisory Committee established under FLPMA played a vital role and was instrumental in creating and fostering a close-working partnership relationship between the public and staff. Other governmental agencies interested in "partnership" involvement will find, as we did, that an active, respected citizens committee is indispensable. Public involvement at this level is expensive and time consuming. There are reports to write and letters and phone calls to answer, meetings and hearings to attend, presentations to prepare and responses to draft proposals (in our case over 8,000 in the draft plan) to review and consider in making decisions. Easily 25 percent of a planning budget will be spent on participation if a commitment is made to expose the process and encourage involvement at each step.

Strengthening the multiple-use concept

The multiple use class approach is an effective tool for managing resources at the regional level. It provides a sound basis for setting priorities, developing more detailed plans, and making decisions covering a wide range of activity. Certainly this approach could be used in other districts. The Class L (limited use) designation could be strengthened through legislation. There is need for a protective designation less restrictive than wilderness which could be assigned to large areas in need of protection. Areas that don't fully meet the wilderness criteria would be placed in this class and managed for protection of sensitive resources. Only compatible uses and activities would be permitted. This would give managers an additional tool and would assure conservationists that not all sensitive areas need to be designated wilderness in order to be protected.

---

1. These laws contain basic policies for planning and management of Bureau of Land Management and U.S. Forest Service multiple-use and for assessing the environmental impacts of federal actions on public lands.

Also Available from Island Press

An Environmental Agenda for the Future
By Leaders of America's Foremost Environmental Organizations

The chief executive officers of the ten major environmental and conservation organizations launched a joint venture to examine goals the environmental movement should pursue now and into the 21st century. Presents policy recommendations to effect changes needed to bring about a healthier, safer living experience. Issues discussed include: nuclear issues, human population growth, energy strategies, toxic and pollution control, and urban environments.

1985. viii, 155 pp., bibliography.
Paper, ISBN 0-933280-29-7   **$6.95**

Hazardous Waste Management
Reducing the Risk
By Benjamin A. Goldman, James A. Hulme, and Cameron Johnson for the Council on Economic Priorities

Hazardous Waste Management: Reducing the Risk is a comprehensive sourcebook of facts and strategies which provides the analytic tools needed by policy makers, regulating agencies, hazardous waste generators, and host communities to compare facilities on the basis of site, management, and technology. The Council on Economic Priorities' innovative ranking system applies to real-world, site-specific evaluations, establishes a consistent protocol for multiple applications, assesses relative benefits and risks, and evaluates and ranks ten active facilities and eight leading commercial management corporations.

1986. xx, 316 pp., notes, tables, glossary, index.
Cloth, ISBN 0-933280-30-0   **$64.95**
Paper, ISBN 0-933280-31-9   **$34.95**

Green Fields Forever
The Conservation Tillage Revolution in America
By Charles E. Little

"*Green Fields Forever* is a fascinating and lively account of one of the most important technological developments in American agriculture . . . Be prepared to enjoy an exceptionally well-told tale, full of stubborn inventors, forgotten pioneers, enterprising farmers—and no small amount of controversy."—Ken Cook, Senior Associate, World Wildlife Fund and The Conservation Foundation.

1987. 189 pp., illus., appendixes, index, bibliography.
Cloth, ISBN 0-933280-35-1 **$24.95**
Paper, ISBN 0-933280-34-3 **$14.95**

Federal Lands
A Sourcebook for Legislation, Management, and State Revenues
By Sally K. Fairfax and Carolyn E. Yale

"In most of the western states, natural resource revenues are extremely important as well as widely misunderstood. This book helps to clarify states' dependencies on these revenues, which in some instances may be near-fatal."—Don Snow, Director, Northern Lights Institute. "An invaluable tool for state land managers. Here, in summary, is everything that one needs to know about federal resource management policies."—Rowena Rogers, President, Colorado State Board of Land Commissioners.

1987. 272 pp., charts, maps, bibliography, index.
Paper, ISBN 0-933280-33-5 **$19.95**

Community Open Spaces
By Mark Francis, Lisa Cashdan, Lynn Paxson

Over the past decade thousands of community gardens and parks have been developed on vacant neighborhood land in America's major cities. *Community Open Spaces* documents this movement in the U.S. and Europe, explaining how planners, public officials, and local residents can work in their own community to successfully develop open space.

1984. xiv, 250 pp., key contacts: resource organizations, appendices, bibliography, index.
Cloth, ISBN 0-933280-27-0 **$24.95**

Land-Saving Action
Edited by Russell L. Brenneman and Sarah M. Bates

Land-Saving Action is the definitive guide for conservation practitioners. A written symposium by the 29 leading experts in land conservation. This book presents, in detail, land-saving tools and techniques that have been perfected by individuals and organizations across the nation. This is the first time such information has been available in one volume.

1984. xvi, 249 pp., tables, notes, author biographies, selected readings, index.
Cloth, ISBN 0-933280-23-8   **$39.95**
Paper, ISBN 0-933280-22-X   **$24.95**

Water in the West
By Western Network

An essential reference tool for water managers, public officials, farmers, attorneys, industry officials, and students and professors attempting to understand the competing pressures on our most important natural resource: water. This three-volume series provides an in-depth analysis of the effects of energy development, Indian rights, and urban growth on other water users.

1983. **Vol. I: What Indian Water Means to the West**
         iv, 153 pp., key contacts: federal, state and Indian agencies, maps, charts, documents, bibliography. Paper, **$15.00**

     Vol. II: Water for the Energy Market
         v, 162 pp., key contacts: federal, state and Indian agencies, maps, charts, documents, bibliography, index. Paper, **$15.00**

     Vol. III: Western Water Flows to the Cities
         v, 217 pp., maps, table of cases, documents, bibliography, index. Paper, **$25.00**

Private Options
Tools and Concepts for Land Conservation
By Montana Land Reliance and Land Trust Exchange

Techniques and strategies for saving the family farm are presented by 30 experts. *Private Options* details the proceedings of a national conference and brings together, for the first time, the experience and advice of land conservation experts from all over the nation.

1982. xiv, 292 pp., key contacts: resource for local conservation organizations, conference participants, bibliography, index.
Paper, ISBN 0-933280-15-7   **$25.00**

The Conservation Easement in California
By Thomas S. Barrett and Putnam Livermore
for The Trust for Public Land

This is the authoritative legal handbook on conservation easements. This book examines the California law as a model for the nation. It emphasizes the effectiveness and flexibility of the California code. Also covered are the historical and legal backgrounds of easement technology, the state and federal tax implications, and solutions to the most difficult drafting problems.

1983. xiv, 173 pp., appendices, notes, selected bibliography, index.
Cloth, ISBN 0-933280-20-3   **$34.95**

These titles are available directly from Island Press, Order Department, Box 7, Covelo, CA 95428. Please enclose $2.50 with each order for postage and handling; California and Washington, DC, residents add 6 percent sales tax. A catalog of current and forthcoming titles is available free of charge.

DATE DUE

MEND	MAY 1 1 2006	
MAY		
NOV 1 5 2000		
MAY 1 4 2007		
AUG 0 9 2012		

DEMCO 38-297